PRAISE FOR *KARL BARTH'S CHURCH DOGMATICS FOR EVERYONE*

This exciting new volume makes Karl Barth's *Church Dogmatics* accessible for pastors, students, and laypersons in a whole new way through an interactive reading guide that is both engaging and easy to navigate. Whether you are new to Barth's theology or a seasoned reader, this volume offers valuable resources for everyone.

—**Kait Dugan**, managing director for the Center for Barth Studies, Princeton Theological Seminary

Like a Mozart symphony, Karl Barth's *Church Dogmatics* has motifs and recurring themes that weave through its pages. However, it takes a gifted ear to hear the themes of Barth's thought in his often paragraph-long sentences. Dr. Marty Folsom is one who has that ear for Barth's music, with the added gift of helping the ungifted to hear it too.

—**Richard Keith**, pastor, Corowa Presbyterian Church, NSW, Australia

I would recommend this helpful book as a companion for the church when picking up Barth's *Dogmatics* for the first time. Barth needs to be read; this resource can provide the encouragement to do so!

—**Cherith Fee Nordling**, sessional lecturer, Regent College

Pope Paul VI said that Karl Barth was the greatest theologian since Thomas Aquinas. That is praise enough to support serious study of Barth's theology. Marty Folsom encourages just that in this new introduction. *Karl Barth's Church Dogmatics for Everyone* provides an accessible and commendable initiation into the theology of Karl Barth.

—**Paul D. Molnar**, professor of systematic theology, St. John's University, Queens, NY

Folsom couldn't be more right! Barth has been admired, and criticized, more than he has been read. In this breakthrough series, Folsom is taking *Church Dogmatics* down from the upper shelf it often fills in the pastor's study, blowing off the dust, and illuminating its pages for the benefit of parched souls and practical living.

Restoring deepest meaning to theology as "queen of the sciences," I hear Torrance and Macmurray applauding as Folsom provides us a lens to introduce us not only to Barth but more importantly to the God who is revealing God uniquely in Jesus Christ, the God apprehended (not comprehended!) in faith, the God who loves us more than He loves himself, the God who is truly *for us*!

One of Folsom's greatest contributions in this series is to provide not only an accessible entre to Barth but also an infrastructure that can be easily utilized for personal or group study. Such a format is only fitting for the discovery of the triune God, who is, in unity, persons in community!

—Jeff McSwain, founder, Reality Ministries, Inc.

This series sets out to communicate with clarity and imagination the insights that define the work of the greatest theologian since John Calvin. Written for nonprofessional theologians, its lucidity makes it accessible to a very wide audience. The additional essays are no less easy to read than Marty's text and are, without exception, outstanding. This series opens a door to the thought of Karl Barth for people who might otherwise miss out on the insights into the faith of this theological giant. This would be an ideal series for church discussion groups who wish to think through the Christian faith in great depth.

—Alan J. Torrance, emeritus professor of systematic theology and founding director of the Logos Institute, University of St. Andrews, Scotland

KARL BARTH'S
CHURCH DOGMATICS
FOR EVERYONE

KARL BARTH'S *CHURCH DOGMATICS* FOR EVERYONE

VOLUME 3

The Doctrine of Creation

A Step-by-Step Guide for Beginners and Pros

MARTY FOLSOM

With additional essays by:
Samuel Adams
Gary Deddo
Cherith Fee Nordling
Will Willimon
Jeff McSwain
Daniel J. Price
Geordie Ziegler
Ross Lockhart
David W. McNutt
Jonathan Lett

Illustrations by Abigail Folsom

ZONDERVAN ACADEMIC

Karl Barth's Church Dogmatics *for Everyone, Volume 3—The Doctrine of Creation*
Copyright © 2024 by Marty Folsom

Published in Grand Rapids, Michigan, by Zondervan. Zondervan is a registered trademark of The Zondervan Corporation, L.L.C., a wholly owned subsidiary of HarperCollins Christian Publishing, Inc.

Requests for information should be addressed to customercare@harpercollins.com.

Zondervan titles may be purchased in bulk for educational, business, fundraising, or sales promotional use. For information, please email SpecialMarkets@Zondervan.com.

ISBN 978-0-310-12573-0 (softcover)
ISBN 978-0-310-12574-7 (ebook)

Scripture quotations, unless otherwise noted, are taken from The Holy Bible, New International Version®, NIV®. Copyright © 1973, 1978, 1984, 2011 by Biblica, Inc.® Used by permission of Zondervan. All rights reserved worldwide. www.Zondervan.com. The "NIV" and "New International Version" are trademarks registered in the United States Patent and Trademark Office by Biblica, Inc.®

Any internet addresses (websites, blogs, etc.) and telephone numbers in this book are offered as a resource. They are not intended in any way to be or imply an endorsement by Zondervan, nor does Zondervan vouch for the content of these sites and numbers for the life of this book.

Cover and icon image courtesy of the Center for Barth Studies, Princeton Theological Seminary on behalf of the Karl Barth Stiftung of Basel, Switzerland.

All rights reserved. No part of this publication may be reproduced, stored in a retrieval system, or transmitted in any form or by any means—electronic, mechanical, photocopy, recording, or any other—except for brief quotations in printed reviews, without the prior permission of the publisher.

Cover design: Brand Navigation
Cover art: © LEOcrafts; John Alberton; Lioputra / GettyImages
Interior design: Kait Lamphere

Printed in the United States of America

25 26 27 28 29 30 31 32 33 34 35 /TRM/ 15 14 13 12 11 10 9 8 7 6 5 4 3 2 1

Dedicated to Ray S. Anderson,
Who has loved God's good creation,
the Church, and the place of the human
as beloved and affirmed. He led the
way as a pioneer in the interrelation
of theology and ministry,

And Earl Palmer,
Who served as a bridge between the
Church, the Academy, and the beauty
of Creation, living with joy, inviting
others into the kingdom of God as
welcoming and hospitable

CONTENTS

Preface xiii

Introduction xv

PART 1   Entering the Hospitality of God in *Church Dogmatics*, Volume 3

  1. God's Creative Embrace 3

  2. God's Hospitality 7

  3. The History of Hospitality 11

  4. Postcards from the Father 15

  5. The Calendared Camaraderie of Hospitality 20

PART 2   *Church Dogmatics* 3.1

  Engaging the God of Creation

Church Dogmatics, Chapter 9, "The Work of Creation"

  6. Acknowledging the Host and His Home 33

    § 40. Faith in God the Creator

  7. God's Groundwork for the History of Love 40

    § 41. Creation and Covenant

  8. God's Hospitable Amen Presence with Creation 62

    § 42. The Yes of God the Creator

PART 3   *Church Dogmatics* 3.2

  God and His Covenant Partner

Church Dogmatics, Chapter 10, "The Creature"

  9. God's Hospitable Presence in Person 75

    § 43. Man as a Problem of Dogmatics

  10. The Host Unveils Our True Human Identity 84

    § 44. Man as the Creature of God

  11. Jesus, the Meeting of God and Humanity for Companionship 105

    § 45. Man in His Determination as the Covenant-Partner of God

12. The Hospitable Self 120

  § 46. Man as Soul and Body

13. The Personal Gift of Time 140

  § 47. Man in His Time

PART 4 *Church Dogmatics* 3.3

  The Accompanying God

Church Dogmatics, Chapter 11, "The Creator and His Creature"

14. He Holds the Whole World in His Heartfelt Hands 171

  § 48. *The Doctrine of Providence, Its Basis and Form*

15. The Lord of Accompaniment 185

  § 49. *God the Father as Lord of His Creature*

16. The Inhospitable Chaos beyond the Shadows...................223

  § 50. *God and Nothingness*

17. Guess Who's Coming to Dinner...............................237

  § 51. *The Kingdom of Heaven, the Ambassadors of God,*
     and Their Opponents

PART 5 *Church Dogmatics* 3.4

  Behaving Like Love Matters

Church Dogmatics, Chapter 12, "The Command of God the Creator"

18. Following Love's Forte Adventure 257

  § 52. *Ethics as a Task of the Doctrine of Creation*

19. Living into God's Hospitable Embrace 267

  § 53. *Freedom before God*

20. Expanding Our Hospitable Embrace toward Others 276

  § 54. *Freedom in Fellowship*

21. A Humbly Hospitable Life Together 301

  § 55. *Freedom for Life*

22. Life's Abundance within Boundaries...........................325

  § 56. *Freedom in Limitation*

PART 6 Voices Valuing *CD* Volume 3: The Doctrine of Creation

The Value of *CD* 3 for Biblical Studies 343

  Samuel Adams

The Value of *CD* 3 for Systematic Theology 346

  Gary Deddo

The Value of *CD* 3 for Embodied Theology 353
 Cherith Fee Nordling
The Value of *CD* 3 for Pastors......................................357
 Will Willimon
The Value of *CD* 3 for Ordinary People 363
 Jeff McSwain
The Value of *CD* 3 for Mental Health..............................368
 Daniel J. Price
The Value of *CD* 3 for Spiritual Formation 376
 Geordie Ziegler
The Value of *CD* 3 for Missions 382
 Ross Lockhart
The Value of *CD* 3 for the Arts....................................387
 David W. McNutt
The Value of *CD* 3 for Science.....................................391
 Jonathan Lett

Afterword..396
Further Reading..397

PREFACE

We have prepared our approach to Christian dogmatics by listening to Jesus, the living Word, heard through the written Word, so we are ready to act and speak His word in the world (*CD* 1).

We turned our ears to hear God speak as the One who loves in freedom, worked out in all God's perfections, and elected from eternity to be for humanity in the person of Jesus (*CD* 2).

We continue with the doctrine of creation and, therefore, turn to God the Father Almighty through Jesus (*CD* 3). He is the One concerned for our existence because He made us and is always with us. He sustains all existence and accompanies all that has been, will be, and exists today.

The cover of this book depicts a waterfall, conveying Barth's image of God's accompanying that comes to us and goes on to water the earth. Also portrayed is a hospitable place to meet with God and others within the beauty of God's creation, following the overarching theme of this book.

Some may think that in this third volume of *Church Dogmatics*, Barth is too human-centered (anthropocentric), missing all creation. Yet Barth centers on the God of the Bible, which leads him to focus on this world (and not the universe), made for companionship with humans (not rejecting the world, but emphasizing those made for covenant), and the God-human relation called the covenant.

We may say that this is a science book focused on persons, not the natural world. Scientists always focus on their subject matter. Across the four parts of volume 3, Barth's investigative work concerns the God revealed in Jesus, who creates a world (*CD* 3.1), makes humans as partners (*CD* 3.2), accompanies all He has made (*CD* 3.3), and discusses the freedom of living with God and one another (*CD* 3.4).

Having climbed the mountain of discovery (*CD* 1) and tuned our ears to hear God's voice (*CD* 2), the metaphor in this volume (*CD* 3) is hospitality—God making time and space for our active life for each other in loving practicality. Hospitality must be thought of as beyond an evening of

xiii

gathering. Here, we will be invited into God's home and asked to sit at the table to be present with God.

Hospitality is not Barth's word. He prefers to discuss creation (making space, time, and everything) as the context of the covenant (meaningful relation with persons made for companionship through Christ, who fulfills the covenant). This pairing of creation and covenant is the overarching theme of *CD* 3.

But this volume is like an invitation to dwell in the home that God has created, to eat at the table that God has prepared. It invites us to rethink who God is and who we are in the world God created so that we might live within the gracious love permanently extended to us. Let it invite you into sharing life with God and others in a creative accompaniment that looks like love in action.

INTRODUCTION

Self-giving love is the dynamic currency of the trinitarian life of God. The persons within God exalt each other, commune with each other, defer to one another. Each person, so to speak, makes room for the other two. I know it sounds a little strange, but we might almost say that the persons within God show each other divine *hospitality*.
—*Cornelius Plantinga Jr.*, Engaging God's World *(2002)*

God's hospitality creates the world and makes room within it for Himself and humans.

Our journey continues through Karl Barth's *Church Dogmatics* (*CD*) with this third volume on the doctrine of creation. Although it says creation in the title, the only way to understand creation is to understand the Creator. So this book is mainly about God, particularly the Father. We cannot get away from seeing Him through Jesus. *CD* 4 will focus on the Son, and *CD* 5 will engage the Holy Spirit. This book is about God's hospitable relationship to all He loves as His handiwork.

This volume also reaches deeply into what it means to be human. But the human can never be understood in isolation, only in relation to God. Thus, this discovery process will explore God as Creator, the human as the creature created by and for God, and the whole of creation as the context for this relationship. This cast of characters sets the stage for the hospitable God to host humanity and for humanity to host Christ in us by the Spirit, along with our fellow humans.

Barth does not devalue or disregard the rest of creation, but the Bible calls him to be focused on God and the human partner, who dance through the Bible in both dialogue and drastic distance.

This volume contains twenty-two chapters, five of which are introductory. From chapters 6 through 22, we continue looking at the "paragraphs" in Barth's *CD* 3, from § 40 to § 56. The § symbol means paragraph.

In your hands is a single volume on the doctrine of creation, covering all four parts of volume 3 of the *Church Dogmatics* as written by Barth. These parts are referred to as 3.1, 3.2, 3.3, and 3.4, as seen in this image:[1]

---

1. This illustration in all its forms through this book was created by Wyatt Houtz.

Karl Barth Church Dogmatics	I/1	1932 (1936 ET)
Karl Barth Church Dogmatics	I/2	1938 (1956 ET)
Karl Barth Church Dogmatics	II/1	1940 (1957 ET)
Karl Barth Church Dogmatics	II/2	1942 (1957 ET)
Karl Barth Church Dogmatics	III/1	1945 (1958 ET)
Karl Barth Church Dogmatics	III/2	1948 (1960 ET)
Karl Barth Church Dogmatics	III/3	1950 (1961 ET)
Karl Barth Church Dogmatics	III/4	1951 (1961 ET)
Karl Barth Church Dogmatics	IV/1	1953 (1956 ET)
Karl Barth Church Dogmatics	IV/2	1955 (1958 ET)
Karl Barth Church Dogmatics	IV/3.1	1959 (1961 ET)
Karl Barth Church Dogmatics	IV/3.2	1959 (1962 ET)
Karl Barth Church Dogmatics	IV/4	1967 (1969 ET)

TOOLS FOR THE JOURNEY

Each chapter in this book will continue the set of tools you have used to understand the previous volumes of this guide to the *Church Dogmatics*.

Chapter Titles: These chapter **titles** orient you to where you are in the process of engaging the hospitable dimension of the book and the picture set before you.

Focus Statement: The focus statements reveal the point of each chapter. They will connect to Barth's hospitable point in this section.

Introduction: The introduction will trace the purpose and a few details of each chapter.

Context: Next will come some helpful details to discern where we are in the creation of God's hospitable life depicted in *CD 3*. There will be a list of subsections that Barth structured within each paragraph.

Text: In these sections, we will engage Barth's text in a simple form. This short synopsis of the sections provides a summary.

Summary: Next is a summary of each paragraph. The text will be simmered down to short sentences and paragraphs. Having read these summaries, you may wish to dive into the actual text of the *CD* to explore the vast detail Barth brings with his creative genius.

Commentary: A few closing comments clarify the key concepts in each chapter.

Conclusion for the Church: Barth's work is dogmatics for the *Church*. Thus, this section includes a statement of helpful conclusions for the Church.

Insight for Pastors: This note for pastors at the end of each chapter invites those serving a church to encounter and know the living God.

Insight for Theologians: Proposals for theologians clarify how we use theology to participate in life with God, the Church, and with the humans God so loves.

Clarifying Questions: Clarifying questions allow us to assess whether we align with Barth as we see the "Yes" of God and the implied "No."

A MAP OF WHAT FOLLOWS

Part 1 of this book, "Entering the Hospitality of God in *Church Dogmatics*, Volume 3," surveys all of *CD* 3 as an introduction to settle us in to *CD* 3 hospitably.

Parts 2, 3, 4, and *5* of this book focus on the specific volumes of the *Church Dogmatics*.

Finally, *part 6* of this book contains a collection of short essays by extraordinary thinkers who appreciate the *CD*. Excelling in their fields of study, each articulates their insights in a brief essay and explains why they value *CD* 3 and its importance for their discipline.

I have maintained the masculine for God (He, His, Him, etc.) because we will encounter this in the original text of the *CD*, and it is best to clarify its use here. Barth does not think of God in male terms; only humans have these gendered attributes. These gendered terms maintain that God is personal and not a force, power, or idea—not an *It*. Jesus was male, but that in no way elevates the masculine. Jesus came in the most humble and lowly way possible. Thus, these pronouns are to be read merely as referring to the personal being of God in three persons.

PART 1

ENTERING THE HOSPITALITY OF GOD IN *CHURCH DOGMATICS,* VOLUME 3

Author	Title	Volume	Year
Karl Barth	Church Dogmatics	I/1	1932 (1936 ET)
Karl Barth	Church Dogmatics	I/2	1938 (1956 ET)
Karl Barth	Church Dogmatics	II/1	1940 (1957 ET)
Karl Barth	Church Dogmatics	II/2	1942 (1957 ET)
Karl Barth	Church Dogmatics	III/1	1945 (1958 ET)
Karl Barth	Church Dogmatics	III/2	1948 (1960 ET)
Karl Barth	Church Dogmatics	III/3	1950 (1961 ET)
Karl Barth	Church Dogmatics	III/4	1951 (1961 ET)
Karl Barth	Church Dogmatics	IV/1	1953 (1956 ET)
Karl Barth	Church Dogmatics	IV/2	1955 (1958 ET)
Karl Barth	Church Dogmatics	IV/3.1	1959 (1961 ET)
Karl Barth	Church Dogmatics	IV/3.2	1959 (1962 ET)
Karl Barth	Church Dogmatics	IV/4	1967 (1969 ET)

CHAPTER 1

GOD'S CREATIVE EMBRACE

FOCUS STATEMENT: This chapter summarizes *CD* 3 in *three words* (because it is volume 3!). We explore the God who exudes His loving freedom in creating the universe. The words *covenanting with creation* will reveal and conceal what we engage.

A question should immediately come to mind: Who is covenanting? The logic of what follows turns our attention to God, not ourselves or the world. He is the Creator who creates the context for understanding creation.

God, in supreme hospitality, makes room for His covenant partner to share life together. Humans are uniquely created as companions, to live in hospitable response.

The image reflects God embracing His creation, held in His heart. The earth is placed near the sun for light and warmth. Nearby is the moon that gives reflected light and moves the tides. This whole picture is a field of God's provision. God's covenant promises to forever engage Him in caring for what He fashions.

INTRODUCTION: This chapter glimpses God inviting and embracing all He has made to live in response. We glance at the spectrum of God's creating and covenanting with it all. God's covenant is a one-sided relationship of commitment and trust, born from God's heart of love. Humans can only unconditionally respond and live within the gift.

CD 3 is a four-volume work (3.1, 3.2, 3.3, and 3.4) labeled "The Doctrine of Creation." Understanding creation begins with the Creator. Notably, it focuses on Jesus, who reveals the intent and scope of the Creator's work.

CONTEXT: *CD* 1 and *CD* 2 set the stage for our current volume. They revealed how God made Himself known and showed us who He is as the One who loves in freedom.

3

4 Entering the Hospitality of God in *Church Dogmatics*, Volume 3

Now, we expand the conversation. We do not look at creation itself. We come to know the One who has created everything with His loving purposes in mind. *Church Dogmatics 3*, "The Doctrine of Creation," consists of four books, divided into four chapters, and expressed in seventeen paragraphs (remember they are chapter-length paragraphs!).

📖 **TEXT:** *CD* 3 in three words: covenanting with creation

🧍 **SUMMARY:**

The theme of *CD* 3 is the relationship between the God who creates and His creation.

God makes humanity His partner. God oversees and sustains all He makes, forging a way for free human response to His covenant. His *covenanting with creation* is fulfilled in Jesus as the Creator becomes human to be with and for us.

To have a covenant relationship, God had to create space for His partner.

The meaningful relationship God eternally intended (covenant) required the temporal field of space and time (creation) to connect.

Covenanting with creation is the logical outflow of the God who loves in freedom.

Humanity is the specifically created partner beloved by God. God's covenant involves a commitment to oversee the field of creation and care for His partner.

The character of creation reflects the unity and distinction within God's life and God's created universe.

🔬 **COMMENTARY:**

In the three words of this chapter, we already have insight that:

- **Reveals the hidden God.** He is the One who covenants.
- **Reveals a relation.** Covenanting is a love-based relation.
- **Reveals a dynamic state.** God is *with* His covenant partner.
- **Reveals creation's context for understanding.** We see God's intent in creating was to make room for us.
- **Reveals what God values.** God's priority in creation is a covenant with His creatures.

🏠 **CONCLUSION FOR THE CHURCH:** The Church has many options for conceiving of its task. We may see a core need to save sinners, bring justice,

God's Creative Embrace

and gather a faithful community to worship. *CD* 3 invites us to begin by knowing the creator God and aligning with Him. Specifically, through Jesus, we know who made it all and gives us purpose.

Beginning with God, we may discover God's intent for the universe and our place within it. God, the Father Almighty, has made heaven and earth. The light of Jesus reveals where we are and directs us to where we are going—living within His covenant agreement. Jesus enables the Church to be a lighthouse that directs, guides, and warns. He is our God; we discover our true nature in knowing Christ, who made us for Himself.

> Covenanting with creation is the logical outflow of the God who loves in freedom.

The Church is a created covenant community. It calls humans to live in loving response to God and enjoy a freeing, loving interdependence with God and all God creates.

In *CD* 3, Barth reveals an essentially personal universe. God personally sustains our lives; the Church is the welcoming team. Pastors tell us that we are not accidents arising from chance. God's history with us demonstrates that we exist to live freely within God's purpose to love and share life as His children.

INSIGHT FOR PASTORS:

The four volumes of *CD* 3 call pastors not to focus on the physical world, neglect it, or begin theology by discerning its concerns from their point of view. The pastor is to bring to our attention repeatedly that God is the Creator of heaven and earth. This call is not an apologetic concern, attempting to prove that God exists. Instead, we are to take seriously the affirmation that the universe, and our place in it, purposefully exist to reorient us to our Creator. As the Bible witnesses, Jesus reveals His Father as Creator, who never abandons His creation or His people. *Covenant relationship* articulates the meaning of Creation. God's covenant is unique in that God fulfills all the obligations. He calls for an unconditional response from humans to live unreservedly in correspondence to His gracious, freely offered presence. Preaching fulfills God's invitational intention to advance in sharing His life.

In human covenants, like marriage, partners mutually submit to each other. Those are bilateral covenants with equal partners. God's covenant is unilateral, fulfilled entirely by one party—God—and enjoyed by others. Many human "covenants" function as contracts. These collapse into conditional agreements *based on fear*, aiming to protect the parties. God's covenant is *based on love*. He guarantees persistent love and unconditionally guides

6 Entering the Hospitality of God in *Church Dogmatics*, Volume 3

with unrelenting faithfulness. This creative involvement is the context for our preaching. God's covenanted presence is the context of our responsive worship.

Living in covenant calls us to live in the world fully. We are not to love God and neglect our environment or communities. The Church grows as a community of learners who want to understand the world and how we serve God in caring for it and its inhabitants. There should be no conflict between understanding the creator God and the scientific service of understanding and nurturing the world.

INSIGHT FOR THEOLOGIANS: As theologians, we stand at a crossroads with the doctrine of creation. If we look at the world around us to discern God and His ways, we will have gone the way of natural theology. We will inevitably select what makes sense and claim it is God's work. But each distinctive of our embodied being brings lenses through which we interpret the world. If you are male, you will see things differently from females, and vice versa. Whatever your context, your lenses allow you to or keep you from interpreting and valuing the world in particular ways.

Consistent Christian theological thinking means understanding God's creative purposes as given by Jesus through the witness of the Bible. We see the eternal God through His self-revelation in Jesus. God's covenant with creation is known in Jesus entering into life with His creatures, especially humans.

CLARIFYING QUESTIONS: Does your doctrine of creation shape your theology of the world based on your observations and your sense of God's work? *Or* does your doctrine of creation begin by listening to the Creator's intentions and what Jesus reveals about what God created?

CHAPTER 2
GOD'S HOSPITALITY

FOCUS STATEMENT: This chapter captures *CD* 3 in *one sentence* to survey God's relation to creation. God's living voice spoke into being a hospitable space for His created companions, a field for intertwined life. Throughout this volume, hospitality depicts God's way of making room for others, to care for them. Humans echo this way of being.

The triune God created a unity—the universe—with abundant particularity. Each unique thing flourishes within the embracing domain of His divine love. *CD* 3 explores how the Creator is the context for understanding all that is made.

God holds the earth intimately close. He still accompanies its dynamic water systems, clouds, and land masses with mountains and flatlands. The flourishing of the whole depends on His interrelation with each aspect.

The dynamics between God and humanity are a contingent system. God created. All else follows as a unique, hospitable place for loving connection where God's providence achieves freedom for His beloved humans.

INTRODUCTION: This chapter aims to see the overarching scope of the God-human relation in *CD* 3. Having established that God loves in freedom (*CD* 2), we now see His love in action through creating and sustaining. His act creates the opportunity for humans to be loved within His roominess. In a single sentence, we will begin to settle into the living room of God—His creation. He is not only the host; He creates us with the ability to return hospitality to Him and extend it to others. He dwells in us, and we abide in Him.

CONTEXT: We are glimpsing the middle of five volumes of *Church Dogmatics*:

> The living God is revealed as the Word of God (*CD* 1).
> The living God speaks, revealing His reality so we may know the perfections of His freeing love and His eternal choice to be for His creatures (*CD* 2).

8   Entering the Hospitality of God in *Church Dogmatics*, Volume 3

Now we see the Father as Creator of His creation and creatures,
triunely caring for them from the beginning (*CD* 3).
In *CD* 4, God acts in Jesus the Son, restoring His lost covenant partners.
In *CD* 5, the Spirit brings to realization the hope of the kingdom of
God on earth.

📖 **TEXT:** *CD* 3 in *one sentence*: **God creates and affirms His world, determining humans as His covenant partners to live within His care, along with all else, accompanying His children everywhere to freely live in fellowship while extending neighborly life.**

SUMMARY:

The doctrine of creation is primarily about the Creator and His creative activity.

The Father initiates creation, the Son facilitates, and the Spirit comes as the giver of life.

Humans are the pinnacle of creation.

The physical universe is God's creation. It has a purpose. It is not without meaning. God's covenant provides the meaning of the universe He intends for His human creatures.

The *external* physical form of the universe finds its *internal* personal meaning in covenant relationships.

> God says "Yes" to all He creates, calling for our "yes" in response.

God says "Yes" to all He creates, calling for our "yes" in response. God says "No" to what disintegrates and destroys His creation. Humans may choose to say "no" to God's "Yes." God still says "Yes."

The futile attempt to avoid God's grace is referred to as *nothingness*. It can have no reality; it is choosing unreality.

When God's affirming embrace is embraced, hospitality works in mutual loving relationships.

COMMENTARY:

- *CD* 3 discusses the God-human relationship's origination, provision, supervision, correction, and intended direction.
- When thinking about creation, we often focus on the field of known things in the physical world. This approach is like seeing art without an artist.

God's Hospitality

- In this volume, covenant will unveil God's unconditional, unilateral act to be the God of His people.
- When defining humans, we concentrate on our capabilities. The image of the head (thinking), heart (feeling), and hand (behavior) dominate our attention. We need a new starting point. We must hear (obey) and receive who we are within God's hug in Jesus (grace in covenant).
- Sin is not about moral failure, wrong appetites, desires, or bad attitudes. It is not about us. It is about missing God. Whatever we choose, other than God's reality, can only be an unreality we will call *nothingness*.

CONCLUSION FOR THE CHURCH: The Church is easily distracted by the chaos of human existence. We believe that we need to fix creation and that God might help. We use what we need from God's creation, thinking God has left it to us. Unfortunately, we often work from human agendas conforming to our ideals.

CD 3 is a call to the Church to begin all its thinking by attending to God's intentions. God is already at work as Creator, sustaining and overseeing the world He loves. We must awaken to His constancy in supporting creation's daily existence.

The Church is to point to the One who establishes our lives and aligns itself within His light. In the darkness, we cannot see where we are going. The doctrine of creation gives the Church a point of view that provides meaning formed within the scope of God's covenant love.

INSIGHT FOR PASTORS: Pastors have the joy of helping people to discover they are beloved children of the Creator. That would be a good outcome from reading *CD* 3. We begin by reading the Bible together from the beginning, exploring the One who speaks and gives us life, health, and meaning. But we must start listening like curious children.

Pastors are privileged to be curiosity creators. We are freed to live with wonder and awe at the world, inviting others to see God's blessings, living in the abundant zone where God furnishes the world to live in freedom—*with Him.*

It is a sin to bore people about God and His creation. We must not pursue a spiritual life detached from the wonder and joy of the Creator. *CD* 3 is a map to get us going.

INSIGHT FOR THEOLOGIANS: Barth follows a logic that unapologetically *does not* look at the created order to discover anything about God. Barth calls theologians to never stop thinking in context: the creation and creature must be understood within the context of God's work. God's work is an extension of His love and will. He covenants with His creation as the ongoing form of His love in freedom. Theological thinking must follow this sequencing: all creation comes from Him. Understand Him, and you will begin to understand creation. Otherwise, theological discussion will become mere anthropology dressed to sound like God. Theology must be faithful to God and not accommodated to human manipulations.

CLARIFYING QUESTIONS: Does your theology of creation explore the world and its beauty to find its meaning, *or* do you pay rapt attention to the Creator, who made it and provides its meaning? Can you see that God creates a hospitable space for us all, even in those places where humans bring chaos?

CHAPTER 3

THE HISTORY OF HOSPITALITY

FOCUS STATEMENT: This chapter captures *the story of the four volumes of CD 3 in one paragraph*. Peering into the hospitable work of God, we see that God creates time, space, and the material world (*CD* 3.1) as the work that prepares for His purposes with humanity (*CD* 3.2). His purpose is to make the way for the restoration of fellowship between God and humanity (*CD* 3.3) and to live in freedom together (*CD* 3.4).

The covenant promises to bring depth to a lifetime joined in faithful love. When the Creator covenants, this is an immeasurable relationship born in eternity. God's history of hospitality makes for a much bigger story.

God initiates meeting, whether in the cool of the day in Eden, in the tent of meeting, on the mountain, in the temple, most fully in the person of Jesus, or with the people of God indwelt by the Spirit. God fulfills covenant love through eating, meeting, or setting out patterns for living a life of wisdom.

In the image above, we see the world as the stage for God's personal interaction and blessing, the context for human history.

INTRODUCTION: God's history is not the story of a rare event within world history. God creates the whole world of time and space for meaningful relationships. We will call this God's *hospitality*. In this book, God must fill out the meaning of this term, not human gathering events or sociable ideas. God creates the place, the purposed end, and the people who will populate God's space. He promises His presence and guidance for those set free in covenant relations.

There are four long volumes in *CD* 3. In them, Barth refers to God's story as a *saga*. He affirms an actual history, but not as told by humans focused on their interests. Saga is a pictorial, relational perspective. It points to God, who sets the context for the human story and is never absent. In Jesus, God enters the human drama and reveals Himself as always involved. Saga provides the most extensive context within which we could understand human history.

12   **Entering the Hospitality of God in *Church Dogmatics*, Volume 3**

▌▌▌ CONTEXT: Thirteen books comprise the *Church Dogmatics*. We are exploring that set's fifth, sixth, seventh, and eighth volumes. These make up *CD* 3. For the whole of the massive *Church Dogmatics*, think of this mapping:

CD 1: 1.1 and 1.2, preparation to meet the actuality of God (getting oriented)

CD 2: 2.1 and 2.2, encountering the God who freely chose us for reconnection (meeting God)

CD 3: 3.1, 3.2, 3.3, and 3.4, *the God-human relation as covenant partners* (discovering God in relation to ourselves) focused on the Father known through the Son, who makes us His own

CD 4: 4.1, 4.2, 4.3.1, 4.3.2 (4.3 divided into two volumes), and 4.4, which includes *The Christian Life* (coming down the road), focused on the Son bringing us home

CD 5: Never written, would have focused on the Spirit known through the Son, completing the homecoming

Pages in *Church Dogmatics* Volume 3:

There are 2,270 total pages in all four volumes combined. The number of pages in each volume is:

CD 3.1, pp. 1–414
CD 3.2, pp. 1–640
CD 3.3, pp. 1–531
CD 3.4, pp. 1–685

📖 TEXT: *CD 3 in a paragraph*:

CD 3, "The Doctrine of Creation," contains four part-volumes. *CD* 3.1 begins the story of creation by the Creator. The Creator fashions the theater within which to play and connect. This external framework is the context for the interplay of His covenant history with humans as companions for God and one another. *CD* 3.2 lifts the curtain on humanity made in God's image. Adam and Eve are introduced, but the spotlight is on Jesus. He is the key to understanding God and our human existence, making God's hospitality available. Jesus lived in our mode of existence as a human for God and as God for humans. Jesus is the source of faithful knowledge, displaying the glory of the creator God and the intended companionship for our creaturely existence.

The History of Hospitality 13

CD 3.3 continues the story of God's contribution, initiating and sustaining a life of accompaniment. God never abandons His preserving presence, even when created beings live in denial. So often we choose detachment rather than gratitude for God's grace in the creaturely world. *CD* 3.4 colors in the possibilities of the unfolding drama. God creates freedom for humans by calling them to loving obedience. God is the host who carries the whole story to His intended end.

SUMMARY:

The doctrine of creation clarifies how we believe in God the Father as the Creator through the Son and Spirit.

Creation, including humans as God's creatures, is understood as God's past, present, and future work. God is always involved.

We do not know God through creation but through His revelation.

The story of Genesis 1 and 2 reveals God's intention for His work in creation.

The story of creation introduces God's human companions, made in His likeness.

Covenant describes God's relation with humans in terms set by God alone.

God's continuing involvement is called *providence*, God's caring and sustaining presence.

When humans conform to the love of God, they live responsive to God's creative purposes, answering God's command to love.

God-human relations, still in play today, mirror the creation story.

We open to God's revealed reality in faith, living in correspondence, not independence. Ethics are the form of our dynamic, faithful response.

COMMENTARY:

In this paragraph, we see that:

- Creation is not a point in the past or a static state. It is the dynamic work of the Creator.
- Creation does not describe the material world as an object of study.
- Creation is the ongoing story of the creator God overseeing the work of His hands.
- Creation is appropriately understood when interpreted in light of the Creator's purposes.
- God's creation makes space for the drama of God's story with His beloved children.

> God's creation makes space for the drama of God's story with His beloved children.

- Jesus is the One who reveals what it means to be a creature as God intended. He comes from love, lives for love, and enables humans to share God's love.

INSIGHT FOR PASTORS: Preoccupation with self is the virus of our age. Faith in God the Father realigns our focus from our struggle and meaninglessness. The covenant God's promises restore us as the healing responses of love are called into action.

Creation's resources are not merely a warehouse to meet our needs. Creation makes available the gifts of a loving Father. This view creates the opportunity to introduce parishioners to the service of God, who has been serving and providing for us.

Church life works best when making the time and place for sharing God's life. We do this in worship, stewardship, companionship, and service; however, we must not begin with what "we do." We must help people have ears to hear God when we attune their hearts to God's heart. Opening to God as Creator births gratitude for who God is and for all He brings in being with us.

INSIGHT FOR THEOLOGIANS: As theologians, we study God, even when studying the doctrine of creation. Studying the world and then trying to discern God's work in it would be a colossal misstep. Creation is orderly, but if we try to interpret its order from our perspective, we will read our sense of order into it and miss God's intent.

Methodologically, Barth is bringing us to understand the Father. Jesus gives us eyes to see and ears to hear what God planned to do with His creative work. He provides humanity the time and space to exist as His children. Jesus opens our understanding of relationships and how we discover meaning. He helps us avoid the futility of pursuing what God has not chosen for us. Barth centers our theological thinking on being part of God's family and acting like it.

CLARIFYING QUESTIONS: Does your theology of creation begin with your experience of creation and then seek to discern what God has in mind? *Or* do you begin with believing God the Father is the Creator of heaven and earth, who will give you the vision and understanding to let Him work through you?

CHAPTER 4

POSTCARDS FROM THE FATHER

FOCUS STATEMENT: This chapter offers a *snapshot of the four chapters of CD 3*. These chapters include God setting the stage with the events of creation, the forming of His creatures, a discussion of their relationship, and how to live in light of His covenant care.

An invitational table is set, as seen in the image. You are included.

- The Tree of Life behind Jesus marks the provision of God's presence in the very beginning. It foreshadows the cross from the garden.
- On the right, the wilderness meeting at Sinai marks God's covenant with His people, including a call for a response with the Spirit's help.
- The Tent of Meeting on the left became a model for the temple, God's Church, and the Father's house of hospitable love.

INTRODUCTION: Remembering the flow of the chapters in the whole *CD*, we stop to glance at the chapters of *CD* 3 in their context following *CD* 1 and *CD* 2.

The seventeen chapters of the *CD* create a logical flow. The chapters of *CD* 1 and *CD* 2 led up to our current chapters:

God is revealed in the Word of God in *CD* 1.
    Chapter 1: The Word of God as the Criterion of Dogmatics
    Chapter 2: The Revelation of God
    Chapter 3: Holy Scripture
    Chapter 4: The Proclamation of the Church

The content of what God reveals about Himself is disclosed in *CD* 2.
    Chapter 5: The Knowledge of God

Chapter 6: The Reality of God
Chapter 7: The Election of God
Chapter 8: The Command of God

God the Father, and His covenant relationship with His creation, is opened for human understanding in *CD* 3.
Chapter 9: The Work of Creation
Chapter 10: The Creature
Chapter 11: The Creator and His Creature
Chapter 12: The Command of God the Creator

These chapters discuss the consequence of God creating everything and never abandoning His companions created for loving, covenant response.

The chapters in *CD* 3 are long and unequal in size. Those dealing with God's work and intention are shortest. The chapters dealing with humans and their responses are longest.

Pages in Chapters of *Church Dogmatics* 3:
Chapter 9: 414 pages (pp. 1–414)
Chapter 10: 640 pages (pp. 1–640)
Chapter 11: 531 pages (pp. 1–531)
Chapter 12: 685 pages (pp. 1–685)

📖 **TEXT:** Four chapters of *CD* 3 as postcards from the Father

---

CHAPTER 9
THE WORK OF CREATION:
WHAT GOD HAS DONE

Dear children,
   This is just a note to let you know what I did and have been doing since creation. I made a place for us to meet. Since the garden, my plan has been to make a meeting place so we could always be together.
                              Love,
                              Your Father

CHAPTER 10
THE CREATURE: WHO WE ARE BECAUSE OF WHAT GOD HAS DONE

Hello again,

    I hope that when I tell you about Myself, it resonates with you so that you will discover who you are created to be. I made you to enjoy Me and each other and embrace the freedom for which I made you!

                  Ever with you,
                  Your Abba

CHAPTER 11
THE CREATOR AND HIS CREATURE: WHAT GOD IS DOING NOW

Catching up with you all!

    In a very real sense, I never left you. Not only do I think of you kindly, but I am personally present and invite you into My life. You may choose to resist Me and end up with emptiness. But I am always chasing you with My love.

                  Watching over you,
                  Your Abba

CHAPTER 12
THE COMMAND OF GOD THE CREATOR: WHAT I AM TO DO BECAUSE OF WHAT GOD IS DOING NOW

My children,

    Hoping you can live today in light of my love, knowing I am with you. I pray your life within My household will be full of gratitude, honor, and rejoicing today. Thinking of you as I pray you think of Me in your every endeavor.

                  Ever caring for you,
                  Your loving Father

18 Entering the Hospitality of God in *Church Dogmatics*, Volume 3

SUMMARY:

These postcards summarize chapters in the story of God giving Himself to us.

In the broader context, God's speaking (*CD* 1) is an extension of God's being in love (*CD* 2) that now takes the form of His creative hospitality (*CD* 3).

The interplay of the chapters of *CD* 3 establishes our reality within the being (Creator) and act (creation/creatures) of God.

These chapters affirm that God lovingly and creatively speaks (3.1) and freely acts accordingly in His accompaniment (3.3).

God's acting creates and sustains the reality of our human existence (3.2) and the freedom for life He offers us (3.4).

COMMENTARY:

- The task of this volume of the *CD* is to think theologically about what is other than God by starting with God.
- To understand the created order, we must engage God's creative act and discover who orders the contingent work of creation according to His purpose.
- God creates out of His loving hospitality to make room for us as His covenant partners.
- God is not separated from what He has made. We can only understand creation in light of His presence and providence (sustaining).
- God is wholly other as the One who makes the universe and is not to be confused with His creation.
- We cannot look at ourselves to understand our humanity. Only Jesus can give us that clarity about who we are.
- God made reality; its absence is unreality, being without substance. To call sin *nothingness* articulates the choice of grasping what God has not chosen, an absence and disconnection that God resists.
- When the light of love opens our vision, we may love as we have been loved. We create space for others, to care for them. Ethics is the outworking of active relations in the light of God's loving intentions gratefully affirmed.

> The task of this volume of the *CD* is to think theologically about what is other than God by starting with God.

INSIGHT FOR PASTORS:

The chapters of *CD* 3 invite us to involve our people in God's story. We open our eyes to see that our lives are meaningful within the context of God's work.

Our lifestyles reverberate with love for others when we act from God's love. When we are selfish and self-centered, we abuse creation, sucking life from it. Under God's sustaining care, we may be creative with our love life, medications, and music (commonly identified as sex, drugs, and rock and roll when acts of rebellion). When aligned with God's creative intentions, our actions connect and heal. Chosen from self-interest, they become an escape, seeking self-satisfaction. The point is how we align with the Creator. He provides the motivation for loving what He has made.

Our job is to reorient our people to the Creator, not to edit sins out of their lives. Teaching self-concern leads to an internal process of fearful judgment that deflects love. This fear casts out love. Perfect love from the Creator attunes us to live within His hospitality and to extend that love to family, clients, customers, and all creation.

We do not detach from the world when coming to know the Creator. We lovingly attach in concrete ways when encountering others as belonging to Him.

INSIGHT FOR THEOLOGIANS: The chapters of *CD* 3 open a crossroads for theologians. Which way do we begin? When pursuing a doctrine of creation, it is easy to want to start with creation. That makes apologetic sense. It seems to point to God and the wonders of His work. However, human sensibilities about the ordering of the world slip in. The "orders of creation" subtly begin to echo cultural values. These Trojan horses twist doctrine to support the values of a group of people. Issues like racism, sexism, scientism, and every other *ism* become branded with a Christian stamp. But they are false starts that do not care about God.

The other option is to start with the One who made it all, to hear what He has done, is doing, and intends us to understand. That is the thinking that guides *CD* 3. These chapters are not isolated statements of "truths." They are appropriate openings to the matrix of reality made by God. If we get this right, we will be theologians; if we get it wrong, we will be illusionists, using sleight of hand with compelling appearances but not pursuing what is actually from God.

CLARIFYING QUESTIONS: Does your theology of creation look at the building blocks and elements of creation to come to know God? *Or* do you come with wonder to God, humbly seeking to understand God's freeing love as it creates the universe, learning to act out His covenant care?

CHAPTER 5

THE CALENDARED CAMARADERIE OF HOSPITALITY

FOCUS STATEMENT: This chapter explores the *four chapters and seventeen paragraphs* of *CD* 3 to echo the *church calendar*. Our variation will not follow the liturgical seasons. Our structure will follow the arrangement of *CD* 3, inviting entry into the experience of God's hospitality.

We will be charting what it could look like to take this volume of the *CD* and translate Barth's understanding of God's creation so it is celebrated in the practices of a people who are invited to live harmoniously within God's creative work. This chapter celebrates God's life within our time and space displayed in a calendar. The four volumes of *CD* 3 correspond with the *seasons*. The *weeks* within each season follow the progression of the seventeen paragraphs (§ 40–56).

Each week is an expression of community life formed under the hospitable care of God the Father. The practices are designed to express each of Barth's paragraphs and will incorporate the dynamics of gathering, remembering, feasting, and creating a spirit of camaraderie. Everyone is invited to participate in the freedom of God the Creator.

Holidays are holy days. All days are holy when lived in the context of God's purposes, as Jesus opens the way to communion with His Father. Jesus calls us to come home to the Father through the Spirit. The sequence of weeks in this chapter intends to create an experience of *CD* 3, indwelling its hospitality. We gather with Jesus at His table as guests who serve together to create a shared experience.

INTRODUCTION: *CD* 3 furthers our exploration of knowing God, specifically as the Father who creates the world and humans as His companions.

The unfolding of God for us comes through engaging His dynamic relationships. Creation is the intentional work of the Creator. It has a

The Calendared Camaraderie of Hospitality

beginning by His will and involves ongoing personal engagement. In these paragraphs, we will see that the doctrine of creation is about a Creator-creature relationship, attending to each pole of the relationship.

We can see relational dynamics in the overarching sequencing of the *seasons*:

> The season of *preparation* (*CD* 3.1) reflects the personal work of creation.
> The season of *participation* (*CD* 3.2) explores being created as God's covenant partners.
> The season of *providence* (*CD* 3.3) creates a life oriented to God's accompaniment.
> The season of *personal presence* (*CD* 3.4) clarifies the dynamics of life together.

The holy *weeks* further express God's hospitality, making a time and place for connecting with humans. Each week is an involving event for the community to embrace God's intention of sustaining humans in a covenant relationship.

Barth had concerns about human attempts at creating festive joy, even within the church year.[1] The weeks of this chapter are lenses to perceive how we participate in God's creative and covenant work, not to humanly create festive joy.

CONTEXT: *CD* 2 used music to reveal God's creative and loving *nature*. Here in *CD* 3, we engage the *activity* of God as Creator and God's *intent* for His creation. *CD* 3 explores the hospitably creative *work* that comes from the person of the Father. *CD* 4 will narrow to the *specific work* of reconciling God and humanity, bringing us home.

> *CD* 3 explores the hospitably creative *work* that comes from the person of the Father.

Pages in Paragraphs of *Church Dogmatics*, Volume 3:
Paragraph 40: 39 pages (pp. 3–41; shortest paragraph)
Paragraph 41: 288 pages (pp. 42–329; longest paragraph)
Paragraph 42: 85 pages (pp. 330–414)

---

1. "At this point a good deal might be said about various forms of human festivity: domestic, social and national occasions; personal and private celebrations enjoyed in solitude or a select company; and even the Christian feasts with which the Church—did it really know what it was doing?—has so richly furnished the so-called Christian year in competition with their worldly counterparts." *CD* 3.4. § 55, p. 379.

Paragraph 43: 52 pages (pp. 3–54)
Paragraph 44: 148 pages (pp. 55–202)
Paragraph 45: 122 pages (pp. 203–324)
Paragraph 46: 112 pages (pp. 325–436)
Paragraph 47: 204 pages (pp. 437–640)
Paragraph 48: 55 pages (pp. 3–57)
Paragraph 49: 231 pages (pp. 58–288)
Paragraph 50: 80 pages (pp. 289–368)
Paragraph 51: 163 pages (pp. 369–531)
Paragraph 52: 44 pages (pp. 3–46)
Paragraph 53: 69 pages (pp. 47–115)
Paragraph 54: 208 pages (pp. 116–323)
Paragraph 55: 241 pages (pp. 324–564)
Paragraph 56: 121 pages (pp. 565–685)

TEXT: The four seasons of hospitable participation developed below

SUMMARY:

Season 1 (*CD* 3.1): The Season of Preparation

The first season focuses on remembering whose we are and how the divine host has prepared the setting. We come to correspond with what the good God has provided.

Faith Week (§ 40. Faith in God the Creator)

Hospitality begins at the door. It starts with trust that says, "I believe in you." This week, plan to practice how you will acknowledge God greeting you. He is always waiting at the door as you enter and exit. The question is whether you will believe it. This week, practice God's presence at doors—like Brother Lawrence did in his kitchen—to help you awaken to the host who stands at the door and says, "I am here for you." Let Him develop faith in you, noticing He is there.

Covenant Week (§ 41. Creation and Covenant)

Hospitality arranges places where we can all live within God's intentions of love. This week, celebrate that each of us has a place in God's family based on His unconditional love. Celebrate each other's differences. Tell stories of how you came to be who you are in the context of daily interactions. Promise to celebrate each other's stories. This week, we make room for creative distinctions and promise to embrace differences, unconditionally accepting others as they are, not as we think they should be—just as God does in making us uniquely.

Yes Week (§ 42. The Yes of God the Creator)

This week, listen for God's "Yes" to all He has made. We are in a week to honor what and whom God honors. Do not listen to your preconceived notions about who is strong and beautiful. Try honoring servants, garbage collectors, and the people who grow your food, but mostly honor God, who has given them the heart to do what they do. Listen for "Yes" moments and what God says "No" to: what distracts your relationships, your valuing of the neighbors, and so on. Make it a week to honor God in little events that awaken you to wonder because of His presence.

Season 2 (CD 3.2): The Season of Participation

Clarity Week (§ 43. Man as a Problem of Dogmatics)

The invitation for the week is to quit measuring yourself, or anybody, by human standards. Spend time acknowledging, "I am your child, Abba. I am your companion, Jesus. I am listening to you, Spirit." This act clarifies who you are because of who God is. Make the week a washing out of the old voices and welcoming the new voice reminding you that proper knowledge of yourself must begin by knowing Him who loves you.

Connection Week (§ 44. Man as the Creature of God)

Mapping our connections helps us to see who we are in the context of our relationships. This week, start a map on the wall using pictures, string, and pins to map out who you are connected to. Include Father, Son, and Spirit. Trace each person's closeness or distance to yourself and the persons of the Trinity. Who you are is all about relationships, starting with God.

Chosen Week (§ 45. Man in His Determination as the Covenant Partner of God)

This week, acknowledge that God has chosen you to be a partner. You have been seen and valued as one personally embraced because that is what He does. Tell one person a day that they are loved. At the end of the week, pass the baton to another person and ask them to tell one person a day that they are loved.

Wholeness Week (§ 46. Man as Soul and Body)

Consider that we are whole beings before God because the Spirit connects us to God and holds us as whole persons, inside and out. This week,

24   **Entering the Hospitality of God in *Church Dogmatics*, Volume 3**

we may also wrap our arms around our bodies and give thanks we are whole beings, body and soul. We may open our souls to all the good in our lives. Consider celebrating God's acceptance of all of you, body and soul. But mostly, it is a week to discover our wholeness in Jesus, who makes us complete by His Holy Spirit.

Context Week (§ 47. Man in His Time)

This is a week to contemplate the strata of time that contextualize your life. It is easy to look at one day at a time or one year. Each layer brings meaning.

On the first day of this week, let the grandeur of *eternity* overwhelm you as you recognize that Father, Son, and Holy Spirit are present in *all* of eternity.

On the second day, think about *created time*, as in going back to the beginning of creation as an act of God preparing for all that has followed.

On day three, think about *human history*, when humans have recorded what is happening. You can read your life in light of human perspectives or allow God's perspective to be the story in which you live.

Day four is about *covenant history*. In this history, God reveals Himself to humans to affirm His covenant relation, into which we are included by grace.

The fifth day is about *Jesus' history on earth*. The point of revelation discloses that He has been here since before day one and ever since. When you cry "Abba, Father," you wake up to His time and your place within it.

The sixth day is to reflect on the *genealogical history* of your life. It is a limited and specific history of people you may never know but were necessary for you to be here.

The seventh day is the *Sabbath history* of you resting your identity in Jesus' affirmation that you belong to Him. You are alive each day because He is with you by His Spirit, always a beloved child of the Father. His time is your home.

Season 3 (CD 3.3): The Season of God's Providence
Intervention Week (§ 48. The Doctrine of Providence, Its Basis and Form)

Intervention is an act of caring to redeem another from destructive outcomes. For one week, celebrate that God comes near, not occasionally to intervene, but continuously. He saves us from self-destructive patterns of isolation and insensitivity to God and others. Discover that daily gratitude is a prayer of acknowledgment for His accompaniment. Set out flowers to remind you that God cares for the flowers of the field and even more for you.

This is a week of "Nevertheless." God maintains our lives even though we have many failures. Nevertheless, He carries us through. That is His providence.

Father Week (§ 49. God the Father as Lord of His Creature)

This week focuses on God the Father, not our human father. We will mainly focus on the intimacy of His care for us. We are wonderfully made as particular persons by His loving hand that sustains us daily. With this Father focus, we may confess that we are His children. All this week, we are awakening to what is beyond and sustaining us—the personal God, who comes near to preserve our lives in His unconditional embrace.

Contrary Week (§ 50. God and Nothingness)

This is a week to consider that a domain exists beyond what we observe. It becomes clear by looking at the cross. The cross confronts all the chaos of humanity. Gratitude for the cross arises from the awareness that God has overcome what God has not chosen.

This week, name the chaos, and acknowledge that Jesus has dealt with it through His cross. The reordering of this world lives from the cross. Open your eyes this week to see the powerlessness of all that claims to be powerful and yet is under the providence of God, who will bring a good end as He made a good beginning.

Kingdom Week (§ 51. The Kingdom of Heaven, the Ambassadors of God and Their Opponents)

We often use the term *kingdom* for faraway countries. Yet God's kingdom is coming, as we pray in the Lord's prayer. Heaven is not far away; it is near and consists of a personal presence from which Jesus and the angels come to us. The angels announce the kingdom and invite us to share its peace.

This week is a chance to affirm that you were made for the kingdom of God. The will of God is that we live with honor for God, our fellow humans, and ourselves. Live with an awakening awareness that heaven is not far away. It is just beyond our seeing. It is another domain. Some have their eyes opened and see the hosts of heaven and the closeness of God's presence. Practice the presence of God by acknowledging that the triune God is here right now, and let that make a difference.

Season 4 (*CD* 3.4): The Season of Personal Presence

Creativity Week (§ 52. Ethics as a Task of the Doctrine of Creation)

God is creative and calls us to live a creative response in a focused manner. The idea of "love the one you're with" comes to mind. God is the One you are with, and life with Him is shaped for love. Ethics involves a day-by-day focus, living love for specific persons. Creative acts express a personal presence with extensive possibilities, limited to those who share your world.

Freedom Week (§ 53. Freedom before God)

This week, consider God as your freeing companion for life. Freedom often means being released *from* others. This week is an exercise in being free *with* others. The point is to be free *with* God. The resulting freedom is the ability to be yourself with someone you love who also loves you.

Think of at least one person you want to be with this week and set up a time together (a holy, set-apart time). Do whatever it takes to say, "I just want to hear your voice and have you hear mine, to let you know I am thinking of you."

Fellowship Week (§ 54. Freedom in Fellowship)

This is a week to think about who you are in connection with others. Each day, take a moment to think about a person and what would be missing if they were not in your story. Think of them as a gift from God and what He intended for you. Freedom is the fruit of connecting by having clarifying conversations about the value of the other. Joy is an emotional form of freedom fulfilled in love.

Openness Week (§ 55. Freedom for Life)

The openness of this week is to consider joy and health as a gift that gives you freedom as you are with others who love you for your unique self. This week, be open to seeing your work in new ways as a participation in the playfulness of God. Let others know they are seen and known by you and the One who made them and accompanies them.

Consideration Week (§ 56. Freedom in Limitation)

This week, ask who you are as a child of God in the time given to you. *Consideration* means thinking about how to meet the needs of others as children of God. Think of one person each day this week as a child of God. See if this consideration brings up any corresponding way to treat them differently to honor who they are as God's child. Consider yourself as the hospitable presence of God's honor. Count them as worthy to abide under the Father's gracious, accompanying care.

 CONCLUSION FOR THE CHURCH: This overview is an invitation to experience this third volume of the *Church Dogmatics* in transformative practices. These are short suggestions intended to translate the theology of creation into rhythms of community life.

 COMMENTARY:
- The Church becomes visible with seasonal celebrations to indwell the story of God.
- Each week is a call to human hospitality within God's hospitality.
- Each week progresses in understanding the continuing relationship of the Creator to our lives lived in the context of His accompaniment.

INSIGHT FOR PASTORS: This chapter is designed as an experiential engagement with theology. Adapt and modify to fit your situation, but always reflect on the intent in the *CD* so that it is faithful to God and your context—in that order.

INSIGHT FOR THEOLOGIANS: This chapter is an invitation for theologians to realize that theology needs to serve the Church at least as much as it serves the academy. In seeing the outworking of theology in these weekly celebrations and calls for participation, we begin to see the intent of God and the participation of humans in the life of creation with the Creator.

? CLARIFYING QUESTIONS: Does your theology prefer definitions and descriptions *or* the upbuilding of a community in the life of God, lived in practical relationships with God and humans?

PART 2

CHURCH DOGMATICS 3.1

Engaging the God of Creation

Karl Barth	Church Dogmatics	I/1	1932 (1936 ET)
Karl Barth	Church Dogmatics	I/2	1938 (1956 ET)
Karl Barth	Church Dogmatics	II/1	1940 (1957 ET)
Karl Barth	Church Dogmatics	II/2	1942 (1957 ET)
Karl Barth	Church Dogmatics	III/1	1945 (1958 ET)
Karl Barth	Church Dogmatics	III/2	1948 (1960 ET)
Karl Barth	Church Dogmatics	III/3	1950 (1961 ET)
Karl Barth	Church Dogmatics	III/4	1951 (1961 ET)
Karl Barth	Church Dogmatics	IV/1	1953 (1956 ET)
Karl Barth	Church Dogmatics	IV/2	1955 (1958 ET)
Karl Barth	Church Dogmatics	IV/3.1	1959 (1961 ET)
Karl Barth	Church Dogmatics	IV/3.2	1959 (1962 ET)
Karl Barth	Church Dogmatics	IV/4	1967 (1969 ET)

CHURCH DOGMATICS, CHAPTER 9

"The Work of Creation"

CHAPTER 6

ACKNOWLEDGING THE HOST AND HIS HOME

§ 40. Faith in God the Creator

FOCUS STATEMENT: In this first paragraph of *CD* 3, we are oriented to know the One who made the universe. The triune God made the world for companionship, gathering His children to Himself. We must start getting to know Him, meeting our host at the door.

Being oriented means coming to embrace the God who has come to us. "Faith in God the Creator," the title of § 40, opens the way to acknowledge this One who is there for us. Faith comes from meeting the Creator. It develops from being in His presence. Faith is a human accommodation to His reality in thought and act, like believing in the sun because it is there and consequently living in its light. Our faith is contingent, reflecting on the givenness of reality in God.

We will consider the universe as a house created by God as a physical structure for His creatures. He makes it home by His personal presence in Jesus. Through Jesus, we come to know God the Father as Creator.

In this paragraph, we engage God's invitation to respond to His initiation. The invitation calls for a response. We are coming home as children to live within His hospitality.

INTRODUCTION: The purpose of *CD* 3 is to reveal the God-creation relation. This text of chapter 9 begins a lengthy discussion on "I believe in God the Father Almighty, Maker of heaven and earth." Barth's methodology progresses by seeing theology through Christ, meaning we have faith only as the Creator makes Himself known in Jesus, who comes to show us His Father.

In paragraph 40, we clarify the meaning of "I believe." This discussion explains the nature of human faith in coming to know God the Father. Faith is not a thought in one's head—what one hopes is true. Instead, faith is contact with reality, a personal connection initiated by the living God to whom we wholeheartedly respond.

33

We have moved from the God who speaks (*CD* 1) to the God who loves in freedom (*CD* 2), which brings us in *CD* 3 to become beloved partners within the time and space (creation) made for us. God built the house and made it a home for covenant connection.

CONTEXT: *CD* 3.1
Pages in Paragraph: 39 pages (pp. 3–41)

TEXT: § 40. Faith in God the Creator

OPENING SUMMARY: The insight that man owes his existence and form, together with all the reality distinct from God, to God's creation, is achieved only in the reception and answer of the divine self-witness, that is, only in faith in Jesus Christ, i.e., in the knowledge of the unity of Creator and creature actualized in Him, and in the life in the present mediated by Him, under the right and in the experience of the goodness of the Creator toward His creature.[1]

SUMMARY:

Let's start by flipping around Barth's opening summary to clarify his point.

The goodness of the Creator provides the basis for human experience. Our faith is not the starting point.

The insight we gain is a given knowledge mediated by God. God's reality creates faith in us. We do not create faith in the sun rising; its rising creates faith in us.

Faith seeks to understand given reality with curiosity—the meaning of faith seeking understanding.

In the person of Jesus Christ, we see the unity of the Creator and the creature. We see heaven and earth together. Faith develops, acknowledging what He claims to be.

Knowledge of creation begins with Jesus. We cannot begin with independent human assessments. Human experience unintentionally sets us adrift from reality.

Throughout *CD* 3, Barth will take a christological approach, learning about creation through listening to Jesus.

Human existence can only be understood by listening to God's revelation; revealing who He is and what He has done develops a reflective mode called *faith*.

---

1. Karl Barth, Geoffrey William Bromiley, and Thomas F. Torrance, *Church Dogmatics: The Doctrine of Creation*, 3.1 (London; New York: T&T Clark, 2004), p. 3. Henceforth, *CD*.

CD 3 is an expansive exploration of the statement "I believe in God the Father Almighty, Maker of heaven and earth," including believing in the Son and Spirit, as in the Apostles' Creed.

When we speak of creation, we consider all that exists apart from God.

We must not skip past "I believe" in understanding God and creation.

Faith is a reception of the divine witness. He lets us see while we are blind and hear when we are deaf. Faith is not blindness; it is what God gives because we are blind and deaf.

We cannot understand by reason or observation the world's creation out of nothing. It is an act revealed by God alone.

> Throughout *CD* 3, Barth will take a christological approach, learning about creation through listening to Jesus.

Concerning creation, we either believe the world developed with a blind progression or that the revelation of God has overcome our blindness. Both are forms of faith. The first is blind faith construed from human reasoning; the second is listening faith attained from the Creator.

There are three reasons we must treat the doctrine of creation as an article of faith:

1. The whole of reality exists, *known apart from God* as His work.

   This belief in God as Creator is a hypothesis that can have no other foundation than God's self-witness; therefore, we respond in faith.

2. The whole of reality exists as *willed by God*; the world and our proper knowledge of it would not exist if not from Him.

   a. An "egological" view of creation contends, "If I exist, the cause of the world must be there for me. Even God must be there for me." This belief is a theological error beginning with the human.

   b. God has to speak to humanity for Himself with His voice and not through the voice of creation. Humans can hear only in faith.

3. A confession of God as the Creator must be *rooted in the Bible's language*, the creed's source.

   Believing someone loves because they tell you so (revelation) is entirely different from silently hoping someone might love you (blind faith). Barth clarifies faith as proper hearing.

How do we know God created heaven and earth?

- We do not ask how we justify our knowing.
- We do not ask about feelings or probabilities to support our case.
- We do not ask what logical necessities support our view.
- We do not ask what comfort and convictions result from our beliefs, no matter how good.

How can we say we *know* it is so? How can we confess God the Father alongside confessing Jesus and the Holy Spirit?

- We cannot begin with philosophical arguments.
- We cannot begin by claiming it as the starting point of the Bible and that it is explained in the Bible, even though this is true.

The basis of our claim is that the Bible states that God is the Almighty Creator of heaven and earth as God's witness to Himself.

To speak of *knowledge* of God, we must look to God with us, revealed in Jesus. This proper entryway overrides all assumptions and philosophies based on human considerations.

Jesus brings the simplicity of divine self-witness, which overcomes the human myths that might lead us away from the God of the Bible.

Jesus reveals the truth of God to us:

- God is not alone. He enters the world-space where He is Lord and affirms its reality.
- He is God not only in Himself but outside Himself.
- He became one with His creature in a free, contingent act.
- Jesus reveals Himself in a sphere (creation) in which God acts and reveals apart from His sphere (eternity). He includes His partners in His actions, through whom He reveals Himself to others.
- God became flesh for His community as Messiah, mediator, head, and representative of humanity before God. He is the Lord over all powers and dominions in heaven and on earth.
- Humanity is not alone. Our sphere of life is not the only one.
- Humans are the work of God's grace, adopted into unity with Him.
- We live because God lives for us and frees us to be God's creatures.
- This Son became a creature and called God Father.
- Jesus stands securely for the reality of humanity in His person and work and for the reality of His Father as Creator.

As Creator, God is unique in His loving omnipotence and has reconciled the world to Himself in Jesus.

Jesus has become the means to know (*noetic* connection) the Almighty Father as the actual source (*ontic* basis) for knowledge of creation. Jesus is the key to the secrets of creation.

Jesus is the known being through whom we have seen and believed and by whom we have faith.

"I believe" means that I have been met by this other reality (Jesus) and may consequently come to understand (the Father and creation).

What kind of faith is it through Jesus Christ that contains the secret of creation, the Creator, and the creature? It is a personal recognition that God's reality is at His disposal as the theater, instrument, and object of His activity.

As we are in Christ, we become new creations. His creation echoes on as He makes humanity new in Himself.

Jesus invites us to know and address God as our Father. As we know this Father, we come to know the Creator, not the other way around.

Faith in Jesus is an entrance into fellowship with God and, therefore, a relationship with the Creator.

 CONCLUSION FOR THE CHURCH: The Church is invited in this paragraph to get its eyes off itself and to engage the God who made everything. He wants to renew our lives. Faith opens the way. Faith cannot be about humans trying harder to believe in a God they do not see. It is a call to the Church to point faithfully to who Jesus is, who He reveals (His Father), and who we are in the context of God's provision and presence. God hosts His Church within creation. The Church hosts God by making Him known. The living host, Jesus, invites all creatures to experience His love through the Church as a community who responds to the Father, through the Son, by the Spirit.

 COMMENTARY:
- The doctrine of creation should not be engaged by looking out the window.
- We begin understanding the creation by listening to Jesus, who tells us He is from the Father, shows us the Father, and restores us to the Father.
- By listening, we come to hear the One we may trust. Faith is created by the reality we encounter.

> Faith is a confidence that the universe comes from a personal act, is sustained for personal reasons, and is understood by hearing God's intent for that which He loves.

- Faith is a confidence that the universe comes from a personal act, is sustained for personal reasons, and is understood by hearing God's intent for that which He loves.
- To believe in God the Father is to set the context for understanding the structure and purpose of all creation—including humans.
- Faith in Jesus is a call to be informed and formed by reality from its source.

INSIGHT FOR PASTORS: As pastors, we want our people to have a vibrant faith. We misstep when we focus on *their* faith-building practices. This paragraph grabs our ears and turns us to face the Creator. We listen. We learn. We hear the heart of the Creator. Faith grows, knowing this Other. Faith is living in the presence of this One who made and sustains us. We are privileged to point to the Bible, pointing to Jesus, who is pointing to His Father, to all He loves in the world, and especially to each child He loves.

This paragraph calls us not to jump to the end but to begin at the beginning—you were made for love. We help our people see and hear the One who has made and ordered the world, who shares with us as we affirm: "We believe in God the Father Almighty, Maker of heaven and earth."

INSIGHT FOR THEOLOGIANS: The task of a theologian is to make God known, especially where God has chosen to be known. Discussing creation, we face the problematic urge to look at creation to discern the fingerprints of God. Please don't do it. Inadvertently, we slip in *our* concerns, detaching creation from the Creator's intentions.

Should we care for creation? Absolutely. We share in the Creator's concern for the whole. Should we care about humans created in the image of God? Yes, but it is so easy to select what we think is the image of God in humans instead of seeing the image of God in Jesus.

We must begin our study of creation by understanding the intent of the Father, the master builder who created space and time for hospitality. He continues as the host. We must think theologically, letting Him host us and hosting Him as Jesus hosted and let others (especially the marginalized) host Him.

Theology provides the lenses to engage the broken world and pursue God's vision of healing, faithfully loving His creation.

Acknowledging the Host and His Home

? CLARIFYING QUESTIONS: Does your theology of creation begin by looking at the complexity of creation to develop a reasonable faith that there must be a Creator? *Or* do you begin listening to the Creator to understand all He has made and let faith be born in you?

CHAPTER 7

GOD'S GROUNDWORK FOR THE HISTORY OF LOVE

§ 41. Creation and Covenant

FOCUS STATEMENT: God's hospitality story begins with the universe's formation. God creates to connect with His chosen creation: humans. In § 41, the theme of "Creation and Covenant" weaves together the "house" of creation, intended as the "home" for God's covenanted children.

In this chapter, we explore the groundbreaking work of God the Creator, who intends to fulfill His love in freedom, preparing for a history of hospitable living together.

The Tree of Life is a silent witness to the presence and love of God. The Tree of the Knowledge of Good and Evil stands nearby as a call to obedience, not a test. The goal is that humans will choose freedom and the life that accompanies it. The garden provides a place of abundance, playing out the richness of God's grace and mercy.

INTRODUCTION: Barth loves the story of the Bible. This section creatively explores the intention of God in putting the universe together. This exploration leads to understanding the meaning of human life in a covenant relationship, meaning to live in response to God's faithful love.

Three subsections investigate the Creator-creation relationship. First, we explore the uniqueness of calling God "Creator" and His comprehensive involvement with creation. Next, Barth explains the creation narratives, revealing God's covenant purposes. Finally, we see God's purpose concerning His creatures, made like Him to love.

This chapter helps us understand the world as God's provision. Creation is purposefully made for humanity, who are God's beloved creatures yet ultimately rebellious. However, God's love never wavers when humans struggle, choosing what God has not chosen.

▌▌▌ CONTEXT: *CD* 3.1
Pages in Paragraph: 288 pages (pp. 42–329)

Subsections
1. Creation, History and Creation History
2. Creation as the External Basis of the Covenant
3. The Covenant as the Internal Basis of Creation

📖 TEXT: § 41. Creation and Covenant

✠ OPENING SUMMARY: Creation comes first in the series of works of the triune God, and is thus the beginning of all the things distinct from God Himself. Since it contains in itself the beginning of time, its historical reality eludes all historical observation and account, and can be expressed in the biblical creation narratives only in the form of pure saga. But according to this witness the purpose and therefore the meaning of creation is to make possible the history of God's covenant with man which has its beginning, its centre and its culmination in Jesus Christ. The history of this covenant is as much the goal of creation as creation itself is the beginning of this history.[1]

✠ SUMMARY:

1. Creation, History and Creation History (pp. 42–93)

The term *creation*, when used in the Bible or by the Church, generally refers to a work of God outside Himself.

The event in creation becomes a revelation of God's glory, an expansive unveiling of God's character.

All things have their source in God's eternal will, the work of God's freedom, as a revelation of His glory.

All God's works fulfill His partnership in His covenant of grace with creation.

The whole universe is the theater where the history of the covenant of grace plays out.

---

1. *CD* 3.1, § 41, p. 42.

The world depends on God, created by the One distinct creator, reconciler, redeemer God, and not by some force or unknown cause.

The God who creates is the Father, Son, and Holy Spirit—this is the freely loving, personal God Almighty.

God's first work, established from God's distinct reality, is set off from God's second work, the sphere of our reality.

Humans participate in a history grounded in and directed by the will of God.

God's covenant in Jesus is not an afterthought, a contingency in response to human action; it is willed and enacted from the beginning.

Humanity is not the center of the meaning of creation; God, with humanity included in the covenant, must be the center.

God created the world to display His glory.

God makes room for a continuation worthy of His beginning, fulfilled in His history with what He creates.

God's covenant can never be seen as contractual laws or lofty ideals. It is God's dynamic, loving commitment to His creation. Through it, He freely embraces, aligns, and calls His creatures to a loving response.

The unified Trinity works in creation, each with particular personal variations.

The Father is the Creator of heaven and earth. He is the origin, the eternal source of the Son and Spirit, the One who brings into finite existence what is other than Himself as time, space, and matter.

The Son and Spirit have no beginning or end. Created being has a beginning and end.

In relationship to the world, God the Father is uniquely the Creator. However, the works of the Trinity are undivided, the work of the Father with the Son and Spirit.

As the One who loves in freedom, the Father connects with creation through His Son, speaking and hearing in a manner worthy of God.

Through the Son, God bears from eternity the curse of all humanity and fulfills the obedient response for all humans.

The Father loved the world as the outworking of His love for His Son.

Jesus is the Lord of all things in that all things were made by Him, in Him, and through Him.

Jesus Christ is the eternal Mediator, who has taken our humanity on Himself as the firstborn of creation. He is the living Word, who was in the beginning and became a historical reality as the Word incarnate.

Jesus is the expression of the inner life of God the Father. From eternity,

God's Groundwork for the History of Love

Jesus was the decree of God's mediation. He bears our nature in His flesh as One loved by God, extending His love through Him to all creation.

All that is true of the Father and Son in creation is true of the Spirit. The Spirit is with them as eternal God. He is in communion with them in their interconnection.

> Humanity is not the center of the meaning of creation; God, with humanity included in the covenant, must be the center.

The Spirit is the innermost secret and the brightest revelation to humans. The Spirit works at the intersection of God's triune life and His creation.

In the Spirit, there exists the fatherly compassion of God. As the Spirit glorifies the Son, the relationship between God and His creatures becomes deeply personal.

The Father creates the creature in harmony with Himself through His Son and for His glorious enjoyment in the Spirit.

True theological history, within which human history resides, is God's history, a red thread in the context of all other human perspectives of history.

We could call God's history "salvation history" if we do not make it into a history of religion. God's history is hospitable to all other narratives. They can never be independent of God's history.

"The covenant of grace is *the* theme of history. The history of salvation is *the* history."[2]

There is no change between creation and what follows. Creation continues in the history of the covenant. God's providence also continues God's creation and covenant with His creatures.

History begins with creation. It is an event. It is not a timeless truth. God is present at every point in time as Creator.

As we believe in Jesus, we believe in the triune God. We also believe in ourselves as creatures who live by grace, which defines our being as God's covenant companions.

Many believe the Bible gives a mythology or a philosophy of creation. But the Bible is a history that sets humans in the light of God's grace. God's meaning and purpose inform the history of fulfillment in what takes place between God and His creatures.

There is a realm of nature, but even it lives within the sphere of grace and points to it.

The creation texts are prehistorical and narrative accounts of God's words and acts. The Old Testament prepares for the history of the New

---

2. *CD* 3.1, § 41, p. 60.

44   *Church Dogmatics* 3.1

Testament. These speak of one Lord and Creator of the world. They have a temporal, this-worldly meaning.

The Bible affirms creation as a historical reality, preparing the story of God with His creatures for the rest of the Bible. Through it, the divine Father speaks to us in His own Son to inform us of His purposes.

God is before, above, and after all time. He is not time; it is really in Him. Creatures live in time, on a one-way road of a succession of days.

Within the history of creation is the history of the covenant, a counterpart to "our" time, with humanity in isolation from God in sin.

God's counterpart in time is the covenant of grace. God accepts us in the grace of a new time where our lost time is condemned and renewed.

God's presence constitutes the new time. Something new has appeared in the resurrection. He heals time and its wounds and makes it real-time.

To have real-time is to live in Him and with Him. We participate in His present. We live in transition from our past into a new future.

History takes place in time. Before its commencing, there is only God's eternity.

No one was there at creation to see it all unfold. Its only content and witness is God the Creator.

All history is limited to the scope of human presence. All of God's history is outside the scope of human history. All human history takes place within God's history.

God's history is more central to what happens than fleeting human history. The resurrection of Jesus illustrates this point.

There can be no history if no historian gives a proper account. If the narrative is human, it is limited to a selected history and cannot reveal the fullness of God's history.

The history of creation is prehistorical; not all narrative is historical (written by human observers).

All human history is nonhistorical (profoundly incomplete and slanted) compared to God's account (the hospitable host of true history).

The modern mind would like to edit out God's history based on a priority of self-confidence in its history. Thus, their history becomes unreal, more of a myth created in their image. This method creates chaos and division.

In addition to the prehistorical, historical, and nonhistorical, there is a depiction in the form of saga. This approach is a poetic prepicture of the prehistorical reality of history. It tells a story within the confines of time and space in a sphere of meaningful action.

God's Groundwork for the History of Love

In saga, the history of God is prominent. Human history enfolds within the story of God.

Liberalism "purified" the Bible to meet its criteria of truth, expelling the Word of God as its living center.

Saga is distinct from myth as well as "history." In myth, the story and characters are not real, but they point to principles in reality and relationships in distinction from history, attempting an "accurate" record from a human perspective.

Genesis 1 and 2 are introductory narratives. The first account recounts the creation of the world created for humans. The second account engages the creation of humans. These prehistorical events deal with the emergence of creation as a saga. Their narration's obvious meaning must be prioritized as creation history, not myth or fairy tale.

Creation myth is a term for literature that depicts events and figures that do not happen anywhere or anytime but that tell a story for enjoyment in an abstract sense or to present eternal truths. These stories may appear to know of creation, but they merely offer one view on a problem needing explanation. These are human productions formed in the cultures of the ancient.

The creation saga of the Bible is not a myth. It points to a historical saga and the history that follows from it. The Bible displays God's activity and confrontation with His creatures.

This saga is a genuine narration of history, not invented by humans. It is the opposite of myth; it speaks of God's active will in creation.

The Babylonian creation myth offers little distinction between the human and the god. The spheres are intermeshed, rising from human imagination.

Genesis 1 and 2 visualize the emergence of the world as the work of God. Creation does not aim at human independence. It aims at God and the world created by Him.

History is a human-*focused* version of a story. *Myth* is a human-*shaped* story, projecting from human experience onto the heaven and gods. As used here, saga points to God, as God reveals Himself in prehistory. Posthistorical literature will take the form of prophecy.

> God's history is more central to what happens than fleeting human history.

Imagination is a legitimate part of all human knowing. To neglect or misuse the gift of imagination is possible.

Imagination is our window to past and future reality and to all that is not present to us now. Therefore, it is a divine gift to be used creatively for God's glory and the service of humanity in engaging reality.

The biblical writers wrote as moved by the Spirit, remembering and speaking under God's guidance. All language requires imagination; not all reveals the truth.

In these creation stories, we see that the Creator encounters humans. The unknown God became known. What is important is not the form of the saga but its object: the Almighty Creator.

The Spirit who spoke to the biblical writers must speak to hearers and readers today to distinguish between what is myth and what is divine witness.

Our interpretation of creation must explore the relationship between God's creation and covenant.

2. Creation as the External Basis of the Covenant (pp. 94–228)

Humans are not self-existent. We are not self-originating (I made myself), separately constituted (I need no one), or self-sustaining (I take care of myself).

We are created by God, given meaning by God, sustained by God, and given dignity by God.

God is free in His love and desires something other than Himself. God does not need His creature but demonstrates His love from eternity.

God's covenant is His love exercised and fulfilled. His creation is the exclusive, external basis of His covenant. He only asks that humans live the covenant purpose for which He created them.

God equips humans to become partners within the hospitable form of creation.

Creation is not the covenant. "The covenant is the goal of creation and creation the way to the covenant."[3]

Creation prepares for the outworking of grace; it is not just a house, but a home built for connecting love.

The story of the world's creation is comparable to building a temple, a meeting place for God and humanity to live lovingly together.

The goal of creation is human participation in God's Sabbath rest and joy.

God and humanity exist in a relationship that displays separation and interconnection in this theater of the covenant.

Genesis establishes God as the Creator, and the heavens and earth are His creations. He made them from nothing.

---

3. *CD* 3.1, § 41, p. 97.

God's Groundwork for the History of Love   47

The story introduces us to the theater's construction, where God's history of hospitality and drama plays out. This includes the earth and heavens. Heaven is God's dwelling place. God gives the earth to His children.

What is ungodly or antigodly can only exist by God's decision. He makes room for the freedom of His creature, even though it means possible rejection of Him.

The Spirit of the Lord is there, bringing life to God's good, creating work. The Spirit hovers over chaos as an eagle watches over its young.

God creates light, which results in shadows. The shadow is not His creation; it is where His light and His will do not shine.

The Lord speaks with His compassionate voice as the Creator. Creation has a personal source; it is not the impersonal movement of energy, a natural impulse, or an ingrained destiny.

God is the living being who precedes all living beings. He creates humans in His image by His Word. Humans may deny His Word, but they cannot remove it.

God speaks. The voice of God is the origin of all reality other than God. "And God said . . ." is the birthing point of all creation.

Israel's history continually draws on the utterance of God with "Thus says the Lord . . ." moving from the past to a new direction. God prepares to guide and sustain His people for a future toward which His purposes flow.

By His living Word, God reveals Himself in the story's unfolding toward which the Bible directs us. The Creator reconciles the cultures of the ancient world and moves them toward redemption.

The Word that creates also speaks in Israel in the Incarnate One and is still today "God with us," in whom we exist and have our being.

God's first work is light that will never cease to shine. Each day He separates the light from the darkness.

Light is a symbol of the revelation of the grace of God. It overcomes the darkness and brings the promise of an encounter with God. It is the "Yes" of God's glory showing concern for His creature as a prototype of His revelation. Light uniquely accompanies God throughout the cosmos.

God creates goodness in the world outside His goodness and makes it the object of His pleasure. God's ordering of the world also stands against darkness and chaos.

In these passages, to create is to separate. Light and darkness meet. Ocean and land coexist. God's separation distinguishes and creates order. Light exists because it is created; darkness is its byproduct without its own reality. This pairing is a limited analogy of the elect and rejected, and an analogy in the "Yes" and "No" of God's Word. The bold "Yes" implies a consequent "No."

God names the distinctions that create our sense of time and the sequence of time. He is Lord over time made by Him.

Our days are not a human invention; they are a divine work. Day and night, evening and morning, are part of the hospitality of God.

The darkness does not escape God. He is the Lord over that as well. God gives it a name and assigns it a place. He upholds the night. He is present there. But we are called from darkness to walk in the light.

Evening comes when His work of separating light is completed. Morning starts a second day to live within God's history. God's Word has taken on the form of time.

"It is this fundamental act of the divine compassion and condescension which becomes apparent in the fact that God not only has eternity but also time, and that now He also gives time to His creatures as the living-space appropriate to them."[4]

On the second day, God orders the theater of life to stand against the watery chaos. In separating the heavens from the earth, God has named the space to live before God.

God speaks. The voice of God is the origin of all reality other than God.

God continues to fashion living space for humanity as the land becomes habitable. By the love of God, the sea becomes a bounded threat. The land is made fruitful so humans can live on the earth.

God provided for all living things. "This spread table belongs necessarily to the centre of the house built by God."[5]

Only God was there to see the world being readied. History begins with God's preparation for His covenant partner.

God made the earth to be inhabited. God makes the home where humans live and die, with joy and sorrow, sin and worship.

Because of the alienation of humanity, the "earth" comes to mean "opposed to God," aligned with human failure. It still belongs to God. There is hope. The promise to Abraham is to bless all the nations of the earth through him.

"The third day is the day of the earth as a dwelling-place and sphere of life; the day of that which is indispensable, of that which is required of the earth, in fulfilment of its destiny."[6] God has provided for humans all that is

---

4. *CD* 3.1, § 41, p. 130.
5. *CD* 3.1, § 41, p. 143.
6. *CD* 3.1, § 41, p. 152.

God's Groundwork for the History of Love   49

needed to eat. There is grace in each morsel. Where there is life, there can be history.

Natural history is a precursor and component of the covenant of grace. Humans need the heavenly bodies and their provision of light. By them, human reason and senses participate and play an active part in the life of the Creator.

Humans named the sun, moon, and stars. These belong to the sphere created for human knowledge, alongside all the animals and plants that humans named.

Modern views exclude discussion of the purpose of the cosmic system, including consideration of the human as the purpose for shaping the world's living space.

While the creation points to God, this does not assume anyone will see, accept, or understand the signs. The heavenly bodies cannot speak or convince.

With all their brightness, warmth, and rhythm of days, the heavenly lights allow humans to have an ordered history with God.

The creation of the heavenly lights on the fourth day makes the way for evening and morning, thus creating days, time, and history.

The fifth day brings the creation of living things, fish and birds to fill the heavens and the seas, all creatures endowed with independent life.

Humans are an innovation within this creaturely realm, inseparable yet unique. We engage the waters and the skies but live separately from these domains.

God blesses His creatures, empowering them with the distinctive promise of success. Multiplication takes place, and the sequence of fathers, mothers, children, and grandchildren in all species. These generations are central to biblical history within the covenant.

God wills His creatures to thrive in the freedom given to them.

The biblical story reveals the human in their particularity, set in the context of the company of living things in this created environment.

Humans and animals are created on the same day. They are all His creatures, but humans are honored and made for covenant companionship with God.

There is no "mother earth" that brings all living things into existence. God brings them forth as His creatures.

The story has moved toward the installation of the occupant for whom the house was prepared. This was very good. The human is not quite the final crown of creation. "Creation is crowned only when God

50   *Church Dogmatics* **3.1**

in His joyful Sabbath rest looks back upon it and down on what He has created."[7]

God created humans in His image. God is the prototype to which we correspond. We are patterned after the nature of God Himself.

The rest of creation is distinct from God, not a counterpart. Humans are counterparts alongside God. God speaks to humans as an "I" and addresses the other as a "Thou." Humans are unique in entering this kind of relationship.

God designed humans as male and female. Humans are beings whose differentiation allows for existing as true partners who are capable of action and responsible relation to God.

Human life is not alien to God, who aimed to create a counterpart capable of harmonious self-encounter, free coexistence, and reciprocity.

The analogy between God and humans exists in the I-Thou relation. God is constitutive and the human reflective. The analogy can only begin with God and be derivative for the human.

Humans are distinct from God even as they are connected. Humans were granted freedom to interact as partners of God and one another.

The Bible is not interested in human possibilities exercising their self-determination. Humans become fully themselves in fellowship with the One who made them.

Humanity is no more solitary than God; they are a duality within their union as male and female.

While humans share the creatureliness of the sexes with the beasts, they stand before God as God's companions.

The human cannot maintain an independent being. The human was blessed initially, but turned away to a curse.

The episode of the fall does not obliterate the image of God in humans. There is a real man in the image and likeness of God who comes on our behalf: Jesus and His community.

The Word, the friend to humanity, affirms the natural being and acts of humanity. He comes with His pledge and hope.

God creates a counterpart to whom He can reveal Himself in a relationship.

Humanity's interrelatedness as male and female occurs in this gifted way. Each is prepared for freedom in response, reflecting the divine likeness.

God is free for humans. Humans are freed for other humans. This image

---

7. *CD* 3.1, § 41, p. 181.

God's Groundwork for the History of Love

echoes the analogy of relations (*analogia relationis*) from God to humans. We may not project concepts of freedom onto God from human intuitions (*analogia entis*).

The image of God is depicted in the juxtaposition of male and female together. They are distinct, yet each cannot be without the other and still be the image of God.

Loving coexistence takes place first in God Himself. God then speaks into being with a summoning "I" to His creature as the summoned "Thou": "I have made you."

In that humans are made in the likeness of God, only God has control over human life. To kill another person confronts the dignity of God, who intends life for His creatures.

The image of God does not mean an *ideal state* anywhere in the Bible. God's free and gracious will is continually fulfilled in loving imperfect humans.

Adam does not possess the image of God; it is God bequeathing to humans a profound mercy. Humans have looked for the image of God in nature, the sun, or their rulers. Paul equates the image of God with Jesus. The Son of God is the image of God and the fulfillment of human existence.

When facing Him openly, we reflect the glory of the Lord like a mirror. We are revealed and transformed into His image at the same time. We see our actual image and simultaneously discover our true image in Him. This happens through the work of the Spirit.

The Son of God is the first bearer of the image of God. We are made conformable to His image. This is not our choice but happens as God's choice, facilitated by Jesus and fulfilled by the Spirit.

The cosmos is prepared as a home for humans and fellow creatures nourished by the existence surrounding them all. God gives food as a gift to all.

God did not originally intend animals as food. God intended humans to be vegetarian. "Creation means peace—peace between the Creator and creatures, and peace among creatures themselves."[8]

> God creates a counterpart to whom He can reveal Himself in a relationship.

The creation story of the sixth day portrays God's intention of a harmonious whole.

All that God made was good, meaning it was properly prepared to provide the framework for God's covenant with His people.

---

8. *CD* 3.1, § 41, p. 209.

On the seventh day, God revealed His freedom to limit His activity, love what He has created, and be the Creator in unity with the world. "The creature finds its completion in the fact that God in His own person has given Himself to belong to it."[9]

God's love willed the whole world so His beloved partner would belong to Him in the fulfillment of love. It is fashioned in an integrated and orderly manner. Each part has an engagement with the whole.

In completing creation, God does not retire. He sustains the world and is active within it.

The Sabbath becomes a divine gift for humans. It creates a time and place to enjoy God's freedom, joy, blessings, and peace.

Rest is more than relaxation. The Sabbath is a day to breathe in and be refreshed by the presence of the Creator. This requires taking a break from human labor, but the main point is about connection and renewal.

God has not retreated or lost interest in His creation. God not only created all things in Christ but with a view to their fulfillment in Christ. He could see it all restored in Christ.

The Sabbath belongs to creation. God gives Himself to it as His own. The Sabbath is an invitation to be with Him.

God is not interested in merely giving humans a holiday. It is time to remove life's daily distractions and open yourself to God's immediate presence.

To become hospitable to His presence, we have to make space for God. As we rest in Him, He rests in us. We are transformed as children of God who no longer live only for ourselves.

God intends a direct connection between Himself and His creature that reaches deep intimacy.

3. The Covenant as the Internal Basis of Creation (pp. 229–329)

We have studied the formation of the house (the earth) God built for His covenant partner.

Now we turn to the purpose for which the house was completed, the relationship between God and His creatures (the covenant). We cannot properly conceive of creation without understanding God's intent.

In the second creation account (Genesis 2), humans do not merely exist; they reveal God's loving intent. Human life is meaningful, the work of the personal God.

---

9. *CD* 3.1, § 41, p. 217.

The creature reveals the glory of God, who makes the human fully alive, being born from God's triune life.

God intends humans to live a life of gratitude. Neglecting thankfulness misses the reason for our existence.

Creation is one long preparation, the road to the covenant, opening to God's freeing love.

God does not just create a space for humans. God fashioned a place to share a history of extraordinary love.

The internal covenant heartbeat is the purpose for making the embodying world.

Historically, creation precedes covenant. Purposefully, covenant precedes creation as its reason to exist.

The second creation narrative is not merely a preparation for the fall. It kicks off the history of the covenant relationship in which God is unwaveringly faithful.

God's personal name is revealed at the beginning of this account. He is Yahweh, the God of Israel, for whom He is Lord of creation and covenant.

The human is made out of the earth to which we are attached. We serve the earth on God's behalf.

Humans are uniquely distinguished as living souls. God breathes life into Adam's nostrils through His most personal act.

The human triumphs over the earth from which we are made. We become its gardener and caretaker.

Adam prefigures Israel as the mediator chosen from among and on behalf of the nations of the earth to take responsibility as God's servant, a sign of hope.

The most profound meaning of this passage points to Jesus:

- He exists for the perfecting of the earth.
- He redeems the earth from its barrenness and death.
- He is the ultimate completion of God's hope.
- He belongs to all creation, all humanity, all Israel.
- He is the personal immediacy to all God has made.
- With Him, we are on the threshold of the history of the covenant.

The second telling begins with bare earth, waiting for fulfillment. The void parallels the waters of the first telling. It is waiting to be made habitable as a sign of its intended future.

The panorama of the whole, especially the inclusion of humans, completes the emerging point of creation:

1. In this story, humans are distinctly different from God as His creation from the earth. But the fingers of God do the shaping, quickened to life by the breath of God.
2. In this story, the human is whole: body and soul, internal and external. Greek thought saw the body as a prison. There was a separation between the physical and spiritual, disgracing the body as a platonic dualism.
3. In this story, we have the Hebrew picture of a human who walks before God as a responsible member of His people.

Humans are one creature in the creaturely world. Humans are neither shining stars nor uneasy guests in this world.

God has made humans citizens of this world, in which they may be a guest or a stranger.

God fashioned the body and what we may call the heart, a "living soul" with a breath of life.

The garden was a place created to give pleasure and delight as a place of abundance. In the middle stood the Tree of Life.

The Tree of the Knowledge of Good and Evil is also in the garden. It is associated with permission and prohibition.

Humans will care for the land, and the land will provide for the human. Each will host the other.

The garden is a supernatural act of creating something natural. This is a place endowed with the personal presence of God. The creation of humans completes the garden.

The story unfolds in geographical and temporal terms. It relates to the earth God created for humans, but as prehistorical history.

God's Paradise is a sanctuary set aside from other places. The Sabbath was a time of rest; this is a place of rest and renewal.

The tabernacle had a center in the holy of holies, so this garden has a center with the two trees. This place is a sacred orchard, and humans are to nurture the fruit.

Paradise is a place of glory. Like the holy of holies, it is a place where God meets with humans for blessing. Like all the trees in the garden, the two trees bear fruit that is good to eat.

The Tree of Life tells the human where he is, to whom the garden belongs, and what he might expect. We do not know if the humans ate from it, only that they were barred after they disobeyed. It represents the life of God's presence and provision.

God's Groundwork for the History of Love

The second tree in the garden is a sign of the possibility given to humanity by God. It is not the Tree of Death. It is the Tree of the Knowledge of Good and Evil. But it has a threat of death, making vivid the wisdom of complying with God's will.

To eat from this tree enables discernment. One can judge between what ought to be and what ought not. This independent judgment is to be like God.

If the creature rejects what God has accepted or accepts what God has resisted, the human prefers self over God. This result is an undesirable possibility.

In eating from the forbidden tree, the human says "no" to the divine possibility of the "Yes" signified in the Tree of Life. Prohibition, it turns out, is an act of God's fatherly care.

Only the Creator properly understands the distinction between good and evil. Only God can decide how the outcome will achieve good instead of evil, life instead of death.

God has willed good and rejected what brings evil. Humans are to stand face to face with the second tree and consciously accept the divine will to love with freedom.

The big question is whether humans will recognize and accept the loving will of God.

Humans must now distinguish what to choose and reject.

> Creation is one long preparation, the road to the covenant, opening to God's freeing love.

We will fail because we are not God. God alone is good, so we pronounce our sentence as we choose what brings death.

The positive possibility of the second tree is to see and obey the sign that says, "Do not enter." This response is life as God prefers. But humans choose otherwise, and we bear the consequences.

Why was divine prohibition not more effective? This tree was an ornament of Paradise for the glory of humanity, and we would be incomplete without it. God acted rightly in placing the tree here. A life in obedience is offered but not made necessary.

God gives freedom for obedience. Humans are not on the brink between good and evil. They are in the garden of God and have one choice that could undo all the good offered. This opportunity was not a test; it was a possibility.

Obedience brings freedom. It is an invitation to confirm God's good will. God does not compel humans to obey.

God has not made humans machines but made them able to decide to obey or not.

Human freedom now becomes an issue here in the garden. Freedom is a dynamic of relation between God and the human when confronted with a decision.

The human is free when confirming the goodwill of God, exercising the freedom to obey the loving God.

This freedom does not remove human decision-making; it is the freedom for fellowship. The humble recognition of God allows us to side with Him without exerting a right to control.

God gives freedom to humans because He desires a true union and connection.

God placed spontaneous obedience before humans, not a constrained, fail-safe world without freedom.

The second tree could only be dangerous if the freedom given were misused.

Israel in the promised land can later be seen fulfilling the original meaning of creation with God's blessings.

The land belongs to God, who makes a place for His people. It is provisional and can become a Paradise lost. There is always longing and a promise of return.

The Tree of Life echoes the presence of God. It is a sign of connection, constantly reminding them to enter where God is wholly near.

Idolatry is the clearest evidence that any nation has taken a wrong path, including Israel.

God's relationship with Adam and Eve amounted to a robbery on the human side, resulting in a curse called death.

Outside the garden, all was arranged for the humans who had eaten disobediently. God loves the humans, who desire what God has prohibited and serve themselves.

The history of human failure, from Adam through Israel and beyond, highlights God's faithfulness to restore fellowship with humanity.

The water from the garden flows out over the whole earth, quenching thirst, healing, renewing, and refreshing, much like the water of life in Jesus, who fulfills God's covenant for the world.

God plants the two trees in the garden, but His primary desire is to give Himself, as evidenced by the presence of God in the garden.

Creation's climax is humanity's completion in adding the female.

Humanity is not created as a single being but as the duality of male and female, with this basic form of association and fellowship.

God reflects the thought to Himself, "It is not good for man to be alone." The creation account is completed with the complement of male and female, reflecting the being of God.

God's Groundwork for the History of Love 57

The whole person is not solitary. A singular human does not fulfill the image of God.

God created humans to partner with Himself and exist in partnership as humans.

Partnership implies both resemblances to another as well as distinction. If the other were the *same*, it would not be uniquely another but only an echo of oneself. If the other is only *different*, the one is still solitary, not met by a corresponding partner.

The man recognizing the woman as partner completed the intention of God as the gift of freedom accepted as grace.

The animals are also created as a background but cannot meet humans' need for God's intended companionship.

Language begins as nouns to name the animals. Language is not the creation of God. Language is a human freedom to relate to our world.

Without the woman, the man was not satisfied. In true freedom, the man must confirm his humanity by saying "yes" to the woman, who corresponds to him with all her differences and similarities.

The man slept while God provided what he needed. Adam had no part in fulfilling what he did not know he needed. This gift of provision is the inner secret of all creation.

There are four things humans know about their completion by God:

1. Man and woman find differences in one another but recognize they belong together in an ordered unity.
2. The man cannot create more of himself out of himself. Each needs the other; they cannot be human without the other.
3. God makes the woman from the man's body, which brings suffering. Healing is needed to restore harmony.
4. God fashioned the new out of the old; the woman comes from the man as a new creation. Each recognizes themselves in the other.

The creation of humanity is the will of God. It is not a natural process. He allows space for the mystery of humanity and the intimacy entailed in human relations.

The saga does not detail how humanity comes into being, but answers how humanity exists as the creature of God.

God concludes His creation, celebrating the woman's existence as the completion of I and Thou.

God creates humans for mutual relationships as agents of joy, revelation, and personal knowledge.

Human freedom comes from recognizing the partner given by God.

In Adam's willed choosing of Eve, he chooses a personal relationship. He finds his being in an encounter with this other as a companion.

Who is this woman? She is the one made to be a companion. She is his completion. They can only be themselves as they partake of each other.

Each is their unique self only with the other. She is not the man's property. They belong together.

This woman is not less than the man but cannot exchange her place with him. She was ordered to come after the man, being taken from him. But this does not mean she has less value, dignity, or honor. She has no shame in coming second; it reveals her glory.

Her creation is the completion of him. Only with her, together, could he be the glory of God and she the completion of this glory, the finality of creation's purposes. He chooses her, and she chooses him.

The man and woman are in absolute unity, but now the man leaves home and cleaves to his wife as a follower to become an integrated whole.

There is a "yes" to God's choice, a "yes" to each other, and a "yes" to being fully human. There is a turn from seeking self to finding the other as a companion.

The man is responsible for expressing his humanity in caring for the woman. He is to remove any cause for anxiety, self-seeking, or rejection. He is assigned to love and to leave his roots to care for her.

Adam and Eve stood naked before God with nothing to add to the work and gift of God. They accepted their innocence before God as His glory and confirmed that God was wholly for them.

Nakedness was the natural garment God had given them, which they embraced as long as they were satisfied with God.

The man and woman became conjointly responsible before God. They stood together as the unity of humanity. They stood naked before God.

They had nothing to hide. There was no shame in God's good work.

> God gives freedom to humans because He desires a true union and connection.

The contrast came when the couple stood apart from God. Guilt and shame swept over them as their enjoyment of God's delight gave way in their attempt to stand alone.

Shame comes when the creature stands apart from God. The sphere of disgrace comes in this alien sphere as the work of the human.

God's Groundwork for the History of Love

Their innocence was in their life before God. With Him came the freedom in which they had rejoiced, with no place for shame or disgrace.

When their eyes were opened, their knowledge was corrupted. They saw from a perspective other than God's. Where there had been acceptance, now there was accusation. Everything was disturbed and disintegrated. Order was thrown into confusion.

Humanity abstracted into soulless masculinity and femininity. The conflict came with attempts at control. Eroticism replaced intimacy. Marriage became a power struggle with a loss of mutual respect.

The corruption of human judgment stumbled in the most intimate sphere of humanity. The glory of human freedom collapsed into hiding and shame.

The Song of Solomon displays delight in eros without accompanying shame, a picture of what we saw in Genesis 2.

Genesis 2 sets the stage for the goal in the Song of Songs. It displays a yearning for union both partners may enjoy within an incomparable covenant.

Although we see the broken covenant for humans, it is still an unbroken covenant for God.

The love between a man and a woman becomes a parable of the link between Yahweh and His people. God is the faithful partner who continually renews His covenant where humans fail.

The election of God is the basis of the human choice of love and marriage.

As Eve was taken from Adam, the Church must arise out of Jesus, bone of His bone, flesh of His flesh.

The Old Testament gives dignity to the sexual relationship reflecting the relationship between Yahweh and Israel, even when Israel is unfaithful. God intends for loving relationships between the sexes that reflect His covenant love.

Jesus intends to be the lover, husband, and bridegroom of His bride, the Church. Here, the groom and bride can be naked and not ashamed.

To become one flesh not only includes physical union in sex but also the whole course of personal life together in the unity of love. This freedom is expressed in openness without hiding.

God's creation completes one humanity in the companionship of male and female.

COMMENTARY:

- God creates the world as a living space for humanity.
- Genesis tells a story of God's deliberate acts to get at the truth of God, not the details of a report.

- Creation implies intention. A listening ear will hear the heart of God in recounting God's masterful work in creating the world from nothing.
- Covenant is a formal relationship initiated, sustained, and fulfilled with God's desired outcomes.
- Covenant for humans is an invitation to live in the freedom of what God has provided.
- The first Genesis story is science in that it reveals the reality disclosed by God. It is not science by modern, impersonal standards. It is the science of the personal.
- The second Genesis story explores the life of persons together, divine and human.

CONCLUSION FOR THE CHURCH: The Church wrestles with making the human the center of theological life. Barth recenters the conversation around the creator God. He does not exclude humans but sets the meaning in a context He has established.

The Church today could help rediscover the universe as personal. It is not a mass of objects without intention or purpose. The Church has the opportunity to clarify the objectivity of modern science by properly including humans as persons, not just another organism or object.

Barth argues that we are created as persons for a purpose. The Church has an opportunity to bring meaningful existence back into view. We are living, interacting beings who share a world made fit for our thriving existence.

INSIGHT FOR PASTORS: The Genesis story contains the original promises of God. It is easy to think of the opening scenes as mythical renditions, but they imaginatively reveal the meaning for which we were made.

The Church is a touchstone for reality. Humans are made as expressions of love and connection, care and concern, companionship and collaboration. We are one family with a multitude of differences. We need to learn to think of people as God's family and strive for unity with our many distinctions as those who love and are loved.

God designed males and females to live in unity with particularity. Differences are good for completing one another. Each male and female is significantly different from all others of their gender, learning to love with freedom. Difference need not mean distance.

We are called to live a life of hospitality, making room for others of a different gender, age, status, ethnicity, and so on. Creation rings with the

God's Groundwork for the History of Love 61

interwoven unity of diversity that more than endures together. It works like the creative household of God. We, as pastors, are not to become parents. We are familial facilitators. We gather around the Tree of Life and tell the stories of who we are, whose we are, and what we are doing here with our loving Creator.

INSIGHT FOR THEOLOGIANS: Creation and covenant are themes that undergird the whole Bible. The themes open up the times and spaces God has set for human participation. Because God has prepared the way, we must read our times and activities within God's context.

We must do good scientific work, exploring the spaces we inhabit in the light of God's purposes. Good theology will participate especially in God's renewal of human flourishing, overcoming the inhospitality we exhibit to one another.

Covenant thinking must be distinguished from legal, contract thinking. Covenant is based on love and seeks love's best outworking. A contract is based on fear and seeks to protect oneself from loss. Fear imagines we can perform well and expect God to treat us well as a reward. Fear makes us selfish.

God is unconditionally faithful to His creatures. His provision sets the foundation for understanding the actualities of God and the possibilities of humans. As theologians, we attune our sense of humble stewardship with people, places, and future potentials to align with God's creative intent.

We cannot fit God or our human ideals into a box regarding how human relationships work. We can only seek to live from God's intentions in the garden. We may become hospitable habitations for one another as God is for us.

? CLARIFYING QUESTIONS: Does your theology consider Genesis an imaginary story or a literal event depicting the history of tension between God and humans? *Or* can you see the story as a God's-eye view, helping us to understand the world's purpose and to echo God's love with it and one another?

CHAPTER 8

GOD'S HOSPITABLE AMEN PRESENCE WITH CREATION

§ 42. The Yes of God the Creator

 FOCUS STATEMENT: Having made the world, God affirms His creation. In § 42, God says "Yes," confirming His presence as an Amen, promising lasting hospitality to care for what He has made.

His "Yes" is a personal, committed sustaining of this world for His covenant partner. This garden world serves His purpose: a place to participate in life together.

God also says "No" to what He has not chosen. Barth critiques all influences that resist God's grace. Outsiders press into the garden with their darkened ways. God is light over their darkness, resisting the void and shadows. His "Yes" finally rules over fleeting things to which God must say "No."

Barth upholds the goodness of God's creation against human assessments of goodness and wisdom. He understands human attempts at judging the world as subjective opinions, estranging the creature from enjoying what God has made good.

 INTRODUCTION: This paragraph closes *CD* 3.1, acknowledging all the benefits of God's creation for humanity as the blessings God intended.

Three subsections focus on what God made good, as affirmed in Genesis 1–2. First, creation is goodness in action, fulfilling God's covenant promise to His creature.

Second, Barth focuses on the fact that the world is truly good, not just an illusion of goodness. It is made good by the most fundamental reality, the Creator, not human opinions about truth or goodness.

God's Hospitable Amen Presence with Creation 63

The final section justifies the claim that the world is good. It is the best world because the Creator made it. Some optimists have had romantic visions about the world's beauty, blind to its challenges. Barth resists this as human tunnel vision, seeing only what the human selects as good. This is not justified.

The world has beauty but also a dark side. God says "Yes" to all that is good and has the final "No" to the shadow side. The light of the "Yes" wins the day. This "Yes" is the covenant of God that sustains all God creates.

CONTEXT: *CD* 3.1
Pages in Paragraph: 89 pages, pp. 330–414

Subsections
1. Creation as Benefit
2. Creation as Actualisation
3. Creation as Justification

TEXT: § 42. The Yes of God the Creator

OPENING SUMMARY: The work of God the Creator consists particularly in the benefit that in the limits of its creatureliness what He has created may be as it is actualized by Him, and be good as it is justified by Him.[1]

SUMMARY:

1. Creation as Benefit (pp. 330–44)

We now engage the meaning of creation and its outworking in our time.

God's creation has a definite, intrinsic "Yes" as God's handiwork, shaped to bring His grace, mercy, and goodness to His covenant partners. God only says "No" to everything contrary to His nature.

God benefits His creatures, working out His good pleasure. He intends us to enjoy what He has provided.

Marcion disconnected the covenant from creation. His Jesus was not a human like us. He could not suffer, speak, die, and rise again. He was separated from creation, disconnected from real humanity and thus became irrelevant.

---

1. *CD* 3.1, § 42, p. 330.

If we do not understand Christ's true humanity, we conceive of Him as independent of creation and disconnected from reality; He cannot touch, much less indwell, the human body.

German philosopher Arthur Schopenhauer disconnected creation from the covenant. He did not argue from God in Christ but from the human itself. The human became both creator and creature, responsible to oneself alone for a place in the world.

Marcion excluded humanity from the covenant. Creation concerns vanished with the focus on an ideal covenant.

Schopenhauer excluded God from the world. He saw an unreal world, abstract and divided from the covenant that gives meaning to it. Excluding God, this world is seen as evil.

But for Barth, what God has created is good. It allows for covenant life suitable for humans.

All humanly developed worldviews emerge with some equivalent to the theological idea of creation. They work with a mysterious background, with systems built in the air.

Theology has the benefit of confessing creation as the work of God because of divine revelation. The object of knowledge is God and then His works.

Nontheological views work with unaided reason, neglecting help from creation. The object of knowledge is the voiceless world.

Christian doctrine is distinct from philosophical systems in that:

1. Knowledge of the Creator and His creation *cannot become a worldview*. To do so would be to abandon its object of study and adopt a philosophy.
2. This knowledge *cannot be based on a worldview*. None can support the investigation of creation.
3. Theological knowledge *cannot guarantee any worldview*. There is no obligation to default to their speculations.
4. A theology of creation *cannot come to terms with nontheological reasoning* because its course of action is mistaken.
5. Theological knowledge *recognizes its object*, acknowledging it is different; its ability is different and does not exclude the other but stands in contrast to it.
6. Christian theological knowledge *stands on the biblical witness* to creation, reflecting on God's faithfulness from what it has apprehended in Christ. It is not embarrassed by its task, nor does it look for support from other worldviews.

2. Creation as Actualisation (pp. 344–65)

God says "Yes" to what He created, which means He graciously gives to reality its being.

Despite all the illusions, appearances, and dreams confronting us, we live in reality as granted by God. God says "No" to all unreality.

Because God exists, we may say, "I exist also, and others exist also."

Reality is not known merely from our consciousness of it. We cannot prove our existence, the existence of creation, or God's existence. He tells us about reality's depths, and our thoughts echo reality.

Reality must exist to be known. We confirm reality in active-knowing encounters. God's order in creation exists in distinction from our perceptions.

Humans recognize that reality occurs all around them. Each person orients themself to what they encounter.

To know God is to engage God's self-revelation as He speaks His reality. Our recognition of His reality becomes the basis of faith.

> For Barth, what God has created is good. It allows for covenant life suitable for humans.

French philosopher René Descartes's philosophy asked questions about the nature of reality. He hoped to prove God's existence and the soul's immortality but failed.

Descartes does not give a clear rule for discovering truth. One believes only what is presupposed. However, as he initially asserted, all these might still be dream truths or opinions. He has only demonstrated he thinks he exists.

The act of thinking does not allow one to escape error. It cannot even establish with certainty that "I am." Apprehending that something is true can affirm only that it is true to me. The human-formed idea of God arises from the treasury of the human mind to create reason. But human reasoning is deficient for discovering truth without doubt.

Descartes asserts the possibility and necessity of God to ground consciousness of the self and world. He cannot prove it. All his knowledge takes place within the fallible circle of human knowing.

Descartes's God is born and locked within the human mind. Descartes can only be a mystic who contemplates and adores in reflection, not in recognizing God's self-giving. He is a self-imprisoned rationalist.

A valid proof of God must be based on God's self-demonstration. This evidence comes from the Word of God, calling us to respond.

The Christian understanding of creation holds that creation is God's work in action and interaction. God has established a covenant with His humans and lives to perform His self-giving.

66   Church Dogmatics 3.1

Creation beneficially provides the sphere for God's hospitality, affirming His choice, acceptance, and care encompassing His good pleasure.

God has said "Yes" so our hearts and lips may acknowledge He is and we are.

3. Creation as Justification (pp. 366–414)

God has given us actual existence and justified His act by His love for us in creating us.

We recognize that we exist by God's work. God's assertions of goodness liberate us from all human opinions.

God's declaration informs our understanding of the goodness of God's creation, including ourselves.

Beauty shines, reflecting the world-affirming goodness of God and the "Yes" of His self-revelation. The many facets of beauty in the world are not its brightest glory.

Humanity needs to be restored from alienation, its negative status within creation.

The "Yes" and "No" of God are never exhausted. God's covenant establishes and maintains communion as He embraces human greatness and wretchedness.

Jesus manifests the majesty and lowliness of God in His exaltation and humiliation.

Indifference to God's reality is the only true ungodliness. Shallow joy and simplistic sorrow are far better than apathy.

In God's affirmation ("Yes") or negation ("No"), God is justified in His acting from His perfect loving existence.

We must affirm God's goodness in His "Yes" and "No." We must be sure we hear Him, not an imposter or supposed surrogate.

God's "Nevertheless" is justified as God's grace in His "Yes" and "No," bringing humans into His freedom as a mirror of His good pleasure. God wills to endure the contradiction of human life.

God knows our incapacity to fulfill our intended place with Him. He is unwilling to leave us alone or unaided. God rescues us to preserve us. As the fulfillment of His "Yes," He says "No" to what would destroy us.

The resurrection is the "Yes" that answers the "No" addressed by the cross. The Creator lives again for humanity, having defended His nature and the needs of human nature.

God has overcome the imperfection of the human by His intervention.

God's Hospitable Amen Presence with Creation

Faith lives by the "Yes" God has spoken to us. God also says "No" to all that threatens us, especially on the cross.

Jesus is involved in the lived drama of history; He is not a mere spectator. He brings meaning to life; we receive it through our gratitude and participation. We confirm what He confirms and deny what He denies.

The "proof of the perfection of the world" set out by philosophers is an abstract idea that *begins with human ideals*. Through natural knowledge of God in the open book of the world, one seeks to know God. This is a misstep.

Barth displays a collection of poems and reflections that celebrate the earth's creative structures as a means to praise God, but all default to human sensibilities.

Barth shares some of the optimism of the theologians of beauty in the eighteenth century, who looked at the magnificence and goodness of creation. Yet earthly catastrophes dimmed the attitudes of the optimists.

The philosophers that followed lost optimism and saw the world in mechanistic and idealistic terms, doubting the perfection and goodness of creation.

For Barth, we need an honest awareness that sin and death create peril for God's creation, held in tension with the goodness of creation.

> God has said "Yes" so our hearts and lips may acknowledge He is and we are.

An abstract, this-worldly *human filter* makes it impossible for optimists to clearly see the dark side of reality.

These optimists are spectators. They do not participate in the life of God, only celebrate from the comfort of their armchairs.

The foolishness of self-confidence was the disease of the eighteenth century. The book of nature was set side by side with revelation. But in practice, nature took over depicting reality. Jesus was not the starting point for its theology.

Christ is the head of creation and is the supreme ground of its perfection and benefits.

The Enlightenment thinkers became more comfortable with Aristotle and Descartes than with Jesus.

We cannot separate who God is from what God has done. Creation and covenant belong together.

COMMENTARY:

- The world has meaning; God created its good purpose.

- Humans have many opinions, pessimistic and optimistic, as filters that miss God's good reality.
- The world is ordered to benefit God's covenant purposes.
- God's "Yes" is not just a simple affirmation; it is God's commitment to sustaining and being present to all He has made.
- God's "No" is the loving freedom to stand against that which is contrary to Creation's goodness.
- Barth avoids discussions of science. However, he lays the foundation to understand what God has made as good, to care for it, value it, provide service, and align with the value God has established.
- Barth critiques as human-centered those philosophers who read their agendas onto the world, not acknowledging the work of God or His purposes.

CONCLUSION FOR THE CHURCH: The Church often discounts the value of the created world. We deliver the natural world over to human agendas. We forget that it is God's gift for our enjoyment and provision.

The Church could honor the world by investing value in science for the good of God's world. We might love the natural world just because He made it for us. Rather than neglecting or overvaluing it, the Church would be well served to hear God's "Yes" to it, act in a manner attuned to its blessings, and resist all to which God has said "No." This ethic of attunement requires an attentive realignment, seeing the world through the eyes of God.

INSIGHT FOR PASTORS: Pastors need to understand that the natural world is the book many read to find God. Barth warns this may replace the Book of God with the values of the observer. With the world as one's text, God's involvement quickly becomes unimportant in the present. Each person will choose what they see as good, beautiful, and worthy of attention. Their judgment overrides what God has made as good, often embracing what God resists.

Barth wants us to begin with what God values—a world created for participation in loving relationship. Too often, people come to church to see how to get what they want from God. They want God to say "Yes" to their "yes." This is backward.

Barth wants the Church to be recentered on God, seeing creation as good in the light of His involvement. Turned toward God's "Yes," we may also align with God's covenant purposes and say "No" to the treasure hunt pursued to meet our own needs. Distracted, we miss the gifts of God and all He has prepared for us.

INSIGHT FOR THEOLOGIANS: If we argue that the world is good because it meets human needs, we make the value of human needs the filter of our thinking. Trajectories matter.

If we want to make God and theology attractive, we will likely default to what those around us find attractive. We will not recognize we have inadvertently made God in the shape of what we value. This course can create some spectacular golden calves and outrageous cathedrals.

Barth wants theologians to cherish that to which God says "Amen." He wants our thinking about creation to value what God values. We need expansive honesty to align with God's "Yes" to all He created. We cannot be distracted by the beauty of sunsets and snowstorms, puppies and insects—all the things we like and those we don't—to think God usually agrees with our evaluations. We must learn to think *with* God about all created things and how to operate as stewards aligned with God.

This paragraph creates the space for theology to establish a context for scientific thinking and operation. The world is not all a mistake, chance, or meaningless. Good science explores the internal structures of reality to help humans to live appropriately in response. Barth gives us spectacles to see the goodness of creation.

? CLARIFYING QUESTIONS: Does your theology view the world as a gift from God left for human use? *Or* do you see God still at work in what He created, valuing our planet as the meeting place for our lives together?

VOLUME SUMMARY: In *CD* 3.1, we have seen that God is the ultimate event planner. God creates space and time (the universe and history) for the event expressed in all His creation. This event is not for a weekend but for all created time, within which He is for and with what He creates. The earth is a special venue for what He plans. He creates the guests, humans, making them suitable to enjoy Him and each other. God made everything good. All of His history with humanity is an enduring event of His loving presence, a free gift that we can enjoy together. All this planning and creating is for a reason: a promised love in a faithful relationship—that is, covenant, the meaning that permeates creation.

PART 3

CHURCH DOGMATICS 3.2

God and His Covenant Partner

Karl Barth	*Church Dogmatics*	I/I	1932 (1936 ET)
Karl Barth	*Church Dogmatics*	I/2	1938 (1956 ET)
Karl Barth	*Church Dogmatics*	II/I	1940 (1957 ET)
Karl Barth	*Church Dogmatics*	II/2	1942 (1957 ET)
Karl Barth	*Church Dogmatics*	III/I	1945 (1958 ET)
Karl Barth	*Church Dogmatics*	III/2	1948 (1960 ET)
Karl Barth	*Church Dogmatics*	III/3	1950 (1961 ET)
Karl Barth	*Church Dogmatics*	III/4	1951 (1961 ET)
Karl Barth	*Church Dogmatics*	IV/I	1953 (1956 ET)
Karl Barth	*Church Dogmatics*	IV/2	1955 (1958 ET)
Karl Barth	*Church Dogmatics*	IV/3.1	1959 (1961 ET)
Karl Barth	*Church Dogmatics*	IV/3.2	1959 (1962 ET)
Karl Barth	*Church Dogmatics*	IV/4	1967 (1969 ET)

CHURCH DOGMATICS, CHAPTER 10

"The Creature"

CHAPTER 9

GOD'S HOSPITABLE PRESENCE IN PERSON

§ 43. Man as a Problem of Dogmatics

FOCUS STATEMENT: In § 43, the host shows up at the door as a guest. He comes to our table, He who made the world and all it contains. God has made space and time for us and meets us within all He has made.

Within God's hospitable context, Jesus comes to show us who He is so we might understand who we are. Meeting Him, we find ourselves an imperfect reflection of Him, but not a shadow. We discover ourselves both determined by who He is—His creation—and missing what gives us our essence as persons—an intimate connection with the living God.

In this paragraph, we will explore humanity as made by God, specifically in the particularity of Jesus, who alone can be the object for studying true humanity.

INTRODUCTION: Having looked at the *whole* of creation in chapter 9 in *CD* 3.1, we now focus on the *crown* of creation, the human, in *CD* 3.2, which is all chapter 10. For this study, we must not look at ourselves; we look to Jesus to see what an actual, unfallen human looks like.

To study the meaning of human persons, we begin with the person of Jesus because all other humans are fallen—only He provides an authentic engagement with a human as God intends, fit for a covenant relationship. He embodies the covenant on our behalf; our true meaning dwells in Him.

This chapter also unveils insufficient, substitutionary ways of studying the universe and humans, subsequently establishing the proper path for appropriate knowledge of humanity as God's covenant partner.

75

76 — Church Dogmatics 3.2

📚 **CONTEXT:** *CD* 3.2
Pages in Paragraph: 52 pages, pp. 3–54

Subsections
1. Man in the Cosmos
2. Man as an Object of Theological Knowledge

📖 **TEXT:** § 43 Man as a Problem of Dogmatics

🔯 **OPENING SUMMARY:** Because man, living under heaven and on earth, is the creature whose relation to God is revealed to us in the Word of God, he is the central object of the theological doctrine of creation. As the man Jesus is Himself the revealing Word of God, He is the source of our knowledge of the nature of man as created by God.[1]

🔯 **SUMMARY:**

1. Man in the Cosmos (pp. 3–19)

The word *creation* includes not only the action of the Creator but also what is made by Him. Similarly, the term *work* includes the action and what the worker produces.

Creator and creation are an integral whole, inseparable in our understanding.

God creates His creatures to live together in a coordinated life.

To discuss the doctrine of the creature—that is, theological anthropology—we must affirm that God creates human nature.

The human is one creature among other creatures, each with a particular relation to the Creator.

Worldviews derive information from somewhere other than the Word of God.

The Bible does not have a specific cosmology that it must explain. This claim is justified in that:

1. The Word of God has not developed a "worldview" and critiques encroaching views.
2. Faith in the Word of God avoids finding its theme in the created world. It begins with God and humanity, not the cosmos.

---

1. *CD* 3.2, § 43, p. 3.

God's Hospitable Presence in Person

3. Because faith focuses on its particular theme, it can only incidentally witness to cosmological presuppositions, thus becoming disloyal to any worldview.
4. When we think we detect a union between faith and a worldview, we have taken a path of deviation from faith.
5. When faith is faithful to God, we recognize the contradiction of associating with other systems with alien worldviews (as seen in Augustine's use of Plato and Thomas Aquinas's use of Aristotle).

Separated from the covenant, knowledge of the world leaves a meaningless, dispensable world. Everything is reduced to a thing, among other things, in an impersonal world.

Dispensing with God, humans reconstruct the world for their purposes, restructuring it to entice the cosmos to fit human ends.

Proper knowledge of creation connects the covenant and the cosmos as the context of God's dealings with humanity.

Heaven reminds us of invisible and inaccessible reality, while the earth is the horizon of our lives.

Heaven discloses the being and action of God, and earth relates to the being and action of humanity.

Heaven and earth contain space for God and humans, meeting for communion between God and ourselves.

The doctrine of creation investigates the spheres of heaven and earth; it is anthropocentric, or human-oriented, and not concerned with the science of the cosmos other than as the setting of God's story.

All actual sciences, natural and theological, share these characteristics:

1. They are not committed to a worldview. They observe, classify, investigate, understand, and describe phenomena and are not committed to constructing a worldview.
2. The sciences investigate and describe from a human point of view, with all the limits of human observation.
3. They recognize two spheres: that which is accessible to human observation and thought, and that which is inaccessible and beyond the limit of the visible sphere. This requires a respectful silence from the natural sciences.

Dogmatics must develop a doctrine of humanity from the Word of God. For this task, God became human.

Within the created sphere, humanity has its domicile, its appropriate residence within the life of God.

Proper knowledge of creation connects the covenant and the cosmos as the context of God's dealings with humanity.

The body and soul of humans have a unity and a distinction that we may speak of analogically, but they are not to be divided into the spheres of heaven and earth.

Humans are on earth and under heaven. We are more than the earth as the object of God's covenant purposes.

God speaks as the Lord of heaven and earth. They cannot avoid giving Him glory; we do not know how.

2. Man as an Object of Theological Knowledge (pp. 19–54)

God reveals His relationship to humanity through the Word of God.

Theological anthropology investigates the God-human relationship, reflecting on God's story in the Bible.

What are humans? God's covenant partner, whom He visits as God in the flesh.

The Word of God does not merely explain the outward appearance of humanity but delves into the inward parts.

Explaining human nature has always been a critical problem in philosophical reflection, including that of Socrates, Augustine, Descartes, and others, who impose their human-informed criteria on all other knowledge.

Two primary forms of nontheological anthropology are distinct but merge into one.

1. *A speculative theory of humanity* extends beyond the exact sciences to create hypotheses about humans. It arises in a system of ideas between a myth and a philosophy of the human.

   The human begins by looking at oneself. Then, using self-judgment, one proceeds to synthesize a system of truth, assuming the capability to know and analyze oneself.

   The investigation reduces to self-inquiry.

2. *Scientific anthropology* also has humans as its object in broader biological, physiological, psychological, and sociological fields.

   These systems are concerned not with the being of humans but

God's Hospitable Presence in Person

with their appearances. They observe the partial phenomena but neglect the inner elements and the whole.

Barth sees the limited benefits of science, as well as what it misses in understanding the nature, limits, and conditions within which humans exist.

Theological anthropology focuses on the reality of actual humanity in light of the Word of God.

Theological anthropology deals with our inner reality and wholeness. We are not merely ideas about ourselves or the sum of our parts as the phenomena of humanity.

Real humanity is not ideal; it is corrupted and alienated, a betrayer of our humanity, and contradictory to God.

In the history of humanity, we are at war with ourselves and are unfaithful to God. Salvation is a remedy for this situation.

We stand before God as humans with body and soul, who can think, speak, act, and work. Satan can only corrupt these enduring elements, not eliminate them.

The Son of God did not assume original sin but took on our sinful nature. He did not sin, but took on Himself the sin of us all to bring humanity to the cross in Himself.

We must hold together that God creates humans and, simultaneously, that we have a corrupted, sinful nature. Both are true.

We need not be frightened by the tension between God and our humanity.

Our anxieties about our nature turn out to be false. We do not know and therefore cannot admit that we are betrayers and enemies of God, which makes us dangerous to ourselves.

It is not self-evident that we are children of God. Yet it is still possible to come to recognize this fact.

Even when we discover we are radically sinful, God pours eternal grace onto us.

God's faithfulness and mercy decide from a place different from what we deserve.

To think of ourselves only as sinful persons is an abstraction, a tragic selection from a larger picture.

We are sinners who participate in the grace of God. Grace is primary; rebellion is secondary.

God's holy fire consumes the sin and self-destruction of humanity with God's love, correcting all that is alien and hostile. Judgment is the "Yes" of God that says "No" to what imprisons. It is light in the darkness.

In sinning, humans deliver themselves to destruction and corruption, splitting away from all that is good. We must be rescued.

Even though we may be blind to God, He cannot be blind to us. Humans did not make the covenant, and they cannot dissolve it.

In the light of God's faithfulness, we see human unfaithfulness. God gives Himself; humans withdraw in concern for themselves.

As we are against God, we are equally against ourselves in forgetting God and choosing the impossible. We have answered friendship with hostility.

God's light does not create sin; it exposes its reality.

What are humans? God's covenant partner, whom He visits as God in the flesh.

Sin resists grace as it turns away in acts of betrayal. We follow Israel as those who became adulterous in their covenant marriage to Yahweh.

We do not fail the standards of a universal law; we rebel against the God who is gracious.

The eternal God became a human creature: this is God's attitude toward sinful humans. We are forbidden to take sin more seriously than we take His grace toward us.

Even with our sinful distortion, we are held in the hand of God.

"Jesus is man because in Him God stands in man's place, and man is one with God."[2]

The ultimate fact about humans is their self-contradiction and self-deception in not recognizing the truth.

Jesus stands against our self-deception and self-contradiction. Jesus ends our illusions about ourselves.

In Him is human nature without sin, self-deception, and shame.

- Jesus is like us, but without self-contradiction, living in faithfulness to His Father and the covenant of grace for which He was chosen. In His purity and freedom, He takes our impurity and bondage on Himself, removing and destroying it.

    All good things come through Jesus to us, including the Holy Spirit. Jesus is the reconciler, prophet, priest, and king, revealing God in our creaturely world.

---

2. *CD* 3.2, § 43, p. 46.

God's Hospitable Presence in Person

Jesus goes before us and makes us like Himself. He is the original; we are the copy.
- Jesus' human nature is not distorted by sin but is preserved in its original essence.

  Jesus is sinless. This makes Him different from us. He is sinless because of His unique relation to God.

  What protects Jesus from temptation is not His specific creatureliness but the way He is a creature. He is God who wills to faithfully take on vulnerable human nature.
- Jesus is the same as us but different from us in that His human nature is revealed in its original form, not concealed as we are.

  We needed Jesus for humanity to become known and hence knowable through Him.

  True discipleship can only be established and worked out in relation to Jesus as He embraces and addresses us, and we follow Him.

Jesus is human in such a way that He could be a brother to any of us. Still, He represents God to us and us to God.

Only in knowing Him do we fully know ourselves.

COMMENTARY:
- God made His creatures to enjoy covenant life together.
- Philosophical thinking, or studying our physical nature, cannot correctly understand our humanity.
- Beginning with human specimens always begins with a corrupted example.
- Starting with Jesus always investigates the truth that only God can give.
- Jesus is the true human who fulfills all that is intended for humanity.
- Even though we have fractured our lives with God, He has not diminished His relationship with us. Even in our rebellious state, we are still His good creation.

CONCLUSION FOR THE CHURCH: The Church is a community of faltering humans pursuing goals and methods to fulfill the destiny of humanity. Barth wants the Church to avoid all shortcuts that end up worshiping the experience of humans to achieve their own desires.

Jesus fulfills His humanity through an intimate relation with His Father, not by pursuing observable perfection. The Church can maintain clarity of thought and action by not idealizing human thoughts (I think, therefore I am) or limiting our physicality (we are nothing but physical beings). The truest human is fully physical and thoughtful *but supremely* oriented as a covenant partner of God.

We must stop assuming that we need better tools to perfect our humanity. The Church is at its best when serving humans, apprenticing with Jesus, restored through His gracious relationship that brings us home.

INSIGHT FOR PASTORS: Barth wants us to understand what it means to be human, pulling back the curtain to reveal all the false assumptions and goals we have used to pursue happiness or manage our physical life. These distractions replace the reality of a personal relationship with Jesus.

Barth insists that we can get a true image from Jesus alone, but not by replicating His behaviors. His starting point was a dynamic relationship with the Father. We too have this through Jesus.

With Jesus as the object of study, we do not merely learn about Him. We listen to and follow Him, loving Him who has loved us, and letting that shape our days and desires.

If our churches are to be appropriately oriented, our people need to reboot into the relationship they were created for. We must let Jesus speak through His Word, giving birth to lovers of Jesus.

INSIGHT FOR THEOLOGIANS: When theology is scientific, it attends to what is real in the world, investigating God's creative experiment with the world, including humans. Some would like to construct a theoretical understanding of human existence. This "common sense" view is not shared everywhere; there are different opinions and sensibilities about what makes us humans.

In the hard sciences, humans are understood in their likeness with the animal kingdom. We share many characteristics and developmental features. Yet we are different. The sciences cannot agree on a proper form of science that treats each person's reality.

Theological science engages Jesus as the One who is not a sample. He brings each person to engage revealed reality, indwelling the life He makes possible with redeeming love.

We need not dismiss our *nurture* or *nature*. We find who we are in the *nexus* of relations that begin with the triune God. This nexus is formed, body and soul, in the context of covenant relations. We are woven together within the life of God, the Church, and our human neighbors.

God's Hospitable Presence in Person

? CLARIFYING QUESTIONS: Does your theological anthropology begin by looking at heroes, geniuses, saints, and scholars to find a vision of true, fulfilled humanity? *Or* does your thinking start and end with Jesus as the only uncorrupted human open for investigation?

CHAPTER 10

THE HOST UNVEILS OUR TRUE HUMAN IDENTITY

§ 44. Man as the Creature of God

FOCUS STATEMENT: Having displayed who He is, Jesus now shows us who we are. Barth shows us how we confuse our understanding and then reengage reality seated with the One who made us.

In the image above, Jesus entertains a hospitable conversation with four guests about understanding human life: a scientist, an idealist, an existentialist, and a hopeful religious person. Each is stuck in their head and misses Jesus sitting with them. For Barth, this detachment is a grand error.

In § 44, we discover that humans select elements from human experience to become a lens to understand what it means to be human. The *scientist* focuses on the body. The *idealist* focuses on ideal morals. The *existentialist* thinks about our existence in context. The *theist* believes we are beloved of "God" as it best serves human ideals of loving. Jesus values each of these, but discloses a deeper existence as love in the flesh, living in intimate connection with His Father and us. We are humans as those deeply beloved, who freely express love and may act as whole beings.

In this section, we identify how to discover and discuss the true nature of humanity as created by God and in which we participate by grace.

INTRODUCTION: This section focuses on being human, a real person, as God intends. Barth launches us by identifying Jesus as one who is for God. (In the next paragraph, He will be for other humans.)

This Christ-focused view contrasts with four major attempts at defining human persons apart from beginning with Jesus. These four are problematic

The Host Unveils Our True Human Identity

because they all assume human observations as their starting point, but each person has a different starting point.

For purposes of illustration, think of a real, meaningful kiss. A kiss signals intimacy between persons. Jesus embodies the original and complete intimacy between God and ourselves (§ 44.1. Man for God). Others try to describe a kiss. The *scientist* focuses on objects (lips), duration, and movements. The *idealist* expresses the ideal kiss through storied and poetic words. The *existentialist* speaks of an excellent experience. The *theist* presents the kiss as a human experience of the spiritual (§ 44.2. Phenomena of the Human). Barth is only satisfied with the mystery of a knowing kiss, with trust, gratitude, freedom in connection, and personal intimacy. Words fail, but the encounter connects and is complete. And it changes us to be who we are in the embrace of love (§ 44.3. Real Man). While only a human analogy, this may open insights.

Barth concludes by discussing authentic humans, living a life of gratitude, freedom, knowing, deciding, and humbling ourselves before God. Jesus is the one genuine human. All other attempts must be reconstituted in the context of knowing Jesus.

This chapter explains how theology gives a scientific understanding of a real person. Barth assumes that *man* refers to men and women, except specific males. Jesus was a male who still embraced all men, women, and humanity. In Him, we find the meaning of our humanity.

CONTEXT: *CD* 3.2
Pages in Paragraph: 148 pages (pp. 55–202)

Subsections
1. Jesus, Man for God
2. Phenomena of the Human
3. Real Man

TEXT: § 44. Man as the Creature of God

OPENING SUMMARY: The being of man is the history which shows how one of God's creatures, elected and called by God, is caught up in personal responsibility before Him and proves itself capable of fulfilling it.[1]

---

1. *CD* 3.2, § 44, p. 55.

 **SUMMARY:**

1. Jesus, Man for God (pp. 55–71)

Having investigated humans within our created context, we now focus on humanity. This topic explores the God-human relation, God-human reflections, human composition, and the human lifespan.

The rest of *CD* 3.2 investigates:

1. humanity as the image of God § 44,
2. how the human exists as a specific image of God § 45,
3. the composition of humans as a unity of soul and body § 46, and
4. the life of a human within the timespan we are given § 47.

Discussing the proper form of human existence must begin with Jesus Christ.

Any abstract ideal will not establish the nature and purpose of humanity; only a history determined by Jesus will do. Jesus' history is known by His coming to us.

Jesus is known as a specific man in definite situations. He cannot be known generally.

We cannot compose a physical image or character study of Jesus. He is known precisely as the Messiah who engaged in His detailed life.

Jesus was a real man, not just one who seemed to be human (as Docetism suggests) but is essentially different. He is born, lives, suffers, hears, sees, speaks, and dies as a human.

The gospel writers considered Jesus a human in history, not before, beyond, above, or hidden from history.

Jesus is the real man born to be the Savior, empowered as the Savior, and in His resurrection and ascension, He is a real man who will come again.

Jesus was like other humans, but not before or outside His earthly history.

Jesus is a human person with a soul and body. However, He does not partake of our humanity, as though we were first; we partake of Him as the firstborn of creation.

Jesus sets limits and conditions, determining and revealing the nature of humanity. Human nature is to be explained by Him, not He by it.

Jesus comes as the One who saves. His act makes whole what needs restoration.

His coming brings destruction to what destroys. He brings life and intervention to sinners and the unworthy. The meaning of Jesus' life is

The Host Unveils Our True Human Identity

to bring life—that is salvation. "For the work of Jesus is the work of the Saviour."[2]

We cannot separate the person of Jesus from His work. Despite being discussed separately in theology, there is no division between the person and work of Jesus.

The New Testament writers saw Jesus as God's work for humanity. Unlike the prophets, who could not act in their own right, Jesus acts as God for humanity. He serves in the name of His Father, who sent Him.

Jesus is the revealer of the Father, speaking of the Father and what He says. They act as One.

Jesus has His being in oneness with the Creator. He stands at the disposal of God. He abides in the bosom (heart) of the Father when coming into the world.

> Jesus comes as the One who saves. His act makes whole what needs restoration.

Jesus exists as a human included in the inner life of the Godhead, coming from the Father for humankind—from above. He returns to the Father for humanity—from below.

Jesus is in the heart of the Father and also of humans. Jesus is the conjunction between God and humanity. He does not occupy separate spheres with God and humanity.

To summarize how we see all in light of the man Jesus:

1. Among all the creatures, Jesus allows us to recognize the identity of God with Himself.

   In Jesus, we see God.

2. God's revelation in Jesus shows He is energetic, active, and resolved to come to us. He wills and works for every person.

   In Jesus, we see God for us.

3. In Jesus, we see that God is the Savior of every human, fulfilling the act of His freedom.

   In Jesus, God has acted for us in space and time.

4. Jesus has a soul and body, but this alone does not reveal Him as real man, only His possibilities.

   In Jesus, we see that God is for every person.

5. The focus of divine deliverance for humanity is not humans; it is God in active grace as the kingdom of God dawns in the man Jesus.

   In Jesus, history takes place as God's history for us.

---

2. *CD* 3.2, § 44, p. 61.

88 *Church Dogmatics 3.2*

6. The distinctiveness of the human creature is that we are for God, for the glory, freedom, and love of God.

    The essence of humans is seen in Jesus, meaning to be for God.

2. Phenomena of the Human (pp. 71–132)

This section aims to define the nature of humanity in general.

Having laid on Jesus our foundation for understanding humanity, we see that we have issues that stand in the way:

1. The state of sin that distinguishes us from Jesus—*our distance from God*
2. The state of Jesus and the mystery of His identity with God—*His closeness to God*
3. The unquestionable difference between Jesus and us—*He is unique as God and man*
4. Our indirect knowledge of who and what we are as those who live in the same world—*we share the same humanity but lack direct clarity*

This subsection will clarify the abstractions we devise about ourselves as humans. We must set boundaries against errors.

Our starting proposition: we must understand every person as a being in some relationship with God.

1. We do not have a self-enclosed reality.
2. We do not have a mere general relation to reality apart from God.
3. We are all open and related to God Himself.
4. Our being in relation to God is necessary and constant, not temporary or accidental.
5. There is no understanding of humans from which God is excluded.
6. Humans cannot be understood apart from God.

Knowledge of God and humans are mutually connected, but knowledge of God must precede that of humans.

From a christological basis, we can define specific criteria of human nature.

1. Understanding persons is conditioned by the priority of the man Jesus, who comes from God and draws all things to Him. *In Him, we are all before God.*

The Host Unveils Our True Human Identity

2. Every person exists in a relationship to the divine rescue that was historically enacted by Jesus. *Jesus is the history of our deliverance.*

3. The divine action in Jesus is freely chosen by God, in whose history we participate. *Our end purpose is not for ourselves but for God.*

4. It is essential to every person that God exists over them as Lord, and each finds freedom under the lordship of God. *We all are free under the lordship of Jesus.*

5. Every person participates in the history in which God is for us; freedom comes in our response to His grace. *We all must exist within Jesus' history of deliverance.*

6. If Jesus is for us as God's Word spoken to us, no person can be understood apart from what God does in Him. *God has attached Himself to us, and we live in responsive service to Him.*

Notice the correlation between 1 and 4, 2 and 5, and 3 and 6.

We discover a theological concept of humans through Jesus, both our differences and what is comparable with Him.

We cannot affirm knowledge of humans derived from sources other than Jesus. However, we may observe human phenomena and their suggestions, but we must examine and critique them theologically.

A firm understanding of Jesus will give us the criteria we need for our investigation.

Our first boundary excludes general descriptions of humanity. These are derived from easily accessible characteristics of human nature, assumed to be true of all.

The person in denial can only present a phantom humanity, holding an empty image lacking appropriate engagement with the real man in Jesus.

When humans claim to be the measure of the real person, they look through a lens of phenomenon and miss their actual being in relation to God and other humans.

In their alternate, phenomenological mode, the observer will select, coordinate, and form a system, thinking their depiction is a real person. This observer will neglect the true nature of a human being. Pursuing the ambiguous, varied symptoms of humans will cloud any adequate answer and create a phantom in the mind.

The phantom person is only a collection of characteristics. These features are passed off as traits of human nature but are arbitrary and temporary ideas.

Grasping at phenomena constructs a caricature, not an accurate understanding of human nature.

One example is *naturalism*, that humans are reduced to animals endowed with reason; intellect is the distinguishing feature for many definitions.

We need not deny that the human is an animal. But is being an animal the central feature of the human, with rationality as a mere supplement? Naturalism and intellectualism took these features and made them primary, to the loss of theological consideration of the whole human.

Being a rational animal is an interpretation of the symptoms of humans, not the essence. It is a "ghost in the machine" view. With humans looking at themselves, arbitrary starting points are chosen for discussions without a solid foundation.

Knowledge of God and humans are mutually connected, but knowledge of God must precede that of humans.

The phenomenon of humanity is important. It provides a legitimate study of relevant aspects for the good of humanity and its symptoms of brokenness.

With the *idealism* of Reformed theologian F. D. E. Schleiermacher, ideas of God and the human were grounded on the pious self-consciousness of the individual.[3]

Arranging a real connection between ourselves and the animal kingdom takes an imaginative philosophy that deals with the vast intellectual, moral, and spiritual differences.

There is a psychological gulf between animals and humans, not to mention the freedom and self-consciousness that sets us apart. Humans function at higher levels than those studied by natural science.

Scientific knowledge studies the world through our sense perceptions. We are different from what our self-perception tells us or what our senses tell us about others.

Thinking relates to sense perception as a contemplation based on what we encounter.

Our knowledge about our knowledge leads to self-perceptions. We limit our interpretation to the phenomenon we observe in ourselves. This reading is entirely subjective.

We think we are thinkers, but we are dependent on sense perception. Even our perception of ourselves is due to our sense perceptions, and our interpretations then follow.

---

3. Barth thought that Schleiermacher was brilliant for trying to explain the Christian faith to the modern, scientific world. In the end, though, Barth rejected his work as beginning in the wrong place, with the consciousness of the human—and not God revealed in Jesus.

The Host Unveils Our True Human Identity

We are not merely thinking creatures. We also will, behave, and act.

To exist as a person is to step into the world of other persons as a doer in what we call human life.

In our thinking, we put ourselves into action. As we decide, we are thinking toward action. Self-knowledge is knowing ourselves in the decision-making process and acting as willing beings. In this personal acting, we are freed from merely naturalistic determinations.

The word *person* must be used cautiously as it quickly defaults to phenomenology, not reality.

A long history exists regarding what being a person means without a conclusive consensus. The many proposals are often about masks, functions, dysfunctions, roles, and representations of humans in their contexts. Limited to these concepts, they are inadequate to understand the nature of humanity.

In one's self-knowledge, one exists in two spheres: one where we *think* of ourselves, the other where life is realized in *action*.

In one sense, we are detached thinkers; in another, we are related actors. Yet we live simultaneously in both.

A ruptured view develops and divides the natural self, setting internal ethical aspects against external physical aspects. These define the human as the thinker *or* the animal self, with tragic outcomes limiting the fullness of human possibilities as integrated persons.

A scientifically restricted approach engages only with sense perception, resulting in naturalistic, observable outcomes.

From the ethical view, we default to individual actors who must make decisions with thinking skills.

The scientific and ethical viewpoints reduce the person to symptoms of human existence. But the naturalistic view of the hard sciences dominates over the humanities where the ethical is considered. Neither agrees with the other or provides a holistic understanding of human nature.

As real humans, we exist with God and other humans, living physically and ethically in response to, and in service to, God and others.

We are left with fragments of human phenomena when God has been abandoned. Freedom is defined in distinction *from* others. But the freedom of God is *for* God and one another as authentic persons (as seen in Jesus).

This phenomenological human is the sinner alienated from God. One's freedom becomes the disobedience in which we are enslaved. We see only a shadow of real humanity; reality is yet to be discovered. We are deceived, missing the relational essence of our existence.

Humans have a body and an ethical character, but these provide no conclusive guide for real humanity nor distinguish real humanity from corrupted humanity.

We aim to discover the reality and not the shadow. We need a real human to clarify the distinction between reality and our damaged and perverted state—the phenomena available to us.

Appealing to our ethical nature cannot help us because it is twisted in self-service apart from God and others.

Reflecting on German philosopher Johann Gottlieb Fichte, Barth sees the failure of human self-understanding. Understanding the human in isolation lacks the other in relation to oneself.

Human knowledge is not reality, so our knowledge of ourselves is inadequate. We engage reality and are shaped by it. But we must *doubt our knowledge* of ourselves, *not reality* itself.

We must have our knowledge informed by what is other than ourselves, true to what we encounter.

Fichte's vision leaves out God and deifies the human in one's mind. This *idealistic view* cannot conceive of the reality of humanity. It is the fruit of human thinking in isolation from reality.

Having addressed the attempts of naturalism and idealism to provide an adequate anthropology, Barth now turns to existentialism.

In *existentialism*, we exist as subjects distinct from the world as objects we observe. Even thinking about our thinking and our physical existence can only be an object of our subjective self.

When we pass from our *nature* to our *thinking* to our *existence*, we still do not escape the subjectivity of our isolated observations and mythological projections. We end up with images echoed from ourselves and not true to the reality of the other.

Humanity is on a long quest to discover itself. We have come from somewhere and are on our way to becoming something. But this discovery process exists in a relationship with a being transcending every human definition.

In the "frontier situations" of death, suffering, guilt, and conflict, we encounter the unavoidable reality that overcomes our defiance. We find the meaninglessness of our resistance, and discover this Other as worthy of our surrender to grant us meaning. Philosopher and psychiatrist Karl Jaspers points in this right direction but misses the actual revealed God.

In time, we may discover that we are not self-contained. We have an "openness, [an] actual relatedness to this transcendent other, and therefore

The Host Unveils Our True Human Identity 93

the experience of [our] real existence."[4] We still have the phenomenon of the human, not the human in actual form.

In the naturalist, idealist, and existentialist attempts at developing anthropology, understanding is pursued with human strength and resources.

Real humanity exists in the history between God and humankind: belonging to God, saved by God for God's glory, and obedient in service to God.

Humanity's natural, ideal, and existential elements should not be rejected. Each contributes at the level at which its claims can be made. But all those attempts combined can create only a caricature of humanity that is a parody of the human, a monster of sorts, but not an understanding of authentic humanity.

There is only one trustworthy source to understand true humanity: God. God has spoken, and we must listen. We cannot forget for a moment that God is our Maker, and we are His creatures.

Our relation to God does not come through any innate awareness of God. Any innate awareness is vulnerable to human constructions based on human attributes and inconsistent with God. This approach is the essence of *theistic anthropology*: acknowledging God but in general experience, not in the person of God's self-giving.

God, as our Creator, must always be prior in our thinking, and we are those who result from the will and acts of God. We cannot look at our good thoughts to find God. The god in the mirror is our reflection.

Accurate knowledge of humanity comes from a *God-centered* (*theonomous*) understanding of who we are in contrast to *autonomous* interpretations.

Humans can be self-determined, think, hear, and be responsible to others. This capacity develops what may be called *human personality*. From this, one may conceive that a human is their concrete choice. They can act and constantly seize their possibilities (Barth's view of fellow Reformed theologian Emil Brunner's position).

But we must not pursue a relationship that misses God Himself. It is natural to have vague ideas of all that is superior and mysterious. This approach does not address actualities, only potentialities.

Real potentiality can only come from the reality of God. Neither a theory of God nor humanity can provide the basis of genuine personal being.

We must recognize the Other with whom we have a relation as the true Transcendent—uniquely self-revealed in Jesus.

---

4. *CD* 3.2, § 44, p. 113.

We get it wrong when all that God gives and does gives us a potentiality that puts the decisions and possibilities in our hands.

Barth believes Brunner holds a detachment for the human, who may accept or reject the commanding love of God. All that Jesus has done is a mere potentiality for human existence. This position puts the human in control in a manner unacceptable to Barth.

> There is only one trustworthy source to understand true humanity: God. God has spoken, and we must listen.

Actual human beings live in response and obedience to the love of God.

3. Real Man (pp. 132–202)

Barth has critiqued four inadequate proposals (naturalism, idealism, existentialism, and theistic anthropology) for understanding the nature of humanity.

Now, Barth offers his proposal for an understanding of "real man," focusing on the person of Jesus Christ. Theological anthropology must begin with Him.

Jesus alone reveals true God and true humanity for all other humans.

- Jesus is the creature in whom God reveals His glory as Creator.
- Jesus is the creature who embodies the sovereignty of God.
- Jesus is the creature who uniquely fulfills the will of God.
- Jesus is the creature who exists from God, in God, and for God and not Himself.

The Bible's message is that this one man stands among all other humans as one like them. He precedes them as a human neighbor, companion, and brother.

Humans have their very being from this Other who constitutes and creates our being. This is God as the divine counterpart of every human. His creaturely being is the ground of every human—in His existence, saving act, and fulfillment of the will of God for us.

Being a human means existing in correspondence with Jesus. We are reflections and representations of this personal God.

We are with Jesus and, therefore, with God. To be with Jesus is the ultimate determination of our being as God's children. From this relation all else is derived.

Godlessness is impossible for humanity because God will not be without His creature.

The Host Unveils Our True Human Identity

- To be in sin is to be contrary to our humanity.
- Humans sin.
- To be with Jesus is to be with God.
- To deny God is to deny our humanity, choosing an impossibility in that we cannot exist without God.
- In rebellion against God, we obscure and attack the continuance of our being with God.
- Every act of God in Jesus is one of correction and restoration of the being of humans.
- Retribution and reward are deeply rooted in the being of humans. Retribution implies punishment and resistance from God in disconnection.
- Reward implies favor with God in connection.
- God rightly rewards and punishes, as He stands with humanity for us and with us.

All creatures are with God. They are not with God as humans are with God.

None of creation is godless, but we are unaware of how all creation is related to God.

Humans are derived and distinct from God, dependent on God, but not identical to God.

In the human sphere, we find clues for understanding the nonhuman world, as the essential being of creation exists in a relationship with God. All being derives from God, but Jesus reveals its meaning to humanity.

We cannot begin to understand creation in itself or humanity from its self-reflection. God reveals the cosmos' meaning and the human's place in it.

Jesus is at the heart of the sphere of humanity, the source of understanding God and humankind in proper relation. We exist in the sphere of His influence as the Lord of creation.

Jesus acts to make His history the space for our history. He does not cancel our freedom, particularity, or actions.

With Jesus, we fulfill every daily activity and every thought, feel every emotion, and live in our relatedness.

Barth affirms that the being of the human is a being with God. How did this come to be?

1. God has elected Jesus to be with us.
2. In hearing the Word of God, He is with us.

For God to elect is to make a *decision* with an *intention* focused on His particular *object*.

The *decision* of God is to live in fellowship with humanity. In Jesus Christ, God and humankind meet.

Jesus is the penetrating presence of God's will, fulfilling His *intention* for His creature.

Jesus fulfills the will of God. His "Yes" prevails over the threat of all that God has rejected. He preserves creation from the irrationality of the human who chooses other than what God has willed.

From the beginning, God determined to preserve His creation, dealing with what causes the undoing of His creation.

Jesus became the kingdom of God in person; eternity entered our history and personally embraced God's creation.

God has addressed us. In listening to Jesus as the embodiment of the divine address, we respond as the counterpart of God. We acknowledge He is the source of our lives as our Creator and Lord.

The *object* of God's grace is His creature, speaking and acting in light of what is heard and understood. We are who we are as those who hear and respond to the Word of God.

Despite problems with Michelangelo's creation painting, he rightly portrays Adam as an actual historical being related to God's action.

Responding to the question, "Who am I?" the answer comes: "I am one summoned by God, addressed by His Word." This reply is valid for everyone.

> Jesus alone reveals true God and true human for all other humans.

Barth affirms that God created the world *ex nihilo*, meaning by someone and without preexisting material. There was no reality distinct from God. God alone is the fountain of life. Humans derive from God and nothing else.

In our creatureliness, we recognize the biblical view of humanity as those made by God.

Creation includes the initiation, direction, and final state of all God reveals, promises, and uses to bring humans to faith. His miracle summons us to hear and respond to His loving will.

Faith is reorienting to our true origin and our true goal.

Regarding the nature of true humanity, we have concluded:

1. A human is a being with God.
2. Humans are derived from God.
3. Humanity exists because of God's election.

The Host Unveils Our True Human Identity

4. Humanity exists as those who hear God's Word.
5. Thus, *humans have their being as history with God.*

Jesus becoming a human reveals the nature of true humanity in history.

Jesus is the fullness of God in human history, showing us who we are as beings in history.

Our personal human history occurs through interaction with others.

The existence of Jesus is God with humanity. He is the history of God's revelation and covenant as it takes place, working toward fulfilling God's will. Our history is a movement within God's history for us.

As the One whose history is the context of our movement, Jesus is the faithful human who relates as kinsman, neighbor, and brother.

As humans, we are not merely like Jesus. We exist in a dynamic history with Him who dwells as humanity's heart. This matter goes beyond similar characteristics; it is living in the encountered history in which God makes and embraces us.

Humans are who they are through a relationship with Him and His movement on their behalf.

Jesus, in His primary history, comes to us. In secondary history, we respond to Him in our actual history.

We live in a state of time, an attribute of our physical being.

As we live in the light of God's revelation, we become helpers and reflect His light. In this way, our history lives within His history. We live in an earthly coexistence with the eternal transcendent God.

God has freely and intentionally made us and covenanted with us so that His history makes room for our history as an embrace.

We confirm our uniqueness as those summoned to hear God and act in response.

Hearing the summons of God's grace and responding means having human existence defined as *being in gratitude*. Gratitude is life in correspondence to the Word as the responsive counterpart of grace.

Humans have their being in gratitude.

To be grateful is to recognize that someone has bestowed a good.

Gratitude is an attitude of acceptance within a renewing relationship.

God is the giver who bestows benefits, mediated to humanity by His Word. Through grace, humans gratefully open to God as He makes a dwelling place in humanity.

Barth continues by examining the meaning of the history of real humanity.

- God first opened Himself to us and extended Himself in grace.
- Gratitude, derived from God's grace, is returned by us to God, its source.
- Humans live in a history of pure receptivity, the object of grace.
- Grounded in grace, the human thinks, opening to God, who has opened first.
- The human exists as a subject whose wholeness unfolds in spontaneous response.

God's history created space for humanity's history with freeing gratitude. Our sense of responsibility arises from the responsive character of thanksgiving.

Humans have their being as responsibility.

God does not force responsibility. God speaks grace that summons a response. When lived with gratitude, this becomes a life of responsibility.

Living "responsibly" is a response to a person, not a state of self-limitations or compliance.

The human also exists as a word, a word of thanks. This echoes the word of grace in Jesus, as connected to it but not identical.

Our life is an answer to the Word of God. A dialogue initiated by Jesus becomes our living activity of address and return, calling us into life together.

In a responsible human life:

1. *Humans have a character reflecting the knowledge of God.*

   God first knows us; we come to know Him as thunder follows lightning. This is not a knowledge of objects; it is personal knowledge between persons.

   We do not come to know ourselves in acts of supposed self-knowledge. We properly know ourselves as those known by the God who wants to be known. Only in affirming "God is" can we state that "I am."

2. *Humans have a character of obedience to God.*

   Responsibility is the active form of hearing God. This active hearing becomes obedience.

   Jesus speaks to us, "Arise, and come to Me. Come to be with Me and therefore to be man, to be saved and kept by Me from chaos. Come to live with Me and by Me."[5] In obedience, we respond, "I will."

---

5. *CD* 3.2, § 44, p. 180.

The Host Unveils Our True Human Identity 99

To obey is to will. We are not carried along like a river. The law of freedom says we will choose who we will be as we stand before the One who summons us.

For Protestant reformer and theologian John Calvin, the highest good for humans is not to be saved but to glorify God by living the most meaningful and purposeful life possible with God.

Obedience is not just reading the Bible but trusting God in His self-revelation.

- It is obeying the Ten Commandments not because they are the Ten Commandments but because they reveal His will to honor Him, our neighbor, and self.
- We pray the Lord's Prayer not because He said to but because He gives us a way to approach Him.
- We worship not out of obligation but grateful for the goodness of God.
- All this occurs as the movement of God invites us to a history of responsibility with the God who speaks and will speak again.

3. *Humans have a character of invocation (asking) before God.*

In all of God's speaking to and being for humans, God exceeds the limits of human existence. We go to God because we need God, who permits us to share His divine life. We come as needy subjects to One who has no need but gives unsparingly.

What we can do is offer ourselves to God. We can thank and respond to God. We can give ourselves, and no less is required. We are empowered to give all of ourselves to God. In this humble state, we find our humanity. Rejecting, we fail to be genuinely human.

We are dependent on God accepting us, which He already has. He calls us, telling us who He is and that He is gracious to us. He has turned to us in freedom and the pleasure of His promises.

In humility, we come to God as an invocation, requesting God's gracious judgment as we offer ourselves. We bring all we are and have, but only as we are summoned, not with anything to make us worthy.

We ask for our lives from Him who supplies them with meaning. We come to God as a request beyond our capabilities, stepping into freedom with assurance and joy, asking God to be our one hope as we entrust ourselves to God.

Our asking corresponds to God's provision. Our request bears no obligation, only submission to divine permission. Our way is not narrowed to fit a constrained path, but is expanded in creaturely splendor. All this comes in our waiting on God in humble submission and arriving with Him. Returning to Him, we complete the circle.

4. *Humans have a character of freedom that God imparts.*

To say that humans have the character of freedom is to say they have personal responsibility before God.

Human responsibility is not a function of God's work; it is ours before God. We know and obey God. We accept responsibility before God, even though God has made Himself responsible for us.

God is free.

God makes His creatures to be free.

As humans exist as God's creatures, they are free.

Humans cannot gain their freedom or accept it from another.

God gifts His creatures to be themselves, engaged in active movement with human freedom. This is not a passive freedom, a state of separation. It is the active being of humans with God, knowing, deciding, asking, and living.

The history of a human is not determined by a person alone, like a cave dweller isolated from others. Freedom is not neutrality in a state of separation; joyous freedom comes from our responsibility before God.

As given by God, freedom is a choice to live in action with the right choice, meaning corresponding with the right choice of God, to be or not to be, to be free or enslaved.

Freedom is never the freedom to sin, to reject one's responsibility. In choosing sin, we lose ourselves, but we are never lost to our Creator.

In looking at Jesus, we can see that humanity is good, not evil. Human freedom for good is lived in the act of responsibility before God. In this way, humans exercise freedom for good before God.

Barth reconsiders the second subsection, "The Phenomenon of the Human," addressing aspects of the human outside what is known in God's revelation, other than in the man Jesus.

The forms discussed can only refer to phenomena. Together they can only give portraits of a shadow-man as these aspects appear to them. Now we

The Host Unveils Our True Human Identity 101

have the reality from which these aspects arise. Now we can see them as actual indications of the human.

We can now say that scientific knowledge of the human has a real object. We cannot understand humanity from our symptoms. The symptoms can only be explained from the being of real humanity.

Our life is an answer to the Word of God.

Theological anthropology can investigate recognizable nontheological knowledge of the human by starting with real humanity. These nontheological topics will not be explored here, only noted to clarify that we cannot begin there. Now, we have real humanity as the object of theological anthropology.

Knowledge of real humans, as the responsible creature of God, enables all other understandings of humanity before God. We are endowed and adapted to live with our capacity as particular beings.

The potential of a human being becomes actualized in a specific life. In this, each person demonstrates that God has created them with the capacity to be human.

The natural sciences seek to present the symptoms of the true nature of humanity. They view humanity in the context of the cosmos and its phenomena. Each person demonstrates the capacity to be a creature of God. *Scientific anthropology* explores this capacity.

Idealistic anthropologies also present the symptoms of humanity. An idealistic ethical vision sees the human rising in moral freedom to exercise a self-initiated history. Ethics addresses this human capacity to act independently. In the light of real humanity, this may be a discussion of proper ethics.

Existentialist philosophy may also address a symptom of real humans. It conceives of the human as open to that beyond human nature and ideals, engaging the unfathomable other beyond human existence. While not abandoning science and ethics, it sees humanity in relationship to this transcendent other as all that exists beyond us. It could be a genuinely scientific enterprise if it pursued real humanity and not being itself.

Theistic anthropology discusses the symptoms of real humans. It sees the human in relationship to a transcendent God. It is God-centered and not self-centered. Humans can rationally perceive God and answer Him with a personal capacity for a history of decisions. This stance may describe the capacity of the human to be genuinely personal as a partner of God. However, theistic anthropology focuses on the human capacity to know God. What it misses is real humanity as known in Jesus, but it is so close. It only needs to have the Word of God reveal real humanity and not begin with human capacity and the God of human exploration.

> As given by God, freedom is a choice to live in action with the right choice, meaning corresponding with the right choice of God, to be or not to be, to be free or enslaved.

These other forms provide a general knowledge of human nature from looking at oneself. They all may have value, but not for knowing real humanity. But they may proceed from an understanding of real humans.

If we can get knowledge of real humanity, we can explore other disciplines that examine the symptoms of humanity. Barth ends by welcoming this possibility.

 CONCLUSION FOR THE CHURCH: The Church exists to fulfill the human as created by God, not to fulfill the ideals of human disciplines. The Church must respect its first allegiance to the true human, Jesus Christ. We are summoned daily to be a community sharing life together with Him. The Church then becomes an invitational community for inauthentic humanity, calling communities away from definitions of success that count bodies, services rendered, or meetings attended. The Church is the gathering place for Jesus to spend time with those who may be shaped in meeting with Him. The Church is a table around which we gather and share a meal—shaping a community in love firstly from Jesus' personal presence.

In this section, Barth recalibrates what we think it means to be authentic humans. We cannot look at our bodies, visions, behaviors, or spiritual selves. We must gather to hear and speak as those falling in love with our true beloved to discover our true selves.

 COMMENTARY:
- Humans are the creatures of God, but Jesus is the only one who can show us what a real human looks like, thinks like, feels like, chooses like, and is oriented toward.
- Only Jesus gives us an accurate picture of real God and actual human.
- Jesus lives a history that spans from eternity. Our history is lived and finds meaning in the context of His whole life.
- Science is valuable in studying the physical nature of the human, but it can only discover partial aspects.
- Ethics and ideals are valuable for the thinking and behaving nature of humans but are often detached from the concrete elements of real life.
- Existentialism sees humanity as concerned for self in the context of the great unknown.
- Theistic anthropology is so close to understanding humanity, but it misses the critical point that God came as a human and is not merely God as we conceive of Him.

The Host Unveils Our True Human Identity

- Gratitude is more than an attitude; it is a whole orientation to Jesus that shapes us.
- Freedom is not permission to walk away to do our own thing; it is life in correspondence with the One who loves us and wills the good life for us.

INSIGHT FOR PASTORS: As pastors, we see all kinds of marketers preying on those outside and inside our churches. They appeal to having healthy bodies, thinking our way to a new future, and seeking self-fulfillment. Many spiritual people want little to do with Jesus but believe we should love one another anyway. Barth points our path to the One who makes us, restores us, and knows the freeing goal that springs from God's will for humanity.

When we preach, counsel, gather the family, or share in friendship, we are actively functioning in the presence of Jesus. We are called to be persons reflecting our experience of living in God's sacred space so we may mirror the glory of God as we have received it.

Barth does not want training programs on how to be fulfilled as humans according to human wisdom. We need to meet the God-Man Himself with gratitude and freedom shaping our interactions. No masks or pretending is allowed. Only be with Jesus. He is already with you. Bring Jesus to people, and let Him be the One who walks with them.

Tell your people they are not on the road by themselves. The science of being fulfilled begins with studying an authentic person, Jesus, who summons us to reality together.

INSIGHT FOR THEOLOGIANS: This critical section clarifies the science of being human. Barth confronts inadequate options used in describing the nature of human beings. He rejects them because they all look at humanity through human filters. Each pursuit (naturalism, idealism, existentialism, and theistic anthropology) selectively observes human "symptoms" and makes that the whole or the key. They neglect other important aspects and are incomplete, driven by their agenda. These methods are not scientific enough for Barth.

Jesus provides an articulate, living Word about what it means to be human. He is Real Man. He lives in an ongoing relationship with His Father, which is our primary, proper orientation. Learning to think theologically means that even the study of humanity must begin with a concrete particular person by and with whom humans are created.

Having established Jesus as a starting point of humanity, we can see the echoes and reflections for understanding who we are. One might not think gratitude and freedom are essential for what it means to be a human, but this is precisely the life Jesus lives and, therefore, offers us as we are in Him.

Barth closes by reflecting on other human pursuits for understanding humankind. He sees a possibility of revitalizing these disciplines by beginning with Jesus as the lens through which to proceed. This redirection opens the way for a disciplined theological science to explore human capacities in the context of Jesus' intentions and actions, understanding His being as the One original and authentic human in the world.

? CLARIFYING QUESTIONS: Does your theology understand humanity by looking for traces of God's design in the human to establish God's purposes? *Or* do you fix your eyes on Jesus, and let that contented and curious gaze open your understanding of what it means to be human, distinguished from views that diverge from Him?

CHAPTER 11

JESUS, THE MEETING OF GOD AND HUMANITY FOR COMPANIONSHIP

§ 45. Man in His Determination as the Covenant-Partner of God

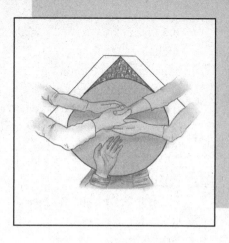

FOCUS STATEMENT: Jesus embodies the meaning of being human as being with others in a personal manner. We are not fully human alone, only with others as an outworking of God's covenant with us.

In § 45, we explore how Jesus is for God and other humans. He extends God's covenant way of being, embodying a partnership for those He creates and loves.

God formed humans to live interactive lives. We are given eyes, mouths, ears, and hands to serve each other gladly. In this formative process, we weave the interrelations that constitute our humanity. We are made like God to reflect His self-giving life in our relations and to fulfill His covenant love.

The image presents Jesus' invitation to hear and come to the table and share life together.

INTRODUCTION: We continue our discussion of humanity as revealed in Jesus, focused now on the human with other humans. We observe Him as One who is for and with others in all He does.

Jesus, as a fellow human in relation, opens our discussion to clarify the structure of human interactions in relating, which is crucial to our humanity.

We live as an *I* with others who are a *Thou* for us. This pairing includes male and female coexistence and Jesus as the head of His body, the Church.

106　　　　　　　　　*Church Dogmatics 3.2*

This relational community extends to the world from God, who exists for and with humankind.

Barth clarifies the concrete existence of life together. He reframes our human existence from being individuals to covenant partners with Jesus in hopeful, loving cooperation.

CONTEXT: *CD* 3.2
Pages in Paragraph: 122 pages (pp. 203–324)

Subsections
1. Jesus, Man for Other Men
2. The Basic Form of Humanity
3. Humanity as Likeness and Hope

TEXT: § 45. Man in His Determination as the Covenant-Partner of God

OPENING SUMMARY: That real man is determined by God for life with God has its inviolable correspondence in the fact that his creaturely being is a being in encounter—between I and Thou, man and woman. It is human in this encounter, and in this humanity it is a likeness of the being of its Creator and a being in hope in Him.[1]

SUMMARY:
1. Jesus, Man for Other Men (pp. 203–22)

In understanding what it means to be a human, we must begin with Jesus as the real deal.

Real humanity is a covenant partner with God—as we see in Jesus.

Real humanity participates in history with God, who instigates life in working together—as we share in Jesus.

Real humanity was created as God's partner—as we are in Jesus.

Real humanity does not live a life without God.

Humans who think themselves godless simply overlook that they belong to God; therefore, they cannot explain real humanity since they lack the essential criteria. They are silent about God and sin since they do not know about either.

---

1. *CD* 3.2, § 45, p. 203.

Jesus, the Meeting of God and Humanity for Companionship 107

Real humanity is a creature *distinct* from God, made to live on the earth and under the heavens and created for life with God, which is the external basis of the possibility of the covenant with humanity.

God has made humans *for* Himself, which is the internal basis and possibility of the human in the covenant in harmony with God. Thus, humans are both distinct from God and connected to Him.

Humans can break their covenant with God and obscure their identity. When this happens, the human becomes disoriented and detached from reality.

The biblical references to inward and outward being, old and new humanity, and the first man from earth and second from heaven all refer to the contradiction when we separate from God, who will not abandon us.

God does not affirm a dualism of being resident in two spheres: we always belong to Him (covenantal) and have our bodily form (earthly).

We cannot blame God for our sins or conclude that we are outside God's covenant. We live as though this contradiction is possible—God is in heaven, and we are on earth—but this is a fantasy.

> Real humanity is a covenant partner with God—as we see in Jesus.

God will hold us and not abandon us, even when we abandon Him.

Who we are as God's beloved cannot be taken away; humans cannot annul God's covenant.

God has made us for correspondence with Himself; this cannot be discarded, even if sinful humans vandalize their creaturely form.

We need the Word of God to know ourselves; we have no natural knowledge of God or ourselves.

Jesus is the authentic creaturely form of humanity, what God intends for human essence, expression, and connectedness. For Barth, anthropology is christological.

In saying Jesus is divine, we say He is man for God. In saying Jesus is human, we say He is man for other humans.

He is particularly and intentionally connected to all other humans.

Jesus comes from God as God, precisely for this purpose of being God for God and humanity.

Jesus cares about humanity and comes for their help and deliverance.

Jesus liberates humans from the devil's threat, sin, and death, as well as the consequences of human loss and alienation.

Jesus' private life is mostly hidden from us, and His public life with others exposes a network of relationships, concrete in His service to God.

Jesus deals with humans at the root of their misery. He puts Himself in their place and makes them His cause and responsibility.

Jesus does not just improve life for humans or alleviate their old life. He helps them gain an essentially new one.

Jesus does not merely relieve humans of their sins, taking their punishment to leave them in a neutral state. He gave them the freedom not to sin anymore, obedient in their new form to live for the glory of God.

Once and for all, Jesus becomes the deliverer, in the most comprehensive and radical sense.

For Barth, the whole New Testament can be summarized in the question, "If God is for us, who can be against us?" "God is for us" takes concrete form in Jesus.

The concrete form of Jesus' humanity has several implications:

- Jesus is *from* humanity, letting Himself be determined by estranged human beings and their infinite need. *His humanity arises from fallen creatures, the fallen Adam.*
- Jesus' movement is *toward* alienated humanity. *His humanity arises to help humans and to intercede actively for Adam.*
- Jesus is *with* humanity, who are all around Him. *Jesus' humanity cannot be considered alone; He belongs to every human, friend or enemy.*
- Jesus is *for* humanity as He is for God. *Jesus lives the twofold law of love for God and neighbor.*
- Jesus *serves* humanity as He is serving God. *He appears as the Savior who restores humanity as His covenant partner.*
- Jesus is *free* as God for humanity while true to His divine being. *Jesus is God for humanity through a freeing relationship.*

In God's inner triune being, a relationship is shared with humans.

God is simple in the unity of His threefold being, coexistent as Father, Son, and Spirit, each abiding in the others in a relationship of reciprocity.

God is the origin and source of every "I" and "Thou." He is the I of One God in three persons. "It is this relationship in the inner divine being which is repeated and reflected in God's eternal covenant with man as revealed and operative in time in the humanity of Jesus."[2]

The humanity of Jesus is the reflection of God Himself. He is the *imago Dei*, the image of God in human flesh.

---

2. *CD* 3.2, § 45, p. 218–19.

Jesus, the Meeting of God and Humanity for Companionship 109

There is correspondence and similarity between the divine and human in Jesus, but the human will always be secondary, a reverberation of the divine. This sequence is an *analogia relationis*, an analogy grounded in God, applied to the human sphere—an analogy of relation.

In Jesus, God is for humanity as He is faithful to His loving life in Himself.

2. The Basic Form of Humanity (pp. 223–85)

Jesus is the image of God, and we are not. No one else can be the image of God as Jesus is.

God's grace is the only thing that can make a human capable of being a covenant partner of God.

Humans exist as those summoned to be God's covenant partners. God's work has made us similar and adaptable for an intended correspondence not achieved from our work.

God did not make humans neutral or opposed to His grace and love.

When we ask, "What is the basic form of humanity?" the primary text and form is revealed in the man Jesus.

> "God is for us" takes concrete form in Jesus.

Barth rejects all abstract views that select and generalize human characteristics.

Conceiving of a human *without* neighbors is not properly grasping what is real. Even considering a human *detached* from others is not seen correctly. Only by seeing each human *with* a neighbor do we understand.

Jesus delivers us from our inhumanity to be who we are made to be.

For humans to wander from the hospitality of God does not mean that God ceases to be hospitable. Jesus never abandons lost sheep.

In forfeiting our neighbor, we deny our humanity. "Every supposed humanity which is not radically and from the very first fellow-humanity is inhumanity."[3]

Without the Christian perspective, the word *human* conjures up an individual looking out for oneself.

This primary perception of humans without God is that we can be without others. Only secondarily are we with and for others on specific occasions.

For the natural human, to say "I am" means that I satisfy myself, maintain myself, develop myself, and expand myself to develop a personality. All this calls on the world to serve my specific human ends.

---

3. *CD* 3.2, § 45, p. 228.

110   *Church Dogmatics* 3.2

From the "I am" of my existence comes the projection of what my fellow human may be for me, fitting within my needs or desires.

Barth offers a colorful discussion on how we shape our relations when working from the solitary self that leads us astray.

Beginning with the I, everything becomes a projection of the I. Consequently, our fellow humans have no actual constitutive involvement in our play; we are for ourselves from the outset.

Philosopher Friedrich Nietzsche was the prophet of *humanity alone*, without our fellow humans. He speaks primarily about himself; he was a projection of himself. The human "will to power" became, for him, the proper form of human existence, a symbol of his willful self.

To say "I am" affirms one's self-existence in the cosmos. One is distinct from and yet connected to the outside world.

Can I say "I" without acknowledging another, a "Thou" who confirms my being? For Barth, an isolated, self-sufficient "I" is an illusion. I am not alone, only distinguished from and connected with other "Thous," who are beings like myself.

I, and others like me, exist in relationship. I am in my sphere, but I share it with others. These other beings correspond with my being. They are not an It, a thing, but a Thou, whom I must treat as a person.

Encounters with others shape us. We limit and impose conditions on each other. We stand within the conditions created by each other. To withdraw is a retreat to inhumanity.

"I am" is appropriately extended to "I am in encounter." I am never outside this encounter, retreating into a world set apart; we exist with fellow humanity, claiming each other's attention.

Jesus is like us as He exists as a being in encounter. Because He is this way, we cannot accept any form of humanity without the other, contrary to modern ideas of individualism.

We are humans as persons due to God being personal as our Creator. We encounter each other as histories of encounters with fellow companions.

Barth turns to clarify the distinctively human categories. He excludes all the activities of thinking, feeling, willing, and acting from being our essential humanity. In all these, we can be human or inhuman.

The question is whether we affirm or deny our humanity in the field where the I and Thou encounter occurs.

That I exist in this field does not make me human; *how* I live determines whether I become true human or inhumane.

Being in encounter is:

Jesus, the Meeting of God and Humanity for Companionship   111

1. An encounter in which each person *looks another in the eye*.

   One sees the particularity of another as one who is a human. One also allows the other to return the gaze and look eye-to-eye.

   We discover the significance of the eye and its seeing, not hiding or refusing to be seen by another. Mutual seeing shapes real humanity through opening to the other.

   Opening is an encounter and not a collision. We know the other like ourselves, and yet they are distinct. We give our uniqueness to the other and gain insight, acting for the other and developing interest in each other.

   "This two-sided openness is the first element of humanity."[4] When we persist in isolation, our lack of participation is our inhumanity.

   The mutually shared look becomes the root formation by which humanity is made possible.

   A dangerous ambiguity arises when we consider humans as a group categorized by attributes. This assessment creates a blind existence that does not look people in the eyes. The actual person becomes invisible to the observer.

   Barth does not use the word here, but the dangerously developed attitude is the essence of *prejudice*. He uses the word *bureaucracy* to discuss this inhumanity in which a person "unwittingly sits and acts all his life in a private bureau from which he considers how to treat and dismiss men according to his private plans, and in the process, he may never see the real men and always be invisible to them."[5]

2. An encounter in which there is mutual *speaking and hearing*.

   Both parties must speak *and* hear one another without a lack on either side, employing human speech for a real encounter.

   The event of speech must become an encounter with reciprocal expression and reception.

   If there is to be understanding, I must express myself, crossing the frontier of mere visibility into relation with the other.

   Words are not genuine if used as a mask to prevent others from knowing us. Our false self gives a dishonest declaration.

---

4. *CD* 3.2, § 45, p. 251.
5. *CD* 3.2, § 45, p. 252.

To hear humanly, I must release my suspicions and allow the other to help me understand their self-expression.

To speak humanly is to talk so that others will hear and acknowledge what we hope to communicate.

We want to experience the hospitality of another making room for us. Likewise, I must make room for others, accepting their address as they knock, asking to be admitted and accepted.

The big question is: What will become of me if I refuse the other, in part or whole, from entering my hospitable sphere? My humanity is at stake, as is theirs.

Health requires we reciprocate in speaking and hearing. Modes of missing each other take on myriad forms.

Speaking without listening diminishes our humanity. "Two monologues do not constitute a dialogue."[6] In our aloneness, we talk past each other with dishonesty that appears to be with the other but speaks merely for oneself.

Dialogue is the encounter of I and Thou helping each other. Speaking without listening is barbaric, yet this is our everyday experience.

Empty words plague human discourse, sermons, lectures, and writings. Usually, it is not the words that are empty; it is those speaking.

3. An encounter in which there is a rendering of *mutual assistance* for one another.

Beyond being knowable, we are called to serve others within limits as a means of being for them.

A life of self-sufficiency, not asking for help and support, is less than fully human. Our very humanity requires our awareness of needing the assistance of others as a fish needs water.

Jesus lives to assist others. His opposite is Nietzsche's Zarathustra, whose idealist vision of a human alone is a sort of maniac.

4. An encounter in which there is *gladness* in the fulfillment of seeing, communicating, and serving.

Gladness is the fulfilling step of humanity, the empowering secret of the previous stages. Without gladness, our actions

---

6. *CD* 3.2, § 45, p. 259.

Jesus, the Meeting of God and Humanity for Companionship 113

and attitudes become mechanical or like a flower detached from its roots.

Gladness is the decisive, animating, and motivating dynamic of true humanity as a covenant partner of God.

In being truly human, we follow our heart's voice, gladly engaging in our encounter with God and others, unburdened by imposed rules.

We must clarify to resist two misunderstandings:

a. We do not *belong to another* person. We do not surrender or neglect our own life to be a slave. We simply need to be with each other. Living together with distinction, we are with each other with true humanity.

b. The second issue is *using the other* for oneself. That is mere conquest; we become a tyrant, violating the other's freedom.

In glad togetherness, we experience human freedom as companions, associates, fellows, and helpmates, indispensable to one another.

We recognize each other's value. This coexistence becomes joy.

> Jesus is like us as He exists as a being in encounter. Because He is this way, we cannot accept any form of humanity without the other.

The secret of being human is this being in encounter—in openness, speaking and hearing, and mutual assistance interchanged gladly in the freedom of reciprocal help.

God has allowed us to choose to be human or inhuman in our hearts. When the "free" choice is for self-destruction, we should call it sin. When our freedom is in seeking the other as a companion, we nurture our created human nature.

Barth will not depreciate human nature. Looking to Jesus, we will understand humans as the object of divine grace.

Human nature is created good. When humans go against their nature by denial and abuse, they oppose and alienate themselves from God. This state does not make evil by nature what God has made as good.

Love is the new gratitude that comes with discovering merciful hospitality as brothers and sisters awakened by the Spirit.

"Christian love is humility before Him, obedience to Him, hope in Him, the commonly received freedom of those who know that they are born and created anew as His children."[7]

---

7. *CD* 3.2, § 45, p. 275.

We do not discover Christian love by looking at humans. Love is the life of those restored by the grace of God.

In preaching the cure of souls, our picture of humanity must embrace them in Jesus, not as we judge them as sinners.

Sinners are capable of freedom with a heart for others. They often put Christians to shame. It is no surprise that they defend themselves when judged.

Eros and *agapē* are often contrasted. *Eros* pictures the fulfillment of human experience. It is love seeking satisfaction.

Agapē is not expected of natural persons, yet they are not impoverished or absent of love.

Our picture of the erotic person cannot be set in opposition to the Christian person. As an ideal set against our natural humanity, Christian love would become disembodied.

We must affirm a form of *agapē* and *eros* as a third way.

1. Christian love is not humanity following their hearts, like the fall, where freedom became self-seeking.
2. Christian love exists as freedom summoned away from serving ourselves, due to the gracious gift of the Holy Spirit birthing *agapē*.
3. God sets human hearts free to serve gladly and freely in connecting with others. Our hearts are determined for this freedom, even if corrupted in the fall.
4. Christian freedom is a love of one another through the gift of the Spirit.
5. Christian love is the fulfillment of humanity: the person loving God and others in the power of the divine "Yes."

Where *eros* could be slavery and tyranny, it can be a recovery of love awakening humanity in how God created us. With *eros* and *agapē* as the gift of the Spirit, an open, joyful, spontaneous love follows, recognizing everything God has given as gifts of the Creator. Without love, they are a perversion.

> The secret of being human is this being in encounter—in openness, speaking and hearing, and mutual assistance interchanged gladly in the freedom of reciprocal help.

We must find the humanity shared in Christians and non-Christians, and gladly love them by the grace of God.

The world needs the Church of Christian love that redeems our humanity in light of Christ and the work of the Spirit.

3. Humanity as Likeness and Hope (pp. 285–324)

Humanity lives as an interconnected community of persons, which is the outworking of our interrelated way of being.

Being fellow humans together means encountering one another. This affirmation holds I and Thou as the form of humanity.

Not all associations are positive, but they are actual in the events of our lives.

The relatedness of humanity is a constant core of theological anthropology. It is also the dynamic within which corruption and alienation arise.

We exist in the encounter of *You and I*, first with God as the originating Other, and second with friend, neighbor, enemy, and acquaintance. We may pretend to live as individuals in isolation, denying our relational composition. That is not reality.

When Barth says "man" or "human," we implicitly refer to male and female. Humanity exists with this togetherness entwined with difference, a duality, a unity with identifiable distinctions that cannot be without the other.

Gender is the only structural form of humanity with visible distinction. It implies another who is different yet essentially compatible for the completion of humanity.

Many variable features, such as race, are part of the structure of humanity and allow intermingling.

Humans share sexual differentiation with the animals, reminding us that we share in creation and are not outside the realm of the animals.

Growing from a child to an adult is a common experience for both sexes. Choosing to be a spouse, to be a parent, or to have a vocation is optional. Male and female are primary as God has made them; all else is secondary within these distinctions.

There is no male except with the counterpart of females, even if a child or single. No female is unaware of the other born male, regardless of how she relates to this other.

No abstract human comes to the world outside the male and female structures. Each learns to coexist and cooperate with varying degrees of success within diverse relational arrangements. Between the two are many forms of conflict and coming together.

Within God's creative purposes, He has made man and woman partners to create children.

Friendship and partnership between the sexes fulfill the call to love the other, but the collaboration in procreation is God's creative correspondence.

Barth resists discussing physiological and psychological structures that become vague, abstract, and prejudicial. Identification of feminine and masculine characteristics are subjective and often prejudicial. Barth warns against these generalizations.

Men and women improperly refer to one or the other as superior or inferior, a head or servant of the other. We must appreciate distinctions, not trying to replace or dominate the other.

Each sex is to the other a fellow human, seeing and speaking to each other to share mutual assistance in meeting the needs and desires of shared life.

The interest, play, and counterplay between the sexes are more significant than sexual love or marriage issues. It extends to parents, siblings, and friendships.

For Barth, there is a special connection in choosing a full-life partnership. Being fellow humans, each becomes the "other" to fulfill the friendship. Each provides the hospitality of making space as companions and helpmates.

The call is that two humans love each other and have each other gladly.

In this sphere of male and female exists the field of sexual encounter, the primary meeting in the domain of I and Thou. To be ignorant here is to miss being human. Whether lived well or poorly, one cannot overlook the sexual dimension of being male and female.

Great philosophers developed understandings of humanity regrettably without serious consideration for the place of women in a man's world.

The only safeguard against becoming dominated by men is good Christology and a cheerful knowledge of I and Thou in companionship with males and females.

The value of male and female is that one sees another like oneself and yet different from oneself. Male and female together are the complete human creature: a duality, meaning a unity with recognizable particularity.

Saying "human" refers to male and female in their differentiation and connection.

There is no shame or cause for embarrassment in what God has created as male and female. Only in falling from God do we experience shame. In our shame, we deny and suppress our sexuality.

The Song of Solomon affirms the place of the encounter of man and woman as God's gift, where each has a voice and is for the other.

The Old Testament has an even more basic relationship—the relationship between Yahweh and Israel, His covenant people. Man and woman reflect this relationship. But the love of Yahweh for Israel is beyond what is possible in human relationships.

The crucifixion of Jesus is God's covenant fulfillment. Jesus' faithfulness overcomes humanity's infidelity. Through the gift of the Holy Spirit, God and humanity are restored to a reciprocal relationship.

The New Testament reaches beyond the Old, grounded in the preparation of God before creation. The hope of humanity is in the Son before creation, not bound to our resemblance to Adam at creation.

In sexual intercourse, the man and woman enact belonging to each other, reflecting Christ's faithfulness, who joined Himself to us.

To use another merely for our satisfaction makes them an "it," an object to be used.

Paul sees the sexual connection between man and woman derived from Jesus' relationship with the Church.

There is a mutuality of men and women in the Lord. The reciprocity of self-giving flows from the gospel, submitting to Christ.

As Christ leads in self-giving love, so should males. The Church and women correspondingly live in loving response, in no way lessened, but as those entirely beloved.

We are dealing with a mystery, with what is both revealed and concealed. The undisclosed becomes an open secret as Christ and the Church, men and women, and the community reflect the hospitality of God's creation.

Humanity's nature is a mystery of faith, unveiled in the man Jesus.

The future of humanity depends on the Church confirming the relationality of humans, not affirming humans as solitary.

As humans, we are distinct from God but have been determined by God to be His covenant partners.

Humans are created with a likeness and image of God, corresponding with Him in the covenant, like Jesus to be for others.

God exists in relationship; so does the human uniquely created by Him.

> Each sex is to the other a fellow human, seeing and speaking to each other to share mutual assistance in meeting the needs and desires of shared life.

COMMENTARY:

- To be fully human begins with being in relation with God and includes appropriate relationships with other humans.
- There is no such thing as a solitary, separated individual. Western individualism is contrary to proper theological anthropology.

118   *Church Dogmatics* 3.2

- We must engage others with assistance and let them assist us in an attitude of gladness, not resistance or reluctance.
- We are created for covenant, which is a commitment to love and be loved by God, and to engage with other humans in a like manner.
- God made men and women as partners in life with a connectedness enriched by the distinctions of the other sex.
- All forms of the human family live an echo of the relation between Jesus and His people, our true family of origin.

CONCLUSION FOR THE CHURCH: The Church needs to create a safe space for humans to become persons. Jesus' priority made room for men and women of all ages and statuses to be included. It is not enough to be a community that teaches doctrine and the Bible detached from bodily existence. To love Jesus is to echo His loving covenant in a community of friendship, valuing distinctions and nurturing relationships, and not solitary spiritual ventures. We are to live as a covenant community with Jesus, not as a collection of spiritual superheroes.

INSIGHT FOR PASTORS: This paragraph calls pastors to nurture the family life of humans. They have been shaped as individuals aiming at self-improvement. Many have adopted beliefs about roles and responsibilities based on sex, age, or other visible features. These abstractions often lock people in boxes instead of opening doors of collaboration and unique contributions.

Jesus called unlikely people to a life of love and serving. Jesus modeled active encounters that granted dignity to each person and invited them to belong. Our churches need the skills of being humans that allow the Spirit to break down walls and weave us together with our differences.

We are called to be covenant people. We cannot do this without listening to Jesus. We must not create an imitation community but reflect God's image in all our relating.

INSIGHT FOR THEOLOGIANS: This paragraph connects the Jesus of heaven with the Jesus who walked the earth. It removes Christology as an abstract discipline unrelated to human life, refocusing us on its interpersonal existence.

Jesus is the most human person alive today. He is with us and for us before we do anything. He calls for an interactive involvement with other humans beloved by Him. With Him, we develop a character of honoring others as though they matter. We cannot reduce anyone to any category of human characteristics.

Our theology must make room for the complexity of persons in their history, including their self-misconceptions and their judgments about others. In this section, Barth proposes rethinking our sense of being human based on knowing Jesus. This process takes theology from the laboratory to our streets and homes. We develop as fellow humans guided by the Spirit to obey the command to love.

? CLARIFYING QUESTIONS: Does your concept of the spiritual life begin with the individual hoping for a worthwhile life? *Or* does it start with Jesus as a covenant partner who shares His love with you and others in a life of knowing and being known, woven into the will and purpose of God as His family?

CHAPTER 12

THE HOSPITABLE SELF

§ 46. Man as Soul and Body

FOCUS STATEMENT: Barth now explores what it means to be human, with Jesus staying central in discovering ourselves as embodied persons. God made us unified creatures with an observable body and an invisible soul, inseparable in constituting us as human persons.

We are not only body and soul. We are given life by the Spirit's animating work, connecting us to God. Without the Spirit's work, our humanity fades.

As God's work in creation is the external form for the internal covenant that gives it meaning, our body is the outward form, with the soul providing inner meaning. All this is God's hospitable handiwork; we are created for intimate connectedness with body and soul.

We are hospitable selves. The Spirit opens us to God, who comes to us, and we come to God as whole beings made to be partners with God and one another. We live in encounters, making possible a hospitable history fulfilled in God's creation.

INTRODUCTION: Understanding the constitution of human persons starts with Jesus, the only unfallen human. The fall impacts all other humans. Jesus is not merely the ideal of humanity; He is the real form. In our alienation from God, we are marred and twisted, shadowy and unreal in our sin.

We have a body. But we are more than a body. An internal element thinks, feels, and relates with others. This component is our soul. Barth argues we must never separate the soul from the body. They are a discernable pair of features that require clarification to understand their unity, distinctions, and proper ordering.

Barth also unveils errors of prioritizing body over soul or *vice versa* and the mistake of choosing one and excluding the other.

By His Spirit, God enables us to participate in heaven and earth. With the Spirit, we live; without the Spirit, we die. The Spirit's hospitality awakens us as persons.

The Hospitable Self

CONTEXT: *CD* 3.2
Pages in Paragraph: 122 pages (pp. 325–436)

Subsections
1. Jesus, Whole Man
2. The Spirit as Basis of Soul and Body
3. Soul and Body in Their Interconnexion
4. Soul and Body in Their Particularity
5. Soul and Body in Their Order

TEXT: § 46. Man as Soul and Body

OPENING SUMMARY: Through the Spirit of God, man is the subject, form and life of a substantial organism, the soul of his body—wholly and simultaneously both, in ineffaceable difference, inseparable unity, and indestructible order.[1]

SUMMARY:
1. Jesus, Whole Man (pp. 325–44)

Human beings exist in covenant with God and encounter with fellow humans. We easily miss this foundational affirmation when we are preoccupied by our human soul and have a diminished concern for bodily existence.

Humans are whole beings composed of body and soul. We can connect human existence within a broader hospitable context, God and fellow humans, who form the field of our relating.

Many pairings express the reality biblically portrayed as soul and body:

- Spiritual and substantial
- Inner and outer
- Rational and sensual
- Invisible and visible
- Heavenly and earthly
- Intelligible and empirical

We begin with humans as presented in the Word of God, particularly in Jesus; moving forward, we can discuss humankind generally.

---

1. *CD* 3.2, § 46, p. 325.

Jesus is one whole human being, "embodied soul and besouled body."[2] Each aspect is never without the other. Jesus is all of this: never divided, added to, or subtracted from. He was born, died, and rose again. He reigns in heaven and will return as the same whole being.

Jesus exhibited a human inner life. We are given few clues as to its nature.

Jesus had a physical life. He had a mother and family. He ate and drank. He bled and cried. That His maleness, celibacy, and health were little mentioned means these are not His defining characteristics. He was a human who embraces what is common to us all.

Jesus' body and soul cannot be considered independently; they are the wholeness of His life.

Jesus lives from His self-grounded intentions. He comes bodily to bring the cosmos to orderliness from its disorder. In this sense, the interior determines His life for and with the others He loves.

Guided by the continual presence of the Spirit, Jesus fulfills the kingly nature of King David, upon whom the Spirit rested. Jesus owes His existence to the Holy Spirit, who enables His messianic mission.

All humans owe their existence to the Holy Spirit, live by the Spirit, and have a spiritual nature. For Jesus, the Spirit is a constant; He lives in and with the life-giving Spirit.

Our human life is transitory, passing in time, depending on the movement of God by the Spirit for our lifetime.

Jesus' personal life in the Spirit displays the divine kingdom present in creaturely form. In the flesh, Jesus lives the fullness of meaning we lack.

Jesus' body is infused with His soul, a consciousness that moves in speech and action.

We begin with humans as presented in the Word of God, particularly in Jesus; moving forward, we can discuss humankind generally.

The relationship between Jesus' soul and body is comparable to that between Himself and His community, the body of Christ. The soul and body of Jesus are original, primary, and basic source in the analogy, which then points downward in the relation.

Jesus is prophet, priest, and king as the soul of His body, preceding those who are the children of God. He originates and builds up this community in Himself.

Jesus is the primary form of wholeness. Christendom can only be secondary and derived from Him within this meaningful analogy.

---

2. *CD* 3.2, § 46, p. 327.

The Hospitable Self

123

As the Spirit is poured out on Jesus, the Spirit will be poured on others, acting as His love directs them.

Jesus will be the norm for all our development of theological anthropology. He is the fixed point for an authentic human in a world of fallen, unstable, and disorderly humanity.

2. The Spirit as Basis of Soul and Body (pp. 344–66)

Barth's essential insight into the uniqueness of humanity's nature is that we have a spirit.

Spirit is not something we possess. It means we exist as God's creation, constituted by our relation to Him, owing our personal existence to Him.

We are not God, but God makes us for God. We can never be without God or understand ourselves without God.

Every nontheological anthropology claims to understand humans without God, proceeding on their grounds as though God were unnecessary.

God makes His creature ever-new, sustained by His mercy and grace.

Humans are distinguished from the rest of the created world, and responsible to God in a manner that corresponds to God's covenant of grace.

God grounds, constitutes, and maintains each human every moment of every day.

When we say, "God the Creator," we refer to the Father of Jesus, the God of Israel, and the One whose mercy makes us new every morning.

Humans stand in a historical existence with God by His covenant, which grounds and sustains our being so His graces enliven our gratitude.

We belong to the visible world of bodies while present with the invisible soul of our bodies.

We share the space of the world with plants and animals. We live in particular places on the land and by the sea, sustained by God.

Each living human is a soul of one body. Each is a bodily soul. Each is a besouled body.

Because we are the soul of our body, we dwell in time inwardly and outwardly, participating in the visible and invisible, implying both the earthly and heavenly.

Barth insists we are a unified duality, unable to be split apart. We exist bodily in the physical, material world. We reflect on that world in our interior life of thinking and feeling, which inseparably refer to the exterior acts of the body.

The human shares in God's life as a soul, and God's work of creation as a material being.

Death reminds us that our bodies do not belong to us. We are always in the hands of God, in life and death.

God meets humans, calling us to know ourselves as those known by Him. We become covenant partners as human persons met by our Creator.

The human *is* soul and body but *has* spirit. Spirit is what comes to humans as something received, not owned. Spirit denotes what God is and does for humans. It might be better to say that spirit has us. Death is the absence of spirit.

The spirit is *not* a third part of humans. It constitutes the human as God comes and makes the soul and body alive. In death, our spirit goes to be with God, as we see with Jesus and Stephen in their dying moments.

"Spirit is, in the most general sense, the operation of God upon His creation, and especially the movement of God towards man."[3]

When we say, "Holy Spirit," we mean the Spirit who proceeds from God. He is the breath who is not distinguished from the source who breathes.

The Spirit is God's action and attitude toward His creation in person. The Spirit brings us into the covenant with God.

The Spirit is the power through which Old Testament people are equipped and commissioned to serve God. In the New Testament, the Spirit equips the community.

By the work of the Spirit, God judges and applies His lordship in the many affairs of humans. He rests on Jesus in His ministry and falls on the New Testament community with tongues of fire.

The community is constituted by the Spirit's gifts and bears His fruit. He comes as the helpful, liberating God.

Each human becomes a new person, born from above, set in right relation to God, and pledged to future participation in the glory of God.

Theological anthropology must attend to the work of the Spirit.

> Each living human is a soul of one body. Each is a bodily soul. Each is a besouled body.

All persons stand within God's covenant concern, granted creaturely reality. God has given everyone His Spirit. Without the Spirit, a person cannot be a soul of their body, much less a member of the body of Christ.

With the Spirit, each person lives as the soul of their body. Without the Spirit, we diminish to a shadow of a soul, a body dissolving into the world.

---

3. *CD* 3.2, § 46, p. 356.

God continually gives the Spirit to humans as a gift. This act is repeated daily so that we may live. The Spirit belongs to God, not the human.

God also gives animals life; humans are unique by participating in God's covenant by the Spirit. They are fitted with soul and body for partnership with God. Humans and beasts are born, but only humans are baptized into Christ.

The Spirit moves humans to cry "Abba," knowing our hearts and minds and interceding on our behalf with the Father.

The Spirit provides what we cannot: life itself, the covenant, creativity, and restoration to life from the dead.

God breathed life into the first human from the earth, and he became a "living soul." Earthly material became an organic body with life aroused to a living spirit with God.

Summing up what it means for humans to have the Spirit:

1. God is there for each of us every moment and with every breath.
2. The Spirit is the One who makes it possible for us to be the soul of our bodies.
3. The Spirit is in each person. Through their soul, He is also in their body. This fact is the most indispensable factor in understanding human existence.
4. The Spirit is related directly to the soulful element of humans but only indirectly to the body. The soul is the life of the body. Thus, the besouled body is the Spirit's dwelling.

3. Soul and Body in Their Interconnexion (pp. 366–94)

We turn to the inner structure of human creaturely existence.
We will look at three subtopics:

1. What is its inner *unity*—soul and body in their interconnection?
2. What is its inner *differentiation*—soul and body in their particularity?
3. What is its inner *order*—soul and body in their ordering?

God stands with humans as the embracing parentheses that establish the content and meaning of a human.

Within the brackets, humans are whole, yet with the duality of soul and body.

Two proposals follow:

Church Dogmatics 3.2

1. The human is a *living* being created for a creaturely life with an individual body. One has existence within this body as a soul.
2. The human is a living *being* with the spatial form of a besouled body. One has a nature that embraces the soul, a body.

Soul and body are not identical and cannot be reduced to the other. Each can be identified. Like distinguishing space and time, both are present and relative to one another.

Creator and creature belong together by the grace of God's will. Body and soul belong to each other by the nature of the human.

The Spirit awakens the soul but is not identical to the human soul. The human soul owes its existence to the Spirit, who grounds but does not cause creaturely action. The human is a spiritual being, interconnected and yet self-acting.

The soul presupposes a body to which it belongs, with the soul as inner and the body as outer.

The soul moves in time in an embodied way. The body moves in space with a soulish experience of thoughts, feelings, and aspirations.

"Soul is self-contained life, the independent life of a corporeal being."[4] This livingness provides the capacity for self-determined action.

Objects that lack the capacity for action, such as a stone or a mass of water, have no soul and are lifeless.

We cannot know whether a plant or a beast has an independent soul. We are only sure of this with humans.

A fellow human can tell me about the acts of their life, including their self-knowledge and capacity for knowing. I can affirm they have a soul.

We discover ourselves and become assured of who we are. As a knowing subject, I return to myself as a known object, alive and acting in thought and physical activity.

We can also be aware of objects other than ourselves. Through our bodily senses, we recognize that they are different from us and distinguish ourselves from them.

We internally know what we engage in the world as a moment in the history of our souls. At the same time, it is a moment in the history of our material bodies.

We feel independent because our bodies occupy a particular space in time separate from others. But there is more.

---

4. *CD* 3.2, § 46, p. 374.

The Hospitable Self

We also can see that we live in space and time sustained within a system of relations in which we participate and act.

Plants have living material bodies. Animals have independent organic bodies. Humans have these, but also a soul that gives knowledge of oneself and others in a compatible manner.

We are not just material (stuff). We are organic (living) beings with a soul (connected with self and others).

When we say "I," the soul speaks for the whole besouled body. I am involved as body and soul in all my expressions and interactions.

> With the Spirit, each person lives as the soul of their body. Without the Spirit, we become diminished to a shadow of a soul, a body dissolving into the world.

I am present as a besouled body in a system of relations, interconnected physically and personally. To deny this can only be a delusion or distortion that leads to disorder in understanding humans.

To say I am a subject is to acknowledge that I am an embodied participant within the network of relations I indwell.

There are three conceptions about the nature of the human we must avoid:

1. The *abstract, dualistic position* holds that two "parts" compose the human; even if they are connected, they are separated. The soul is valued, and the body is opposed as a lower part.

   Soul and body coexist as two substances in this view, with the soul being the highest level distinguishing animals from humans through their moral capacities for understanding goodness and truth.

   The soul becomes separated as the eternal, spiritual element, and the body is mortal and material. The body is eventually cast off so that the soul might be united to God.

   The final result of the dualistic position is the separation of body and soul. It elevates the soul and humiliates the body.

2. The *abstract monistic, materialistic position* suggests that the body is the primary substance of the human. The soul is diminished to the point of saying there is no soul or spirit element. Only the bodily, material, and physical component is real.

   In this view, thoughts, feelings, and behaviors are merely functions of the body, the result of processes in the brain and nerves. The soul is reduced to a mythical notion.

This materialism is a sober counterattack against the dualistic older traditions. It bases its thinking on modern individualistic life more than science.

Where the Church has favored the soul, this modern view dominates with the body. Both are inadequate to reflect biblical richness.

Psychology has become a branch of physiology. Experience, emotions, self-consciousness, and the like are discussed as functions of the animal organism.

Scientific naturalism became a philosophy accepted by a more common sense view. It did not offer a scientific approach that explored the complexity of the human, leaving room for inquiry into the soul of the body.

3. The *monistic spiritualist position* takes the opposite view from the last and sees the soul as the sole substance of human reality. The body is pure appearance, and the soul is the real thing.

The body becomes a garment covering the soul. Only the spiritual can be valid; the rest is appearance, a symbol of the real.

Science becomes the synthesis, with human perceptions discerning external forms. These assessments become psychology, a science of integrating human perceptions (generalizations).

Barth agrees that real humanity is naturally a soul. The soul is as real as the body.

Materialism, with its denial of the soul, makes a human subjectless. The personal self is lost.

Spiritualism, with its denial of the body, makes the human objectless. The body is devalued and dismissed.

Both materialism and spiritualism seek unity in humans. Each holds a one-sided view that does violence to the whole of the human person.

Historic Christian doctrine tended to lead to spiritualism, focusing on the soul.

Materialism reacted to Christian views, exclusively pursuing the body and material world as valid.

When either the soul or body is minimalized, we have an abstraction. An absurd conclusion results, neglecting the actual human in the fullness of body and soul.

We live as those alive with the Spirit, who holds us together as whole, personal beings.

4. Soul and Body in Their Particularity (pp. 394–419)

Barth now explains the differences between soul and body, noting the uniqueness of each.

The unity of the human is in the interconnection between soul and body. The soul is the enlivening factor enabled by the Spirit. The body is that which the soul enlivens.

We cannot say much about how souls and bodies work in animals' lives. We cannot live within the limits of their being to understand their inner world.

With humans, we can discuss the uniqueness of each aspect since this is not hidden from us.

Humans have God's Spirit and are thereby capable of meeting God and being persons in relation to God.

Humans can be self-aware, understanding themselves as distinct from the world and the Creator. At the same time, they can know they are interwoven with the world and connected to God's life.

We can recognize our responsibility to God and others and respond as the Word God speaks to us.

The Spirit qualifies, prepares, and equips us for daily activities through the Spirit's ongoing presence.

Barth continues with the particularity of the human as the *soul* of one's body.

Humans stand before God, who speaks our name and calls us His own. Even in our response, we are independent and in partnership with God. We make our own decisions.

We are conscious of our existence and aware of our place in our world and our relation to God. In this way, we are the soul of our body.

From this center, one engages the periphery as a body with attitudes, making choices and representations consistent with who we are.

> We live as those alive with the Spirit, who holds us together as whole, personal beings.

We have a center and a boundary; we are inward and outward simultaneously. We are capable of being a particular person with a unique personality.

As soul and body together, one is a person: the animating and the animated element made alive before God by the Spirit.

As the human stands before God, Barth unfolds two propositions:

1. *Humans are capable of interacting with God and the world.* We can meet God, hear His Word, know His will, and live with an orderly response.

God has made humans aware that they are partners in the world God creates.

Humans are not merely self-contained beings; we can perceive and receive others into our consciousness. One can acknowledge the presence of another person and oneself in relation to them, plus the connective response of the other in reply.

Humans have an *immediate* experience of the world and *reflective* abilities to think about it. To say that humans are perceptive is to include both. We see and know at the same time.

We do not perceive with an act of pure thought *or* pure awareness. Our thinking awareness opens the door for receiving another into our human consciousness.

To have the Spirit is to perceive God and the world He creates. Responding to God's claim as His own is the proper stance for humans regarding God.

With a unified perception, one may recognize *awareness as the bodily* function and *thought as the soul's* task.

Sensing deals with bodily organs, and thinking extends this detection to the act of perception in the cooperation of body and soul. We are bodies that think.

Through the *soul* of one's body, one prepares for awareness. As the soul of our *body*, we prepare for thought. The two are different but always act in cooperation.

That others have bodies makes it possible for them to enter our consciousness. Our soul discerns their presence through outward perception.

The body is the outer side of perception. The openness of the soul comes through the body to perceive and receive the other.

The soul is the inner side of perception, the openness of humans to themselves, aware of themselves in their bodies. It enables transparency for the self to be with the other; they are, in a sense, "in us," embraced within.

The Bible is not interested in the abstract rational nature of humans. It is interested in the human standing with God, believing that God is for us and in us and that we can perceive God and His purposes. This attitude is the rational nature of humans making sense of God and His world.

Rationality comes from being a partner of God, acting within the covenant God has established for humanity.

The Hospitable Self

In the Bible, observation, recognition, knowledge, and perceptions reflect on the human capacity to be open to the will and actions of God.

Correctly perceiving the world begins with recognizing God. Knowing God takes place within the context of the created world.

God is mediated through His Word, works, and ordinances in a world of objects radically distinct from God.

To have general knowledge of the world is good, but it is not to be confused with knowing who God is. He is the context for understanding His workings.

Humans in the Bible are sinful people who would like to escape God. Thus, they contradict a rational human nature found before God.

Rational nature derives from knowing God as Creator. Other knowledge is abstracted from human experience, becoming improper when estranged from its proper grounding in God.

The story of the Bible recounts and facilitates God's self-giving of Himself in the world He creates.

Humans learn to listen to the One who comes to us so that His hospitality might be complete, renewing, and restoring in the face of our needs.

God is in us as we perceive Him in hearing, thinking, and following Him.

Completely externalized or internalized religion goes astray as a human act that misses sharing life with God.

With a priority on the soul, we live before God as embodied whole persons in a world created by God, who informs our understanding.

Who we are comes with recognizing how we stand with God. *What* we are comes with awareness of our embodied self in a world distinct from ourselves.

2. *Humans are entrusted to be God's partners, walk with Him, and thoughtfully respond to Him.*

Having perceived God, one can act accordingly. Knowledge alone is not enough; there must be fellowship in action. Personal knowledge implies decisions.

Action implies free movement as an agent intends to move toward others.

Objects are not self-moving, much like a rock. They are not doers but can be acted upon by an agent who moves them.

Humans can be moved or move themselves and others. Humans can will or desire within the range of possibilities given to humans.

Pure *will* would only be an internal exercise with no external activity.

Pure *desire* remains external as something entirely sensed but incapable of activity.

To say that humans have spirit affirms they are *first* active with God and, therefore, *second* active to all else.

Existing as persons, humans execute their actions—they shift from perceiving to a movement that fulfills a desire.

Attempting to live only in contemplation or only in activity can only lead to forms of inhumanity.

Like sensing and thinking, desiring and willing are inseparable components of human nature. Desiring is uniquely related to the body, and willing to the soul. But both are soulful and bodily.

Desiring is bodily in that it arouses our liking. The brain's nerves engage a sensible experience with an urge that confirms our appetite (or possibly aversion!) with a material act. Without our body, we could not desire or shun at all.

Willing is a matter of the soul. We have an intention that comes to a resolution with movements corresponding to desire.

Where there is no desire, there will be no will. All that we desire, we will not necessarily will. To will is to make up one's mind, united with the physical, to determine our activity toward fulfilling or avoiding our desire.

Desiring, with the will, leads to an attitude toward the object of our attention. The body does not determine our action and attitude; that is the will's work.

In willing, our desire empowers us to act as our soul moves the body.

We stand before God as those who desire, will, and act. God covenants with us, and we affirm or resist, will a response, and act with obedience or rebellion.

God calls humans to:

- Hear God as One who speaks
- Believe God as He gives Himself in Jesus
- Love God as the One who first loved us

The Hospitable Self

- Live within God's covenant
- Do this because God made us able to respond

Israel acts in the world as God's world. God gifts Israel all that constitutes its being in a total life relation. It grows by the promise and presence of God. The gift of God is to be a blessing to the nations through Israel's witness.

There is no general human activity sphere or a separate sphere where God acts. This split is a human division of the world alien to God's intentions.

The Bible affirms that all humans relate to God in either acceptance or resistance. Christians acknowledge Christ and connect through His self-giving.

The Bible acknowledges the human attempt to withdraw from God. Human rebellion creates a closed circle where desires and willingness, working and gathering, are held in a human space against God.

In their closed spaces, humans strive for well-being, self-made greatness, and command of one's life uninterrupted by God.

Further, each individual becomes self-enclosed with their desires, willing an autonomous existence, with occasional private or public activities separated from everyday life.

The Bible sees the disconnected life as false and deficient in its desires and doings, empty from a lack of acknowledging God.

The autocratic life has a false self-contentment, unable to surrender to God, seeking to supplement life with religious and enlightened activity.

The Bible identifies sickness with human attempts to conduct life as though it has nothing to do with God.

Sound human activity exists when God is respected and honored, desiring God wholly, genuinely, and properly, which means loving Him.

Proper desiring can only be a desire for God. All other desiring is a form of seeking self-satisfaction.

Desires gone astray from God will be irrational and corruptible, like the prodigal son. Desire can be heard in Jesus when He wishes to celebrate Passover with His disciples. Desire is not the problem; the object and goal of desire are at risk of corruption.

We are made to love. We must not confuse the love of God with our inner human desires.

God comes to us outwardly, strange and mighty, that we may know Him as He is. The Bible speaks anthropomorphically (God is like a human), so we will come to know Him amid His created world and be attuned to His self-giving actions.

It is not enough to desire or perceive God, which is only our inner activity. We need an outward response, oriented to the One to whom we belong.

In our obedience, we will what He desires. In our disobedience, we disregard His desires.

With obedience, we are shaped by God. In disobedience, other desires steer us away from God.

As we will to love and belong to God, we will that from which all other decisions come.

God chooses us so that we may desire Him in return.

Who we are comes with recognizing how we stand with God. *What* we are comes with awareness of our embodied self in a world distinct from ourselves.

We live in a constant state of saying "yes" or "no" to God.

Desire and decision combine in a single function as the whole human person engages in living before God by His Spirit.

5. Soul and Body in Their Order (pp. 419–36)

Barth now orders the two elements, addressing the meaningfulness of our response to God as embodied souls.

The nature of humans as soul and body is not accidental. Our ordered union reflects intention, not chaos.

The soul provides reasonable guidance, and the body includes our service in action. God also sends His Spirit to guide the soul and empower the body.

For Barth, reason implies a meaningful activity in the human as both soul and body, accurately perceiving and acting in a manner appropriate to reality.

Rationality is a comprehensive engagement with reality and is not limited to thinking. It includes soul and body since the body participates in our rationality.

God obligates humans to become rational, choosing God's election for them and not choosing disordered nothingness that rejects God.

Theological anthropology compels humans to look from God's perspective.

The Hospitable Self

God treats humans as rational beings because He made them that way.

Barth discusses what it means for humans to be rational under three headings:

> The Bible affirms that all humans relate to God either in acceptance or resistance.

1. If humans are to be understood, they cannot understand themselves in the *distinct forms* of soul-having, thinking, *or* willing subjects.

   We are not pure souls; we direct our thinking and living in the *sphere of our bodies.*

   By the Spirit, we are *spiritual souls* living before God as souls and bodies.

   Humans live and serve in the *sphere of their souls* with their bodies.

   The Spirit of God awakens us to be living beings, summoning us to live with God.

2. If humans are to be understood, they cannot understand themselves *exclusively in the form of the body.* We are not merely sensing and desiring beings.

   The body lives in the *sphere of the soul* as a living being, animated by the Spirit.

   The human lives in a broader sphere than oneself, the hospitable *sphere of God* and the world.

   With one's body comes the freedom of serving and ruling oneself.

   As a body with a soul, one is *immediately with God* by the Spirit.

3. If humans are to be understood, they *cannot understand themselves as dual* but only as a single subject.

   We cannot think about cooperation or coexistence between body and soul. A person is a soul from head to toe.

   Humans exist in their life-act, always with the ruling soul and the serving body.

   Human existence is characterized by the order and rationality that permeates the whole of creation as intended by its Creator.

   God has willed to keep company with humanity so they may live within God's order.

Barth rejects the materialistic and spiritualistic doctrines of the human. These assert either an all-material body, all spiritualistic soul, or any combinations that maintain a split between soul and body, no matter how connected.

Psychophysical parallelism and alteration theories draw Barth's critique (psycho-soul, physical-body).

The *first falsehood* of psychophysical theories is the belief that they can discuss humanity in abstraction from God.

The *second falsehood* is that humans can be addressed not as a unity but with soul and body alongside one another.

The theory of *parallelism* holds the psychical and physical elements of the human as parallel but independent. They correspond with each other but have no influence or direct connection.

A theory of *intercommunication* extends the idea of the two sides of human existence. This view perceives an interconnection and mutual influence on both sides.

Questions for these theories are: Who is the actual human? Who or what operates from one side or the other?

No matter how close the interaction may be, if it maintains an essential separateness, it comes under the same critique as other parallelisms.

There is no bridge between the purely physical and purely psychical world.

Those who see soul and body in parallel are shortsighted. They divide the one human and then try to put them back together.

Does science require us to look only at the body and deny the soul? What right does anyone have to make the outer phenomenon the measure of all things?

Why can we not investigate the rational existence of the human as rational (soul) and physical in one person? Why not explore real humans as a whole?

Psychology, physiology, and other sciences are authorized to investigate the connections, functions, and interactions that explore the interrelated issues of human elements. They establish and evaluate the facts. We do not shut our eyes to them.

In seeing the whole human, we can turn our attention to each element in relation to the other components.

Extensive work needs to be done in the psychological, physical, and biological sciences to address the full scope of what it means to be whole humans.

The Bible only knows humankind in the context of their interactions and interconnection with God.

The Bible affirms the body as the locus of the activity of the soul; we live as integrated, spiritually activated, material beings with God.

According to the Bible:

> The body lives in the *sphere of the soul* as a living being, animated by the Spirit.

- Our flesh cries out for God, longing for Him.
- Our innermost being is open to God as our bodies communicate human emotions to God.
- Poetic language can give accurate depictions of humans before God.
- The heart is the center of human existence, the whole person in miniature, encompassing all our thinking and acting.
- To be pure in heart is to see God. To have a hard heart is to reject God.
- The heart reveals the human as soul and body, a rational being.

 COMMENTARY:

- Barth does not use the terminology of bipartite or tripartite. The human is unified with discernable elements of soul and body and made alive by the Spirit.
- We belong to God, who made us soul and body. We are made alive by the Spirit, who is not part of our constitution but connects us to God.
- The human body is our most observable phenomenon, but we cannot live without the soul. The soul is our inward being that thinks and interprets through our body.
- As embodied beings, we have a historical existence.
- We are soulful beings open to God and others in living relations.
- Other anthropologies portray humanity based on human observations of the human, and leave us with autonomous self-rule rather than as beings created in freedom by God.
- To develop a Christian view, Barth focuses on concrete reality, not an ideal or a fragment of human existence. Jesus is the concrete reality from which to explore.

 CONCLUSION FOR THE CHURCH: The Church is easily seduced into generalizing about what it means to be human. It is hard work to clearly describe what it means to be human because so many ethical issues follow.

Issues of gender, chosen identities, human capacities, age, and many others come with associated judgments. These lead us to categorize humans based on mental or physical capabilities or attributes for which we have no agreed terms as to what constitutes a whole and healthy person.

Barth calls the Church to be clear by beginning with Jesus as the One

138   *Church Dogmatics* 3.2

human who can determine what a fully alive human looks like. We cannot be spiritually oriented without consideration for our bodies. Equally, we cannot default to thinking that bodies alone make us human.

In Jesus, we see that God creates and sustains human bodies. He also gives each a soul as a component of human existence to observe, reflect on, and participate in the world and with other personal beings.

Barth's anthropology is clear and concise as it leads the Church to know itself in light of its head and with hope for His body. All other theories are selective and miss the whole.

INSIGHT FOR PASTORS: As a pastor, one guides a congregation of diverse humans. Barth does not want to overlook those distinctives but wants us to recognize the inclusiveness of a human before God, as seen in Jesus.

Barth does not want to downplay or disregard the human body—God took on a body to be with us. We need to value the body as He does. Jesus also had a soul, with the capacity to think, will, and act. In Him, we have a companion who can transform our alienated souls, restored by being with Him who knows us.

We cannot give the world the task of defining a meaningful life. Our preaching and teaching must direct our attention to Jesus so He can do His work of loving us to His fullness.

Barth is concerned that church leaders acknowledge the Holy Spirit at work in our church families to open us to the Father and Son. We must not take the place of the Mediator. The Spirit wants to make us whole in body and soul as a community by spiritually being face to face with Jesus.

We need insight to expose other voices permeating our expectations and inclinations, to take another look and begin again at the beginning.

INSIGHT FOR THEOLOGIANS: As theologians, God calls us to speak truthfully about God and all God has made. To clarify the human constitution, Barth begins with Jesus to address the soul and body of a human. Barth will resist any other starting point.

Jesus took on a body. He lived in it entirely as a human all the days of His life on earth and then ascended bodily to heaven after His resurrection. Jesus also had a soul by which he thought, made decisions, and caused His body to engage in everyday activities. His unified existence clarifies how a whole person exists: it is not up to us; it is up to the One who made us.

The Spirit makes us alive daily with every breath and is an essential yet neglected aspect of being human. The Spirit connects us, transforming our thinking—that we are individuals detached from God and each other—to existing as persons who live with inseparable relations. The Spirit works in our spirit to restore us as we discover the love of God for us revealed in Jesus.

Theology opens us to hear whose we are and who we are. We discover the extent of God's rational and orderly knowledge, which explains our wholeness as body and soul. Proper theology opens the way to a Spirit-informed, Jesus-focused discovery of who the Father has made us to be as those who belong to Him as our Abba.

? CLARIFYING QUESTIONS: Does your theology think of the human as made up of different parts, with some good and bad features? *Or* does being a human mean that God makes your body and soul like Jesus through the work of His Spirit?

CHAPTER 13

THE PERSONAL GIFT OF TIME

§ 47. Man in His Time

FOCUS STATEMENT: God created time as a field, giving humans space to live. Barth distinguishes our existence within God's time. In § 47, Jesus displays how He is like us yet living in our history as God, present at all times.

Jesus is not limited like we are. He is present in the past, present, and future. Saying He is Lord of time affirms He is hospitably present as He holds us within the gift of His loving presence—even before and after we die.

Barth wants to expand our limited sense of time based on our experience between birth and death. God gives us time to live as covenant partners within His good creation.

Jesus is the person who acts throughout all times to fulfill the loving will of God. Jesus cannot be merely the person of the year; He is the One and Only God who embraces us from and for eternity.

INTRODUCTION: We have seen that God made humanity as His covenant partners to live in the context of created time.

The meaning of human existence transpires as our time intersects with God's eternity met in Jesus, the Lord of time.

Jesus reveals a proper understanding of humanity's existence in time. God gives an allotted time to live. We can either be frustrated with its shortness or recognize the gift. What matters is what we do with our limited time within God's end goal.

This paragraph is the last section of chapter 10, "The Creature." It provides insight into issues that arise when we formulate our histories in the light of Jesus. Jesus embraces all times. We cannot know our future, but Jesus is the One who deals with what is beyond our natural life and holds our future.

CONTEXT: CD 3.2
Pages in Paragraph: 204 pages (pp. 437–640)

Subsections
1. Jesus, Lord of Time
2. Given Time
3. Allotted Time
4. Beginning Time
5. Ending Time

TEXT: § 47. Man in His Time

OPENING SUMMARY: Man lives in the allotted span of his present, past, and future life. He who was before him and will be after him, and who therefore fixes the boundaries of his being, is the eternal God, his Creator, and Covenant-partner. He is the hope in which man may live in his time.[1]

SUMMARY:

1. Jesus, Lord of Time (pp. 437–511)

To understand the constitution of humankind, Barth explores how we exist as embodied souls in the time made by God.

Human life unfolds as a series of activities accomplished within the gift of time.

Without time, humans would have no life. Time is necessary to exist as body and soul.

God also lives with time. His eternity is authentic time, the source of our time. God's time is uncreated and exists with past, present, and future in a simultaneous, not successive, relation.

As His creation, "created time" is distinct from God, further shaped by the corresponding movements of His creatures.

Human time is ours to the extent that it is not God's eternity. It has a fixed span and succession where the souls of our bodies live before God.

We must set our bearings on the human Jesus Christ in His time. His life displays indwelling created time as a human who stands with God.

As the Lord of time, Jesus lives in time as a human, like all other humans.

---

1. *CD* 3.2, § 47, p. 437.

Jesus also lives His life as God, for God, and with God. He lives for humans and with humans. He represents God to humans and humans to God.

Jesus brings God's kingdom, making the relation between God and humanity right.

The content of Jesus' life addresses and embraces everyone. He is contemporary to all humans who will ever live.

Jesus can live in relation to others' times because He expresses the character of God's eternity as the Lord of time.

Jesus had a lifetime marked by His birth and enduring His death. The content of His life was eternal but lived as human life, once and for all.

Jesus is the presence of God, Creator and creature, the life of God in the lifespan of a man.

Jesus' life is a historical event of the Word becoming flesh and dwelling among us.

Jesus has a further history beginning on the third day after His death, a second history. This history refers to the Easter story and extends to His ascension.

The resurrection event is the prism through which the disciples saw Jesus as the One who is and is to come.

Theologian Rudolf Bultmann demythologizes Scripture by removing any references to miracles, thus rejecting the resurrection as an historical event; instead, he attributes belief in the resurrection to the witnesses' faith, not the event's reality.

The resurrection is the "eschatological event" in which God appears in His glory, encountering unbelief and creating belief through His appearance to them.

Barth continues to affirm that we must accept the resurrection of Jesus and its appearance as a historical reality in the language of its own particular time.

That God was in Christ is the truth that dawned on the disciples. The decision for faith was grounded in the reality of Jesus' presence, not an abstract faith in His ideas.

For the disciples, the resurrection affirms the indisputable fact that God is present. Their recollection is their commission to preach the gospel to all nations.

In the Gospels, we see the One who was dead and lives again. That is the core of the gospel's historicity.

The empty tomb and the ascension mark the limits of the Easter period. The disciples thought they had lost Jesus. Instead, they were found by Him.

The resurrection is more important than the empty tomb. We do not

The Personal Gift of Time

pursue the empty tomb. We follow the living Christ. The empty tomb points away from itself as a sign of the resurrection.

The ascension is a sign that points upward and forward. Jesus enters the hiddenness of heaven right before their eyes. Yet Jesus did not cease to be a human. He is the man who lives on the Godward side of the universe.

The ascension points to the time that is to come when Jesus will return. Jesus is still alive. He is not to be found here. He lives in the hiddenness of God, looking forward to His conclusive revelation.

This resurrection story is a once-for-all event that differs from all other histories as God's incomparable salvation history.

Barth's view is against all forms of Docetism, which detaches our knowledge of God from the humanity of Jesus so that He only seems to be human. For Barth, this risen Christ is the fully human Jesus in all His glory, changing history in person.

Time is a hospitable gift to make way for God's covenant with humanity. God created time for this particular time.

God utilized holy times in the Old Testament to display His time in history.

Minor forms include the Sabbath year once every seven years and the year of Jubilee once every fifty years. These are seasons of rest, restitution, restoration, and liberation that point to Jesus' time on earth.

The primary anticipatory time is the Sabbath. The Creation story shows that on the seventh day God looks back and sees what He has made as good. It is suited for His future purposes.

Sabbath was a day for the Lord with His creatures in covenant connection. It is a time of freedom, festivity, and joy. It is a day of release, not obligation; rest, not task.

The early Christians adopted the first day of the week as the holy day they called the Lord's Day. Jesus' resurrection rearranged the meaning of time around God's activity within it.

The Sabbath day looks back to creation, centers on the resurrection, and moves the Church forward to enjoy God's rest.

We must look at "the fullness of time." God sent His Son at the right time to fulfill the adoption of His children. All other time is fulfilled because of this entering of time by God.

Metanoia is a changed orientation; the whole self turns to the One who has come to us in our time.

Jesus knew when the hour of fulfillment had come and could utter, "It is finished." Time was finally fulfilled at Easter time.

Jesus' time is also different from other times, with a beginning, enduring, and ending. We call these past, present, and future. He was, is, and will be.

Barth notes what is the same, different, and distinctive between our time and Jesus' time.

Like all times, Jesus' time occurs once and has a beginning, duration, and end. Some were with Him, for some He is past, and for many He was future. He lived in time as we do.

What is different between all other times and Jesus' time:

1. All other time begins and has a future. It does not exist before it begins.
2. All other time endures as a present moment contemporary for an observer.
3. All other times end; at a later point, they no longer exist. They have passed.

Jesus' limitations were removed since He is eternal God. For Him, time is a gateway. The distinctives of Jesus' time are:

1. Jesus' life began, and so had a future. But Jesus existed before that life began. He already existed before the time of His lifetime on earth.
2. Jesus' life had duration and was present in His lifetime. But His present reaches back to when all was future and reaches forward to when all will be called past. All time is included in His present.
3. Jesus' life ends. It became a past. But His end is always present and future. Jesus was as He is and will be. All time is the time of His renewed presence.

Jesus' time is not only humankind's time; it is God's eternal time. He created time and rules over it.

The resurrection of Jesus is the starting point for

As the Lord of time, Jesus lives in time as a human, like all other humans.

thinking about the real meaning of Jesus' existence in time. Jesus is not timeless but is concretely present in all time.

Jesus' life embraces the past, present, and future. He exists in all three dimensions simultaneously.

He is the I am who identifies with Yahweh in the Old Testament.

The Personal Gift of Time

Jesus rose from the dead and lives so that all time is His time, and He is in it all.

Jesus Christ is not merely a man of yesterday. He is alive today. He is present in every possible future. He belongs to all times at the same time.

Barth continues with a study of Jesus regarding His past, present, and future.

1. *Jesus is a past being. The New Testament community believed Jesus was present in a distinctive, invisibly close manner revealed in their past.*

   Jesus' history cannot be seen as a thing of yesterday; it is also part of today.

   The Holy Spirit has been given to bring the yesterday of Jesus to our present engagement.

   Jesus becomes our contemporary so that His past life, death, and resurrection have significance for our current existence.

   Jesus is personally present in baptism and communion. He knows us and we come to know Him and His purposes in the activity of the sacrament that points to Him. He is present as God and human, body and soul. His presence is not restricted to the "sacraments." We gather around Him even apart from worship.

   The royal freedom of the children of God comes with the leading of the Spirit, who guides them to go with Jesus.

   Jesus also opens the way of anticipation, grounding us in the hope of His future.

   Jesus includes all things that will be in His history and the fact that it is "not yet." In the present, we live "between the times."

   Jesus disclosed the intimate connection between His name and history when He stated in His first sermon that He had fulfilled all Isaiah envisioned.

   Jesus still calls His Church today to proclaim and live the year of the Lord, still at work by His Spirit. The event of Jesus' yesterday is the vitality of our today.

   The conversion of Paul is one example of the appearance of the resurrected Jesus in person. Paul's ministry depended on Jesus' presence, as did all the apostles.

   The life of Jesus makes possible the time of the Church. The first time gives the second meaning and substance to unveil the revelation of God.

146 — Church Dogmatics 3.2

To talk about the ministry of Jesus as though it is history is to lose heart, as was the case on the road to Emmaus before the disciples recognized Jesus. We cannot hold to mere recollections instead of a living Lord.

Only in eating and praying with Jesus are eyes opened to the living presence that transforms. The Jesus of the past became a present reality.

Gospel has concrete meaning in witnessing to the Jesus of history, sharing His story as a present unveiling. The past interrupts the present as He makes Himself present.

2. *Jesus is present but not restricted to the present.* He is also a being of the past. Jesus has been in history in such a way that His today includes His yesterday.

When we look at Jesus' past, what do we see? We see the story of His pre-Easter life. This story is like a stream flowing underground that surges to the surface in the post-Easter time, swelling to become a great river in the apostles' witness.

The power of today's mystery is derived from Jesus' yesterday. There, we hear of the kingdom. We are met at the cross of reconciliation. We become His community and are invited into His family. There, God becomes flesh and becomes all He is for us today.

We cannot say that the Old Testament was a "not yet" of Jesus in that He revealed that it all already spoke of Him. Jesus was there already. In the same way, we cannot say He is "no longer" present; He is still here for us.

Although the meaning of Jesus' death was concealed from the onlookers, it was revealed on Easter morning. Jesus stood alive after being judged but was now delivered.

Jesus fulfilled the promises of the past. Ancient words rang out anew like never before. Even the meaning of the sacrificial system came to life as the witnesses saw who Jesus was as He fulfilled the reality of the divine covenant.

The Old Testament pointed to Christ so that He could say we would find Him in searching the Scriptures.

3. *Jesus is a future being, in addition to being a past and present being.*

Christians live just as much in expectation of Jesus coming as in recollection of Jesus' presence. He is equally present in all three dimensions.

The Personal Gift of Time   147

Jesus never faded into the background for the apostles. He was present to them with all His grace as the Holy Spirit brought them to share in His life as His body.

The New Testament always speaks eschatologically, seeing all things related to the One who is with them to the end of the age.

Seeing Jesus in the future does not mean working toward creating a utopian society that appears to be the kingdom of God. This well-meaning fabrication can be pursued without Jesus.

The New Testament does not look for an improved world improvised by humans but for its living Lord, the Resurrected One, present daily to His own.

The apostles saw what Jesus had done for them and the entire world. At this point, as witnesses of the resurrection, the apostles became the foundation of His community.

Hope, detached from Jesus, is merely wishful thinking. We need patience in the form of perseverance, living with continual expectation.

If we forget the Jesus of the third dimension of time, the future, we become satisfied with Jesus' past, and the future goes dark and becomes disconnected.

Christians stand between two choirs, the prophets on one side and the apostles on the other. They both sing from the past into our present about the mystery of things to come.

The events of Easter, ascension, Pentecost, and the *parousia* form what we might call a single mountain range in the time of Jesus' existence.

To look to Jesus' future is to look at His actual revelation; the kingdom has already come.

God's judgment is salvation for all humans and the whole cosmos. Ultimately, He will be the triumphant Lord of His community and world.

At the kingdom's conclusion, there will be a Messianic banquet. Unlike the Last Supper, this will not be in anticipation of sacrifice but a celebration of completeness.

The Passover meal becomes an Easter meal, filled with joy in a singleness of heart that does not argue over the nature of the bread and wine.

In standing before the Sanhedrin, the point of the passion story begins. The Messiah from heaven is found guilty of claiming to be

God (blasphemy) in the eyes of the Messianic court with earthly authority.

Jesus stands before His accusers at a time open for Israel's greatest opportunity. As a "yes" to God's covenant, they could call Him King and the anointed One. That is not what happens.

We see here the final clash between salvation history and world history. The King waits to be acknowledged for who He is, and the world resists with hearts far away.

Israel rejects its King. Ultimately, He is not in their hands; they are in His.

From the time of His resurrection to the time of consummation, the Holy Spirit gathers Jesus' community and nourishes them throughout this time of expectation.

The waiting community of Christ is to apprehend the self-witness of Jesus by the Spirit. They are to stand with Him in all their inadequacy so that the Lord is witnessed, not human heroic efforts.

The Spirit seeks new dwelling places in humans to become hosts and good-news givers. The time of the Church is a giving and inviting time. It is not a time to be content with guarding and defending, which may sometimes be needed.

The end of kingdom work is to sit at the banquet with the King and enjoy all He has set in motion and brought to its fulfillment.

We are not left alone to do the best we can. It is a time for those who go with Jesus to serve and speak to those without knowledge of the Lord.

In the last judgment, we see a parable of sheep and goats. We cannot judge from the human perspective. The judge invites sheep into the hospitable space prepared before the foundation of the world. Jesus judges at the end. He is waiting now with the hungry, outcast, imprisoned, and estranged.

Jesus waits with the least, representing the world for which He died and rose again. He lives in solidarity with them. One cannot call Jesus Lord unless one treats the least as part of the family whom Jesus loves. We, too, must help the world in its suffering to align with Him.

A core question for the community of Christ is whether we see with Jesus' eyes of compassion or our glance of judgment.

We must avoid two errors during the waiting time:

The Personal Gift of Time

First, we may *underestimate* the majestic presence of Jesus and the Holy Spirit in the interim.

Second, we may *overestimate* the greatness of our community, self-satisfied and deaf to the critique of the Holy Spirit, who wants to move the community toward its Lord as we wait.

Hope for the future is set aside when the Church claims equal dignity and authority with Jesus, leaving Him aside in His "absence."

Where some churches teach that a second visible coming is uncertain, Barth contends that the New Testament holds this as the greatest certainty because of the resurrection.

When the Church is enamored with its estimation of itself and all it does for Jesus, it will "de-eschatologize" Christianity.

> Jesus' time is not only humankind's time; it is God's eternal time. He created time and rules over it.

Both in its underestimation and overestimation, Jesus is deemed absent. The Church sees Him working at another time. They clear the ground for a humanly constructed church. Jesus becomes a figurehead of the past, as though He was vacating the present and the future.

2. Given Time (pp. 511–53)

We must understand the being of Jesus in His time to understand humans in our time.

Jesus' time embraces all previous and subsequent times; He is the source and end of all time as the Lord of time.

Human time is quite distinct from Jesus' time in that He is God, and we are mortal. In Him, eternity entered our time in an unrepeatable fashion and gives it meaning.

Our time is different from Jesus' time:

- Our *past* is the time we leave and no longer dwell within. It is a great flood of forgotten reality with a few islands of memory.
- Our *future* is the time we do not yet have and might have if all goes well. It is not our time yet; we are moving in its direction. We live with anticipation that may conflict with our expectations.
- Our *present* is the most obscure of all. It is a momentary step from the "no longer" to the "not yet." It drifts from what was and grasps for

what might be. The past and future can have duration, but the present is a fleeting time between the times. It is experienced as a moment that is never fixed.

We live in the riddle of human temporality, experiencing insecurity in losing our past and uncertainty regarding our future.

In Jesus, God became a man, the Creator became a creature, and eternity entered time to resolve our insecurity. Therefore, God has time for us.

For Jesus to live in the present is not fleeting; it is resting and lasting. His past is not lost in the shadows. His future is not dark and empty, waiting to be filled. It is filled with His present and past.

God fills our present with stability from the security of His past, present, and future. He takes our disintegration and integrates us into Himself.

In Jesus, our true nature has not been corrupted or invalidated by our corruption. We cannot find our true nature in ourselves, but we can find it in what God has willed in this One human. We discover our true being as His companions.

The good nature in which we were created is not taken from us. He preserves us so we may share in His time.

Time is the gift of God as the stage where real life is acted out. Time is the form of existence in which all that is created finds its order and is sustained by God.

Everything exists within God's hospitality. Humans only have access to the time given to us; without time, we cannot live.

The interrelations of the acts of God and humans are an ongoing sequence of intention, execution, and completion played out in time.

Our relation to God and other humans is formed in a history of actions that shape our particular being.

God loves us and chooses to involve Himself with us as our light and life in a history that sustains and corrects us in every aspect of our lives. Our hearing and responding, whether in faith or resistance, occur as we live before God in our time.

We also encounter each other as a historical reality. We are concrete beings who may impact each other for good or ill, but we are not separate from each other.

Each character in the Bible has a unique part to play in the story. God is not distant, above the cares of humankind, but accompanies each person as He gives responsibility.

The Personal Gift of Time

Covenant is the meaning of all created time and history, including our particular times. This determines our anthropology as we reflect on how humans accept or resist God's covenant.

We exist in the time given to us. It might be better to say that time has us and forms us as we move along in dialogue with it.

That humans exist in time is a silent song of praise to God. Our living in time is our interplay with His gift.

> A core question for the community of Christ is whether we see with Jesus' eyes of compassion or our glance of judgment.

The rustling of the Holy Spirit surrounds us and urges us on with our own lives.

God's eternity is a dimension of God's life, which is the simultaneity of the past, present, and future.

Barth examines the being of humans in time:

1. That humans exist in time means that we are *always in the Now*, between the past and the future.

   It is always now that we respond to our world. Now we know, feel, possess, and react to all the surrounding elements. It is now we actually make decisions.

   From our standpoint in the present, we understand the totality of what has gone before and the possibility of what is yet to be.

   We live in time as God's gift of hospitality rather than the wisp of each moment. Apart from God, humans lose the meaning granted to their existence.

   Our past is similar to our now, and our future will also be comparable. Thus, the present now seems to be the primary form of time.

   Barth proposes that God's Now is the essential and enduring Now. He made all that exists and is Now present to it all, constantly faithful, not just now and again.

   The human now is secondary and dependent on God's Now.

   God is Now in His eternity. We are in our passing time.

   God steps from the enduring state of His eternity into our passing time. He acts for our sakes, to be for us so that we will be for Him in loving connection.

   God gives us the gift of the *present*, living each moment with Him.

   God gives us a *past* that shares in His past for us. We live out of the gift of His past, where He has always been for us.

   God gives us a *future*, giving meaningful hope to the future where He is already. We need not live in the "not yet" because He fills our futures with His love.

Humans live in the Now that is real because it is the present of the eternal Creator. He goes before us, is with us, and will not leave us alone.

2. Humans sense they have been, as in "I am *Now* one who *has been.*"

My many transitions to this point have sculpted who I am.

The past's prejudices, assumptions, and expectations have varying influences on my current and future existence.

My accomplishments and breakdowns belong to the pages that mark my story. I am because I have been.

Changes may happen in the past that transform us. Parts of who we are do not exist in the same manner as they existed back then. I am the same person in the new form that I am today.

We attempt to restore the past with memory, extending its fading reality to capture a time now gone. This attitude is the substance of historicism, romanticism, or science that clings to what was. An ideal past is conceived of to grasp what one wishes were real.

While past events shape us still, our memories are untrustworthy in giving us real-time, and we become victims of illusory life. The ghosts in our heads haunt us.

Seeking "the spirit of the age," each generation wrestles with being free of past practices. They think progress is salvation from what has been, replacing memories with imagination.

There is a *Then*, a genuine past in God's eternity so that our past is not left behind.

The real being of our history is held within God's eternal embrace. He will not abandon our past but will be faithful to us even through seasons of past unfaithfulness.

> God's eternity is a dimension of God's life, which is the simultaneity of the past, present, and future.

We need not shut our eyes to the past. If what we see is encouraging, we should rejoice. If dishonorable, we should be modest and humble.

To avoid the memory of our personal history is to be an escapist, dismissing reality and running from God's grace. It is living a lie to cover our tracks. But God holds all our actions and memories, deals with our shame, and gives us cause for gratitude. Running from the past is blindness to what has shaped us.

The Personal Gift of Time

On the other hand, we must not live in the past. To run to the past constantly is to close our eyes to the present and future.

We must resist being reactionary to our past, either living in denial or attempting to restore it idealistically.

It is tempting to misrepresent the past to cast a better light on ourselves, making ourselves the victim to gain sympathy.

Our memories are limited, giving us only filtered glimpses, not reality itself. Only God's eyes can see what is happening; it is a hidden reality for us.

Fortunately, we are free from the paralysis of positive or negative judgments that live from fear. We are secure in the hands of God.

All that has been is now in the hands of God. God never forgets, but we need to forget. We must be released from the weight of our human failure and inadequacy, which can crush us.

When we try to conceal what God has not, these buried thoughts become the source of psychological problems. To try living with *suppression* of memories is as bad as *only* living in the good memories of days now gone. Both deny the reality that shapes our present and future.

3. Humans intuit that a time is *coming*, and we shall be there in due time. This state also begins with a specific reference to our present, then moves to a second state toward which we progress.

Our eager waiting and grasping for the future begins now. The experience of Now is full of the future as a time of possibility, just as Now is full of the past as a time remembered.

Our orientation moves us in the present, coloring our thoughts and feelings with hopes and fears; we act as a reaction to what we think and feel may be coming.

Like a farmer, each season requires us to prepare for the next. Our present is always pregnant with the future.

In a nutshell, I am what I shall be, not only what I was.

We take for granted that "I shall be as I was and am." A day will come when that assumption is not valid.

We could shut our eyes to the future or face it honestly. Becoming an optimist or pessimist is always a possibility. Both lead to a dead end.

We may think we can choose unreflectively and ignore all

future challenges. This tactic is a life of avoidance, but the task of facing our fears is real.

We do not acknowledge or reflect well on our anxiety about our future.

The future may become a source of anxiety or lead to depression. The dead end is our internalized trauma shut down by the imagined trials to come.

Beyond the gloomy predictions of what may come, we may express the free spirit of a child; the future will have its way despite our forecast.

Pessimism is not preparation; it is limitation looking through the lens of fear.

Beyond the unreflective and reflective life, focused on our fate, is the future in which God is faithful in the next moment and beyond.

God provides the genuine Then that is coming. It is part of God's faithful eternity.

Our relation to God stands under the cover of what God will be and do in working out His will with us. We are those loved by God, who has given us time to live.

The future is dark and triumphant. Dark because it is unknown and steamrolls over all our preparations. Triumphant because light will come in unexpected ways, astonishing as the brightness interweaves with our story, making us feel like children turning the pages of a wonderful book.

God's goal is for us to have confidence in Him, cast our fears on Him, and live joyfully within the gift of His hospitality.

Going with God is the only adequate way to proceed into the future, living responsibly and with gratitude.

We should fear God, who has intervened in our brokenness with all His mercy. From eternity, He has been our covenant partner and friend. He is not a judge to be feared. He will rule over us with His grace.

We are both fearful of God because of our inadequacy and fearless because He is our comfort and joy.

We live in time as our soul lives in our body as the natural realities of our lives.

Jesus is not hidden from us in eternity; He has been made known as the Lord of time, who was, and is, and is to come as the eternal God for us.

The Personal Gift of Time

Jesus is our starting point to understand God's intervention and work and to encounter the One to whom our concepts can only point.

3. Allotted Time (pp. 553–72)

God creates human time in three forms, past, present, and future, creating space for human life.

We looked from the inside to understand the *experience* of the human in time. Now we will look from the outside to *observe* the human in the succession of movements through time.

Time is a field for interaction and interconnection with other humans.

God gives us time, but it is not unlimited. Each person has a lifespan unique to them. The time between birth and death is God's allotted time.

We are called to accept our allotment of time as a gift received with gratitude and joy.

Human life is a mystery created by and for God on the vertical level beyond our observation. On the horizontal level, we are created in and for relationships with other persons.

All life on earth comes to an end. It is natural to crave more time. God gives us our allotment, even when we waste and warp our lives away from God's loving intentions. In our complaints, we trash the time we already have, robbing ourselves of God's blessing in what He has given.

Human life needs time to live a definite life before God and with other humans. Why are we not given unlimited time?

1. God lives in His own time, called eternity. It has no limits to its span, measure, or margins. He is its only measure. God's time differs from ours, not merely time with no beginning or end.

   Humans live in time, created and given by God. Humans are not eternal; they are limited as God's creation.

2. Humans live in allotted time because unlimited time would not serve humans in bringing ultimate fulfillment.

   Humans want unlimited duration and fulfillment. We are human and inclined to serve ourselves in our self-limitation.

3. With unrestricted time, humans would continually grasp for their most total sense of fulfillment in life.

   An unrestrained state could be the definition of hell. We are ill-equipped to deal with the threat of endless yearning without the ability for complete fulfillment.

4. For time to feel adequate, it must lose the character of restriction. The promise of what is ahead must invite us. Our urge for adventure must override our need for security.

   Fear must yield to trust, and complaints must be transformed into gratitude. The positive attitude must rest in the person of God and His provision, not as a form of human coping.

   It is best to focus on the God who allots time to us, not a God who limits us.

   Our lives will have limits and boundaries, but they must not define us.

   He cares for us by allotting time to be with us rather than setting us adrift with unending time.

5. God is determined to give us life. This commitment partly creates the craving for a long and fulfilling life. But we cannot bring the desire to a successful completion, though we do have a part to play.

   In Christ, the possibilities for our lives find fulfillment.

6. The God who gives us our allotted time is gracious. He is the God who is with us and for us in our allotted time.

   God enters into solidarity with humanity, making human life His concern.

   We live within the nearness of God's free grace. He alone is our help, comfort, assurance, and hope, even with its limitations, as He allows us time on earth.

The life of the eternal God who came into our restricted time displays what a life lived in the grace of God may be. Jesus shows us that limited time is fulfilled time.

Jesus reveals the purposes and meaning of human time as the place where God meets with humans to share life as a gift. We cannot understand human nature except in the light of this one human.

4. Beginning Time (pp. 572–87)

Time given by God as an allotted time has two facets: it begins and ends. The beginning is a fixed frontier from which we have come. The future is an unknown but certain frontier. The future looms before us, and the beginning of our lives recedes into a forgotten past.

People are concerned about who we were in the past, as evidenced by human interest in history. This curiosity is not only about our personal history; it extends to spheres beyond our own.

Rather than coming from nowhere and being a nobody, we want to originate from a vigorous, passionate past that gives us meaning.

We did not always exist at a time, but that does not mean we come from nothing. We come from God. He has preceded us in time and before time. God was for us from eternity. God will be with us the whole span of our lives.

> Jesus is our starting point to understand God's intervention and work and to encounter the One to whom our concepts can only point.

God is with us from generation to generation. We live as family members in a history accompanied by God.

Yahweh is the God of a family: Abraham, Isaac, and Jacob. Their family history binds Israelites to the One who covenanted with them and gave them their identity.

The command to honor father and mother is the call to live within the past that binds one to God. Father and mother represent God's blessing received as God's gift. We live within a family tree story.

Rebellious parents can pass on destructive attitudes. Even there, God forgives and heals the family.

God redeems families from their past to be His family. Blessing is God's power to pass on good things from generation to generation.

Through Abraham, all the nations of the earth are to be blessed. This commitment unfolds as He lives out His covenant of grace to all humans.

The New Testament does not make obsolete the history of the Old Testament. Jesus reveals that the world's Savior is inseparable from Israel's Messiah.

The rituals and influential figures of the Old Testament point to the ultimate high priest known in Jesus.

All prior time in history is nailed to the cross. We are raised to present and future hope in Him as He completes human history on our behalf. His Spirit brings us to share in this life so that His presence today is faithful as it was yesterday and will be tomorrow.

In the Old Testament, God reveals the coming salvation. In the New Testament, the same gracious God reveals that salvation has appeared.

The Church has one service: pointing beyond itself and sharing God's goals for every human life.

We do not become the children of God because of our families or church. We become the children of God by being born of His Spirit and calling on His name as our own, acknowledging that we belong to Him.

Barth proposes that baptism replaces the meaning of Old Testament blessing. It extends the blessing of God to be part of the family initiated by God and connected to Jesus.

The Church becomes confused when it regards itself as a repetition or renewal of pre-Christian Israel. It forgets its identity with the crucified and risen Jesus.

When the Church thinks of itself as a community born of the natural bonds of kinship and neighborliness, they depart from the freedom of the Spirit. This situation is the case in what we call the "Christian West."

For Barth, baptism is a freedom of the Spirit, a personal response to Jesus as part of His family.

When answering the "Whence?" of life in Christ, we need more than being told we were baptized. We must not obscure what Christ has done and what we do in response.

Being a Christian can create a stale past or bring triumphant joy. For many, ignorance of Jesus' story must be corrected. Jesus' story brings recognition of who we are in Him, who is the powerful presence of God incarnate. We cannot merely default to being members of the status quo of Church tradition.

5. Ending Time (pp. 587–649)

The time given to us will end. We are disquieted that our lives will end.

The past diminishes in our rearview mirror, and we find the future looming larger before us.

We strive against our limitations to make the most of future time, rushing toward the ending time. We will die. Time passes, and death comes.

The shadow of death creates anxiety in life. Death is a door we cannot see through.

Death deprives us of our future and may rob our present if we fear death's coming.

In the Old Testament, God speaks to His people in the land of the living. Especially in Jerusalem, the people of God meet with God as the mainspring of their lives. Death is associated with the wilderness and places like Egypt and Babylon.

Death in the Bible is an inhospitable place where people are bound or need keys to be released. It may include silence, dust, and darkness. It is comfortless, a lonely wilderness.

Death is like a darkness that may spread its shadow in sickness, depression,

The Personal Gift of Time

isolation, loneliness, or estrangement. The lost, imprisoned, and those in peril taste death's threat. Laments are a response to these dire situations.

The Old Testament sees death as a threat and alienation from life now. The New Testament considers death as a judgment of humanity. It also sees death as defeated by Jesus.

The end of our lives can only be seen as a threat if seen as a negation of our lives as persons.

However, there is a possibility of being spared the finality of death.

Another has suffered death for us. Thus, while we are like a tree marked for felling, God did not create us to live under this threat.

Jesus reverses the impact of suffering and sickness, resisting the shadow of death in the land of life. He comes with healing victory as the representative of the positive will of God.

The dying of Jesus is the climactic event to which all the miracles point.

Jesus stands between God and humanity with justice, suffering what humans deserve. He caused judgment to fall on Himself in the place of many guilty sinners, not needing to suffer the punishment they deserved.

In the death of Jesus, He declares death to be His enemy as well as ours. He stands with humanity so that we do not suffer that fate.

Humans still die as a sign of the judgment against them. The wages of sin is death. We cannot forget this as we accept that our guilt is forgiven.

God has acted to remove the judgment on us. Death entered the world through sin; it is not God's determination for us. He seeks life and love, even in defeating death.

The cross is the central viewpoint of the New Testament. The writers saw the seriousness of sin and the finality of God's deliverance offered.

There are biblical revelations on the death all must face:

1. Death overshadows every human greatness. Even Jesus faced death.
2. Death implies the threat of eternal corruption. Jesus suffers for us all in the depths of eternal alienation and torment.
3. Death is the result of living without God. The person who abandons Jesus walks toward death.

The cross measures humans by what God has done for them, taking their place to bear the burden of alienation from God so they may have peace and restoration.

No human articulation can capture the profound

> All prior time in history is nailed to the cross. We are raised to present and future hope in Him as He completes human history on our behalf.

"Yes" of God that underlies the "No" of the cross. God's act is powerful in addressing the problem's depth and respecting the strength of God's answer.

Were it not for the answer of God in the person of Jesus to deal with the human condition, we would rightly fear our extermination in death.

The God who awaits us in death is the gracious God. We give ourselves to Him as He has given Himself to us.

God is the One we need to fear more than death but also the One in whom we find comfort no other can offer. We cannot cease to be the objects of His love.

The joy of the resurrection dances on coffins and ashes, bringing light to fading memories as heaven's Word speaks life to restore us.

In the New Testament, God comes as our Helper against death. God has given us the promise of His loving solidarity with humanity.

God has triumphed over death, both in dying and rising again. He does not bring condemnation; He brings hope.

In Jesus, death is disarmed, dismissed, and rendered impotent.

Fundamental to the Old Testament is the fact that Yahweh has triumphed over death.

The Old Testament tells of the faithfulness of God, who will meet us even in death. It does not look for life after death.

The New Testament attests to God's faithfulness. Jesus has become the fellow and brother of every person, taking our guilt and overturning it for our restoration to His Father.

To believe in Jesus Christ is to see death behind us. We have already died with Him. Jesus' burial is the original of our baptism, by which we are included in His life.

The resurrection of Jesus is the starting point of the end of time. The old is past; the new has come. We live in the event of the last day.

The New Testament hope makes three points:

1. The *crucifixion* and *resurrection* show that death is conquered and time is fulfilled in Jesus.
2. The *resurrection* and Jesus' *return* in glory display that the former inaugurates the Church's life and times and the latter its culmination in time.
3. Humans are *born again* in Jesus' resurrection to share new life, *revealed* in glory as the goal of the time made for them.

There is an end, the last time, when God will be all in all. This finale will be a historical event.

The Personal Gift of Time

To say that our lives are limited is to acknowledge we die. It is hard for us to see the good in this. Death means a contradiction of life. Therefore, we live in fear of death.

The judgment of our guilt is not the end of the story. The God we stand before as judge is the gracious Creator and the Lord of the covenant. In it, God has determined, even at creation, that He will be faithful even when humans are unfaithful.

Death is not a friend, and what Jesus suffered is not what God planned in creating humanity. He made us for life together.

God does not choose death. God overcomes this warped existence, returning humans to their created nature. In the end, God finally triumphs over death and sin by taking the consequences of sin on Himself in Jesus' death. He stands for us in our place.

Each *human life ends*, and this is the result of the fall, the first death. Jesus died on the cross as a physical death identified with our humanity. There is a "second death," *a standing under God's judgment*, as Jesus does on the cross before God on our behalf.

Jesus suffered His death as atonement. Whereas sin calls for death as an acknowledgment of the negative state of humanity, Jesus dies as a positive act of love. He freely accepts His death for the many.

Jesus is the firstborn of all humanity, releasing all from sin's bondage. He is God's faithfulness despite human unfaithfulness.

Our mortal bodies still die, but we know we belong to Jesus in life and death, so all threat is gone.

In the end, we do not stand under the wrath of God's judgment; we are held in God's grace that originates and acts from Him.

Jesus had to be able to experience human death. All humans come to this boundary, but Jesus had to be able to meet it and step over it. He had to identify with our end and deliver us from death.

We could sin infinitely and multiply our guilt if we had an endless life. In death, redemption takes effect and completes what Christ has done for us.

To belong to Him and not be left to ourselves, we must have a finite life born of Him and, in the end, embraced by Him. Thus, a limited life is not evil but a provision made by God's hospitable grace.

Natural human existence has no beyond; it comes to an end. But God is our beyond, who has been our life counterpart and will be in death.

We are claimed by, belong to, and are grateful for the gracious God who saves us from eternal death; this One is our true beyond.

Life ends as well as it begins. This scope creates a playing field that is vital for ethics. We do not merely set our hope on life beyond death. Instead, we must consider our current acts in the presence of the living God as foundational for ethics. This dynamic is the crux of *CD* 3.4.

Death is an enemy because humans lean away from God, attempting to escape responsibility to Him. It is an end in nothingness without meaning. Without God, the human future is a forgottenness that snuffs out every trace of once being alive.

We are not left to chaos in death but to the reordering of creation embraced by God as good.

The first death is the end time of the human in their *natural* existence on earth. It does not carry the weight of judgment of the second death, which deals with our corruption, alienation, and what is *unnatural* to us.

The second death may be abolished, in that a person who naturally and physically dies is released from death for eternal life. Jesus does not reverse our physical death, even for Himself. He overcomes the separation from God, which is the more severe and lasting death.

> The resurrection of Jesus is the starting point of the end of time.

Death wears a disguise as a threat, but we can now look it in the face and see our beyond in Jesus.

The biblical term "to fall asleep" refers to the natural death of a person released from the second death. Jesus intervenes on the far side immediately. Jesus is the first to fall asleep and rob death of its sting.

The message of salvation is that God has made a way to be with Him in life and beyond in death.

Jesus sacrificed His life to rescue us from destruction. He accepted life's limitations to demonstrate God's love.

The hospitable God has given us a perishable tent for this lifetime. We may look forward to an imperishable home with the Lord.

We should not fear death, nor should we hope for it. We choose life with Jesus here in His service and let the hope of being with Him when we die sustain us.

Life here and now is lived in joy and confidence that, in Christ, we already have, or rather are held by, our great Beyond.

COMMENTARY:

- Humans are inclined to think about time from their experiences of a lifetime and the rhythm of days. Like natural theology, this misses the proper starting point to see time as created by God.

- To understand time, we need to look to Jesus as the One who creates time, indwells all time up to our time, comes after our time, and is present within our time—all simultaneously.
- Barth wants us to see all time as a gift that allows us to live.
- God may seem absent in our future, but when acknowledged as present, we live as covenant partners until our death. This alignment brings meaning to life, acted out within the gift of time.
- Death stands as the end of our bodily existence. This culmination is a natural event for all, including Jesus. But Jesus, in His crucifixion, has shown that He deals with our past so that we have a future beyond death. His resurrection attests that He lives beyond death, and we will live with Him.

CONCLUSION FOR THE CHURCH: Barth wants to recalibrate the Church's thinking about time. For the Church, time is about the life of Jesus. However, it may be reduced to the self-management of the Church focused on itself.

Human history, Church history, and the lifespan of each human all have limits: a beginning, an end, and a time between. We miss living within Jesus' time.

Humans do not live in our time for us to manage. God creates the time and space to live in covenant love with God, neighbor, and self and to be personally present to all of it!

It is easy to think humans must manage their lives. We struggle to fit Jesus into our lives. Barth turns this on its head and proposes we are fit within Jesus' time, shaped by His love.

Jesus brings eternity to embrace our history by indwelling the story of humanity. The Church points as a lighthouse in a dark world, guiding us home so we may live in the light of His allotted reality. Otherwise, we live in the illusion that time is ours and abandon His presence.

This final section of *CD* 3.2 looks beyond our embodied existence to our context within God's meaningful time. Time is not just hours and years that we may control. Time is our relation to God and one another, sharing the hospitable context God has given. The Church must pull back the curtain and invite others to live in the fullness of time gifted by Jesus, the Lord of time.

INSIGHT FOR PASTORS: Barth wants pastors to point to Jesus, calling people to abandon the sense that "we own our time," managing it for ourselves or "for Jesus." Barth wants humans to give up the idea that we live parallel to God and each other in separate storylines.

The new possibility is indwelling the gift of time as we share Jesus' sustaining lifeline. He knows our traumas, guilt, shame, brokenness, and past. He heals us by embracing our story within His story on the cross. He does not crucify the events of our lives; He remembers them all within His reconciling time and acts.

Barth sees Jesus as the Lord of time, and we are not. The Bible is a window into the story of God that encompasses eternity, including today. When we see our days in context, meaning in Jesus' presence, we may participate in the life of grace and love.

Time is not a significant point of discussion in many pulpits. But it is a central biblical theme. God provides a history and a lifetime for human existence. Pastors need to help us see that the time in which we live is within the time of Jesus, here now, with us, and for us. Your church is an alarm clock to awaken people to the joy of a shared life with Jesus and His people.

INSIGHT FOR THEOLOGIANS: Time is not always a focus in theology, but it should be. "In the beginning" already addresses time. Barth insists that we not neglect that we are time-integrated beings. If we miss the gift of time provided by God, we have the real possibility of disintegrating our lives. God's redeemed time has already embraced us with His eternal presence in our times.

God has created time and space as the laboratory of His love. He occupies time by being present to all times. He occupies time in human experience, opening us to God's gift of allotted time from birth to death.

God is concerned with the history that precedes our birth and the generations of family who shape us. He is attentive to our personal history. He is interested in our living entirely by His Spirit in the time we have on this earth. He will sustain our being beyond death.

All aspects of time fall within the field of theological investigation. Each includes the life of the person of Jesus, and our part within the strata of activities that we call family, culture, civilization, and so on. If we start investigating our interpretation of history, we will read our concerns into history and God. We will miss the actuality given by Him. This selectivity is the problem of the search for the historical Jesus that limits Jesus to human lenses and records. This selectivity misses more than it finds, creating a caricature of Jesus, not the Lord of time.

As always, we must begin with Jesus and what He reveals about time as His medium for engaging humanity. He wants to restore humans to bring us home, not just to a place, but within the time He has for us—all the time.

? CLARIFYING QUESTIONS: Does your theology include time as a fundamental element in relating to the life of Jesus, or is it merely an assumed field of human experience? *Or* is time the gift of God, enveloping a proper reading of human history within God's time and His persistent engagement with you?

VOLUME SUMMARY: In *CD* **3.2, we have seen that God is the ultimate event organizer. He shows up in person to ensure we know what it means to be free and loving humans in the event of our lifetime, within the larger event of His history. In encountering Jesus, we do not focus on ourselves. And yet we are freed to be more ourselves as whole beings, body and soul. Jesus organizes the space and time within which we live so that we will have not only a great time but a meaningful time—because we go with Him. His organizing does not control us in the least; He prepares all that is necessary to know who we are as whole beings with Him.**

PART 4

CHURCH DOGMATICS 3.3

The Accompanying God

CHURCH DOGMATICS, CHAPTER 11

"The Creator and His Creature"

CHAPTER 14

HE HOLDS THE WHOLE WORLD IN HIS HEARTFELT HANDS

§ 48. The Doctrine of Providence, Its Basis and Form

 FOCUS STATEMENT: Within the space and time God gives, He establishes a relation of caring accompaniment, providing all we need. God does not control us; He supports every aspect of our existence. This is the meaning of providence. Paragraph 48 unpacks the benevolent relationship as God's gracious coordination, inviting humans to a free and loving response.

God's sustaining presence is not a hopeful wish but a direct reflection of what He provides in fatherly care. Barth rejects any idea that God has left or become absorbed into the world. God gives life and keeps creation moving with His loving intentions as a distinct and present Creator.

The image of holding expresses considerate and compassionate involvement. The Father, Son, and Spirit provide time, space, and an open field for humans to learn the life of freedom. Sharing His freedom is the purpose for which God creates and sustains the sphere of human history within His covenant history.

INTRODUCTION: We begin a new volume (*CD* 3.3) and a new chapter in the overarching scope of the *CD*. Whereas chapter 10 discussed the human as a creature created by God, chapter 11 further explores God's relation to what He has created. This study extends to investigate God's involvement with all He makes.

This paragraph (§ 48) clarifies what we mean and do not mean when saying God is the Lord over what He creates. The doctrine of providence is not the beginning of God's ways. That is election, God's *intention* for action.

171

172   *Church Dogmatics* 3.3

God's providence works out of His covenant history, *sustaining His creation*. Human belief reflects on God's acts through ongoing interaction, responding to God's intentions and actions.

▌▌▌ CONTEXT: *CD* 3.3
Pages in Paragraph: 55 pages (pp. 3–57)

Subsections
1. The Concept of Divine Providence
2. The Christian Belief in Providence
3. The Christian Doctrine of Providence

📖 TEXT: § 48. The Doctrine of Providence, Its Basis and Form

✝ OPENING SUMMARY: The doctrine of providence deals with the history of created being as such, in the sense that in every respect and in its whole span this proceeds under the fatherly care of God the Creator, whose will is done and is to be seen in His election of grace, and therefore in the history of the covenant between Himself and man, and therefore in Jesus Christ.[1]

✝ SUMMARY:
1. The Concept of Divine Providence (pp. 3–14)

In *CD* 3.1, we dealt with God the Creator, His relationship with His *creation*, and the relationship established in His *covenant*.

In *CD* 3.2, we explored the nature of the *human* in light of the person of Christ.

In *CD* 3.3, we engage the continuing relationship between God and humanity, investigating *how God is present* to His creation and provides direction without interfering.

Providence is God's relation with His creature in time, maintaining what is distinct from Himself according to His loving will.

Providence highlights God's active provision. It is not a passive watching of what happens.

Predestination (God's intent) presupposes providence (God acting out His intent).

---

1. *CD* 3.2, § 48, p. 3.

He Holds the Whole World in His Heartfelt Hands

Predestination happens in eternity; providence plays out in history, acting out the election of Jesus. The first originates within God's character, and the second extends that in time.

Providence is the tree of provision that grows from the rootedness of God's election. We must see them as essentially interconnected and explore them in the proper order.

Creation and providence are not identical:

- In creation, the world is established. In providence, the world continues.
- In creation, we see the function of the Creator giving and the creature receiving. In providence, we see a reciprocal relationship of participation.
- Creation takes place at a specific time. Providence is the rest of time to its end.
- Creation's basis is in the will of God alone. Providence has its basis in the freedom of God and includes the creature in response to its Creator.

God does not merely manufacture things. Human artisans can leave what they create. God cannot. His creation leads to His connection to those He has made.

God does not need others to complete Himself. He places humans alongside Himself to preserve them. Providence is the eventfulness of God's hospitality.

The power of God is at work in the continuance of the world as much as its creation. Without acknowledging God, the universe appears cold and lifeless.

The ancient philosophers had forms of the gods who abandoned the world to itself without a personal presence.

> Providence is the tree of provision that grows from the rootedness of God's election.

According to Barth, Augustine proposed a world made by an architect that no longer needs to be involved. Aquinas saw God starting a world in motion like a clock that no longer needed him to continue. These and other arguments propose that the world endures with self-maintenance without God's persistent sustaining.[2]

Providence affirms that God has associated with us as the Lord of our history ever since the first act of creation.

---

2. *CD* 3.3, § 48, pp. 11–12.

2. The Christian Belief in Providence (pp. 14–33)

Belief in God's providence means having confidence in God's care and being joyfully obedient on the grounds of this perception.

Barth finds clarity in the Heidelberg Catechism, questions 26–28, and follows up with commentary:

1. *Belief in God's providence comes first with hearing and receiving the Word of God.*

   We do not speak from our experiences and convictions regarding God's involvement.

   Since the eighteenth century, humanity's history has moved toward looking away from God's providence in what Barth calls the great apostasy. In the shift from faith in God, everything depended on human certainty in self-assurance. Those beliefs quickly come and go.

2. *Belief in providence is strictly faith in God, who wills and works to sustain the world.*

   We exist on the horizon where God's existence sustains and controls our own. He is Lord over good and evil; all things occur within the realm of His care.

   We often say God controls, but unconsciously, we think of creation and its life as being in control or on autopilot.

   Creation is the mask of God as the history of the glory of God. We do not see His face but discern the hidden history of God's glory taking place. It is only in unity with Jesus that God revealed Himself fully.

   Humans inevitably conceive of other explanations to understand the nature of the universe and history. An imagined picture will develop with selective judgments of self and others who share the story.

   From their unique, highly developed point of view, each person assesses their past life, builds expectations, and develops desires and fears regarding the future.

   Providence does not exclude human recounting to reflect self-expression and understanding. These become the lenses of interpretation through which we create masks of God or what we call idols. Humans hide behind their lenses that become protective walls, building our own masks to keep out of sight from God and other humans.

To believe in God's providence is to hold one's history as a hypothesis, accompanied by humility, humor, and the freedom to adjust or abandon what we have believed.

God calls us to believe in His providence and not our documented history.

- Affirming God's providence is not to be confused or equated with a philosophy of history. We do not believe in a worldview, even a Christian worldview; *we believe in God, who rules over history.*
- We must avoid listening to our internal interpretations and *not follow any scheme of history unfolding with a specific process.* Figures such as Lessing, Hegel, and Marx are but a few who have claimed to understand the forces in natural history. To follow them is to worship false gods.
- *When we have faith in God's providence, we look at history with open, attentive, participating eyes.*

The history of created beings fulfills the history of God's glory. We see the rule of God in the world. We know the work of His hand in specific events, relationships, possibilities, and collaborations that call for our obedience.

3. *Christian belief in providence is faith in Christ Himself.*

The history of the divine presence in Jesus acts in its own category, but it makes room for all other accounts.

Barth compares the Christian view of the providence of God with that of Judaism and Islam:

- In Judaism, there is a history of salvation as the meaning of history. But it is a history that has not reached its goal and still strives for accomplishment. Its God has a strangely hidden character, which leaves adherents with an anxious concern.
- In Islam, the hidden God has been made a principal who becomes a caricature.
- These ideas lead to a history in which God's relationship with humanity is lost.

By electing the Son to be for us, God the Father has elected to be our Father and for us to be His children.

With God the Father, we are not strangers in strange hands. We are His children through the Son, who is for us so entirely that He becomes one of us.

This fatherly hand, which is kind, friendly, and loving, rules the world.

Human fatherliness can never be the measure of God's. We grasp His eternal fatherly fidelity as He shows it to us in His Son.

We have been brought home to live within the hospitality of our Father by His Son through the work of the Spirit.

Some theologies propose abstract characteristics of God to outline God's providence. Barth sees these as empty shells void of the content revealed in Jesus. The principle of lordship has replaced the person.

- Older Protestant theology tried to appease and speak to the reason of the world.
- They became "liberal" by not listening to Jesus or the witness of the Word.
- They became an "enlightened orthodoxy," replacing the voice of God with human-centered thinking aligned with the Enlightenment.
- Liberalism came to mean free from faith in Christ as the Word of God who teaches us at every point.
- The Trinity, the Church, and the witness of Scripture came to have no meaning for the orthodoxy of Protestant Christians.

Christian belief in providence must be specific, as seen in Jesus as the Lord. Providence, or God's power in the world, cannot be a general concept, or everyone will claim the providence of God supports their cause, even someone like Hitler.

> Christian belief in providence is faith in Christ Himself.

Providence is a cornerstone of the Christian faith. But it must arise from Christ, not from a mutiny, searching for control and pretending to serve God.

3. The Christian Doctrine of Providence (pp. 33–57)

What we mean by a Christian doctrine of providence must be worked out from Christ.

- It is clear what God wills of His creature as the Lord of our history: His action's meaning, purpose, and goal.
- It is not plain when *we* lift the veil of history to uncover its secret.
- It is not plain because we have determined and planned it for ourselves.
- It is clear because God has revealed it in His Word.

He Holds the Whole World in His Heartfelt Hands

God has revealed His will by revealing Himself as the triune God:

- He is the Father who is over us.
- He is the Son who is for us.
- He works in the Spirit who creates our lives under Him and for Him.

God wills that His free grace rules in the world, radiant through the revelation of His love in the will and work of Jesus.

- In Jesus, we see the eternal will of the Father.
- In Jesus, we see the life-giving will through the Spirit.

Faith in providence is faith in Jesus Christ. He can see His glory through to its end in our history as its Lord. This is our starting point for all that follows.

All things have their existence, order, and coherence in the Son. All would dissolve if not sustained by Christ.

From the early pages of Genesis, God acted as the Lord of the covenant, looking ahead to the One who would come and die to give life as the God who provides. Providence undergirds the history of salvation.

Christ entirely determines the history of the covenant within the scope of human history. It is a narrow path through the course of history. There are crisscrossing trails, but the will and purposes of God converge in this One Trail known through Jesus, that is Jesus Himself.

Having been addressed by God, humans participate in His covenant. God completes what He has started with His protection and provision. Humans live within the gift.

God integrates human life within the coming of His kingdom. God does not work generally and inattentively. God works specifically and concretely.

All humans stand under God's offered and realized relation. One cannot be neutral in response. We live within the gift or run from it. This choice shapes a human's life, meaning, and freedom. In any case, His love never wavers.

Those who complain about creation's imperfections are those who want to control it and cannot.

All creation's beauty exists because God has made its goodness, and its beauty gives glory to Him.

We perceive creation rightly when we see the purposes for which God has made each thing in their coordination.

Church Dogmatics 3.3

Since God's providence is the actual work of God in the world, we have to do every step of our lives with God.

The impression that we have an autonomous existence is called into question by the free self-giving of God in the person of Jesus.

Humans have limited awareness of reality. We look at the appearances of the order and contingency of nature, the cleverness of humans, and the goodness and badness of humans and think that is all there is. But God is freely and mightily at work before all human observations.

Nevertheless captures the freedom of God in the face of human failure and resistance. Nevertheless means God's grace will triumph.

When we look at the turmoil in the world and the history of humanity's chaos, it is easy to protest any belief that God cares for the world's concerns. But in those cases, we are overwhelmed with our human perception of human problems.

God does not intend chaos. We must not confuse human anarchy and unrest with the freedom and grace of God. We are self-seeking creatures. Nevertheless, He is self-giving.

We confess "Nevertheless" as the gracious providence of God that loves despite our inadequacy.

God's "Nevertheless" came before human failure. It is a proclamation of the unstoppable love that endures Nevertheless.

Nevertheless embodies an awareness of the human plight. God's "Therefore" is not a response to the human predicament but a proclamation of God's fidelity.

Grace cannot be grace if it is not free. Any conditions would violate the nature of grace. We cannot condition God into loving, sustaining, or restoring us.

The covenant of grace is wholly *for* humans but not mediated *through* them. Only One can offer grace—God Himself.

Barth wants to clarify the relationship between God's role in the history of the covenant and the human interface.

- With a lord and a servant, the lord's intention provides the incentive that directs the servant.
- The servant participates in the lord's work, involving their particular function with their sense of time and place.
- This place of service echoes the relation of humans concerning God's action as it works out His grace.

He Holds the Whole World in His Heartfelt Hands

- The metaphor has inadequacies. As humans, working within our limitations, we still have a range of freedom to work within the work of our Lord. And we are not wholly selfless!

A second metaphor takes up the image of the human as an instrument.

- God uses instruments to fulfill His specific intentions.
- The instrument does not know the purpose for which it is made. It cannot make use of itself.
- Someone who knows how to use a tool must pick it up and use it for its intended purpose.
- Humans are instruments to fulfill God's good purposes.
- This explanation is also an inadequate metaphor in that the tool is passive and depends entirely on the initiative of the Master.
- In reality, humans are not passive in the hands of God but come with their intentional activity.

God coordinates and integrates His creature within the history of His covenant, which is knit together.

God did not *find* the creature to use as His *tools*. God *made* humans to be His living *companions*.

While these images and metaphors are inadequate, they are sufficient to show that God hospitably provides time, space, and opportunity to reveal God's intention in the world.

The first creation story displays God's provision of a house for humans to inhabit. The sixth day pointed toward the seventh day, where God's intended rest includes humans within the embrace of His covenant.

God's final intention is that humans be inhabitants delighting in His creation by sharing in His covenant. In this way, following Calvin, creation is the theater of God's glory; space and time provide the stage for His love to play out with humans.

God is never alone. He is with His creature in such a manner that the creature exists outside and alongside Him.

God's creation is not an end in itself; it is the necessary context for His history with humankind. God's service provides the content as God's care, which informs the doctrine of providence.

The human story does not play out in an empty and meaningless place. It is not God's fault if we do not feel at home in the world.

Church Dogmatics 3.3

When our eyes open to see that God has created our home here, we also understand we are made to be members of His family.

Since God's providence is the actual work of God in the world, every step of our lives we have to do with God.

"We are in the house of our Father, in a world ordered according to His fatherly purpose, as we are in the created cosmos, under heaven and on earth, and ourselves cosmic creatures."[3]

With joy and gratitude, we understand God made us for Himself, and we are at home. The images of theater and home are not adequate because they focus on material provisions. The focus must be on personal provision and participation.

How may we understand human life acting in coordination with God's providential care?

Our creaturely accompaniment takes the form of a reflection, like a mirror. In this illustration, we can see an *interconnection*, one inseparably preceding the other. There is also a *distinction*; one is not the other, even though it is related.

The original is the working of God in the history of His covenant.

The mirror reflection of the human adds nothing to the original but derives its life from it. The reflection gives correspondence and a likeness.

Creaturely history is a reflection of salvation history, where the great acts of God occur and then reflect in the lives of humans.

The Father's house is not our focus; it is the Father, known through His Son, not His house. We recognize the house because we know the Father who brings us home.

True human meaning can only be discerned within covenant history. Meaning pursued outside the covenant comes in the form of natural theology. Such "meaning" becomes isolated, nonreflective, human self-fulfillment looking away from the Creator.

God's revelation is dynamic. Jesus lives the history of the covenant to claim us as His own. Detached contemplation has no place, only a call to respond to His direct address.

A mirror's value is in making the original visible. When we seek God through the mirror without reflecting God, we will only see ourselves or some other object—this is like the analogy of being that misses God as it looks away at the world.

The appropriate approach to knowing God is to acknowledge His Living Word (the analogy of faith) or respond to His relating revelation (the analogy of relations). These methods always seek to know the original.

---

3. *CD* 3.3, § 48, p. 48.

He Holds the Whole World in His Heartfelt Hands   181

We have looked at four portrayals of the life of humans with the being of God:

- God is the Lord, and we are servants, though we maintain our ability to act personally.
- God is the Master Craftsman, and we are tools in His hands, though we are made as active companions.
- God has made the world as His theater or home; we are participants in His story, not dispersed to live on our own.
- God is the original being whose life may be reflected in ours, but we must maintain this order, or we will miss God and become enamored with ourselves. We become like Him as we reflect Him.

These analogies must be taken together, pointing to a deeper reality with a personal connection.

Our lives are nurtured from the source as children of God.

God has an original, universal, eternal rule in all of creation. What is made *may become* the servant, instrument, theater, and mirror by the intention and action of God. What is created is coordinated by God's sustaining presence and fatherly care. This includes His creatures.

The hand of God never rests and never gives up. His faithfulness never ceases. God does not owe us His love. We participate in His love and glory and reflect it back to Him.

Under God's gracious providence, we correspond with God's benevolent will. The implications are:

> God coordinates and integrates His creature within the history of His covenant, which is knit together.

1. *God's free love gives existence and meaning to all.* Nothing created can have independent cooperation by which it acquires a place in the covenant of God. All is grace. The creature's creation, preservation, reconciliation, and redemption are all the active outworking of the Creator's good pleasure.
2. *Created history provides the external context for covenantal history to give its meaning.* Without God's creation, there would be no place for God's covenant.
3. *We cannot understand how the world is ruled without understanding the world's ruler.* All practical systems originate and find their meaning within God's gracious activity. To encounter the world in its created reality is faith.

4. *The world is the dynamic work of God.* The Holy Spirit gives us the freedom of faith to correspond with God's life. To be stuck in a static, fixed view is to be stuck in the past, resistant to God's ever-present providence. God invites us to awaken to His gracious ruling, aligning with His freeing reality.

COMMENTARY:

- Providence is proper doctrine only so far as it begins with God's gracious will, not the exercise of His power.
- Providence is not sheer power but the outworking of God's care for the world He created.
- Providence will never overpower human choice; it involves the creation of the space for humans to come into being, grow, and find fulfillment entirely as a gift of God. Humans can also rebel in the same space and still be loved by God.
- Metaphors for the God-human relation will always be inadequate yet will make the point that God's original action determines the responsive action for humans under God's care.
- Providence means that God came near in Christ and still comes near as the Father through the Son in the Spirit; God still allows us to occupy the personal presence that sustains us in love.

CONCLUSION FOR THE CHURCH: It is easy for the Church to forget that God goes before the Church and with the Church as the source and sustainer of its ongoing life. Further, it is tempting to think we must build the Church because God is not obviously involved.

God's providence affirms that the existence and flourishing of the Church can only exist as it reflects what God cares about. This focus calls us to be enamored not with the world but with God Himself. Thus, the Church's faith in God's providence will not merely be a doctrine to affirm; it is an awakening to God's orderly involvement, reoriented to His creating and covenanting with each person every moment of every day.

INSIGHT FOR PASTORS: Providence is absent from many churches' everyday language. Its meaning may be assumed; unfortunately, we leave people with the impression that God is absent, which leaves them to think, "God helps those who help themselves." Helping themselves excludes acknowledging and accepting what God gives daily.

He Holds the Whole World in His Heartfelt Hands 183

The role of pastors is to awaken people to Jesus' promise, "Surely I am with you always, to the very end of the age" (Matthew 28:20), an assurance of presence and fatherly care. The Spirit persistently brings us to participate in this life of familial love.

The lofty ceilings of cathedrals, or the call for Jesus or the Spirit to come, may communicate that God is removed by some distance. If *we* have to call, *He* must be otherwise engaged, not already present with us. Barth loudly proclaims that He is always providentially present.

Providence acknowledges the Father's ongoing relation to what He has created. As Christians, it is easy to focus on Jesus' work of salvation while neglecting the fatherly care of God.

The Lord's prayer intends to connect us daily to God's providence. Otherwise, it will all feel like waiting. When we see the Father's kingdom come and His will done, the providence of God becomes our present reality; this means to know Him in the space in which we move, the air we breathe, and the embrace by which we have our very existence.

INSIGHT FOR THEOLOGIANS: In pursuing the science of God, we must rightly evaluate how God is involved with humanity. If we begin with *our* day-to-day experience, we may conclude that God is absent and the universe is on autopilot, as is the conclusion of deism.

Many think God exists but at an unimaginable distance. Alternatively, many think God collapses into the dynamic structures of the world, like Mother Earth or the Force in *Star Wars*. Biblical providence affirms God's closeness and personal involvement in all His creation.

As theologians, we must let God's self-confession clarify His level of involvement. For Barth, no part of the created world is not under God's care. Rather than beginning with human evaluations of how the world develops, we are invited to acknowledge God at work. He has guaranteed creation's future ever since it began. He will continue caring until it reaches God's point of culmination.

Providence removes the wondering about *who* keeps the world working but does not answer the *how*. The natural sciences may explore *how* things work but cannot fathom *who* made it. In affirming God's providence, we submit to the orderly sustaining of all things and, with gratitude, acknowledge God's overarching care. Faith in God's providence is not a leap into the dark; it believes the author whose history gives meaning to our own.

? CLARIFYING QUESTIONS: Does your theology of providence hold a view of God as the Creator who generally controls all He makes, as an absolute Manager? *Or* do you recognize God as involved in caring for every aspect of daily life, as a passionate Father whose love sustains the freedom of His creatures?

CHAPTER 15

THE LORD OF ACCOMPANIMENT

§ 49. God the Father as Lord of His Creature

FOCUS STATEMENT: This paragraph further awakens us to the relationship of God with humanity. Providence is not God controlling or watching from a distance. In § 49, we join the journey with our Creator, who brings His family to Himself.

God is for His creatures, preserving and maintaining their existence throughout their lives. He accompanies them as a companion, graciously together with His family.

God rules over His creatures, but not as a tyrant. He sends angels as helpers so that heaven's kingdom touches the earth's inhabitants.

God's universal lordship means He tenderly loves the community He establishes. He invites His people to share a freeing space for inviting friends to find safety and refreshment within His embrace.

Life together is like a pilgrimage, attentively exploring healthy spaces and, along the way, finding God has always already been at work because He considers them family.

The symbol of pilgrimage is the scallop shell, a natural gift easily used for scooping water or other provisions. Such is the character of accepting the provision of God in His providence.

INTRODUCTION: This section continues to clarify providence, distinguishing it from abstract conceptions. Chapter 11 of the *Church Dogmatics*, "God and His Creature," draws together how God is ever-present for us, providing what we need in the God-human relationship.

This paragraph corrects abstract ideas about a distant and controlling God. Instead, a passionate and ever-present God accompanies us with love

185

186   *Church Dogmatics* **3.3**

and concern. He journeys with each of us, "ruling" as an act of love that calls us to submit to His care.

The life of intimacy under God's providence is one of faith, obedience, and prayer. Each of these is ignited by God's presence (providence) so that we live responding to His initiative, never forced or constrained. This facilitates a life of freedom, meaning embracing God's loving presence entirely and living into His lordly welcome.

Providence is a profoundly inclusive hospitality. Barth wakes us to the reality that surrounds us. We discover that we are preserved, accompanied, and watched over, and we find the depths of fatherly love as His beloved children.

CONTEXT: *CD* 3.3
Pages in Paragraph: 231 pages (pp. 58–288)

Subsections
1. The Divine Preserving
2. The Divine Accompanying
3. The Divine Ruling
4. The Christian Under the Universal Lordship of God the Father

TEXT: § 49. God the Father as Lord of His Creature

OPENING SUMMARY: God fulfils His fatherly lordship over His creature by preserving, accompanying and ruling the whole course of its earthly existence. He does this as His mercy is revealed and active in the creaturely sphere in Jesus Christ, and the lordship of His Son is thus manifested to it.[1]

SUMMARY:
1. The Divine Preserving (pp. 58–90)
God fulfills His fatherly lordship through His providence. Preserving is one of God's concerns for His creation.

Having created the world, God sustains and upholds it through His wise and powerful care.

God is attentive to each creature with its particular existence, not sending it away but allowing it to live under His care. This status requires God's preservation.

---

1. *CD* 3.3, § 49, p. 58.

The Lord of Accompaniment

Jesus is the divine preservation who enacts God's grace to preserve humans in their humble state.

God is for His creatures. His fatherly lordship expresses His mercy to facilitate freedom as His choice, not left to chance. Whatever fatherly lordship might mean, it is an act of love for His beloved. With His "Yes," He stands against whatever menaces humans through His "No."

Barth approves of the concept of *conservatio*, which speaks of preservation by God in the face of what threatens us. Other terms that could work here are *permansio* (abiding, permanent presence) and *manutenita* (maintaining).

With *conservatio*, there is a twofold sense of service (*servatio*) that could be mistaken as a relation of equality, as side-by-side cooperation (*con* implies "with"). Barth rejects this equivalence but affirms the primary conservation, an original service by Jesus with an acceptance by humans preserved by His service. Like the mirror, the original reflects in the secondary receptor.

Barth discusses four considerations for understanding in what sense God preserves His creatures:

1. *Humans are given a finite time as mortals, wherein He cares for them.* They are preserved within the history of Jesus Christ and His people. God arranges human time to correspond with His eternity and gives each creature what is proper to it.

2. *God mediates His free acts of conservation within the web of human interaction.* Indirectly, God uses humans to care for each other and the world. God acts toward the world and within it through His creatures.

   Through His Church, God mediates His witness in a missionary manner. "The Church is either a missionary Church or it is no church at all."[2]

   God is the Minister, and humans are the assistants. Medicine and healing alone do not heal a person; God's hand is at work, even while providing servants to work through.

3. *God elects to confirm what He began in His election by preserving His creature.* Barth has moved beyond continuous creation (as in *CD* 1.2, p. 688).

---

2. *CD* 3.3, § 49, p. 64.

Church Dogmatics 3.3

What God makes, God loves. God continuously cares for what He creates, making space for surprise, wonder, praise, and thanksgiving as we meet Him face-to-face.

God has faithfully attached Himself to His creatures so they might be securely attached to Him in faith.

4. *God elects to maintain the humans He created, preserving them from what stands against them.*

What God wills to create is good; His preservation sustains it. What God does not create, Barth calls nothingness. God does not maintain it; He rejects it.

Before God created, there was nothing. There is still a threat from what God does not will. At this point, we must notice that providence sustains us by opposing the nothingness.

What God positively wills, Barth refers to as the will or election of God. This intentional activity is the work of God's right hand. At God's left hand is what is negative and harmful, which He has not willed and, therefore, must reject because it stands against His will.

Jesus is the divine preservation who enacts God's grace to preserve humans in their humble state.

Nothingness is that to which God says "No." It is only identifiable as what God has not willed and so rejected. This sphere of nothingness includes the devil, the father of lies; demons; sin; evil; and death as the enemy of life, not including natural death.

God does not turn His face from evil. He meets it with the power of His grace and love to establish and maintain what He wills as the good that He intends.

Humans depend on God's power; without Him, we would crumble or be in the absolute dark as if the sun had disappeared.

Nothingness does not exist by chance, above God, or without God. It exists by means of God. Without God, it could not be present. It is present because God said "Yes" and "No" in His wisdom.

God marked off the hospitable space where humans could enjoy life with God and one another. Outside that space exists inhospitable resistance to God's grace and election. His judgment dispels it.

The nothingness is not an opponent to God but is a threat to humans. It is a radical problem for the creature that we cannot face alone. It is a whirlpool into which we sink and vanish.

The Lord of Accompaniment

What is the basis for claiming that God preserves His creatures amid great danger?

By His merciful will, God has become one of us to take up the cause of His creature. He stepped into the middle of our contradiction and defanged its power.

"He tasted and suffered the whole onslaught of sin, the devil, death and hell, and in so doing, He broke it, blunting its weapons and depriving it of all claim against the creature or superiority over it."[3]

Jesus completed the work of grace ("Yes" in love) and wrath ("No" to sin) in His one act. In this way, He gifted us His freedom as already decided in Him.

The mercy of God gives glory to the beloved Son, whose service is our final judgment so we may participate in His gift of salvation. In this way, God preserves us.

Because God elects to serve (*servatio*), He creates (*creatio*) and therefore preserves (*conservatio*).

Why do we need to be preserved by God?

God has shown us our need in the extent of His service. He deals with our shame and needs and fulfills us in Him. We are freed from alienation to participate in the covenant of grace.

We cannot complain about God for our situation; He has removed our shame and made us His own with all dignity.

The ministry of Jesus in the Bible is abundant with the language of preserving, maintaining, keeping, assuring, establishing, and guarding. We need Him to accomplish this service in all its forms.

The people of God found comfort and security in their concrete experiences with Yahweh, who acts as Lord of His covenant.

We depend on God's activity, who gives us autonomy. We owe our existence to Him. We are not overwhelmed by the chaos of our self-determination; God's fatherly care sustains us.

The Creator initiated a life of delighting in which the creature can participate. This course of life is the free and magnificent mystery of God's preservation. This provision includes God's care for the universe and the most microscopic elements.

Within this sustained existence, we may use our senses, think, be creative, eat and drink with joy, experience the full spectrum of emotions, and

---

3. *CD* 3.3, § 49, p. 79.

190   *Church Dogmatics* **3.3**

live a fulfilling life as whole persons. We may have free hearts, a sense of worth, and a conscience at peace.

God allows us to be the persons for which He created us by being faithful to His love. He neither prevents us from living nor misses out on life's events as though He had more important things to do.

Nothing can escape God, past, present, and future. In eternity, everything is present and open to God. This proposal does not miss the point that in space and time we have creaturely limits. But even then, temporality will be preserved in God's eternity.

"Nothing will escape Him: no aspect of the great game of creation; no moment of human life; no thinking thought; no word spoken; no secret or insignificant enterprise or deed or omission with all its interaction and effects; no suffering or joy; no sincerity or lie; no secret event in heaven or too well-known event on earth; no ray of sunlight; no note which has ever sounded; no colour which has ever been revealed, possibly in the darkness of oceanic depths where the eye of man has never perceived it; no wing-beat of the day-fly in far-flung epochs of geological time."[4]

2. The Divine Accompanying (pp. 90–154)

God fulfills His fatherly lordship by accompanying His creature.

In all that follows, the word *causa* (cause) must not be reduced to an impersonal cause but is God's personal, intentional partnership with His creatures.

This section addresses how humans can operate autonomously in the context of God's gracious operations that sustain them. Are humans really free?

The first act of God is to provide for and maintain the human as His child. The second is to accompany His child every step of the way with fatherly care, not domination. God is not passive, indifferent, or partially interested as an uninvolved person.

To say God accompanies humans can be misread and needs clarification:

1. God continues to *preserve His child* and does not abandon anyone. He accompanies for the entirety of His child's life.

2. God *recognizes and affirms our distinct activities*, respecting and affirming who we are as His children. He makes a place alongside Himself for us.

---

4. *CD* 3.3, § 49, p. 90.

The Lord of Accompaniment

Accompanying is a precise term that reflects the appropriate ordering. God offers His presence, and the human abides within His attentiveness in His covenant of grace.

3. God goes with His creature as a *unique kind of companion*. We live as the work of God by the gift of God. God does not treat humans like puppets, tools, or objects.

   God rules over us in a manner congruent with a world of freedom. God does not force us to do anything.

   If we say that humans depend on God, it cannot be a mechanical relation; it must be personal and interdependent, with God always a step ahead.

   It comes down to this—God loves His children. He recognizes and affirms who we are in ourselves and what we do by ourselves. He loves us so much that He freely gives Himself to us without merit or accomplishment.

   His love compels Him to solidarity with us. He is our God, and we are His children *by His choice*.

Another term for this accompanying is *concursus* (*con* meaning "with," and *cursus* meaning "running"), a movement accomplished together or being brought together.

The Bible is full of examples where God is at work, and so we are at work even as His workmanship. God is the living Lord in the relationship in which the human is accompanied, differentiated, and ruled over in love.

> We are not overwhelmed by the chaos of our self-determination; God's fatherly care sustains us.

There are misleading conceptions that might confuse us:

- We might think of an unmoved and passive God and a moved creation.
- We might think of an active and working God who moves creation from the outside, implying a passive and unaffected creation.
- We might think of God acting in the invention and establishment of the creation as a perpetual motion machine, leaving it and humans to run their course.
- Finally, we might think of the relation between God and creation as undifferentiated, where all its movements are interpreted as indistinguishably integrated or fused.

Barth rejected all of these. We need to see how the Bible juxtaposes God and His creation.

God's actions set in motion our creaturely actions; as one movement, there is a primary and secondary cause.

The history of interaction begins at creation, and the history of humanity flows from it in cooperation or rebellion. All our actions are responsive within the history of God's covenant.

Humans may secondarily cause actions, but God is the cause of all causes. Without God, humans could not cause. Therefore, we may consider human motivation as participating in God's cause (or rejecting it).

Two corrections need to be made to the older orthodoxy:

1. Those theologians abstractly proposed the relation between the Creator and creature with a distant and featureless God. This proposal corresponds to featureless, general humans.
2. The pursuit of cause within the God-creation relation could easily collapse into synergism (an intertwining of cause between God and creature) and monism (a unity that fails to distinguish between God and creation). This loss of personal distinction creates a system missing the personal interaction between God and His creatures.

Barth lists five conditions for God's role in causing things to happen for personally involved reasons.

1. *God's causing cannot be understood as an automated, mechanical act on God's part.* Modern science defaults to this conception of cause and effect in a systematic, impersonal world.

2. *We must use the term* cause *of God and humans only if we speak of them as persons, not as "things."* Things need to be observed and analyzed to understand their cause.

    Persons *reveal* themselves and what they cause. We know objects by examination and persons by revelation.

3. *When we use the term* cause *with God and humans, we cannot hold them as variations of one common idea.*

    God's causing is self-causing as the triune God who loves in freedom. He is not limited.

God's gracious act causes humans. We are not puppets with no choice; we live with freedom in response to others, especially when responding to the freeing love of God.

We must maintain the absolute distinctness of divine and human cause. God is self-grounded, and humans are grounded in God. There is no common denominator. When we try to make them similar, we constrain God with human limitations and therefore lose God's true nature.

4. *When using the term* cause, *we cannot default to any philosophical concept that appears similar.* We must discern cause, as applied to God, from God's activity in biblical revelation.

Theology must maintain priority over philosophy. Philosophy defaults to human wisdom and departs from understanding the Creator. Christology must guide our discernment in how God causes things to happen.

5. *When engaging the concept of cause, we must speak positively of God's embodying of the conception of divine accompanying as affirmed in the first and second articles of the creed.*

The God who creates in love (first article) becomes the One who causes our salvation (second article).

The secondary cause in the world is the creation in which we live. This realm is a subsequent context in which we live under the primary care of the Creator. The secondary is never without the primary cause of God.

> All our actions are responsive within the history of God's covenant.

We must return to the operation of God in the world, beginning with God's operation with His creature.

God's power is entirely different from that of humans because God is love.

- God's love is primary. Humans can only be loved by God and possibly return the love.
- God's love is essential, as Father, Son, and Holy Spirit exist in love and overflow with love for God's creatures. Humans can only accept this love.
- God's love is eternal, extending into time to embrace His creature. Humans are limited to loving within their allotted time.

Church Dogmatics 3.3

God accompanies His creature with unquestionable superiority. We must be clear that this is the supremacy of love.

God preserves human reality, which is constantly changing, and He accompanies it as such.

That God is present and active in the world is more fundamental than any natural law or mathematical axiom.

God is immanent as He gives Himself as our companion, excluding the idea that God is simply present in creation.

We cannot speak of God in nature or history as though He is one of the properties of these elements. That approach depersonalizes God and makes Him a principle.

God collaborates with nature and history only by allowing them to cooperate with Him. They can only respond to God's initiation toward them.

When God actively associates with nature and history, this does not mean that nature or history becomes God. He is present without losing Himself to them.

We cannot speak honestly of God by ourselves. However, God can speak through us as we submit to His operations, working His love through us.

We cannot propose that God accompanies and causes *all* human activity. We cannot broadly suggest that the world is divine so that nature becomes a nature-God and human history is merely the history of God. God is distinct and at work in the world. Pantheism collapses God into the world and loses the distinction between Creator and creation.

When political systems assimilate the Church into their systems, a cult of power develops. The leader is considered a world leader and Jesus a servant of the new order. But Jesus is the only true world leader and will not share this honor.

Humans love to make idols of people and ideas.

- The *spirit* was idolized in the first half of the nineteenth century (Hegel).
- In the second half, *matter* was revered (evolution, scientism).
- The profound focus on *human existence* started in the twentieth century (existentialism).

Barth then discusses the Reformed doctrine of providence. He affirms the uniqueness of their doctrine of Christian providence but not the content of their approach. They were logical in their character but pointed into the dark by missing the nature of God as the defining motif.

The Lord of Accompaniment

The Reformers had *formal* concepts of God but not *personal* ones on this point. Thus, the relation of God to humanity pointed to the overarching supremacy of God and the resignation of humans. The Calvinist picture of God made it appear that any individual human activity was an illusion.

Barth contends that Catholics, Lutherans, Arminians, and, later, Modernists left the biblical God for their philosophical, abstract arguments. Their approach brought a sickness that put these groups in the theological hospital. Having forgotten grace and justification, they lurk in philosophical shadows without substance.

To rightly understand God's accompanying of humans, we must begin with God's intentional activity that finds fulfillment through the activity of His creatures.

When we say "God," we must refer to the three persons of the Trinity, who exist in One loving life and cause all that is created.

When we say "the will of God," we must include the Father's good will, expressed through the election of Jesus from eternity to bring His creatures to Himself and sustain their existence.

When we say "the work of God," we must understand the history of the covenant of grace. That includes its fulfillment in the sacrifice of Jesus and the Holy Spirit, who confirmed us into a life of faith and obedience. They sustain the whole created sphere.

Our thinking must be transformed:

- We must drop the harmful, impersonal notion of cause, operation, and effect.
- We must know:
  - Who God is
  - What He wills
  - How He works

In the Bible, we learn who this invisible, ruling God is who accompanies all things.

We will not yield in an apathetic surrender to the inevitable, a life of chance.

Holding fast to God's grace in Jesus, we can never dream of setting humans over against the working of God, like a constrained second person in a contract whose hand is forced and bound.

Our freedom is found in corroborating and confirming what is done for us.

Church Dogmatics 3.3

Our freedom is found in corroborating and confirming what is done for us.

1. God actively *precedes humans in every way*, the meaning of *praecurrit*. This word is the first of three terms clarifying God's accompaniment. His eternal love paves the way with His almighty will and work.

   "Always and everywhere when the creature works, God is there as the One who has already loved it."[5]

   God operates as the sovereign Lord of His creatures by accompanying His creatures from His sphere. He orders all things from eternity in time.

   God has been working in eternity, and Jesus follows in His footsteps. We must pay attention to God's preceding activity, not just His foreknowledge. God is not a passive spectator.

   God's divine activity upholds all human activity, including the environment surrounding each human; God accompanies and hosts all human activity.

   There is a similarity between the work of God and the living systems surrounding and sustaining all creatures. All human activity occurs in conditioned contexts.

   God's work takes place on a higher level, sustaining all things, including the personal lives of humans.

   Human activity occurs on a lower level, within God's hospitable space. The dynamic relationship between God and humans is firm on God's side and flexible on the human side.

   Our actions do not function in a closed, absolute context. We are accompanied within the network of God's covenantal activity—His being before us, with us, and for us.

   We operate in a field of forces within which we function materially and personally. This sphere is the creaturely world gifted by God. We acknowledge the gift but not yet the giver.

   God gives the world independent operation and cooperates according to His will. God does not overrule His creatures. He determines to make space for humans to cooperate with His loving will by His grace.

   The human is an instrument in God's hands, chosen to live in particular freedom. Our lives derive from His and are set free by His presence.

---

5. *CD* 3.3, § 49, p. 119.

The Lord of Accompaniment

We do not have to do with a vital force in the universe but with God Himself.

When Barth speaks of the creaturely nexus, at a minimum, he refers to our whole environment in the physical world, our historical context, and the network of human relations.

We can expect human life to occur within the framework of the norms of human existence with its many laws. It is a mistake to equate these laws with God's activity that prepares for human existence.

God can work without limitations in any sphere. The laws of nature are limited to function within their fields, such as gravity, light, electricity, water, and so on. There is no reason not to regard the laws of nature as valid insofar as we can understand them. But they fall short of the eternal laws of God by which He freely operates.

The laws of nature derive from human perspectives. They recount the form of the world as it occurs for us. They set the context, limits, and possibilities within the physical world as we experience it.

Our limited concepts of order can only point beyond, toward God's unlimited choice and actions to create a world for God's purposes. We cannot project from our ideas of law to discover the divine directives in creation.

We are never indirectly before God; He is ever-present and accompanying us. We are never directly present to all the operative laws of nature and life. Even though it all seems to surround us, we are profoundly limited.

God is the sustaining law of all that occurs in the world. What we see hinted at as natural laws can only point us to Him, who provides the constancy and continuity of the created world.

> We are never indirectly before God; He is ever-present and accompanying us.

We live and move and have our being in God's presence and freedom, not our self-determination or a system of ordinary occurrences.

The Father of Jesus is the Lord over all things and is always present to us by His Holy Spirit. This God is not against us in a broken relationship where God is aloof.

A second term for clarifying the one movement of God's accompanying is *concurrit*. It affirms that He goes with us hand in hand, walking with us. God comes as a companion, the presence of God as Emmanuel, God with us.

2. *Concurrit* means a concurrent working together of two persons who are not equal in their simultaneous movement.

Barth calls this corresponding movement a "single action" involving two agents. When God speaks, authors write what becomes the Bible. The human collaborates with a superior partner.

God enters the sphere of human existence and accomplishes His will. He is not absent, inactive, or restricted. As with one action in writing, both hand and pen are guided. The action of the human is enclosed within God's.

God and human functioning are not the same; they are asymmetrical. Because God acts as God, we can act as humans. This ordering is not reversible.

God stoops down to His creatures and brings them close to Himself as the secret of grace. In this embrace, He neither adds to nor takes anything from His child. He allows us to be just what we are. It is an open meeting of two beings of different orders.

God's power over His creatures is unique for each one, giving what is proper to each in their time and place. God is not a commander who has everyone doing the same thing.

God is not a schoolmaster, officer, or bureaucrat who controls a group by a set of rules for their purposes. He is benevolent as a noble person, in the sense of one who cares for others without fear for their authority.

God is one in the unity of His life of love as Father, Son, and Holy Spirit. God coexists within the wholeness of His creation. He gives space for all to exist in their particular place and time.

Our relation cannot be reduced to mechanics, principles, or infusions of some divine essence. Our understanding must point to a genuine encounter that engages the rich mystery of God.

God wants to be known and encountered, so we cannot be satisfied with being ignorant.

The missing element in all philosophies is understanding how the cooperation of God and humanity occurs. We cannot merely observe an event and then contemplate what has happened to describe it.

God will never fit within the boxes we come up with and call philosophy. Philosophies come up with generalizations of what is true. God can only be known as the specific Creator who makes all we attempt to generalize.

The Lord of Accompaniment

We understand God in the specific events of speaking to humans who hear Him by the Spirit. We resist all proposals of general knowledge that are not attentive to God's speaking.

We are persons responsible for living a genuine life before God in our particularity.

We must never doubt the spontaneity of human actions. God does work in and with human activities, empowering rather than excluding humans in their acting.

God is not merely the Lord of human activity but also the supporter and helper. Lordship confirms the freedom of creaturely movement in all the varieties of their particular acts.

a. In understanding the God-human relation, we must first *understand the character of God.*

A fear complex constrains humans. This perception is a spiritual twisting of our thinking regarding God. We mentally experience God as a stranger or enemy. Thus, we think marking off our territory and excluding God is necessary for human freedom. Some merely restrict God, while others abandon Him altogether.

Humans take a defensive stance in fear, thinking God's claim on them is dangerous. But there is no basis in God's being for this tragic belief.

God the Father is nothing like the father complex that plagues many. He is the Father of Jesus Christ and our Father who loves us.

Unfortunately, much of Christendom and theologians of every tradition and denomination have hardened human hearts, "protecting" others from God rather than letting Him free them. Thus, humans barricade themselves against the Truth, even while "truths" pass over their lips.

"If our Christian perception and confession does not free us to love God more than we fear Him, then it is obvious that we shall necessarily fear Him more than we love Him."[6] This dilemma is the root of human sin.

If our fear of God is a fear *for* ourselves, we will be imprisoned in self-isolation.

---

6. *CD* 3.3, § 49, p. 147.

Church Dogmatics 3.3

Clarity will follow in our understanding of God only when shedding the habit of fear in our prayer.

We cannot mark a boundary where God's freedom ends and the human's begins. A free person will find freedom in pursuing God's heart.

God is the Master of all things. He is the One who makes what is possible. From beginning to end, He allows time and space for spontaneity. We have every reason to celebrate the Lord who made it this way and permits us to live within His hospitality.

b. In understanding the God-human relation, we must also understand that *God makes space for us while He is with us.*

The activity of God over His creatures remains His own.

The activity of the creature before God also remains our own.

In this relationship between God and humans, there is no:
- Absorption
- Assimilation into the divine
- Disintegration of the human
- Destruction of the human in favor of the divine

Instead, there is:
- God's free grace from above engaging humans
- Condescension, as God stoops to be where humans are
- Support of the variety of human activities
- Affirmation, deliverance, and glorification of God's creature

Knowing the true God will remove the fear that humans will have nothing left to do under the lordship of His simultaneous presence.

We respect God's unconditional grace, and He also respects the creatures to whom He is gracious. There is nothing better for humans than to be held by the astounding grace of God. To lose it is cause for fear.

c. In understanding the God-human relation, we must *receive the richness of His activity toward us,* offered in His Word and Spirit.

The riches of God flow from His eternal life as Father, Son, and Holy Spirit. There is no reason to think this activity will destroy human freedom when the Father sends the Son and Spirit to make us free.

The Lord of Accompaniment 201

Only ignorance or forgetfulness of the Word and Spirit can leave us with a poverty of spirit instead of enjoying the riches of His grace.

3. A third term for clarifying the one movement of God's accompanying is *succurrit*. This accompanying is God's following human activity to bring it to good effect—God works all things together for good.

The one eternal operation of God has multiple dimensions, going before, with, and after us.

Humans cannot control the outcomes of our activities or guarantee that the result will be the desired one.

God has the freedom to work with human acts to fulfill His purposes. He goes where we cannot go, accompanying the vapor trails of our actions.

All the activities that precede today stand accompanied by God. Each occurrence helped bring about the here-and-now we are experiencing.

Once we have acted, what we produce is no longer ours. We did not create the action apart from God but with Him. He alone appoints the meaning and scope of the outcomes that follow.

When we speak, the word is ours that goes out. But we cannot control how it will be interpreted, received, or repeated. It will still be my word, possibly not affecting others as intended. The word instantly has its history that I cannot control; the hearer also brings their history to it to provide meaning.

God oversees the impact of my words and their effects on others.

God oversees all our activities so that no human activity is in vain, coordinating them to conform to His will.

He also brings about the results He desires in the actions of Jesus, acting as the Father who loves us and every one of His creatures.

3. The Divine Ruling (pp. 154–238)

Having begun under God's fatherly care, accompanied by His care, we now see the goal of God's intent is to return us to Him.

God accompanies as a Father with a will to specific ends. This *telos*, or goal, is set by Him, guided by Him, and He is its final aim.

The Old Testament used the term *king* to describe God ruling over His creation. The New Testament develops the idea of a Savior-King, who is coming at the end and setting all things right.

We engage the kingdom (βασιλεία; *basileia*) of God as already present and yet to be fulfilled.

"The βασιλεία is here, and yet it is not here; it is revealed, yet also hidden; it is present, but always future; it is at hand, indeed in the very midst, yet it is constantly expected, being still, and this time seriously, the object of the petition: Thy kingdom come."[7]

The kingdom is a complete fact in Jesus, yet it is moving toward its fulfillment, which is still hidden.

God makes Himself the goal appointed for His creatures. Those created by God, accompanied by God, must return home to God.

All the activities that precede today stand accompanied by God. Each occurrence helped bring about the here-and-now we are experiencing.

God laughs at our attempts to see His rule with the eyes of human reason.

Jesus reigns now in distinction and relatedness. He rules in eternity and also in our history.

God is always doing something new as the God of miracles. All the marvels of the natural world are also the work of His rule.

God loves law as well as freedom. He loves the well-to-do and those who wander with little to their name. He is a God of peace and not disorder. He loves that two plus two makes four.

God's governance may take the form of permission. God uses this for the salvation of humans, as with Joseph, when sin led to saving for the nation.

Ultimately, God is far above every contingency and necessity and, therefore, over every idea of fate or chance.

God rules. What does that mean? It means there is a definite plan when things take place. God directs this plan through constantly changing circumstances. This involvement brings order, so God's operation over history maintains His will in organizing its events.

God is not a prisoner to His plans. He freely works out His activities according to His good ends.

God controls human activity as the free action of His creature. There is no contradiction between God's control and human freedom in the sphere where freedom is given by grace.

---

7. *CD* 3.3, § 49, p. 156.

The Lord of Accompaniment

God provides a framework of divine permission. The meaning of human activity comes from the gift of God's ordering, directed by His permission.

God controls everything that happens, while granting His permission. He guides all toward His goal. Nothing will be ironed out of our lives to be replaced by a unified plan.

Jesus' freedom joyfully accepts and affirms our unique particularity. This plan embraces everyone.

God takes nothing from His creatures. He gives everything to them, directing their free activity.

God preserves humanity from a descent into chaos, abandoned to the effects of mere individualism.

God not only preserves from chaos and individualism but also coordinates the life of humans in mutual relationships. We are all brought into relationships of giving and receiving with other humans and our environment.

We are each like a word within a sentence or paragraph. This setting is firstly proper vertically in the context of God's ongoing purposes. Then, it works out horizontally in the context of human activity.

In ourselves, we are nothing; we have no meaning and can do nothing. All derives from God. While we are nothing without Him, we are everything with Him within His determination to be for us.

We exist firstly by our relativity to God and only derivatively in relation to other humans. Also, we are not dependent on the universe as a whole, only its Maker.

When we say humans belong to the universe, the state, or the community, we introduce categories by which humans find their value other than belonging to God. And if we must "belong" to any of these groupings as the means to follow God's will, we have taken a wrong turn in submitting to another power that seeks to dominate.

The kingdom of God means an order that does not infringe on the activities of His creatures.

God's ruling subordinates all things to Himself without prejudice, dealing with each person directly and personally. In our submission, He lifts us up. In our being ruled, we are coordinated into life as God intends.

God is not interested in unholy hierarchies where we are lost in the collective whole of any group. Within God's wholeness is the dignity of each person, honored for who they are. Each person fulfills their own life to fulfill the common good. We are never a drop in the ocean or a brick in a pyramid. For God, each is a beloved child.

God does not despise the little things. He cares about the thread hanging from a beggar's coat. He cares for the grass of the field and the birds of the air. They are valued for the little things they are to God, who counts the hairs on our heads if we still have them.

When we address God as King and Father, it means the King of Israel, the King of the world. He is the One who says "I am" in both the Old and New Testaments.

The God of the Old Testament is the "I am" who made a covenant with Israel as His people. He initiates the history of these people and guides them in distinction from all other people. He gives Israel His Word as a commandment, full of promise and warning.

Israel's history is marked by failure to recognize its true King and shows that they are ungrateful and disobedient, unfaithful to God, and seduced by the idols of the surrounding nations. Israel rejects the God who elected Israel.

By rejecting its King, Israel places itself in the sphere of the legitimate wrath of the King. Thus, we see ongoing judgments by the One, still their King with unalterable faithfulness. He continually speaks to them through His prophets. He preserves a remnant who recognizes His favor. These set their hope in Him.

The God of the New Testament speaks as the same actualized "I am," who is Lord of the same covenant. He removes what is incomplete and fulfills what was promised. Where Israel has been unfaithful to the covenant, God faithfully maintains the covenant Israel had broken.

The King steps onto the stage of history from an obscure outpost called Nazareth in Galilee. From there comes the Prophet to whom all the former prophets pointed.

This new King was born in Bethlehem, where David was born. This fulfilling King is faithful as the Lord of the covenant. He achieves what Israel had failed to do.

Israel rejected this Prophet, who was also its King. Only by His mercy do they receive their final restoration.

> God laughs at our attempts to see His rule with the eyes of human reason.

"King Yahweh Himself has come into the midst of His people on behalf of His people, to turn this people to Himself, to confirm in His own person its election and calling, to vindicate His kingly honour."[8]

---

8. *CD* 3.3, § 49, p. 180.

The Lord of Accompaniment

In the Old Testament, the King proclaims to His people, "Hear, Oh Israel." They hear of His election, will, and love in the command to respond.

In the New Testament, the King has come. They may behold and respond to His glory as He speaks and teaches in a manner decisive for furthering their relationship.

Jesus' servants spread the news that the King has appeared, is appearing, and will appear.

Throughout the Bible, the King is faithful, and His people are not. The King's faithfulness overcomes the unfaithfulness of His people.

The history of created reality exists concretely as a stage for particular events that reveal God's glory. The events are not an end in themselves; they provide opportunities for humans to participate in God's rule as sons and daughters.

The King of Israel is the focus of divine ruling, not a system of oversight or the sphere of Christianity. Jesus is His name, and He is Lord over all.

Why does God rule alone? He alone is the faithful One whom our unfaithfulness cannot thwart. He gives Himself in the Son. He is the fountain of mercy from the Father. He is the source of the Holy Spirit, whose power rules above all dominions. In all this, He is the King of Israel and the world's ruler.

How might we understand the relationship between God's ruling and His creatures' activity? At the same time, God directs humans and does not suppress their distinctiveness in the process. He affirms them.

We are not chess pieces moved around on the board. We live in a relationship where the One who loves in freedom grants us freedom daily. We are neither controlled nor abandoned.

Does the divine rule establish into a single whole a horizontal ordering of relationships? The Holy Spirit brings a peace that brings the many together as one body. This arrangement creates a unity that affirms human particularity—both by the work of God.

The individual and the community coexist so that neither diminishes the other.

The world's occurrences are unlike a shoreless sea of sameness flowing back and forth within itself.

God has a face, form, history, and name. He is not an empty, original monad. The world has a self-ordered unity that He set on its way. It has order granted to it, alongside God's overseeing, which we refer to as divine governing.

Within the economy of God's work in the world, there is a continual differentiation that is the ordering process. There is before and after, above and below, and so on. There is authority and subordination, advance and withdrawal. There is a purpose for everything; nothing is lost.

The world's occurrence is like a river with waterfalls that supply but cannot be scaled. It has a source (God), a course (history), and an estuary (interface of histories).

Barth is criticized for a lack of engagement with nature. He emphasizes that reality rests in God, and the derivative and natural elements are secondary. These analogical echoes may point to God as their source.

Barth uses living things as an echo of the ruling of God: "The true image of the cosmos which is ruled by this King is undoubtedly that of a natural structure, a living plant perhaps, or some other organism, in which the various parts, root, stem, branches, leaves, buds and fruit are all mutually ordered, in which the presence of all the others demands that each one should have its own place and function, in which they all have a different place and function and are therefore different the one from the other."[9] This sentence illustrates a theology of nature, not natural theology. We understand nature because we begin with God rather than trying to understand God through nature.

Barth notes Paul's use of the body with many parts as an image of the cosmos ruled by the living God. There is a unity (the whole) with particular parts (the individuals) empowered by the Spirit to participate each in their unique way for the good of the whole.

We must never hold images of natural life before our knowledge of God. We must begin with the Word addressed to us. He informs us of who He is and how the created order reflects His majesty.

Attempts to understand God through observations of nature would amount to idolatry. The "god" revealed would be constructed according to our sensibility.

We must begin with the Creator of the concrete world. Then, we may understand God's administration over all events that set the context for human life.

God questions all our presuppositions so that we may discover what is true.

The individual and the community coexist so that neither diminishes the other.

The history of the covenant is the context in which this economic interaction occurs.

All world history works in the context of this activity of God.

---

9. *CD* 3.3, § 49, p. 193.

The Lord of Accompaniment

Barth affirms that God has penetrated the world and left constant reminders of His ruling presence, even where God is hidden.

1. *The history of the Bible* allows us to encounter God Himself through this witness. The original witnesses are reliable spokespersons of God's Word and work.

    The original writers were free to be living, acting, and speaking persons who still talk afresh in every age to every person who will listen.

    The history of exegesis is a continual return to God's presence in the world, seeking clear articulation of God's rule within it.

    All commentaries and sermons are echoes of those original voices. They are not of the same quality but spring from the same source.

2. *The history of the Church* is another sign of God's present ruling. It results from the voice of the Bible, which is the foundation of the Church. The Church is integrated into the history of Scripture through the witness of the prophets and apostles.

    The Church extends the testimony of the first witnesses.

    Church history is the story of God's gathering of people who will point to God's world governing.

    The Church proclaims the King of Israel on the strength of the biblical witness. We meet the One who is present in the ever-changing constellations of history. The Word and work of God seek new realizations from generation to generation.

    The historical sphere of the community of faith is not one among many histories; it is a unique sphere where one can see a trace of God's world governance:

    o The Church is in service to the rest of the world, acting as a trace of God's history.
    o The Church has had to resist history's oppressive and hostile elements, believing what the world cannot accept.
    o The Church has the power for renewal. It is forever being reformed, so we recognize God's guidance as a trace of His ruling.

3. By itself, *the history of the Jews* is not a demonstration of God's ruling. It has a King, Jesus of Nazareth. It is hard to turn away from the history of the Jews without theological explanations for insight.

What was preparatory has become final and determined. The Jews have outlived the empires from that time and ever since. They were small and the underdogs but have lasted.

The Jewish people have a mysterious, persistent presence as strangers, guests, and aliens among the nations.

The Jews can only be understood as a distinctive, one-of-a-kind people.

The existence of the Jews is a mystery and a riddle. One may construe these people as similar to others. They may be assimilated into world history as another story among many. However, one may concede that the ruler of the world has given them a special place as a trace of His divine ruling.

In light of the Christian message, Barth holds that we must see in the Jews a valid trace of God's benevolent governing revealed through these stubborn people.

Israel wanted to be like other nations, but God had other plans as its faithful Lord. God chose to take the place of this unworthy partner on Golgotha to ratify His grace toward them.

Israel can only be a people as the people of God. Jesus is the world's savior as one of these people, despite their unfaithfulness. In this way, they become the history of humanity with God—resistant to the end, but God's acceptance is more significant.

The history of the Jews is the embodiment of God's "Yes" and humanity's "no" as the theme of world history.

A Jew is a person who belongs to this elected people. They are not worthy of election. They wanted to elect another king. But their true King elected them.

Like with Israel, all our attempts to be grand and glorious must be stripped away. These endeavors come in the form of religion, culture, language, and race, all sculpted into formal attempts to replace grace with human achievement.

The world has not been hospitable to the Jews. They are strangers at the door, outsiders like Abraham and Moses, who wandered with God. The prophets, the Son of Man, and the elect of God have nowhere to call home other than as God's servants and family.

Why are the Jews so mistreated?

- In them, *we see ourselves*, reflecting who we are, like in a mirror, so we see how great our need is.

The Lord of Accompaniment

We can make room and excuses for our neighbors to conceal their sins. But the cloak of the Jew is stripped off. Their revolt, disbelief, disobedience, and self-interest are apparent; we find in this other what is also ingrained in us. We deflect and point to their failure, blind to our self-interest at work.

We must see that we are all enemies of God, turned from His grace. The trace of God's ruling is evident even as we resist it. Our resistance to His elect people is resistance to Him. We are committed to our attempts at self-rule.

o In them, *we see God's electing grace* as the sole basis of human existence. We are annoyed because they mirror divine grace for those who have persisted only by God's mercy. They have not merited grace; they are unworthy in our eyes—yet they persist because God loves them unconditionally!

This possibility offends us; it sets aside all we have done to merit grace. We depend on God's grace and must let the King judge others without considering our judgments.

The Jews reveal something. No one has a home in world history; we are all pushed about as strangers full of insecurity. Only in the life of the eternally hospitable God are we securely at home.

We can no longer console ourselves by looking at our efforts. We can no longer judge others by their failures. The Jews have attained a place in God's history as His chosen children, not by earning this status and in spite of often rejecting it. They are His children by grace. Because of who He is, He will never reject them.

One Jew, in particular, is elected on behalf of all. We can only be elected in and with this Other.

The One Jew Jesus looks at us from the desolation and difficulty of the Jews and says, "I am for you too." He is the new head of the human race.

4. *The limitation of human life* is a sign of God's rule. He is the One who conditions human life, ordered by the God of the Bible, throughout Church history, and as King of the Jews.

The history of Scripture, the Church, and the Jews are objective facts that must be discovered as clues of God's work in human history.

Even if we have never heard of the Bible, the Church, or the Jews, or if they have no impact on us, we are aware of ourselves and the limitations of life.

Being conscious of ourselves and our limitations is a sign of God's world governance. All of us live within limits set by God, with all their variations.

Within the limitations, we are under the lordship of God.

- We have a spontaneity of life under God's lordship, gifted and liberated to be free persons. This life is within limits while still spontaneous.
- We live under the sovereignty of God, not belonging to ourselves, within which we are limited. There is life outside our lifetime, before and after our lives. We "recognise the hand of His in which we are held, and in which we are both secure and free because it is the hand which preserves all creatures."[10]

We now discuss angels as appropriate for our current focus on God's care provision.

God created the heavens, which are more closely related to His existence.

Our earthly history has its source in the creation of the universe. It proceeds as the history of God's covenant and salvation. Subsequently, in our lower realm, the glory of God is magnified. The Son of God is not a man who rises to a divine state. He is God coming down to take on human flesh.

The will of God is done on earth as it is already done in heaven. Heaven is where God sets out to establish His order and glory.

Where God is, heaven is there to serve Him. He brings the kingdom of heaven to us. His servants enter the world and become active in it. They do not act on their own behalf but fulfill the will of God.

Angels are heavenly messengers called for service. They have flexibility in obedience to fulfill the word of God in our concrete realm.

Angels do not exist as humans do. They operate entirely within their cooperative function within the will of God. They are heavenly beings who belong to the Word and work of God in Jesus.

---

10. *CD* 3.3, § 49, p. 235.

The Lord of Accompaniment

Angels appear, fulfilling the work of God and declaring in speech or actions God's words on the boundaries of our existence. They are watchers, speaking and singing when the time comes to stir those who are sleeping or half awake.

Only in knowing the primary sign of God's speaking, Jesus, can we apprehend the second, angels. If we do not accept angels, we will dismiss their voices and all they reveal in the Bible, Church history, the history of the Jews, and our own life story.

Where God is, there are angels. Where we deny angels, we exclude God. Angels serve in their office as messengers, and we must be grateful for their role in the divine-human relationship.

4. The Christian under the Universal Lordship of God the Father (pp. 239–88)

We have seen that God the Father cares for His creatures as the basis and meaning of human history, preserving, accompanying, and ruling them.

Now, we must explore how humans participate in this relationship. Humans do not look on from without like other created animals preserved and accompanied by God.

Humans may perceive and acknowledge God's care. They have the opportunity to affirm God's provision with thankfulness. They can conform their lives to the will of God in joyful obedience.

The free human sees God's work and perceives the traces of God's providential ruling. The traces are easily missed. They must be pointed out.

There are persons with a specific nature and attitude to discern the divine preserving, accompanying, and ruling. These are Christians, living members of a Christian community.

Christians may join in confessing God's providence because they are aware of and participate in God's present care as reality. Seeing God at work in the world is as evident to them as a person looking out a window.

Humans may have confidence in the almighty Companion, who embraces their whole being. Not all humans know this. Christians acknowledge and accept they are not different from other creatures other than by saying "yes" to being a creature ruled by God.

Rather than follow the innumerable illusions humans have about themselves, Christians hear the call to live under the lordship of God. Some people want to be more than a creature, yet apart from God.

Christians denounce a life separated from God and others. They confess they are creatures made by God with all the joy accompanying the claim. This acceptance makes them creatures who know who and what they are.

Rather than being ruled by natural law, fate, chance, the devil, or self-elevation, the Christian lives under the care of the One who is God the Father.

God organizes and sustains the processes of life, which are made visible in the person of Jesus Christ. Seeing Jesus as the fullness of humanity and ourselves belonging to Him, we are delivered by Him into life together and placed at His disposal.

The Christian community is a gathering of those whose eyes are opened to the fact that they are children of the Father. Christians are open-eyed people.

God's rule is not a burden or oppression; it is for the human to be unreservedly under the grace and loving lordship of the One who has given all. There is nothing to fear. There is no need to run or rebel.

If we see the relation between Creator and creature in Jesus Christ, then Jesus shows us the highest possibility of human freedom and contentment.

We walk through an open door that we have not opened. Inside is a banqueting hall. We take our place at the table with all manner of beasts, human and otherwise. We find camaraderie with them all in that we are as they are, made by God. But we also see, where others do not, the Creator as the One who invites and opens doors.

The Christian alone knows about providence and the lordship of God and consents to be embraced by God's ruling love. All others benefit from the providence and lordship from the outside without knowledge.

> Only in the life of the eternally hospitable God are we securely at home.

Like all humans, we still face the challenges and opportunities of daily existence. With appropriate wonder, we live with a sense of surprise.

Curiosity and wonder find their source in trusting the One who opens the way.

Knowing the Father is a science and an art, a knowledge that claims the whole of us in an engagement with this Other. Through the relationship, knowledge encounters and transforms us.

A dynamic attitude develops as we are claimed and participate in God's work. We are ready to cooperate with thankful hearts.

The overseeing lordship of Jesus becomes actual in faith, obedience, and prayer as three forms of the Christian attitude. If you are missing one, it is not a Christian attitude.

The Christian attitude cannot be pure theory or practice; it embraces both, joining knowing and acting to bring an insightful working out.

The Lord of Accompaniment

Believing, obeying, and praying are interwoven without one being superior. The inward and outward are elements of one Christian attitude. Faith, obedience, and prayer do not come in a specific sequence; they come together.

Analogous from the three persons in the One God, the three elements of the Christian attitude are included inseparably in one Christian. One may say that each component is the others, so faith is obedience and prayer, prayer is faith and obedience, and obedience is faith and prayer. Together, they echo a kind of perichoretic mutuality (the interactive indwelling of the persons of the Trinity).[11] It is also valuable to discuss them in distinction.

> In faith, one finds they are a child of God the Father, participating in the relationship God has provided for His creature under His care and ruling.

1. Faith means hearing and receiving the Word of God. It is a confidence that acknowledges that a Word from God has been spoken and is now being affirmed by the Christian.

   Faith is the opening point for the Christian attitude. It has a priority only in its ordering, not in importance. To have faith in Jesus is to be a Christian.

   In faith, one finds they are a child of God the Father, participating in the relationship God has provided for His creature under His care and ruling.

   All that follows comes from the opening of faith to hear and respond, the working out of faith.

   Faith is not a magical quality that surpasses the capabilities of nature. It is not something humans can produce by themselves.

   Faith is not blind subjection to an external law forced upon humans. Neither is it a conviction about a set of facts established by humans.

   Faith is an awakening to what it means to live within the sphere beyond our creatureliness. This state is what we see in Jesus, who displays the outworking of faith as He embodies the highest restoration of human existence in the sphere of His Father's love.

   Faith does not close our eyes; it opens them.

   Faith does not destroy our intellect; it captivates it for development.

---

11. *CD* 3.3, § 49, p. 246.

Faith does not break down the will; it sets it free in movement.

Faith is entirely the work of God and altogether the work of humans.

The Christian participates by faith in God's world governance. As faith in Jesus as Lord, it is also faith in the power of the Holy Spirit.

By this Word, the Christian awakens to faith. In faith, one lays hold of the faith of the Word alone that has laid hold of them. Faith alone makes the Christian life possible.

- o Faith alone opens the Christian's eyes to see.
- o Faith alone allows us to resist false systems.
- o Faith alone allows us to be held over the abyss and led through the waves.
- o Faith alone brings courage, patience, and cheerfulness.
- o Faith alone enables us to be willing and ready to live as Christians.

Genuine faith depends on participating in the life of Christ, from this relationship alone, drawing out the implications for life together.

Our faith cannot be in ourselves, looking inward at the power of our affirmation, enamored with the beauty of the system of Christianity, or borrowed from others for security. These all create imitations based on what we see in others.

Our impersonations attempt to produce from human capacities that which can only genuinely come from relating to the Word.

The Christian is a person of faith, even if only a pitiable fragment, who knows they are with God as a child of the Father who inherits His glory.

The Christian has a Lord. What is lacking is simply a complete revelation of the Lord, whose presence rules over life's challenges and issues.

Faith is the work of God and then the work of humans. God gives to humans by awakening their faith.

Christians believe because God has moved toward them. They are not spectators; they have a personal response of recognition: "This is my Father, and I am His child. I am at home with Him." Hospitality has found its goal in this homecoming.

We are leaving the life of separation and independence. We are giving ourselves to Him, who gives all for us. We cannot continue as we were before.

We have a Lord who calls us to obedience to His lordly love.

The Lord of Accompaniment

We are made friends and intimates with God. We abandon our waywardness as we accept the embrace of the One who makes us courageous, patient, and cheerful.

We become free lords of our lives under the freeing Lord. Our attempt to resist is a return to slavery that leads to death. We willingly lose our lives to the Lord so He may give them to us afresh. Thus, we are free. Faith is liberation.

To believe from the heart is to give our whole being. The heart is the whole of a person. We love this Lord with all our heart, soul, mind, and strength as the life of faith.

We can see that faith implies obedience. As we submit to the Lord, we are free to obey Him. However, we cringe because all other acts of obedience we have seen lead to tyranny.

We hear this Lord speak and entrust ourselves to His care. We surrender by following Him in the direction He takes us in the walk of love born of His presence.

Faith also includes prayer, in which we are directed to God. We are thankful and give praise for who He is. We acknowledge our inadequacy and ask for His help. We honestly lay all of who we are before Him, giving ourselves to Him.

Prayer is the act of reorientation, awakened by God to His presence. Therefore, it begins as an act of God, who surprises us and gives us the freedom to act in response. We are amazed at all that is shown us:

- God is our Father.
- We are children of this God.
- We belong in the Father's home.
- All is an unearned gift, including the ability to believe.
- This includes our inability, unworthiness, and incapacity to believe.
- God is near.
- There is a wealth of God's goodness.
- God covers our shame, fills our hunger, restores us from our shortcomings.
- We knock on His door, and He answers.
- He brings us to participate in the life of Jesus and His universal, sustaining lordship.
- He gives us the freedom for genuine faith.

Humans live in this movement of prayer. Faith as prayer is living in the conversation initiated by God and daily returning to Him.

2. Obedience means doing the Word of God.

Humans hear the Word by answering its call in surrender. This response is obedience that includes the whole Christian in the encounter.

Belief is an act of awakening to the Other, becoming a Christian. Obedience is the act of responding to the Other, being a Christian. This person does not just contemplate the work of God; they cooperate with Him.

Obedience is not separate from faith and prayer, but is a unique feature of them.

Obedience does not give an advantage in God's judgment, promises, or assistance.

Obedience is the obligation one places oneself under in becoming a Christian. This dynamic has analogies in marriage and friendship. In entering the relationship, one obligates oneself to act consistently with the connection. It is not forced; it is freedom in loving.

Jesus is obedient to the Father because He is the Son. He cannot choose to deny being the Son or reject His Father's love for Himself or humanity.

Obedience is the fidelity of relation that aligns us with the One who has loved us.

The Christian's only master is the Holy Spirit, who binds us by the Word of God and speaks from the living Word as the Spirit of the community.

Following the Spirit is the opposite of pursuing freelance opinions, self-formed attitudes, or resentments. The Spirit leads us to live within a community to provide acts of fellowship, service, and mission. The Spirit guides us to be for others.

The Spirit does not make us better as individuals but as friends and companions in the community. This connection forms obedience as a journey with the free Spirit, who takes us where He wills and compels us to love in each new circumstance.

The Spirit never gives us autopilot orders. We always go together in each new situation.

The event of salvation for a Christian is an entry into this life of cooperating with this living Lord.

Obedience begins at the cross as we find that we do not belong to ourselves but to Him. We, along with the world, are loved by Him and called to follow Him into His restoring mission.

The Lord of Accompaniment

At the cross, we affirm that what Jesus did was His obedient decision for us.

The Holy Spirit sees to it that we may believe, indwelling and guiding us as members of Jesus' body. We become incorporated into the life of service and find the life of responsibility that develops inwardly and outwardly in sharing Jesus' mission.

Obedience continues as we stand with Jesus. He has claimed not only the sacred sphere but the secular sphere as well. He works in the Church and the economic, political, academic, and artistic arenas. They all belong together in Him.

There is no place for choosing between the spiritual and material worlds. He rules over both.

In the general sphere of the world, only through the Holy Spirit will the Christian be appropriately governed with its systems of rules and regulations. The unbroken Word of God accompanies, drawing from what one learns in the school of Jesus.

God is at work by His Holy Spirit to work out obedience in us as His creatures.

Christians are children of God and accomplish His works as servants. The will of God is at work. All we must do is listen. Someday, we will learn how it all worked within His will.

Christian obedience is possible because disobedience was excluded at the source. God has already justified us with His profound mercy. He has claimed and determined us by His Spirit. We live with a personal obligation to give thanks to God.

Faith is the root of our actions of obedience. Only as the Christian believes does one begin their whole life at the foot of the cross where the decision of God's love was made for them. One finds confidence that Jesus is Lord of all and follows Him.

Even here, the Christian is hidden in the sphere of God. We need confidence in the one light of the revelation that endures, renews, and is new every morning.

Despite the weariness and weakness of the Christian, divine mercy forgives; Jesus forbids us to despair in light of ourselves. God is all the closer in His grace when we see our failing.

All we need is confidence in the faithfulness of Jesus Christ. Our human spirit will attempt to substitute itself for the Holy Spirit. But He is the leader who frees us.

By the Spirit, we acknowledge the Word of God spoken to us. This speech is Jesus Himself in His revelation that addresses us.

Obedience includes prayer as the most intimate act of Christian action. Everything else follows and derives from prayer. When desiring to act obediently, the Christian lifts up praise and thanksgiving, yielding in weakness to the One who is our only help. This stance is Christian obedience in a nutshell.

Prayer inwardly renews and empowers the Christian as a breathing of the soul.

In prayer, we are free to answer the Father who addresses us. We enter the surprise and wonder that God is our Father and that we are His children.

Prayer is the act of obedience from which all other actions spring as the answer to the One who meets us.

3. Prayer is the essential form of faith and obedience.

While prayer *is* faith and obedience, we must distinguish it. It may be described in the following sequence:

- Prayer that does not focus on *our* attention but on *His* majesty and mystery.
- Prayer that includes our worship, praise, and thanksgiving but never begins or ends at this point.
- Prayer that may include confession and repentance as honesty before God, admitting our neediness and self-made illusions. But this also cannot be the starting point. We cannot focus on our lowliness as humans but on the light that shines in our darkness and humility.
- Prayer that leads to petition, seeing God as the One who provides. We give thanks, admit our shame before God, and then ask for what He provides. Petition is the crucial element of the Lord's Prayer. Praying is asking.

It was for intimate and direct nearness that Jesus became a human. Jesus was born, crucified, and resurrected so we would be close as Father and children.

In answer to the light of Jesus coming to us, we accept the freedom given to us. This does not mean thinking deeply about our worthiness or unworthiness. It means turning to Him and receiving what only He has to give.

The Lord of Accompaniment

Without anxiety, one sees the majesty of God, what one lacks, and how we have been distant.

We need not be afraid to draw near to the One who has come to give us everything. We can tell this God what we would like to have from Him.

The most intimate thing in the Christian life is that we may ask of God. This is not just permitted; it is commanded. True worship is expressed where the human takes what God gives—Himself and all that comes with Him.

The biggest surprise for humans is not merely the majesty and mystery of God but that God is for us and acts accordingly.

The one great gift given to humanity is the person of Jesus Christ. In Him, God has concerned Himself with us:

- He has made the world and us.
- He has taken on flesh and pledged Himself to us in covenant love.
- He has accepted solidarity with us and delivered us to His eternal glory.
- He has personally made Himself the Lord, guardian, and helper of the world and humanity.
- He has become our peace, controlling all occurrences, upholding, accompanying, and ruling us.
- He has helped the world since creation, providing all that is needed.
- He is the One from whom all things come and to whom all things return.
- He is the Savior of the world who is absolutely for us.
- He is the One in whom the answers to all our prayers are made available.
- He has given Himself for His people, His community, His body.

Prayer is an enduring participation in Christ. We are connected to and compelled by Jesus in daily living, integrating our lives within the will of God.

In prayer, we consent to God's covenantal reality, His promise, action, and faithfulness to us.

Jesus gives Himself as the answer to every human prayer.

The first one who asks in prayer is Jesus. He taught His disciples to pray by leading them in prayer.

What Jesus did in the Lord's Prayer is what He asks us to do.

Because one has faith, one turns to Him. In prayer, we transcend our limitations, asking God who has given Himself to us.

Prayer is a dynamic response to God's self-giving in providential care.

The life of faith, obedience, and prayer is the heart of human existence, lived under the universal lordship of God, given a share in God's life.

God is free as the living Trinitarian God who will not be without His creatures. He is free to live with us and be affected by us in our lives together, with all our distinctions.

God's sovereignty is so great that He may embrace human activity. Our freedom does not compete with God.

We are permitted to live in the freedom created by God to be His friends.

God does not surrender to humanity. He maintains Himself as Lord and King even over disobedient children, whom He calls to intimacy as friends.

"In obedience the Christian is the servant, in faith he is the child, but in prayer, as the servant and the child, he is the friend of God, called to the side of God and at the side of God, living and ruling and reigning with Him."[12]

The One who originally stands before God, listens to Him, and answers with a Christian attitude is Jesus Christ. Without Him, there are no Christians, and there is no Christianity.

There is Christ.

There are Christians.

There is Christianity.

There is discipleship in Christ.

There is faith in Christ that leads us to His Father.

There is obedience to Christ.

There is prayer, asking together with Him.

There is participation in Christ: in His priestly, prophetic, and kingly offices.

The Spirit never gives us autopilot orders. We always go together in each new situation.

We are lifted to the place of God's hospitality in heavenly places and on earth.

The Christian is in Christ, a child and friend of God, and a member of His body.

---

12. *CD* 3.3, § 49, p. 286.

Whenever the Christian believes, obeys, and prays, concealed within this movement, the finger of God moves, and the hand of God holds the scepter that rules the world. Even more, the heart of God moves, full of love, wisdom, and power.

COMMENTARY:
- Providence is a personal presence, not a sheer power over humans or creation.
- The fatherliness of God in the world upholds and sustains all He makes.
- As the Lord, God is the servant who maintains all He makes.
- In conceiving of God's providence, we must think of His loving power that creates time and space to share with His creatures, not as a playground for us so He can do His work elsewhere.
- When Jesus says that His Father is at work to this very day and that He is doing His Father's work, this includes His ongoing care and attentive sustaining of all God makes.
- The ruling of God is to bring His creatures from their self-destruction to live within His loving will as a family.
- God rules from a kingdom in heaven and intends to fulfill His will on earth. He sends angels to bring echoes of heaven to this world in messages and manifestations of God's intentions.
- The Christian attitude is not self-chosen.

CONCLUSION FOR THE CHURCH: Today's Church has a management problem and a success distraction. If the Church could listen to the wisdom of this section, it would be less concerned about making a name for itself, its tradition, or its denomination. We may pray, "Thy will be done," but often leaders feel that they must implement God's will in their own time and way. Aligning with God's providence means practicing God's presence because that is more real than anything else.

Providence is about God in action, not in His observatory in heaven. When the Church is concerned about God's providence, it becomes a listening Church that asks what God wants. God loves the whole world. Our attitude toward God's providence makes the difference. Missing Barth's vision of providence results in a coup of chaos which leads the Church astray.

INSIGHT FOR PASTORS: A pastor cares for those within their sphere of influence. But they represent the greater sphere of God's influence, as discussed in this section. Cathedrals once fascinated persons who entered their towering pillars and witnessed their beautiful art. However, leaving the building meant leaving God in the sacred spaces. Reminding people about God became an impersonal replacement for God.

The pastor who is awake to God's providence will pull back the curtains we have put up to shield ourselves from God. We will lead people to the Source and Sustainer of everything. We will look more deeply to see the world as a dynamic provision for sharing God's story. Then we will go with them out the door hand in hand with Jesus wherever He is at work.

INSIGHT FOR THEOLOGIANS: Providence can quickly become an abstract topic. Worse yet, it can distract us into thinking God has set the universe on autopilot. God then becomes distant and abstract. That focus reduces God to the cause of what God is supposed to have set in motion. Any view of providence that separates God from God's ongoing presence has departed from doing theology. It becomes philosophy, a discussion of cause and effect that misses God's will. The Lord's Prayer aims to orient us to His providence.

As with all good science, we ought to be able to operate more adequately in the world because we are more aligned with its actuality, not blinded by illusions of chance, fate, or necessity to run our lives.

CLARIFYING QUESTIONS: Does your theology of providence focus on how God can be in control and yet leave the world to run its course? *Or* do you stop and remember that Jesus has promised to be with us to the end of the age, realizing that providence is God's active presence each day?

CHAPTER 16

THE INHOSPITABLE CHAOS BEYOND THE SHADOWS

§ 50. God and Nothingness

FOCUS STATEMENT: Outside God's hospitality is a chaotic dimension of existence—that which God has not chosen. This "realm" is not merely the absence of light that creates shadows. Beyond the light and shadows is the nothingness outside God's creative providence.

The image of a threatening hand with no apparent source is a faint glimpse of nothingness. Shadows may leak from this dark dimension, but Barth looks beyond all shades of darkness, engaging what God has not created nor sustained.

God creates and sustains all that exists through His loving will. Some choices and events are the shadow side of created reality (divorce is the shadow of marriage; death is the shadow of life). All the shining and shades are within the scope of God's creative activity. Beyond that is the nothingness He does not will; He resists it through His love.

Beyond God's creation is the threat of what God has not created. We cannot see it directly; however, the purpose of the cross was to defeat its power. God says "No" to nothingness that invades our space and to our "no" that contends with God's will. He does all this from love, for love, and within His place as Lord of the universe. In § 50, we look through God's act in Jesus to peer into the utter madness of what God has not willed and wills to defeat— the chaos beyond the shadows.

INTRODUCTION: Discussing nothingness, Barth takes us into challenging territory. Barth takes this paragraph to whisper about what God has not made. Nothingness refers to all that is overcome by the cross. We cannot directly point to nothingness (*nihil*), but we can see that God has overcome the threat.

223

224   *Church Dogmatics* 3.3

We are dealing with providence in *CD* 3.3, not yet focused on a doctrine of sin. We address God and His creation, including what God has not willed. This realm impacts His creation and needs consideration.

If we let God's logic reveal an enemy implied but not seen, we will recognize the chaos of evil that God overcomes. We cannot grant it status as created by God or as an equal opponent. But it is there. In a world sustained by love and creativity, death and destruction echo in love's absence.

Nothingness exists as the backdrop for sin, suffering, and death. God intends none of this. Barth will not satisfy our curiosity regarding evil's source and sustained presence. He wants us to know about God's lordship over everything—even the menace of evil exposed by His Word.

▦ CONTEXT: *CD* 3.3
Pages in Paragraph: 80 pages (pp. 289–368)

Subsections
1. The Problem of Nothingness
2. The Misconception of Nothingness
3. The Knowledge of Nothingness
4. The Reality of Nothingness

▢ TEXT: § 50. God and Nothingness

✠ OPENING SUMMARY: Under the control of God world-occurrence is threatened and actually corrupted by the nothingness which is inimical to the will of the Creator and therefore to the nature of His good creature. God has judged nothingness by His mercy as revealed and effective in Jesus Christ. Pending the final revelation that it is already refuted and abolished, God determines the sphere, the manner, the measure and the subordinate relationship to His Word and work in which it may still operate.[1]

✠ SUMMARY:
1. The Problem of Nothingness (pp. 289–95)

God is sovereign, as the Lord of His creation. Even so, the Bible reveals an opposition and resistance to His intentions.

We may refer to nothingness as an aspect of being from which God withholds His preservation or accompanying. It is more profound than a

---

1. *CD* 3.3, § 50, p. 289.

The Inhospitable Chaos beyond the Shadows

shadow—the consequence of blocking light—standing against what God has made; it is a bullying threat.

God says "No" to those elements that He has not willed. Willing His "Yes" for the world, He logically resists what His "Yes" excludes. Saying "Yes" to one choice implies a "No" to other options. That is the case here.

Barth relegates nothingness outside God's creating acts. A shadow is part of the created world, understood in relation to light; we cannot provide the same level of existence to nothingness.

God does not accompany or preserve nothingness that has broken away from His will. Those alien elements oppose His will for creation. He must resist them.

We must acknowledge there is an opposite to God's election. It is not from God or for God; it stands apart from God.

Nothingness threatens to enslave creatures who turn from God. God preserves from nothingness. It appears as an autonomous choice to go away from God. "Lead us not into temptation" points out this threat. That is the path to enslavement.

God's will liberates humans for fellowship with Him, for knowing and being known.

In Jesus, God became a creature set against nothingness. God's action revealed instances of what opposes His will.

We cannot try to engage nothingness independently. God's providence includes standing against what resists His love.

All things are affected by nothingness, entangled with it and bearing its scars.

These scars include sin, guilt, punishment, suffering, and death; nothingness cannot be explained as an act of God or the human.

Jesus Christ has judged nothingness. It cannot kill or destroy, but it can still injure. Jesus must deal with it.

Nothingness is a break arising between humans and God. It contradicts God's intended relationship as a hostility incompatible with God's goodness, forming a clash point like the meeting of water and land at the shore.

God's providence is observed in His *dealing* with the break. Theology can only secondarily be concerned with the hostile blackness that intrudes on what God intends with humans.

God's dealing with His creatures is a history of the break between God and humanity. Theology may study the brokenness between God and humans as a report, not a logical system. It must be derived by reflecting on God's loving actions and engaging what is broken.

226 Church Dogmatics 3.3

2. The Misconception of Nothingness (pp. 295–302)

It is easy to confuse nothingness with what Barth calls the negative element of God's work.

Light exists, as well as darkness, as seen in shadows. God's creation contains both positive and negative. Neither element should be mistaken for nothingness.

One created element is positive (day or light). The other is negative, only as the limiting of God's work on the frontier of creation (night or darkness). Notice that God wills and includes the separation of light and darkness at creation, embraced within His will.

This "negative" aspect is created, distinguished from the "nothing," which is not created. The negative is within God's will, an element of the world God creates. God does not make nothing; it is exposed as it opposes His will.

Shadows and night are not opposed or resistant to God's will; they are a relative element within God's good creation. The night reveals God's starry expanse and the moon as lesser lights. Darkness is not always difficult.

In Jesus, God deals with our creaturely positive and negative aspects. He deals with the antithesis within our humanity, simultaneously obedient and disobedient.

The negative aspects of creation point to the danger and corruption of nothingness—but they are different.

Light and dark were created good. They are the work of God's right and left hands. His love works throughout the spectrum of our human existence.

God knows what He is doing; who are we to complain? If we only praise God in the good moments, we miss the point of going with God throughout life.

In our selectivity, we often only look with favor on what pleases us to assess whether God cares for us, missing God's perspective for us.

Barth turns to Wolfgang Amadeus Mozart as a person, even as a theologian, who revealed the goodness of God's creation through his music. Mozart had a heart that found peace in the face of the world's tragedies and human reasoning.

Mozart saw the harmony of creation. He could see shadow that was not darkness, sadness that was not despair, trouble that was not a tragedy, and a lack in life that was not defeat. He saw the light shining brightly in the shades of darkness. He could hear the whole of creation embraced by this light.

Mozart heard the positive notes more strongly than the negative. The

The Inhospitable Chaos beyond the Shadows

negative was nuanced with the positive. He could listen harmoniously and not hear abstract thoughts separated from each other. This inclusiveness provided completeness to his music.

The music Mozart composed was not his own; it was that of creation as the harmonious praise of God. He had no program or agenda to promote. He was free of the need to be absorbed in self-expression.

Mozart drew from the voices of all creation, expressing the emotions of humans and the praise of creation. He was an ear that could hear the melodies of praise and providence and then mediate for other ears to hear.

Mozart lived to express God's good creation within the limits of human life. His music includes a "Yes" and a "No": oriented to God on one side and nothingness on the other.

Mozart gave order to the totality of creation for those with ears to hear, better than any science could present to us.

In our misunderstandings about providence and nothingness, we fail to recognize nothingness for what it is. We consider it a necessary part of existence. While being aware of the *negative* side of God's good creation, we are still unclear about the true adversary, the nothingness that corrupts us in our confusion.

Considering nothingness within the context of God's creation is dangerously easy. Nothingness becomes harmless and innocent. We come to consider deep, destructive sin as a temporary mistake.

Nothingness is present and active as sin, evil, death, and the devil. Because we are blinded, we may not see it where it occurs. It goes unnoticed, ignored, or forgotten.

The more we attempt to sanitize our world by leaving out sin and the devil, the less we see its danger. Confusion results as the Creator and nothingness are both turned into fantasy. The confusion becomes a masquerade that disregards the Creator.

Nothingness is a force that deceives; we may think we are listening to wisdom but end up following human common sense, which is self-serving folly, not recognizing God's voice.

Without desiring to do so, we serve nothingness because we accept it as normal. We have confused it with the negative element of creation.

Only by knowing Jesus can we recognize what contradicts His way of being in the world.

3. The Knowledge of Nothingness (pp. 302–349)

The source of all Christian knowledge comes from Jesus Christ.

In Jesus, we see the "Yes" of God's intentional work and the "No" for the sake of the "Yes."

Through Jesus, we learn about nothingness as an adversary distinct from God's creation. Humans cannot comprehend nothingness by themselves.

Nothingness is real but contradicts creation. It is the antithesis of God's work. It cannot be synthesized with God's good creation.

Humans fell under the influence of this alien power and could not find their way home.

> Mozart had a heart that found peace in the face of the world's tragedies and human reasoning.

The Creator became our kind of creature when He took on our flesh. He took it as an attack on Himself and delivered us.

Human acts in contention with God's grace reveal our sins. Sin is human refusal to live in freedom and gratitude. It is human arrogance to be one's own master.

We are sinners, victims, and servants of nothingness.

We cannot know nothingness by looking into ourselves. We only learn as we know Jesus and what He encounters and confronts by dying on the cross.

We cannot know nothingness through abstract ideas of sin. Only Jesus can tell us the truth about our sinfulness.

On our own, we figure we are primarily decent. We only know we are authentic sinners when told so by God. To understand nothingness, we must turn to the heart of the gospel.

We have rejected God's grace and His command. In our self-justification, we rupture our relationship with God and our neighbors.

The will of God that humans reject is His merciful, generous, and patient will. We refuse the goodness of God and go our own way.

God created us for fellowship. We run from His freedom and goodness. We sin against the law of God's unconditional grace. Jesus' law is not full of requirements.

God acts for humans enslaved to the rebellion of nothingness. He overcame that which resisted Him.

Jesus' judgment of sin reveals His grace. He pledges His faithfulness to prove His mercy is unconditional.

Sin is the concrete form of nothingness. Each act of human self-will opposes God, and we bear the responsibility for our actions. We surrender to the enemy's power, injuring and destroying our human nature.

Real suffering follows our rebellion in the form of evil and death. There is a real devil and hell.

The Inhospitable Chaos beyond the Shadows

Jesus opposed His enemy in the crucifixion. He suffered death for the forgiveness of the sins of humanity. He conquered death, the last enemy. His resurrection confirms that it is complete.

God's command does not call us to reach lofty standards but awakens whole-hearted gratitude for God's mercy, freeing us to do His loving will.

When evil is seen as the corruption of good, evil becomes mere human deficiency, not a force that needs to be dealt with by God.

Humans may be content with an ongoing process of removing imperfections. God becomes unnecessary or even unhelpful. Misunderstanding nothingness diminishes our relationship with God.

For Schleiermacher, knowledge of sin arises in self-consciousness. Because we have God-consciousness, we are open to sin-consciousness as our resistance to God. The freedom God gives us creates sin so that God becomes the source of sin. Barth rejects this.

Schleiermacher started his doctrine of nothingness from the standpoint of Jesus as One who has negated nothingness. But he quickly departed, not understanding the Jesus of the Bible, defaulting to focusing on human consciousness.

Schleiermacher's God is a doctor who prescribes medication for a patient with no intention of testing or taking it. Evil has no existence for his God; it is a human problem. It operates in our consciousness as opposed to His will. He is aloof and untouched.

Is sin a reality for God? Has He accomplished anything on the cross?

For Barth, when our consciousness of sin follows consciousness of grace, it awakens our need for redemption and the gratitude that it is already offered and completed.

"God's grace is mightier than sin, evil and death. They are together the enemy of whom it can be said: 'One word shall quickly fell him.'"[2]

For Schleiermacher, sin and grace are just two states of Christian consciousness. Sin became a state within the human and not about God. Grace became a resolve based on human consciousness, not a gift of God. His religious consciousness was not open to the Word of God and was limited to humans.

Philosophers Martin Heidegger and Jean-Paul Sartre are examples of modern thinkers whom Barth thinks we must consider when dealing with sin and nothingness.

---

2. *CD* 3.3, § 50, p. 332.

The predominant concept of Heidegger's work is "nothing as something that must be reckoned with." It is dynamic and active. It diminishes what "is so" in our lives into an attitude of dread.

For Sartre, the human starts from nothing and projects oneself into being something, a deliberate rising to become a project willed into being.

Sartre can only affirm existence that starts with the human. The human is "God," projected as a mythical phenomenon arising out of human ideas.

We must question the place of God in Heidegger and Sartre. Heidegger denies he is atheistic. He is an atheist in principle, but his teachings include the functions of deity in a different dimension. Sartre considers humanity from a hidden viewpoint of the being of the divine, an imitation of God.

In a sense, for both Heidegger and Sartre, God is not dead. They each provide a substitute, and God is in the shadows: God is on a retired list. Yet the biblical account of God is considered in both their proposed mythologies.

The God we are discussing is not the God Heidegger and Sartre rejected. They are concerned with nothingness understood from vastly different portrayals from what we consider nothingness before God. Yet they cannot escape the problem of God.

All those we have been discussing are children of their age, building from an arbitrary human standpoint. Confidence in the thinking self dominates the presuppositions of their systems.

4. The Reality of Nothingness (pp. 349–68)

How may we speak of nothingness being "real"?

1. Nothingness exists.
   - We cannot argue that nothingness is nothing.
   - Besides God and His creation, nothingness is a third way of being.
   - It is a problem God strives against with His whole being and overcomes.
2. Conversely, nothingness cannot be equated with what is not God.
   - The "shadow side" of reality is all within God's will.
   - The nothingness is outside His will.
   - We share a border with nothingness but stand within God's care.
   - When creatures cross that border, nothingness invades the creaturely world.
   - We cannot affirm that nothingness is necessary to God or the creature, nor can we say it is derived from their being.

The Inhospitable Chaos beyond the Shadows   231

3. Nothingness cannot be known by insight into what is accessible to the human.
   - Nothingness stands before God as His adversary but cannot be discovered with human capacities.
   - While nothingness is an objective reality humans encounter, it is not an object of our natural knowledge.
   - Nothingness misrepresents God and His work and its own nature; it wants to be seen as aligned with God.
4. In the Bible, God's election by grace displays the context for the nothingness He rejects.
   - God is holy and therefore opposes as He separates from what He has not willed.
   - In the Bible, God elects; therefore, He rejects what He does not will.
   - God is Lord with His right hand and Lord with His left, holding nothingness under His control with wrath and judgment.
   - Nothingness is an impossible possibility, an intrinsic contradiction in its own paradoxical, improper way.
   - The chaos of nothingness is not part of the separation within God's days of creation.
   - The sin of humans in Genesis 3 is what God did not and does not will. It confirms the existence of nothingness. Humanity has fallen victim to chaos.
5. God stands against the threat of chaos and acts to negate and reject it. Nothingness is unique in its particular nature.
   - Nothingness is evil. God wills what is positive in His creation and preservation in the history of His covenant.
   - It lacks God's grace. Therefore, He rejects it out of jealousy for what He loves.
   - It is chaos. It is what God passed over and set aside.
   - It is the attempt to defraud God of His honor to be gracious. It also robs the creature of its salvation, which is living by the grace of God.
   - It is disorder, calling out the refocusing of God's holy work.
6. God's concern with nothingness is one of conquest and removal and is His alone.
   - The creature is powerless against the threat of nothingness.
   - In the form of sin, the creature opened the way for nothingness by thinking and acting contrary to God's grace.

Church Dogmatics 3.3

- Human alignment with nothingness resulted in guilt, death, evil, suffering, disturbance, destruction, and grief.
- Even as victims of sin, we still belong to God; He does not abandon us.
- We cannot contend with sin alone but are invited as co-contenders to join His cause.
- God's power can empower humans to resist this adversary. This takes place in Jesus.
- When humans sinned, it was not because of a built-in capacity or freedom.
- The humans made the impossibly self-willed choice to become enslaved, trying to be like God instead of accepting His grace.
- To say God condescends is to say He comes down to surround us and intervenes on our behalf. He does not merely look down on us from above.
- It is a dangerous heresy to say that God is unaffected by nothingness. This belief is much like the error in thinking that humans could take on nothingness independently.

7. Nothingness does not endure.

- Nothingness cannot last because it was not created or sustained by God.
- The triumph of God's love is boundless, and He will bring an end to His enemy.
- God only allows His enemy to be for a while; it cannot be an eternal enemy.
- "He does this by giving Himself in His Son, by Himself becoming a creature and as such taking on Himself the sin, guilt, and misery of the creature."[3]

Nothingness has defaced the hospitable space of God.

The only serious fact we must consider is that Jesus is victor.

The problem of nothingness arises concerning the fatherly care of the Creator over His creation.

God acts for humans enslaved to the rebellion of nothingness.

We must engage how the world operates as a history under the rule of God. As a shadow cast from the chaos, it calls into question the goodness of God and His creatures: this is called *theodicy*.

---

3. *CD* 3.3, § 50, p. 362.

The Inhospitable Chaos beyond the Shadows

Barth outlines the many problems of theodicy in the classical presentation as follows:

- God is good but not powerful enough to stand against evil.
- God is powerful but not good concerning evil.
- Humans are good but imperfect against evil.
- Humans are perfect but limited in resisting evil.
- The God-human relationship is orderly but not good.
- The God-human relationship is good but disorderly.

We can only think these ways from an abstract and detached point of view.

We must look from the relationship of God's rule in history with His creatures in their history under the covenant of grace and salvation. Thus, we begin with concrete history and not abstractions.

1. Nothingness must be reviewed looking back. It is interpreted based on what has been judged. The hostility of nothingness is displayed in human history by God's defeat of it.
2. All that remains of nothingness is a shadow of corruptive power that Jesus Christ has destroyed. It took place in Him, once and for all.
3. Nothingness exists now only in the hand of God, inescapably in His divine grip.
4. Nothingness is forced to serve God, honoring the Son in the proclamation of His triumph over evil. Nothingness reminds us of what used to be, that the one who had the keys of prison is defeated by Him to whom we flee, who now sets us free.

Even nothingness is one of the things that God can now work together for those who love Him.

COMMENTARY:

- Nothingness is real, but we are not to be frightened by its presence.
- When God creates, His positive will is at work. Even with our failure, we are in the space God sustains.
- When God creates, there are things God does not will. He does not will death, yet it is there as an enemy to His life.
- Sin and evil are not synonymous with nothingness but result from nothingness.

- In the Lord's Prayer, we ask that we be delivered from evil.
- Nothingness has power and is also a defeated power. The cross always stands between nothingness and us as the triumph of God over it.

CONCLUSION FOR THE CHURCH: The Church needs hope grounded in Jesus Christ. Too often, hope is in new programs, affiliation with political powers, or some other replacement for God's freedom, instead of dealing with spiritual darkness.

We see evil and death. We wish for hope, seeking human answers to the violence and fracturing in the world. Barth wants the Church to see the evil in the world and not look for its causes in human failure or God's neglect. He wants an honest acknowledgment that God has made a good world (including humans) and that there is still a world of chaos beyond human control that God addresses.

We must acknowledge that there are forces in the world God must deal with, and only He can. We cannot throw our hands up in despair; we look to Him as the victor He already is. The Church is not to confront evil head-on; we must turn to the One who has conquered death, forgives and reconciles all divisions, and will bring an end to all corrupt authorities.

Evil exists in our neighborhoods. We function best as the Church when we listen to God and our neighbors, joining the love of God as light in the darkness. Our questions of concern bring light to the worry and pain that hide in the nothingness of fearful and traumatized souls.

Hospitality with God diminishes the darkness of inhospitality in the streets. As a community following the Spirit, we come alongside others as the Spirit has come alongside us, not submitting to the threat of nothingness. Light takes the form of active love, shining into each home to extinguish nothingness, in its states of meaninglessness, with God's gracious embrace.

INSIGHT FOR PASTORS: God does not intend sin nor see it as the outworking of His will. A pastor cannot blame God or deny evil's pervasive presence. The pastor's position is to point to One who has taken on human flesh on the cross. He deals with the full force of what evil brings, like a tsunami of destruction in many lives. God's love reveals the neediness of our situations.

Pastors are pressed to explain human experiences of tragedy. How could God allow pain and suffering in the world? Barth knew loss as well. He lost his son Matthias in a mountain climbing accident when he was just twenty

The Inhospitable Chaos beyond the Shadows

years old.[4] The "now of loss" lives for him on the border of "then in eternity," when now and then are united.

Barth affirms that Jesus taught us about life and death and His victory over that which we fear. Because of the resurrection, evil is defeated. Barth will not give space to nothingness in the face of his loss and pain. The voice of Jesus accompanies the tears and calls us to find rest in Him.

Nothingness is not the final word. The death and resurrection of Jesus bring words of hope and final consolation in the face of a fallen world. God has not abandoned us. This acknowledgment will not stop the pain but allows us to give to God what is out of our control.

Pain and suffering are a given in life, as is death. But the first word is the life of love from God. The last word will be that final embrace of love. In between, God goes with us; pastors are reminders when nothingness becomes forgetfulness of God's faithfulness.

INSIGHT FOR THEOLOGIANS: Dealing with evil often begs us to look at the tragedies of life, like showing up on the scene of a horrific crash. Tragedy is everywhere. Barth will not let us begin here. Theological thinking must persist in looking at the realistic way God cares for His world.

A fascination with the battles of good and evil fills our screens and minds. Considering what is wrong cannot begin to explain evil. We must start by asking what God has done to confront what He considers evil. Only in that way can theology guide our understanding.

Nothingness can seem abstract, as can any relationship, especially broken ones. The younger generations see broken marriages and conclude marriage is pain or a prison. Experience has told them it is nothing to embrace. If we select what threatens us and let it drive our decisions, we will be controlled by fear, and the threat of nothingness will haunt us.

Barth does not want nothingness, sin, or evil to be a set of abstract ideas. They are the concrete reality, force, threat, and invasion inconsistent with and opposed to God's loving will.

If we make our problems appear to be God's chief concern, we will also accuse Him of not doing enough about them. God has dealt with nothingness and all the forces of deep darkness and chaos.

---

4. Eberhard Busch, *Karl Barth: His Life from Letters and Autobiographical Texts*, trans. John Bowden (Eugene, OR: Wipf & Stock, 2005), 311.

? CLARIFYING QUESTIONS: Does your sense of evil make you question whether God is at work? Do you look at evil and try to understand God, *or* do you look at God to see His relationship to evil? Does it matter that God has already defeated death and pain on the cross and triumphed in His resurrection?

CHAPTER 17

GUESS WHO'S COMING TO DINNER

§ 51. The Kingdom of Heaven, the Ambassadors of God, and Their Opponents

FOCUS STATEMENT: Barth now discusses how heaven and a few uninvited guests come near. Heaven, angels, and demons show up in paragraph 51. God, the host, invites a host of angels, stirring our awareness that God is present and providing.

The table is set for feasting. In the shadows beyond the table are unseen enemies, constrained and made powerless. They are liars who seek to take and never give. But the focus is on heaven's hospitable personal presence.

This paragraph discusses God's nearness, how he comes close to His servants. The room fills with grateful music, resonating with angelic voices. All is fashioned for festivity, circling around Jesus.

Barth debunks misconceptions of angels, including all those paintings on ceilings across Europe. The proper place of angels is at the table of God serving us. They are sent to ensure all is well and welcoming for our experience of heaven here and now.

INTRODUCTION: Heaven is off the map for most people, far away or coming later. This section draws back the curtain to help us recognize that heaven is near. Heaven and earth are one creation.

This section of *CD* 3.3 explores God's creation of the heavens and the earth. The angels are part of that creative work. They are mouthpieces and ambassadors to speak to humans.

Barth insists we move past all the cultural projections about angels and get to what the Bible says. Heaven and earth have a paired nature. Angels are part of God's provision, acting out providence's meaning.

Angels come announcing and accompanying us as God's representatives. They never show up in place of God; they facilitate His presence and invite us in.

Some beings, similar to angels but from the dark side, oppose God. Our study of nothingness allows us to see these are agents of falsehood. They try to corrupt and invade the earth; their power lives in their lies, mimicking heaven but void of its provision. They are powerless unless we buy into their deceptions.

For many, heaven is insignificant. We are so earthly minded we seldom think of heaven. Barth brings heaven to earth as the kingdom of God, fulfilling the will of God here and now.

CONTEXT: *CD* 3.3
Pages in Paragraph: 163 pages (pp. 369–531)

Subsections
1. The Limits of Angelology
2. The Kingdom of Heaven
3. The Ambassadors of God and Their Opponents

TEXT: § 51. The Kingdom of Heaven, the Ambassadors of God and Their Opponents

OPENING SUMMARY: God's action in Jesus Christ, and therefore His lordship over His creature, is called the "kingdom of heaven" because first and supremely it claims for itself the upper world. From this God selects and sends His messengers, the angels, who precede the revelation and doing of His will on earth as objective and authentic witnesses, who accompany it as faithful servants of God and man, and who victoriously ward off the opposing forms and forces of chaos.[1]

SUMMARY:
1. The Limits of Angelology (pp. 369–418)
Barth is concerned about treading into this territory. The footprints of those who have gone before caution him.

We are susceptible to being led away by the speculative mythology of the ancients or the demythologizing sterilization of modern thinkers.

We can only have imperfect knowledge of the realm of angels. Angels

---

1. *CD* 3.3, § 51, p. 369.

are not independent subjects like God and humans. God alone can give us insight into their service.

Angels are sent from the kingdom of heaven. Barth makes five points about angels:

1. We must *stick to what the Bible says* about angels. God includes angels in the biblical witness of revelation.
2. Our task is to listen to the Bible, *not delete* what we do not understand. We must ponder how angels fulfill the purposes of God.
3. We must *explore the doctrine of angels theologically*, not with general ideas about angels.

   Thomas Aquinas was famous for discussing angels. Barth found him inadequate for theological work. His scholastic system is a giant ladder to the heavens.
4. We must focus on angels through the Bible and *think out of its light from heaven*. We must resist all other foundations, aims, and interests that deflect our attention.
5. We need *not be anxious* if we remember to search the Scriptures regarding angels. We are best at theology when we avoid "probable arguments."

The Bible makes available the history of God's covenant of grace. The study of angels must be considered within this context.

The angels stand in a once-for-all relationship to the once-for-all event of God's coming.

Many theologians would like to give a "shrug of the shoulders" to angels, looking for explanations only in natural causes. The existence of angels is questioned and then dismissed. Barth's long list of examples displays this discounting.

Modern theologians lost their respect for the Bible and could not accept all it revealed, including angels.

Theologians made angels pre-Christian, buried in the Old Testament, a shadow too far for their version of Christian thinking, attuned to the sensibilities of the modern mind.

2. The Kingdom of Heaven (pp. 418–76)

The biblical witness includes the dynamic relation of the Creator and His creatures and thus the dynamic of heaven and earth. We understand the place of angels within this dynamic.

To speak of God is to point to heaven. To consider humanity is to point to earth. If we are to speak theologically, we must talk about heaven and earth while prioritizing heaven and acknowledging that they are not equal.

Angels are best understood in the relationship between God and humanity. If we abstract their nature, turning it into an imagined concept, we will go down blind alleys or shrug our shoulders and make them insignificant.

To say *heaven* is not the same as saying *God*. God is the Creator; heaven is created.

Angels come from heaven, but they are not divine. They are created.

Heaven and earth are under God's care and rule, but the world is under heaven. Heaven always has precedence over earth. They are only equal as God's creation.

> Angels are not independent subjects like God and humans. God alone can give us insight into their service.

Neither heaven nor earth can contain God. Heaven and earth will pass away, but God will not.

The heavens are created, so angels, like humans, are vulnerable to rebellion. They are not to be worshiped. Angels are designed for service and will never be released from this service.

Heaven and earth are the home created by God in which we become His children.

What takes place between God and ourselves is an event in our relationship that is both heavenly and earthly. God initiates, and we participate.

Heaven exists as a counterpart to the earth. What takes place in the sphere of our existence occurs in participation with this other sphere, heaven. What happens in our sphere is open to this other.

Earth is the sphere where we live. It is visible and comprehendible. We have access to what is around us.

Heaven is beyond a boundary marked off from humans. It is invisible to us and, therefore, incomprehensible. It is beyond the limits of human capacity.

Human pride reaches to extreme heights, hoping to storm heaven, only to fall. The people of the Bible are not intent on teaching us the nature of heaven.

The Creator enters the world as its King, who comes in person to be its ruler, helper, and deliverer.

Heaven and earth stand within the constant movement of God's

Guess Who's Coming to Dinner

covenant relationship. "God speaks and is heard; He reveals Himself and is known; He comes and is present; He goes and comes again; He acts and effects; He gives and takes; He hastens and waits."[2]

The loving inner life of God within the Trinity is the basis of God's external working that expresses His love. As His honor dwells in the world, it becomes the theater of His glory.

Heaven is where God acts for His children, to be with and for them. God is not at work above the world but in the world. He lives in dialogue with the world, between heaven and earth.

God has a relationship with humans characterized by the name *Father*, which reveals the essence of heaven.

The *kingdom of heaven* describes the kingdom of God when it enters the circle of human vision. In its coming, the benefits of God pour out on humanity in gifts, insight, and help. He can also warn and correct from heaven. But the most significant gift is the Word, addressed to us as the Lord of His covenant.

Heaven is a place. God is at the same time above the world and present within it. His concrete covenant history ventures out to us from this place.

We begin the Lord's prayer, "Our Father, who art in heaven."

Heaven is God's glorious habitation, the place of the throne of God. It is also the Father's house of love that Jesus prepares for our arrival.

Jesus has come from heaven and is now in heaven since His return. Heaven is where Jesus is seated and exercises power.

Jesus is not a privileged spectator of divine activity. Jesus is the active agent of God who pours out His Spirit.

The Son works, following the Father at work. They cannot function independently of each other. There can be no conflict between them.

The *Father* is the One true God who exists in heaven.

The *Son* is the same faithful God who became human to live on earth. He was born, suffered, and died.

Jesus rose from the dead and returned to heaven, bringing humanity and fulfilling God's loving intention.

By His *Holy Spirit*, God is present on earth through His Word. God is not remote.

Heaven is beyond our observation as a mystery. We must not say

---

2. *CD* 3.3, § 51, p. 429.

too much with misplaced speculation nor too little with inappropriate skepticism.

The theme of Christian proclamation is that God has come to earth as the kingdom of heaven, seen and known.

God's coming from heaven extends toward His creation, restoring its brokenness to harmony, reintegrating life together.

God is revealed in the Old Testament as the Lord of hosts. Heaven is not empty; it is filled with a multitude of angels to serve God's purposes.

The hosts of the heavens can include the sun, moon, and stars. These also serve God and humanity and are not to be worshiped.

We know these hosts are from God and interrelated in His work. We know little of their separate nature, relations, or distinctiveness.

In relation to Jesus, angels are to the heavenly sphere what apostles are to the human sphere. Each uniquely functions within God's service.

Angels watch, speak, guard, and act on the frontiers between us and them. They guard Paradise and speak words of praise in God's holy presence. They may be called *cherubim* and *seraphim* according to their tasks. They may have names like Gabriel and Michael.

Angels not only show up as a chorus; they come personally to meet with humans like Mary (Luke 1:26–38).

Angels cannot do independent work. They cannot create, reconcile, or redeem the world.

If angels act independently, they deny their nature as servants of God and become demons. There is a kingdom of falsehood and darkness.

Angels are created by God, coming and going as they maintain the freedom of God. If they turned to serve themselves, it would lead to wild anarchy.

The proper service of angels is witness, an appropriate response to God's existence, address, and actions.

Praise of God begins in heaven. God rules. Angels witness to Him. All creation joins in response.

Revelation 4 and 5 allow us to look through heaven's open door. We see the throne of God surrounded by a heavenly gathering. In the middle is the Lamb, given a book that reveals world history.

Those gathered around the throne are dressed in white as they stand before the multicolored radiance of God. It is God, not the creatures, who make these gathered around the throne to be bright. All those gathered around Him represent the relationship of God to His creation, as heaven with earth.

This scene is not a special moment; it is the everyday life of responsive living. It is the liturgy of loving correspondence to the God of grace. It is a liturgy employed in regular events in the natural world.

The cosmos is invited to join this song of heaven. All heaven blesses Him who has come and will come again.

The book, the Lion of Judah, and the victory of grace resound from heaven, impacting the creaturely realm. The Lion of God becomes the Lamb for humanity.

> The theme of Christian proclamation is that God has come to earth as the kingdom of heaven, seen and known.

3. The Ambassadors of God and Their Opponents (pp. 477–531)

The kingdom of heaven comes to earth as the kingdom of God.

When we pray for God's will to be done on earth, we request an echo of a heavenly happening.

There are not two happenings, one in heaven and another on earth. The hospitality of heaven makes waves of grace that encounter and embrace God's creatures.

Where God is, His heavenly angels are present, acting within the purposes of God. They mirror heaven to us, opening the mystery of God.

We cannot speculate about the experience of angels apart from their service to God.

What does God intend through the operation of His angels on earth?

God makes His presence known in a form appropriate to God, able to represent Him so that He is available and personally accessible.

God mediates Himself through these servants. They never act independently. God Himself speaks; in this way, He is gracious and patient on earth.

Angels belong to God; He has created them as faithfully His.

God takes angels with Him as companions on His way to earth. They share in His speech and actions. They only come to the world with God. They have no history of their own.

When angels appear, God Himself is at work speaking and acting. If an angel spoke independently, it would be lying, a demon impersonating heaven for its benefit.

Demons entice humans away from God and to themselves. Such is the character of all those masquerading as God's servants, seeking their own glory, attention, and adoration.

Heavenly beings come to our sphere of existence from heaven. These angels continually see the face of the Father of Jesus, which we cannot see. Thus, they speak with a pure witness.

"When an angel says anything, although he is not God, it is God who speaks. When an angel acts, for all the infinite difference between God and heaven or God and the angel, it is God who acts."[3]

In their eloquent quietness, angels point away from themselves to God, so heaven comes to earth, and God's hospitable presence opens so that He is revered and loved as God.

Angels cannot replace or contribute to the work of the Word of God or His Holy Spirit. Angels can only direct us to the source and sustaining presence that gives life.

Angels have no cause of their own. Their reciprocal relationships all conform to God's relational being with no independence. Therefore, their lives and being are an eternal, harmonious hymn of praise.

Barth discusses the Angel of the Lord as a figure we must understand. The early Church supposed this to be a preincarnate Logos of the Godhead. Some have seen him as a replacement for the presence of God. He becomes an angelic mediator of God, prefiguring Jesus and the Holy Spirit.

Barth says that the angel of the Lord is related to Jesus and the Holy Spirit but should not be identified as the same being, a prefigurement, or a temporary substitute. The angel of the Lord is a witness to God but is not God Himself.

Like the covenant, the angel of the Lord points to the living Word of God. The angel of the Lord assists God, announcing, restoring, protecting, and advocating for God's people.

Angels have an advantage in knowing what God says with firsthand knowledge. They share God's address.

Angels are temporary and cannot replace the prophets, apostles, or community. They work with God to ignite humanity with grace throughout the earth.

Angels form the hospitable heavenly context for the outbreathing of the human witnesses proclaiming the Word of God on earth. When we are in God's presence, we are also in the presence of angels.

Heaven is concurrently watching earth so that joy fills the angels when someone turns to God.

The light of the angels is like a candle outshone in the brightness of the noonday sun. Or we may say they fade like stars with the rising sun. Like John the Baptist, they must decrease as Jesus increases.

---

3. *CD* 3.3, § 51, p. 484.

We honor angels by thinking of Jesus. We dishonor them if we give them independent functions from Jesus' work.

Angels are evangelical. They announce the good news. God's grace radiates through the angels over the dark earth, revealing a baby is born. Heaven has come to earth in a child, inviting us to find the child who has come.

Angels do not act in the event of God's arrival; they point, announcing to the human race, calling attention to God in the flesh. They start with humble and ordinary folk.

Angels help us recognize that God has entered the world, stand with appropriate wonder, and enter a relationship with Him.

> The hospitality of heaven makes waves of grace that encounter and embrace God's creatures.

Angels also announce the risen Jesus to the women who come to honor His broken body. They are the first witnesses of the resurrection.

The angels, women, and disciples are all witnesses directing our attention to the living presence of the Resurrected One.

After Jesus ascends, the women and disciples are given the kingdom of heaven—God's Spirit empowers them.

God, as Holy Spirit, not the angels, moves the story along as a community guided by His presence.

Angel is a fitting term in that it describes their function. Their function is to witness uniquely in the service of God. We cannot discuss their nature, number, or ordering in heaven.

Is the ministry of angels only relevant within and limited to biblical history, or do they work in our current history?

If angels belong to the history of the covenant, they are present in all other events before and after God's coming in Jesus. Our history has its meaning and center in Him.

By His Spirit, we share the history of the covenant as house-fellows, connected with all our companions.

Wherever God is at work, the kingdom of heaven is at work, including His angels. They show us the mystery of God, meaning God Himself.

National angels were a concept used by the Third Reich (Nazism).[4] But nations and states are ordered by humans, usually protecting national interests. True angels support the interests of God.

---

4. Barth opposed Hitler and the Nazi Party's various ways of manipulating the Bible, theology, and the church.

Some traditions portray guardian angels, each assigned to one person. However, Jesus stands with us, mediated by angels; angels do not replace Him. Why not affirm that all the angels watch over us? That is more likely the case.

We can only consider demons in contrast to angels with a glance. We stand on the edge of an open crater, imagining what might have been. It is not good to look too long at demons or too seriously. Demons want us to find them interesting and give them our attention.

Demons belong to a different sphere than angels. Heaven and hell have nothing in common. They have no common root or reality. Unlike black and white chess pieces, they cannot return to the same box at the end of the game.

There are no good and bad angels. Demons belong to a different category. They exist as an antithetical contradiction.

Nonsense is not comparable to sensibility; it is what stands in contradiction to it. Sense overcomes nonsense. There is conflict between them. This illustrative contrast is the only way to understand the devil and demons.

Demons are opponents of heaven and God's kingdom on earth. They are related in contradiction as chaos and creation, evil and good, death and life, impenetrable darkness and revealed light, and destruction and redemption.

In the light of Christian truth, demons are the lie that is the basis of all other lies. How can one relate to a lie except as unreal, not giving it merit?

The origin and nature of the devil and demons are found in nothingness. All we said of nothingness is true of demons.

The Bible understands demons and the devil as alien elements. They are a kingdom seizing power. God treats them as invading enemies to be stopped.

Understandably, one might want to compare the kingdom of heaven and demons, but we cannot. One is building for good; the other sabotages all that is good. They are not only dissimilar but opposites.

Nothingness is a falsehood, a lie based on what is real. It cannot build; it can only malign and destroy. It appears similar but is only a façade. It belongs neither to heaven nor earth.

Nothingness lies when it:

- presents itself as similar to the kingdom of God,
- pretends to belong to this world created by God,
- wants to rule alongside God,

Guess Who's Coming to Dinner

- wants to be a fellow ruler with humans,
- feigns that it is for God and humans,
- assumes form and power for its destructive purposes,
- moves with the intent to invade and assault humanity,
- represents itself as a kingdom with rulers and forms of government,
- opposes the kingdom of God,
- lines up its messengers, demons, and the devil as a team as opposed to God and His angels with similar appearance and activity,
- pretends that it, too, comes from heaven so that its will might be done in place of the will of God, and
- trivializes and hides, concealing itself with optimism for being allowed to be present to declare and maintain its power.

Nothingness represents itself with appearances. We need not be afraid in the face of it.

Nothingness rejoices when it notices it is not detected. It hides under a cover, beautifully concealed, while humans take on what they consider more significant threats:

- morality and prejudice
- medicine and its future
- psychology and mental health
- aesthetics and the place of beauty
- progressive politics and conservative politics
- new philosophies to tickle the interest

All these have their place but serve nothingness when they distract us from God and make us miss the unraveling consequences of pursuing what God has not chosen.

The other attempted triumph of nothingness is in presenting itself as though it is not a lie. It appears as though it could contribute to our lives, calling humans to exercise their rights against God's lordship. We are called to admire our independence.

To achieve our autonomous status and power, we unthinkingly integrate the liberated human "freedom" to side with the devil in opposition to God.

We love ongoing cycles of "enlightenment," ridding ourselves of old values as outdated myths.

We hand the future to the priests of medicine, morality, politics, media, philosophy, and even religion. All these leaders claim to be true liberators.

But they keep the dominion of nothingness intact as everyone does what is right in their own eyes.

We cannot ignore demons. They will deceive us with their concealed agendas. We must call them out. He has dealt with them. We hand them back to Him.

Like the kingdom of God, the demonic is an invisible kingdom.

It imitates creation, redemption, providence, and authority. It plays with law and gospel and false forms of grace and judgment. With falsehood it mimics all God does.

We cannot deny that nothingness is successful in its plot to deceive and disrupt. Everywhere we look, we find that this is the case. We see the dis-ease deep in our hearts.

We find our relationships with others in disarray or broken as we hide in self-protection. Fracturing occurs in our individual lives as well as our attempts at mutuality.

Conflict is present in culture, science, art, technology, and politics. It disintegrates classes, peoples, and nations.

The life of the Church and theologians is not immune from the play of pretenders who claim authority. Like the tentacles of an octopus, demons are at work—but angels are also present and at work for God's good.

The demons' only real power is falsehood, the ability to tell lies. Their imitations and mimicking of God fool many. They are powerful with their lies; we may dispel them by pointing to the truth. Many people are imprisoned by the lies that bind them.

The power of God's love and truth sets people free. The truth of God unmasks the forces of falsehood. A lie exposed becomes powerless.

God calls us free children, released from the puppet wires that control us and from the slavery that imprisons us.

Released from the lies, we may find joy. We laugh at the limitations fabricated by lies that steal our lives. The lie loses its last breath as we breathe in the grace of God.

The kingdom of Satan is unmasked and disarmed. Truth has triumphed over their falsehood. Jesus has triumphed over demons. In the face of the cross, demons have nothing to declare but defeat, and they lie about that as well.

The power of God's love and truth sets people free. The truth of God unmasks the forces of falsehood.

Barth does not affirm any battle in heaven that prefigures the fall of humanity. We only know of the actual fight Jesus won on the cross and in His resurrection.

The devil was never an angel who became a fallen angel, as some assert.

Every good and true gift comes from the Father of Lights, including the Light of the World, who dispels the darkness and accompanies humanity to share His light and life.

COMMENTARY:

- God's providence includes the heavens, created for God's habitation and mission.
- Angels are not just cute cherubs or fiery seraphim; they are personal messengers who work for God.
- Angels are still at work, bringing heaven to earth as God's concern for human needs.
- Heaven is home for God and the angels; it is invisible to us but is where God's will is done and from which God speaks to humans.
- Angels are not independent like humans; they exist to do God's will and serve His mission.
- Demons exist, entirely devoted to a life of falsehood. They imitate what God does without substance.
- When humans live with and propagate lies, they cooperate with the demonic, even in the Church.

CONCLUSION FOR THE CHURCH: Heaven is mainly off the Church's radar except at funerals. But heaven is where God dwells today. We need to be aware of what it means to be citizens of heaven. We are not just getting our visas ready. It is our citizenship, even while we are abroad on earth.

Defaulting to the seen is seductive. We easily miss the mystery Jesus reveals about reality. Earth is for now, so we unconsciously think heaven is for later. But heaven always reaches out to us, attuning us to the love of God.

The Church is alive to the work of God when it believes God and His angels are still at work—we are not alone. Jesus is in heaven as ascended Lord, not far away; He is with us, bringing the kingdom of heaven into our midst by His Spirit and angels.

The demons in our world come as lies in the Church and all the world's systems. We must take Jesus seriously enough to hear Him speak the truth and expose the lies that divide and destroy the Church and our neighborhoods. The guiding question is whether our compelling motivation is protecting something (fear-based) or loving. When love rules, we live on earth as it is in heaven.

INSIGHT FOR PASTORS: We pray, "Thy kingdom come." How can we help people live the Lord's prayer? First, we must learn to live in the presence of the Father. He is in heaven, which means, here in His present, living relationship. Second, we must learn how His will in heaven informs our living on earth as He speaks to us. Prayer is our personal connection with heaven, so we can listen. Angels help us get the message as they serve God, allowing us to hear heaven.

Prayer can awaken congregations to know the accompanying God.

Charles Dickens was aware of the sphere of the spirit. Scrooge was visited by spirits (who were not quite angels), and he saw the unseen world where angels care for the needs of humanity. Maybe this section allows pastors to contemplate the unseen, readied to partner with the angels in serving unrecognized needs.

Demons are also worth taking seriously. The demonic invades our families and neighborhoods through deceit and division. If we hide behind masks of propriety or survival, we will not see the kingdom coming. We will live in prisons of fear. Demons live in the whispers that build beautifully destructive walls of self-protection.

Heaven and hell may be closer than we think. Barth wants pastors to become attentive to angels' work in keeping us focused on Jesus. Hell might be whatever distracts us from Jesus and lets other priorities reign as our lives lose direction.

 INSIGHT FOR THEOLOGIANS: As theologians, we easily gravitate to the big topics: God, salvation, the Church, missions, and so on. But Barth wants us to consider heaven, angels, and demons that may appear optional.

Heaven is not just where dead people go after they die. It is where God dwells, from which He comes as Son and Spirit, and where He brings us home. Heaven refers to the domain of God and His servants.

We glimpse the seduction that lures theologians to explore what God has not created. Demons, for theologians, appear as roads taken to find new insight for humans but depart from God. Science, art, healthcare, politics, and even economics can echo the concerns of heaven.

It is easy to quit listening to God and seek what makes sense to human sensibilities. These become nonsense. They arise to mimic God's work but hand control to humans. They serve human powers and interests. They do not build community or serve humanity. They make signposts for demonic theology and miss the God who is with us.

? CLARIFYING QUESTIONS: Does your theology of heaven focus mainly on what happens after death as a mystery? *Or* is heaven as close as the air you breathe, filled with angels who are invisibly there, bringing your attentiveness to Jesus?

VOLUME SUMMARY: In *CD* 3.3, we have seen that God is the ultimate event patron. He provides all that is necessary, acts as guardian and guide, and supports the creative activities of humanity. The event of God's history provides what is necessary for humanity to thrive. Providence involves providing and watching over His human guests in His provisional space. Creation has a caretaker who is always present.

PART 5

CHURCH DOGMATICS 3.4

Behaving Like Love Matters

CHURCH DOGMATICS, CHAPTER 12

"The Command of God the Creator"

CHAPTER 18

FOLLOWING LOVE'S FORTE ADVENTURE

§ 52. Ethics as a Task of the Doctrine of Creation

FOCUS STATEMENT: God has acted in creating us and invites our human response to our Creator. Consider Jesus, who has already answered God's call for us and is now with us.

Humans love to argue about right and wrong actions. Unfortunately, they are arbitrary, based on different human values. Some work from grand ideals like peace and love; some want to protect themselves to survive. Some think of ethics as a mind game, and others as a set of rules. These are adventures in human control.

In § 52, Barth explores ethics from the impact of being in the presence of the compelling Creator. "Special" ethics will explore human life in response. Jesus leads the way with undeniable love.

"General" philosophical ethics works like a fence, with a system of rules that litters our emotional and behavioral landscape. "Keep Out" or "House Rules" signs exist for property or our private lives. Rule breaking implies getting in trouble. This approach is impersonal, generally creating a climate of forced obedience for some or rebellion for others. Rules and regulations don't care about persons. They make for faceless and unfriendly spaces.

For Barth, the Creator is transforming us to wholeness as personal beings. His presence in Jesus stands in for us, including us in His renewing, loving life. This personal epicenter shapes what Barth calls special ethics, anticipating our actions in each specific setting as a response to His presence. This is the dynamic ethics of life together with the ever-present God.

INTRODUCTION: Having studied the work of God the Creator (*CD* 3.1), specifically His creature (*CD* 3.2), and God's accompanying of His creation

258   *Church Dogmatics* 3.4

(*CD* 3.3), we now turn to how we behave in response to the Creator in daily life (*CD* 3.4).

Barth resists all attempts at rules and regulations that depart from God speaking to us. Ethics is about being faithful to God rather than to any moral theory or system.

Chapter 12 of the *CD* is "The Command of God the Creator." Paragraph 52 introduces and clarifies what ethics will and will not pursue. Barth discusses life practically lived in response to God and all He creates. The following paragraphs (§ 53–56) in *CD* 3.4 will engage domains where we practically articulate ethics in action, echoing from our God-relation, sharing life in its many spheres.

Special ethics attends to particular activities in daily life, not general theories. The Spirit makes us free in and with Jesus.

▊▊▊ CONTEXT: *CD* 3.4
Pages in Paragraph: 44 pages (pp. 3–46)

Subsections
    1. The Problem of Special Ethics
    2. God the Creator as Commander

📖 TEXT: § 52. Ethics as a Task of the Doctrine of Creation

✠ OPENING SUMMARY: The task of special ethics in the context of the doctrine of creation is to show to what extent the one command of the one God who is gracious to man in Jesus Christ is also the command of his Creator and therefore already the sanctification of the creaturely action and abstention of man.[1]

✠ SUMMARY:
1. The Problem of Special Ethics (pp. 3–31)

Christian proclamation points to Jesus and the covenant between God and humanity. This engagement compels us to discuss how human actions are appropriate in response.

God's Word informs theological ethics.

---

1. *CD* 3.4, § 52, p. 3.

Following Love's Forte Adventure

Because God is good, His Word to humanity is good.

Goodness can only be measured in relation to Jesus Christ.

His command expressed is good.

Human action is good as humans listen and obey the Word of God.

Ethics cannot merely look back at what humans have done. We must see ourselves in light of God's actions.

"General" theological ethics focus on the claim, decision, and judgment of God, as seen in *CD* 2.2.

"Special" theological ethics investigates how humans act in light of God's command.

Special ethics deals with concrete situations. Humans daily choose what kind of person they will be.

In human experience, our intentions are at work in every act, particularly in deciding to pursue or abstain from obeying God's command.

Special ethics is not tied to biblical texts with universally binding directions. Those rule-bound traditions developed in Western Christianity, claiming universal validity and morphing into a human legal code separated from God.

In this mistaken view:

1. Special ethics becomes like a country's laws; *statements of law* cover every aspect of human activity.
2. Laws are *applied to specific cases*, judging what should be done. Armed with moral definitions, humans appeal to their conscience and others' opinions; thus, humans decide right or wrong.

This clarifying process *seems ideal* for special ethics, following formal logic to advance reasonable outcomes. It provides moralists with decision-making strategies.

Barth refers to these law-based forms of ethics as *casuistry*. For example, Rabbinical Judaism seeks to provide the right decision in every imaginable situation based on the Torah.

Barth contends that casuistry lacks confidence in the Holy Spirit, who gives guidance corresponding to God's command.

Barth examines some examples of early Christians who developed systems apart from God to guide the human conscience.

> Goodness can only be measured in relation to Jesus Christ.

The Reformation moved back toward the God of Scripture. But it faltered, using natural law and the Bible to develop rules for human action. By the seventeenth century, the trend shifted back to legalistic readings of the Bible with additions from Greek and Roman antiquity, once again apart from God.

The ethics of Puritanism, Rationalism, Idealism, and Romanticism focused more on a person's internal motives, not external conformity to laws. The individual became a judge.

Casuistry has a grain of truth. When "conscience" is understood as an encounter with God's command, from which human action flows, the conscience is aligned correctly.

The problem with focusing on the individual conscience is the lack of consideration of our relation to God or other humans.

We must learn to talk and listen to the Spirit in life's concrete situations. Fixed rules attributed to the will of God imprison us in impersonal systems. We need to follow the dynamic command of God.

"Special" ethics should not try to be casuistic because:

1. *They create moralists who take the place of God.* Humans become the judge.
2. *They develop rules that replace the command of the living God.* God's command is petrified into regulations.
3. *They destroy Christian freedom, calling human rules the command of God.* The command of God brings freedom but not self-serving freedom.

The vertical relationship with God intersects with the horizontal of human action.

The intersection of the vertical and horizontal is a lifeline in a shared event.

Special ethics studies humans existing with God as a constant presence, claiming our lives for a loving response.

The living Word of God is the constant command of God as the context of our decisions.

Emil Brunner's concept of "orders" focuses on the horizontal, losing its proper rootedness in God, hoping to derive ethics from the world around us, which is a small step in the wrong direction.[2]

---

2. *CD* 3.3, § 52, pp. 19–20.

Following Love's Forte Adventure 261

Mistakenly, one looks to human spheres of life to find divine ordering. It appeals to laws of nature.

Lutheran theologian and pastor Dietrich Bonhoeffer speaks of mandates from God that are not derived from human sources but address the horizontal sphere. They come from God; they do not emerge from perceived "reality."

Still, Bonhoeffer's doctrine of mandates hints at German patriarchalism. Mandates problematically take on a hierarchy of meaning with veiled, definite order.

We must know the living Word to whom the Scriptures lead us and not the deposit of "truth" within our consciousness.

Every act of an ethical life has God as the primary focus for humans.

The human is secondary, acting in response to God; He is concerned for the freedom of His creature.

To say God is primary is to say He is present in all times and places for humans.

The human is secondary as those God treats seriously as autonomous in partnership with Him.

Both God and humanity are revealed in the Word of God, Jesus Christ. We begin by asking two questions:

1. Who is the commanding God made known in the Word of God, Jesus Christ?
2. Who is the human who acts as one made known from the Word of God, in Jesus Christ?

To the first question:

1. He is the One who created heaven and earth. He placed humans under the heavens on earth. He is the *Creator*.
2. He is the One who reconciled humanity to Himself. In this action for humans, He embraces the world He made. He is the *Reconciler*.
3. He is the One who liberates humans for eternal life. He deals with our danger and conflict. He makes us perfect in His love. He is the *Redeemer*.

To the second question:

1. He is the *creature* God had in mind when He created heaven and earth, a covenant partner who would participate in His eternal life.

2. He is the *sinner to whom God shows His gracious freedom*, to those who broke His covenant, denied their nature, and missed their calling.
3. He is the *child of the Father*, led *by the Spirit*. He is, even now, one who lives in the presence of God's future as the time of conflict and contradiction nears its end.

This disclosing of the nature of God and the form of humanity is not so much a description as telling the story of which God makes us part.

We understand our ethical life as actualized within this story. The human is what it is and does what it does in the context of God's overarching personal presence.

The task of special ethics is to focus on the history of the encounter between God and humanity, exploring the journey of accompaniment from creation to redemption.

God creates a hospitable field in which we may look at special ethics. He is the host, chef, and server; this does not mean we do not dine with Him as a companion.

God's one will and command call for responsibility. Laws require a person to do wrong or right according to an external principle. That is not what Barth is pointing toward.

Command calls for internal, willing obedience or acknowledged disobedience. The command calls for relational correspondence as the outworking of love and grace. The ethical takes place within our relationships.

The Spirit's assistance must not be corrupted into imprisoning laws that kill us with detailed instructions.

We will follow where love compels us to go moment by moment. We are never out of earshot of the One who loves us in freedom.

2. God the Creator as Commander (pp. 32–46)

All creation is God's work. Humanity is a covenant partner sharing God's house under His fatherly care.

The house becomes a home when we learn to live in it together. The meaning and end of ethical thinking is how we live together. This ordering is how dogmatics becomes ethics.

God is One and yet acts in many ways out of the singularity of His will. This will is known through the Son, who shows us the Father and reveals the Spirit.

Following Love's Forte Adventure

God, as our commander, impacts all spheres of life.

The *first sphere* is in the history of the one commanding God, our Creator.

God's unified *perichoresis* (making space for each other, mutually indwelling) does not violate the independence of each person of the Trinity. Unity does not exclude particularity.

> This disclosing of the nature of God and the form of humanity is not so much a description as telling the story of which God makes us part.

We know God as One here and now. We live in this sphere as:

1. The Creator God commands us in the person of Jesus Christ.
2. This God commands as the Creator.
3. His command sanctifies our human action, and his action precedes and impacts our activities.

God and humanity do not live in separate spheres. God is the sphere in which we live. We are those addressed by His command intended to fulfill our being, our sanctification.

What is the secret of the sphere in which we are operating?

1. *Jesus Christ includes being God* the Creator (true God), the command of God as Word to humanity (God-human relation), and the fulfillment of our being (true human).

   In Jesus, we know God's deep internal working and life. Creation lives within the "Yes" of God.

   God takes on a specific form of gracious friendship in Jesus Christ.
2. *Jesus is the one command of God* given to humanity. He has already sanctified human action.

To understand ethical humanity, we need a firm starting point. All human attempts are hypotheses, claims without foundation:

- a *natural being* in the context of other natural beings
- an ethical *rational being* able to master distinctive human nature
- an *active being* with the ability to limit and transcend one's existence
- a *being who exists within the historic community*, both experiencing and making one's history

Church Dogmatics 3.4

These aspects of human existence do not provide a common denominator for understanding the whole of the human.

For Barth, a human being is one to whom God is gracious in Jesus Christ. This affirmation does not extinguish other phenomena of human existence.

An authentic human is the object of God's grace; we neither question nor confirm any of the old views. We see humans in the simplicity of who, how, and what they are. But we must think of Jesus Christ first.

In Jesus, we can say, "Behold your God!" At the same time, we can say, "Behold the Man!" The true God reveals this true Human. He reflects the fatherly heart of God while embodying the particularity of being human.

From Jesus, we learn that we are sinners pardoned by God's grace and that we are children of God. We can only know this from Jesus, not from ourselves.

In the mirror of God's grace, we know we still wrestle with sin and are beloved children forgiven by God's grace. God does not destroy us with His grace; He stands against devilish corruption to preserve us in His Son.

Who we are must be understood from the incarnation of Jesus Christ:

1. We are *historical beings* whose beginning lies in the election of Jesus, who are then summoned by God, and who continue as those enabled to be responsible to God.
2. We are *relational beings* who live in encounters with other human beings in a Thou-I friendship that reflects the image of God.
3. We are *embodied beings* who know ourselves as the soul of our body in an inseparable unity that, by God's Spirit, is a particular knowing person.
4. We are *whole beings* with allotted time on earth and with hope in the God who has made us this way.

Jesus shows us this historical nature, relational constitution, embodied soul, and the limitation of life before God on earth.

We need family and community to give us a history. We need doctors for our bodies. We need therapists for our mental health. We need help planning for the span of our lives. But not one of these tells us who we are or what we are here for.

> From Jesus, we learn that we are sinners pardoned by God's grace and that we are children of God.

Real humanity is a pardoned sinner and a child of God who lives in hope. We do not start by focusing on being sinners. God made us for shared life; that is who we are.

Jesus made it possible to live in the sphere of God and the sphere of creatureliness. God commands us in both spheres to free us and make us whole.

Sanctification and liberation describe what God has done in making us whole for loving enjoyment throughout our lives. God's command is to share freely with Him in His ongoing work as Creator, Reconciler, and Redeemer in Jesus by His Spirit.

COMMENTARY:
- General ethics generalizes ethical concepts. Barth resists this methodology as abstract and susceptible to human dominance.
- Special ethics begins with our particular life with Jesus.
- Our life is a response to God's ongoing involvement as Creator, Reconciler, and Redeemer.
- The command of God is not a constraint; it is a call to live in freedom with God.
- Jesus shows us the God who calls and the human who responds to God's call.
- Jesus lives a fully human life in response to the love of God on our behalf, and we live in Him.

CONCLUSION FOR THE CHURCH: The easier road for guiding sheep is to set up fences with signs and slogans to manage their behavior. However, Jesus calls His Church to be compelled by His love in response to His presence. The question is not what Jesus would do but what we will do because Jesus is with us.

The Church needs to find the freedom to know that Christ is in control but not controlling. Setting standards for church behavior misses the point. We need a passion from the Spirit to awaken us in pursuing loving obedience with Jesus, one situation at a time.

INSIGHT FOR PASTORS: Pastors are sources of wisdom and can often offer good advice. They can also develop a sense that there is one Christian way to do things. This system stifles nurturing what it means to be children of the Father, to know His heart, hear His Spirit, and go step by step with His Son.

At our best, we help people discover their identity as the Father's children and with Jesus as their brother by the Spirit. We may also help them recognize that there is no standard Christian life. Each person will reflect Jesus' love in a different way. That is what special ethics does.

Barth wants our people to know our Creator, who sustains His work. We are restored by our Reconciler, who reminds us of His daily healing. We are made new for love by our Redeemer and made free for loving encounters. Seeing ourselves at the nexus point of God's work allows us to find meaning, empowerment, and courage to echo His accompaniment.

INSIGHT FOR THEOLOGIANS: It is easy to think that theology must be systematic. But for dogmatic theologians, shedding the system releases us from fitting our theology into a prefabricated grid.

Barth rejects general ethics because it fabricates a broad framework to categorize actions. By applying human logic, general ethicists hope to discern how they fit specific situations into their evaluation systems. These approaches are not theological; they depend on human values, not working out of the ways and works of God.

Once we see what it means to be an ethical person in Jesus, He becomes our centering point for the embrace that forms us. Barth contends we must know ourselves as those who stand before Jesus and accept His grace. All other attempts to evaluate and propose ethical development are arbitrary. The evaluator, judge, or therapist will only choose specific phenomena to consider. We only develop as whole persons with Jesus, to become ethically whole by grace.

Barth does not exclude any approach for evaluating humans. He sees their profound limitations in determining how a whole human might behave. He does not throw out psychology, medicine, or other systems that pursue health for humans. They each may do their limited part. Knowing who made us and for whom we are restored hones our behavior within His loving presence.

Special ethics is concerned with hearing and following the One who acts in love toward us. No cookie-cutter ethics will do, only fresh apprenticing with the Master, who shapes our intuitions to follow Him with creativity and never depart from His guidance.

CLARIFYING QUESTIONS: Does your theology incline toward principles tied to historic Christianity and Bible-based prescriptions for how to live a godly life? *Or* does your sense of right behaviors and attitudes feel like a daily adventure, going with Jesus to serve in a freeing, creative life bathed in grace?

CHAPTER 19

LIVING INTO GOD'S HOSPITABLE EMBRACE

§ 53. Freedom before God

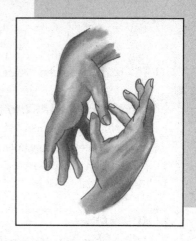

FOCUS STATEMENT: Ethics implies conforming to God's embrace, not a set of rules. He invites us into His space and time for connection. Jesus reaches out; we receive and respond at the listening point.

Freedom is practiced with God. The holy day facilitates intimacy. Confession declares our delight. Prayer aligns us with the One who gives all.

Thus, § 53 is about fulfillment through an interwoven life. Ethical activity radiates from the love born of God. It displays itself in behaviors extending throughout our relationships with others.

INTRODUCTION: Ethics is a developing arena. By His Spirit, Jesus meets us to be our delight, providing what we desire and need from Him.

Sabbath provides time to honor God by connecting with Him and others, not as a day of avoiding work. Confessing is about rejoicing in the grandeur of God, not declaring our sin. Prayer is about honest asking and believing God is present and provides for what we desire. Ethics becomes a lifestyle sculpted by love for the God who is present—this is freedom before God.

The Lord's Prayer forms a backdrop for this paragraph. It bids us focus on the God who cares for the world, echoing back God's care coming from heaven to meet our daily needs.

CONTEXT: *CD* 3.4
Pages in Paragraph: 69 pages (pp. 47–115)

Subsections
1. The Holy Day
2. Confession
3. Prayer

268   *Church Dogmatics 3.4*

📖 **TEXT:** § 53. Freedom before God

✝ **OPENING SUMMARY:** It is the will of God the Creator that man, as His creature, shall be responsible before Him. In particular, His command says that man is to keep His day holy as a day of worship, freedom and joy, that he is to confess Him in his heart and with his mouth and that he is to come to Him with his requests.[1]

✝ **SUMMARY:**

1. The Holy Day (pp. 47–72)

To be appropriately human is to stand before our Creator and acknowledge God *as He is*, not *as we wish He would be*. He is not like us. He is wholly other, our Creator who made us. However, His holy day invites us to be with Him.

God compels us to enter His Sabbath rest, which nurtures togetherness and engenders freedom with God.

Love for God and the world are connected. In love for God, we do *theology*; in love for the world, we engage in *sciences*. These two related spheres are the focus of the command to love God and neighbor and call us to action.

God's love engages us in parallel activities. We *pray* to connect with God and *work* to connect with the world. We *serve* God as an act of love and extend *practical* love to help our neighbor. We share in our *church* family but also the life of the *state* and *neighborhood*.

Sabbath becomes the womb of the ethical life born of God. His love develops our lives as the children of God. The tomb of Jesus was the womb of the resurrection, and the Lord's day is resurrection day remembered and shared.

Barth concentrates on one day among many, set apart from other days to be with God—*the* holy day. This emphasis does not mean God does not claim all our times; this day is a special time within our times.

The Sabbath interrupts our daily work. It redirects us to the heart of God, giving meaning to our other work. We are reoriented to His love and activity for us, restoring the pattern of our lives to reality.

God rested on the seventh day because He had completed everything necessary for His covenant history to unfold.

Every seventh day echoes through creation the affirmation that God has created everything for Himself and His creature. That day is a breathing

---

1. *CD* 3.4, § 53, p. 47.

Living into God's Hospitable Embrace

space for celebrating and rejoicing in God's completed creation. We praise God's completion, not human accomplishments.

We rest with God. His restful ending begins our participation in His covenant history. Our acts cannot earn His favor. We rest with God and then go to work.

In the New Testament, the Sabbath transforms to celebrate the resurrection of Jesus, fulfilling His covenant for humanity. The move away from calling it the "Sabbath" celebrates humanity's response to the completed work of God in Jesus. Now it is rightly called the "Lord's Day."

Sabbath is a day filled with the "Yes" of God. We are to embrace the "Yes." We may wrongly think of the Sabbath command only as a "No," a stop to our action, but that misses the point. His "Yes" propels us into the other days of the week.

Our future does not lie within our power to create but within the creation that God gifted us. It is not a day of self-improvement. It is a day to surrender to God's renewal.

The Sabbath day invites us to connect with God's creative and restorative purposes. Grace is at work as God gives us Himself. Providence is at work as God accompanies us.

> God compels us to enter His Sabbath rest, which nurtures togetherness and engenders freedom with God.

The Sabbath is inclusive, inviting all peoples to interrupt their histories and acknowledge the Creator's provision. All are called to this Sabbath rest.

The Sabbath points us to the culmination of history. The day of the Lord and the day of Yahweh depict the completion of God's restoration. Sabbath allows that future to shine on us today.

This Sabbath life is a kind of mysticism, an adventure that fixes our ears on Him to hear and obey. This approach is a mysticism of yielding to the Holy Spirit.

We must avoid the mysticism that attempts to shape ourselves with practices in search of God.

The Sabbath command has two significant benefits:

1. We are freed from the pressures of daily work.
2. We are freed for God and given space to hear the Word of God.

In addition to deepening our lives with God, the Sabbath gives rest to our bodies and minds. It allows time for connection with family and friends. It meets real human needs.

270   Church Dogmatics 3.4

The holy day frees one for participation in praise and worship, attentive to hearing and speaking of the Word of God with shared thanksgiving and prayer. Beyond rest, it celebrates the festival of mutual service among the gathered.

The Word of God becomes the sanctuary in which we gather. We do not focus on the building but on being brought together as those who are His body and temple.

We must be sure human rules do not replace God's command. We prepare to serve God and our neighbor for another week.

The command is to hear and respond to what God speaks, living in freedom as those who have spent time with Jesus.

How can we think appropriately of the Sabbath as a holy day?

1. *This day belongs to God.* It is made for humans as God's gift, but we do not own it.
2. *The meaning of Sabbath is a feast to celebrate the joy of God's freedom.* The fruit of His presence is joy as we share in His meal. He is not gone. He is more than a guest; He is the host at His table.
3. *The Sabbath is a day for relationships with those dear to us.* It belongs to the neighborhood, the community, and society who need its benefit, a day for closer contact, opening, listening, hearing, and giving help.
4. *The Sabbath completes its work when it brings meaningful light to the rest of the week.* Sabbath is the stream of joy from openness to God and our fellow humans.

Sabbath renews us. From our busyness, we will find rest. From our daily struggles, we will find peace. From our commitment to work, we turn to find renewal in prayer. We do not abandon everyday life; we find meaning by giving ourselves to our loving Lord.

2. Confession (pp. 73–86)

Confession is participation in the delight of who God is as He is for us and with us. This activity captures the freedom of authentic, joyful praise of God. The focus is not on confessing our sins—we profess the honor of God's goodness.

Confession gives voice to the fact that we are God's creatures, confirming that one is created and belongs to the Creator.

God commands us to be His witnesses, revealing what is hidden. God extends Himself through us as embodied grace and love.

Living into God's Hospitable Embrace

Praise is the climax of all human action toward God, joining all creation in praising Him. We acknowledge He has known and loved us. We rejoice that we may love Him in return.

As we proclaim God's glory, the history of God's covenant shines forth, and we are freed to speak of our relationship with Him in word and deed.

God will give us opportunities to speak. By His Spirit, He gives us words. We are never alone in our witness. God will teach us what to say.

How can we think appropriately of confession before God?

1. *We will desire to honor God with no motive but to make Him known.* We confess for sheer joy, even though it may appear useless.
2. *With a confident faith, we will protest against unbelief and heresy when God's honor is confronted or questioned.* We stand with God's "Yes" against the human "no." We must stand against false claims and speak God's truth.
3. *We confess the faith of the Christian community.* Our hearing and speaking let Scripture speak with fresh directness in an open, public attitude.
4. *God's free grace makes confession a free activity breathed by the Holy Spirit.* We confess what the Spirit of Jesus, the Spirit of Scripture, and the Spirit of the community compel us to convey in our context.

We are not constrained to speak in the words of the Bible or current Christian lingo. We may use those forms or an entirely secular language.

> The command is to hear and respond to what God speaks, living in freedom as those who have spent time with Jesus.

In the act of confession, we are free before God. We live from love and speak of the source of that love even as we live it out.

3. Prayer (pp. 87–115)

Prayer is the life of living alongside God, turning to Him directly.

In confession, humans turn to honor God. In prayer, humans come to God, seeking and asking for what we need.

Confession and prayer point to knowledge of God as the basic act of human reason. God created the world. He draws humans to live reasonably in its context, as His ordered work.

Humans connect with God, whose renewing happens continuously, like breathing in and out so that we are grounded in the One who loves us.

Prayer attends to God. It is personal communication oriented to address God, not impress humans.

Confession is the praise of God for the ears of the world. Prayer is for the ears of God.

Prayer is to be honest, without fear of what others think. It does not have to be beautiful or theologically correct. It is not an art but the opening of the heart concerned with God's answer.

No matter how we stumble, God will hear and accept our attempts at prayer as acts of obedience.

Prayer is God's underlying accompanying, upholding our human actions. Prayer overcomes our forgetfulness.

We pray because God invites us. He expects us to return, to answer and converse.

Real prayer requires a degree of inwardness and outwardness in the community. By the Spirit, we hear and respond as God intercedes and helps weak humans.

Barth now clarifies what he means by true prayer:

1. *That we may pray to God is the beginning of human freedom.*

    Barth proposed that anxiety is the opposite of prayer and competes with prayer. It will teach us to beg, curse, resign, or try to fix the issue ourselves. Analyzing our asking is a block that sabotages our freedom. It is like sitting on an exercise bike and going nowhere.

    Our only question is whether we are praying according to God's will.

    We pray beside and behind Jesus, coming in His name through His mouth so that we see that He intercedes for us.

    We belong to Jesus and pray with Him as we pray in His name. This connection is confirmed as the Mediator works through the intercession of the Holy Spirit to join with the Father.

    There is no reason for us not to come to God in prayer. Our sin is never too great; His love has already overcome that excuse on the cross. Only our fears stop us.

2. *That we may petition God is decisive for understanding prayer.* It is a pure, unconditional request. We come with empty hands to be filled. Prayer is not cleansing, deepening, or preparing ourselves for God.

    Thanksgiving is the root of prayer as the grace of God invites us into His freedom.

Living into God's Hospitable Embrace

Repentance is the honest realization that we do not deserve what we request—all is grace. God gives us a new heart and renews our spirit.

Worship is our turning to the revealed God, who gives us the freedom to pray and answer His summons to us.

Asking follows His command that we come. To ask is to be humbly obedient.

3. *We are each only a person who prays appropriately as part of the "we" of the community.* We pray "Our Father" in the Lord's prayer. The "we" who pray is a fellowship open to all. This community has its holy day, common confession, and shared prayer life.

We share in God's cause for the world that He loves. As we pray united with Him, we are for the world, and He is for us; we belong to Him, whose prayer is true prayer.

> Confession is the praise of God for the ears of the world. Prayer is for the ears of God.

4. *True prayer is confident that God hears and answers.* We may doubt the sincerity of our asking, but not God's hearing.

When we pray "in Jesus' name," we follow Him, asking Him to bring us to His Father.

Believing that God's unchangeability means He cannot answer our prayers is tragic. God is unchangeable in His mercy and commitment to be for His creatures.

5. *Prayer takes on the form of orderly action.*

First, we should always *intercede on behalf of the world*, the greater Church, and our local community before we ask for ourselves.

Second, we should pray in *free orderliness* before God. It will be active with definite thoughts and words, whether silent or audible.

Third, we must continually *learn to pray*. This affirmation justifies formulated prayers that echo the Lord's Prayer.

Fourth, it is best to keep prayers *relatively short* so they may penetrate our hearts and not get lost in many words.

Fifth, it is good to have *regular patterns* for prayer, to make a habit of coming to God, praying in free, hearty, and spontaneous obedience.

It is better not to pray than to be bound by methods where we show up with our mouths while our hearts are far away.

We need to connect with the communion of saints from the past, praying their prayers. We also must connect with present contexts, speaking their language and inviting participation.

Prayer must never become a museum piece. It must serve the current requests of the gathered people of God.

Prayer must awaken people from their sleepiness, invigorating them in refreshing rhythms.

COMMENTARY:
- Freedom before God is an interactive, nurtured, ongoing response to God's pursuit of us.
- Sabbath is a day of action celebrating God's presence.
- Confession in ethics is continually refocusing and speaking our beloved God's truth.
- Prayer is a communication connection with God as we awaken to His presence and provision.
- God wants us to ask, believing He is willing and able to answer.

CONCLUSION FOR THE CHURCH: The Church exists where Jesus lives. It also exists as a community at a particular place in time. It acts weekly and daily to remind people to live in response to God's love.

The Church must be careful not to exist as a set of traditions focused on human experience, neglecting the Spirit knocking at the door. Freedom before God calls the Church to be an interactive observatory (Sabbath) with auditory capacities (confession and prayer). God may be seen at work and heard in His address.

In sabbathing, confessing, and praying, we break free from the stagnation of life in a forgetful world. God has invited us to meet Him eye to eye, to hear and speak, and to know the other. We walk out the door with gratitude and gladness to serve God.

INSIGHT FOR PASTORS: Ethics develops from spending time with Jesus and becoming His servants. Who we *are* is shaped by who we are *with*.

The education of the heart can never begin with human self-reflection. Like falling in love, it happens because the other is there; we yearn for a nurtured life with another person.

As pastors, we help our people to find that they are found by God, enabled to return His loving gaze and live in His presence.

People become disciples by being with Jesus. Barth's special ethics lays the foundation for being with the living God. When the activities, not just our words, reflect being with Jesus, we become an ethical Church, the beloved family of the Father.

INSIGHT FOR THEOLOGIANS: Barth believes humans function ethically by living in the context of God's patterned life together. We must begin with God's provision, followed by human participation in reply.

Barth envisions the Church as a laboratory to discover God, where we are continually shaped by the One we encounter. The science of theology is not merely through statements but in ongoing engagement with the personal reality that shapes our acting.

In knowing God, the Sabbath is a space for shaping human experience within divine presence. Transformation happens in God's renewing process with regular encounters. From this stance, observing the Sabbath, confession, and prayer become practices that reframe the Church from human-centered traditions to God-centered communities. That is theological ethics in action.

CLARIFYING QUESTIONS: Does your theology of a freeing ethical life before God persist as a set of rules and regulations that function like an owner's manual? *Or* do you think of each week as a rhythm of interactions, aligning with God's presence as He fashions you freely to reflect His nature?

CHAPTER 20

EXPANDING OUR HOSPITABLE EMBRACE TOWARD OTHERS

§ 54. Freedom in Fellowship

FOCUS STATEMENT: God fashions us to be hospitable to one another. Behind the curtain of observing one another is deep interconnectedness. Barth sees this in the mutuality of males and females made with and for each other. Parents and children likewise live in collaboratively created unity.

Near and distant neighbors extend our humanity by choice, not built into our nature, as with gender and familial relatedness.

The relational dimension of humanity is called *fellowship*. Our companionship fulfills the purposes of God as our interwoven lives enrich our uniqueness.

Freedom is what we experience when relationships are lovingly and functionally fulfilled. Thus, § 54 discusses the outworking of love with other humans—hospitality in action.

INTRODUCTION: This long paragraph explores the relation of humans to fellow humans. Having discussed the *created form* of humanity in *CD* 3.2, we now explore the *relatedness* of humans as God's creatures. Ethics is proper relatedness.

The three subsections of § 54 investigate how God made humans to exist and act toward one another. The first affirms the primary form of humanity as male and female.

The image of God requires both male and female considered together, not separately. A male or female alone cannot be the image of God; they display a complementary unity with the possibility of loving fulfillment.

The second section discusses parents and children within God's creation of humans.

276

The final section acknowledges that we are to love our neighbors, some near and some far away. God orients us to respect and honor neighbors wherever they are.

Freedom in fellowship means relations aligned with God's love. God's command seeks tangible expressions responsive to love.

CONTEXT: *CD* 3.4

Pages in Paragraph: 208 pages (pp. 116–323)

Subsections
1. Man and Woman
2. Parents and Children
3. Near and Distant Neighbours

TEXT: § 54. Freedom in Fellowship

OPENING SUMMARY: As God the Creator calls man to Himself, He also directs him to his fellow-man. The divine command affirms in particular that in the encounter of man and woman, in the relationship between parents and children and outwards from near to distant neighbours, man may affirm, honour and enjoy the other with himself and himself with the other.[1]

SUMMARY:

1. Man and Woman (pp. 116–240)

Barth reminds readers of § 45 that humans are beings-in-relation, made as male and female in the likeness of God. And in § 41, he discussed covenant relationships, including males and females.

God directs us to live fulfilling relationships in an I with another who is a Thou covenant partnership.

God invites us to freedom through sharing our fellow humanity. If we fail, we become inhuman.

The first distinction within the unity of humanity is being female and male.

The relationship between men and women called *marriage* corresponds to the biblical relationship between Yahweh and His people and Jesus and His Church body.

---

1. *CD* 3.4, § 54, p. 116.

Being male and female is the only structural and functional distinction within the relations of humanity. They are both human. Each has differences unchanged by aging, becoming a parent, or other relational distinctions.

To say "humanity" is to say man *and* woman (including all) as well as man *or* woman (one or the other), to coexist with the other, and to value the other sex.

Discussing morality begins with God and radiates to every aspect of human life.

We are met with a triple action by God to shape our response:

1. Our heavenly Father *rules* us in the sphere of our humanity. He is concerned for our relationships as male and female.
2. Our heavenly Father *relativizes* us regarding His commanding presence. We act in obedience to Him.
3. God will *direct us to His freedom*. He gives us the freedom to accept our humanity as sexual beings before God.

Barth discusses five views to be questioned:

1. *Schleiermacher* affirmed a form of "romantic love." However, Schleiermacher collapsed the sexual experience into an experience of God. Sex becomes sacred worship. The human experience becomes central.
2. The *Roman Catholic* and *Eastern Orthodox* traditions make marriage a sacrament. Marriage becomes a means to grace, the natural link to the supernatural.

   But here, the marrying partners mediate grace through words of commitment.

   Schleiermacher's and sacramental positions both begin with the natural human and then project a heavenly or supernatural benefit in marriage.
3. *Modern views* attempt to wed religion and eroticism as two sets of relationships needing to overcome their estrangement. Their synthesized God-human agenda transforms humans by making religion erotic and eroticism religious.
4. We must not dismiss the erotic, as the Church has tragically done. We must always see the loving encounter of male and female as real humanity created and blessed by God.

An evangelical theologian, *Theodor Bovet* rightly affirms that marriage is a sign that echoes the relationship between God and humanity. Bovet begins well with divine love filling human life. But then he asserts that only in the experience of eros can one be transformed by divine love. This proposal makes marriage and sex the vehicle of renewal, not God's grace!

5. Finally, *Henry Leenhardt* does not fall into the error of exalting eros. Still, he defaults to the institution of marriage as a sacrament of redemption, as an embodiment of grace, echoing the Roman Catholic position.

God claims the entire human for wholeness. Sexual life, in the narrower sense, lives within our understanding of humanity as male and female.

In the duality of male and female, humans either honor or dishonor God in their embodied life, as the sex life of humans takes place as partners.

Sex is an aspect of our relatedness to others, whether or not we are engaging. But this aspect should not define our relationships.

> Discussing morality begins with God and radiates to every aspect of human life.

We must pay attention to our sexual existence because it is often the source of shame, superficiality, or meaninglessness.

When being ashamed defines our existence, we have isolated one aspect and made it the whole. The ethic of shame is the opposite of an ethic of freedom.

God has created us sexually as male and female. We should not live in denial.

Our sexuality should form an integral part of relating as male and female. If we see others as sex objects, we dehumanize ourselves and others.

When sexuality dominates our relating, we resist God, demonizing sex as a human right, missing it as the gift of God.

God is not merely concerned with our sex organs and desires. He wants our sexual determination to be aligned with our whole being as the spirit-driven soul of our body in a manner consistent with physical eating, drinking, and sleeping.

The question is who and what we will be before God. Sex can shape who we are as physical beings, but it is not to be the whole or to define us.

Sex cannot be the central motivator for a couple's life. Sex is honorable when permeated with love, as the communion of spirits working together through life's challenges and joys.

280

Church Dogmatics 3.4

When planning sex, we must ask what we want for each other. Is this a meaningful act sustaining life together in a future full of promise?

Loving commitment is the challenge of God's command. Unlawful acts arise from an unwillingness to orient to this fellow human appropriately in love.

Two become one, not as an aspect of their particularity, but as one in their nature, becoming what they were not. To love one's spouse is to love oneself because the other is part of us. This engagement is *agapē*, godly love, not merely sexual desire.

The psychology of Sigmund Freud and the writings of D. H. Lawrence explored the suppressed emotions in the unconscious unleashing of the sick soul. Function and dysfunction were understood through manifestations of the libido. That stage of research has passed, but its effects linger.

Writers like Carl Jung and Alfred Adler corrected this limited focus on the sexual to understand the human as a whole.

The sex impulse gains power when determined by the Spirit in love. The biological urge becomes genuinely human, connecting in the realm of spirit.

Sexuality is a partnership that celebrates the communion of the body and soul. Human life is not merely biological, a step beyond the animals; it is endowed with mental and spiritual life.

If we lose the value of the other in sex, we default to intense self-centeredness, pursuing a flight to self-service. Sex must be mutual self-surrender.

We need sanctification of the sexual life grounded in theological freedom and not biological urges alone.

It is helpful to understand the physiology and techniques of sexual activity, but that alone cannot make a great marriage. We need honest information where we usually get vague allusions. We need to see the unity of sexual impulse and love, looking beyond the psychophysical dimension of the human to the spiritual.

Barth provisionally defines *marriage* as "the encounter of male and female in which the free, mutual, harmonious choice of love on the part of a particular man and woman leads to a responsibly undertaken life-union which is lasting, complete and exclusive."[2]

The sphere of male and female is more extensive than marriage. God's command pertains to the unmarried, widowed, divorced, and those with other limitations.

---

2. *CD* 3.4, § 54, p. 140.

Expanding Our Hospitable Embrace toward Others

We all live before God as humans. This relation is central, as the form of humanity before God, with marriage as a particular case.

The ethics of modern marriage consider the crisis of marriage, monogamy, and divorce, almost forgetting the unmarried state.

Roman Catholics make singleness superior to marriage in celibacy. Some Reformers make marriage about procreation as the purpose of marriage, setting human traditions above the Bible.

The creation of male and female in Genesis displays an integral connection between male and female and love and marriage. The two shall become one flesh points to marriage as the focal point of the male-female relationship.

The Genesis account introduces the gracious covenant relationship between God and Israel. Yahweh is the faithful Lover. He is husband to an unfaithful wife. God intends mutuality, which Israel does not fulfill, and Israel constantly slips away.

The Old Testament presents male and female covenant relationships as an echo of God and His beloved people. In the New Testament, this theme continues in the relationship between Jesus and His Church.

It is not a disgrace to be unmarried. Marriage is to be honored, but being unmarried is also honorable: Jesus had no bride other than His community. He honored marriage but did not require it.

In heaven, there will be males and females, but not marrying.

Marriage is justified to avoid the sexual temptations of lust and prostitution, a life of unfaithfulness. But we are *intended* to join together as a form of faithfulness to God and each other.

Marriage is for having children and also the personal life of love. Marriage is a gift and calling from God to be entered for love's fulfillment.

Marriage is a life of reciprocal adaptation. One lives to please the other as an obligation from love's caring heart.

Singleness can be freedom to serve the Lord and others. It is a valid calling. We are not obliged to God to get married, only to be faithful in love when we are married.

> Marriage is a life of reciprocal adaptation. One lives to please the other as an obligation from love's caring heart.

- Barth's *first principle* in understanding humanity is that they are male and female in a unified duality (pp. 149–63).

    God said that it is not good to be alone. He made another of the same species fundamentally different. The I has a Thou to constitute a relationship.

God wills humans not to be alone and created woman. This pairing is a parable of partnership.

The man and woman came to exist as I and Thou for each other. They were naked and not ashamed. They did not envy each other, conceal from each other, resist each other, or complain about each other.

There is no shame when we cling to the nature of how God created us, even in our nakedness.

When noting the distinctives of man and woman, we must avoid generalized, prejudiced definitions based on human experience. "All women" or "All men" are inadequate launching points.

We notice differences in gender, age, family systems, and all the distinctives of each individual. But we remain blind to the mystery of who we are, standing before God, known wholly and uniquely.

Man and woman *together* are the image of God, a unity in the likeness of God, made for loving responses to God and each other.

Barth lists a parallelism of what people think of males versus females. Barth is not affirming them, just illustrating the problem.

Half-true caricatures should not be made into ideals or norms for males and females.

Barth avoids introducing masculine or feminine standards as a theological starting point.

Schleiermacher envied the fairer sex's life, who better lived his ideals. He does not follow theological reasoning.

Barth questioned the feminist movement of his time as an attempt to reverse the roles of women with men. He sees this hopefully changing in the future, not reverting to traditional roles or what men find suitable for women.

Women need freedom to be themselves as beloved of God and not try to be other.

Barth does not see value in transcending our humanity, becoming sexless, bisexual, or attempting to rise above our particularity as male and female to achieve higher purity or freedom.

Humanity's form reflects the image of God. The Trinity is One in three persons. Humanity is one as two sexes.

Humans share God's likeness as male and female without requiring marriage. Each is for and with the other in distinction yet also as their complementing counterpart.

Neither gender should think of themselves as the better sex nor believe their particular sex a burden to bear. That moves toward

Expanding Our Hospitable Embrace toward Others 283

inhumanity, abandoning God's command to understand oneself as God's good creation.

Barth critiques Russian theologian Nicholas Berdyaev for losing distinctiveness in the unity of humanity, with a vision of an androgynous human borrowing male and female characteristics, a sexless compilation within the conflict of wrestling natures. This is the history of humanity. Barth rejects "the great anthropological myth," identifying it as the neutering of humankind.

Barth affirms removing masks and myths of domination. But Barth believes this creates a new mythology, denying physical existence to pursue wishful thinking.

- Barth's *second principle* for humanity is that "there is no such thing as a self-contained and self-sufficient male life or female life."[3] They are oriented to care for each other (pp. 163–68).

With their counterparts, men and women become what they are in themselves. Yet each is not self-centered but is expansive and open.

Freedom forms in the unity found in Jesus Christ, who breaks down the walls between men and women, bringing equal footing.

We must be committed to the interrelationship of man and woman. Isolating men and women from each other is inhumane.

Barth is not bashful about his views on homosexuality. Based on the affirmation that humanity is male and female in collaborative completion, he cannot accept a man with a man or a woman with a woman. Of course, writing during his time may have influenced Barth's thinking. Yet he consistently views humanity and the implications for sexual relations as the outworking of the intended state of humanity in Genesis.

We cannot merely dismiss his view; we must engage it with serious thinking in reconciliation and redemption before God and not default to political positions. Barth's "Nevertheless" means God's love will always persist.

1. consider one another,
2. hear the question that each puts to the other, and
3. provide responsible answers to one another.

To elaborate:

---

3. *CD* 3.4, § 54, p. 163.

Church Dogmatics 3.4

1. To consider one another means to want to know about one another. This means not assuming one knows or doesn't need to know the others.

   Consideration requires a generous heart, ready to learn something new about the other with eyes that have no judgment.

   We have legitimate questions to ask of the other sex to understand them.

   Wondering is not unreasonable; working out our capacities, interests, and tendencies leads to joy. We need the other to discover ourselves.

2. Having heard the other's questions, we are encouraged to act responsibly toward each other.

   This means mutually accepting differences, honestly revealing ourselves, and being empathetic toward the other.

3. Self-revelation must desire to be with the other with mutual respect.

- Barth's *third principle* is that men and women live ordered lives, valued in their mutual interrelatedness (pp. 168–240).

  Men and women are equal before God. There is a sequencing, an *A* and *B*, that cannot diminish the dignity of either, equal but distinct, without any advantage given.

  Males are not granted privilege over women, nor women over men. Men are not self-sufficient or in command. Any domination or oppression of women is contrary to God's ordering.

  In acknowledging she is *B*, a woman does not give up dignity or value in subordination to the man. Barth believes in the importance of service that follows the path of Jesus in valuing women.

  Barth interprets the biblical statements about women with men as mutual coordination. They are to submit to each other as they submit to the Lord (Ephesians 5:21).

  The conduct God requires will not stay the same for all people everywhere. We cannot shackle God in any system concerning men and women.

  Men must devote themselves to the care of the dignity of women. Women must partner with men for the good of both.

  A tyrant controls the other person. This attitude is a denial of humanity. It is a warped pleasure to seek honor by dominating the

Expanding Our Hospitable Embrace toward Others

other. In every sense, it is a lie that separates and devalues the other, taking advantage of them.

Equally problematic is going along with the tyrant, adapting to their lie. A false persona masks the fading self, living in silenced compliance with the controller. Expectations, rather than conversations, define the relationship between them.

Forms of hierarchy built on power will fail in rebellion. The tyrant will weaken, and the rebellious partner will increase resistance.

A mature woman will never take the role of a compliant wife. Her strength will support a strong man's strength.

Barth engages marriage as the central point in ethical thinking, the highest state of loving encounters between men and women.

Marriage is a life partnership where both give and receive in the mutual choice of love in a deliberate union. They commit for a lifetime, desiring and affirming each other. It is interwoven with a community, as expressed in a wedding.

Barth acknowledges that there are psychological, social, hygienic, and legal aspects of marriage that he will not discuss. He pursues the theological ethics of marriage as how we stand before God's command.

The relationship between God and humanity is the reality for which the human relation of marriage is its subsequent analogy.

Humans stand before God as man and woman, as a single humanity in the image of God. Marriage fully expresses the human connection when lived in love and companionship.

> The relationship between God and humanity is the reality for which the human relation of marriage is its subsequent analogy.

Barth diverts in his outline to discuss the elements that make up marriage (pp. 181–240).

1. *Marriage is a divine calling* (pp. 183–87). God has not commanded all to be married. Some choose to be married, and others decide to remain single.

   Humans are freed for marriage; it is not an obligation. It is a response to God's grace in providing the other with the completion of love.

   Marriages may be disastrous when people do not ask about the will of God but act out of their biological needs or societal customs.

   In marriage, the Holy Spirit frees two humans for an extraordinary, fulfilling relationship with another human. It is not about self-fulfillment; it is the context of the

Spirit's work in developing love in human relating. It is not a human institution; it is a divine participation under the guidance of the Spirit.

Marriage is not child's play. It is an entrance into a holy sphere. So is the life of celibacy. Each call responds to God, not seeking to be self-fulfilled.

Christian marriage often focuses on the problems and does not pursue its positive aspects, the institutional limitations, and the theological blessings. The discussion has become legalistic and not realistic.

Marriage lives with intimacy and companionship, becoming a "We" that practically engages throughout the waking day.

Marriage is fulfilled as each day echoes the "Yes" of love.

2. *Fulfilling the life partnership is the focus and task of marriage*, requiring the contribution of both. Marriage must be a priority (pp.187–89).

Love is the source that feeds the work of mutual accompaniment and reciprocal understanding. It is reasonably made together, not defaulting to others' expectations.

The two create a work of art, forming their shared world. No one element, such as sex, children, or a job, can dominate the other aspects of the whole together.

Marriage takes priority over the family. Children are secondary and need a loving marriage. Marriage is a sphere of fellowship with or without a family.

3. *Marriage is an all-embracing fellowship of love for life.* It fulfills the task of togetherness (pp. 189–95).

The two must leave their parents and become one flesh.

Barth notes Schleiermacher's three forms of what this does not mean:

- The hideous marriage is one united in strife and fighting. *Love is missing.*
- The conscious marriage is a contract without joy, where unity means avoiding fighting at all costs. *Belonging together is missing.*
- The negative marriage is a dead union, accustomed to each other after a long time but seeking life elsewhere. *A positive connection is missing.*

Barth sees these as lacking genuine embrace of each other, only keeping up appearances. Schleiermacher's proposed marriage ideal is that the partners become identical in thought, feeling, and so on. Barth rejects this form of oneness that loses the uniqueness of each.

Marriage should free men and women to be who they are in their particularity. Their unifying love frees them to be dear to each other, not equal or identical in thoughts and activities.

Married love is the fellowship of freedom that embraces differences. One cannot lay down the law for the other. That is a bondage of control.

Marriage must work toward the freedom of both partners. This freedom does not mean they will understand each other.

There is a mystery in love. Marriage is the unity; understanding is not. Love holds all along the way, and respect allows for differences.

Sexual intercourse is the affirmation of one by another.

"The concern in marriage is with emancipation for this reciprocal and practically experienced awareness of each other, this orientation on one another, in which there is mutual acceptance and co-operation, and in this way (and this way alone) mutual affirmation and therefore faithfulness and love."[4]

With this coexistence, a house of love is faithfully built. This orientation nurtures the hospitality of marriage, making space for the other to belong. God established this space after making humans—marriage was made for humans, not humans for marriage.

4. *Marriage is an exclusive life commitment* (pp. 195–202). It lives uniquely within the network of other relationships. Marriage must be prioritized and protected.

The marriage partnership does not exclude friendships with men or women but tolerates them, acknowledging the exclusivity of the life partnership.

---

4. *CD* 3.4, § 54, p. 192.

Barth rejects bigamy, although he can see that society may change its laws and customs as it abides by its changing authority. Theologically, God is the authority and excludes bigamy.

Barth reasserts that marriage is born of the love of a man and a woman. Simultaneously, loving more than one is not possible or permissible.

Love compels us to discover that we belong, are meant for each other, and choose each other.

Once the choice to be married is entered, that choice is behind. The path ahead involves learning how to be faithful in the partnership born of love and lived in love.

In marriage, God reflects His unity as the loving God of the covenant of free grace lived in faithfulness. Monogamy is an echo of this enduring love.

Deuterogamy, the marriage of a person after the death of a spouse, is affirmed by Barth. Marriage does not extend beyond death as an obligation. The marital limits have reached their end and free one to marry another.

On the mission field, polygamy is apparent. It is not our task to change the culture. Their intent may be termed monogamous in its intent of faithfulness in answer to the command of God to love and obey.

5. *Marriage is to be an enduring partnership* (pp. 203–13). Divorce in the Old Testament appears permissible, but not in the New Testament. Marriage is for a lifetime.

What is love but a mere experiment if it is temporary and expendable? Society, the state, and the Church did not invent permanent marriage. Marriage was discovered in the faithfulness of the covenant God.

We cannot say any marriage is "made in heaven" or is without promise.

It may be that divorce becomes inevitable, but it should not be easily pursued. There must be faith that divorce is an obedient form of acknowledging God's judgment to end the marriage. The marriage is dissolved as permission when not living under God's command. It must come only when there is no alternative.

Divorce for a believer is not forbidden but a bitter path

Expanding Our Hospitable Embrace toward Others

to walk. Divorce may be the only way to return to healing and new obedience. This path includes the possibility of blessing a second marriage and not the scorn of being polluted persons.

6. *Marriage requires a free and mutual love based on God's freeing love* (pp. 213–24). It is a mutual choice to recognize a love that brings reciprocal freedom.

God calls a corresponding partner for marriage and equips both by joining them in choosing to love.

Other humans ought not to be the ones to choose for us. We need to be personally involved and act in love.

The love of Yahweh elects to make a covenant with His people in covenantal faithfulness. Jesus continues this with His Church.

The center of the biblical message is God's covenant election (marriage implied) to love His bride (people and Church) unconditionally. This focus has implications for every aspect of life, including the choice of a partner.

Israel's persistent infidelity in breaking the covenant contrasts with God's unconditional love. The idea of mutual love is a painful reminder of how Israel has failed God, joined by all of humanity that follows Israel's pattern.

What is the love that sustains a marriage? It is the free, mutual choice to engage in understanding, self-giving, and desire gifted by God to live for one another through their lifetime.

One should only marry with authentic love, which requires mutual understanding, self-giving, and desire. This engagement is the full breadth of *eros* fully expressed.

Eros should not be reduced to desire. It is the joy of being willing to belong to one another. God sanctifies desire in the context of God's love indwelt.

Affection is an inclination, a movement toward the other that is not yet a decision. It is the seed from which love grows, full of possibility. It opens two lives to each other without binding them together. It is not yet adequate for marriage but moves toward its potential.

7. *Marriage is a public relationship* (pp. 224–40). It has an outward engagement with those who surround a couple.

This transition may include a wedding or be seen through some event, facilitating the new relation to the surrounding community as a couple. Marriage is not isolated from the event, but through the event, a union is integrated into an immediate community.

Having a wedding does not equal being married. Tradition locks people into an institutional form, which can be legalistic. A ceremony is not a complete companionship before God. It is an artificial replica needing real shared love for a lifetime.

Marriage has a *public form* that facilitates recognition and affirmation. The couple stands with their parents and family as their nearest neighbors.

Marriage also has a *legal form* that validates the legitimacy of the union in the state. But the declaration of the state cannot constitute the marriage, only confirm its existence.

Finally, marriage has a *churchly dimension*. The church ceremony declares the union before God to know His promises and blessings.

Who is free in marriage in obedience to God (pp. 231–40)?

- One who listens to the command of God as the voice of the Good Shepherd, rejoicing in whatever it may mean as valid for life. We are freed to love.

- One who knows they cannot create or achieve freedom without Jesus. From Him alone streams the freedom to obey the command of love that surrounds and shapes us. We all have emotions and eyes that turn away and destroy relationships. All need His grace to restore us with humbled hearts. We are freed to be open and not judgmental.

- One who allows themself to be lifted by the wonder of grace. Encountering God, our shadowy, resistant, hidden side is exposed. But divine grace sees us and removes the shame and judgment. We are freed by God's forgiveness to forgive.

In the sphere of men and women, all have sinned and fallen short of God's loving intentions. But all may be led by God's loving command. God's kindness leads us to turn from self-centeredness to serve in the embrace, being accepted by God and freed for the other.

Expanding Our Hospitable Embrace toward Others

There can be whole-hearted love in relationships that do not blossom into marriage but bear its loving marks. Ultimately, we are all justified sinners in male and female relations and as sexual beings. Jesus has made way for renewed life living under His loving command. We live by grace.

2. Parents and Children (pp. 240–85)

- We are creatures created by God.
- We are conceived by a mother and father and born into the world of other humans.
- We exist in a sequence of generations as a child.
- We may become fathers or mothers.

This context of creaturely existence is the second sphere of human relationships. We must hear and respond to the divine command as it expands to this horizon.

Barth assumes that each person has the capacity for sex with another to produce children. Having children is not required, but available for building the generational staircase.

As a child, we uniquely relate to two persons who may or may not nurture us at this second level within the first community of males and females.

We also may marry or be involved in a child-bearing relationship that develops a further level of communal life, creating a life history woven together or unraveling from this initial point.

A couple engages in sex, whether married, in love, or pursuing one of many variations of sexual arrangements. They may engage in sex and intend not to have children. Parents are likely to have planned their children, although this is not necessarily true.

Children become a symbol of life history for a couple, sometimes with pain. A web of relations may expand with brothers and sisters, aunts and uncles, grandparents and great-grandparents. Barth's concern focuses on parents and children.

Barth avoids the concept and word *family*. He is concerned that the word *family* implies bondage for those who belong to a lord, as is evident in patriarchal societies.

> Love compels us to discover that we belong, are meant for each other, and choose each other.

Parents instruct children in life. Children are to accept. The parent-child relationship implies hearing and obeying the Word of God.

Honoring parents includes respect, gratitude, agreement, devotion, and the willingness to learn. Parents are God's primary representatives for children insofar as they correspond to the intentions of God.

Only God the Father can give proper meaning to this name. Human fathers should further the mercy and grace of God to their children, corresponding with God's primary care and connection.

God is Father for the whole human family. Human fatherhood humbly sits alongside unparalleled divine fatherhood.

Because Jesus is our human brother, every human child is a child of God. God is our true family of origin.

Parents, through their actions, are responsible for bringing children within God's actions. They are God's representatives. God speaks human words intended for parents to hear; they are God's means of communication.

To be born of God is to become His child, attached through the name of Jesus.

In the Old Testament, being a child of God meant being one of the people of Israel.

In the New Testament, being children of the Father is mediated through Jesus. We are children rooted in Jesus, made members of His body, the community of the Church. We are awakened to this reality by the Holy Spirit guiding us to know who we are in Him.

Our human parents stand in the foreground of our historical existence. But our childhood is more deeply grounded in the fatherhood of God and the restoring work of Jesus. Our relationship with God shapes our identity. Honoring our human parents is not abolished but put into perspective.

Human parents have limited authority; proper authority belongs to the Father through Jesus. Human parents point to Him. This reflects the first commandment, to have no other god or authority before God.

The fifth commandment affirms that children should obey their parents to honor God and for His glory. Our parents are to teach us to love God over themselves.

The youngster, adolescent, and adult child follow their parents insofar as they are God's representatives. This honoring of parents continues even after death.

A time comes when honoring our parents means going our own way. The season of learning has passed; following the Spirit is the path before us. Parents become senior friends.

There are many ill-prepared, oppressive parents. All parents have inadequacies, not always reflecting the fatherhood of God. We are not to hold any illusion of perfect parents.

Expanding Our Hospitable Embrace toward Others

A human parent can only live by God's forgiving grace. We are not to be our parents' judges. We must avoid the dangers of imitating, despising, or thinking their deficiencies reflect God's character. We must learn openmindedness and patient understanding.

Children may never recognize the divine mission in their parents, which God has called them to provide. We all need eyes of grace to see beyond human perceptions and judgments.

Jesus alone fulfills the command of God. Parents and children live within the obedience that Jesus offers the Father on our behalf. Despite our failure, He has restored us by His grace that transforms by the power of His love and Spirit. This gift is His order amid our chaos.

Beyond our human horizon as children and parents, we thank God that He intervenes with healing grace. Beyond our blindness, we see the divine command to live before Him as our true horizon.

Jesus has obeyed God's law and commandment on our behalf. We must recognize the consequence that the kingdom of God has come to us, and we live in His presence. He foreshadows the end that is to come, revealed as perfect obedience in the sphere of the parent-child relation.

The kingdom of God must be our orientation above all earthly relationships. We owe faithfulness to the kingdom even when leaving behind familial relations.

Barth discusses those who never have children, whether by choice or otherwise. While parenthood is a joy, children are not required for happiness. Others should not consider having no children a misfortune, although it may cause pain and loss for those who desire children.

Having to have children is a burden lifted from us. "Parenthood is now only to be understood as a free and in some sense optional gift of the goodness of God."[5] The childless must let themselves be comforted by God since the Child who needed to be born was born for them too.

Those without children are empowered to build their lives in their particular way in a life of caring.

Barth discusses birth control and choosing not to have children. He asks whether "Be fruitful and multiply" still applies to New Testament Christians.

Birth control is reasonable when viewing the increase in the earth's population.

---

5. *CD* 3.4, § 54, p. 266.

Sexual intercourse may complete the command to become one flesh in marriage indicating a desire or readiness for children. Barth wants to maintain the goodness of God in giving children.

One must have a clear conscience before God, whether the decision is made in obedience to God or out of self-interest. Barth acknowledges there is no absolute denial of birth control.

What options are there for a couple not wanting the responsibility of children?

1. Refrain from sex. This method challenges the psychological dimension of the relationship.
2. Engage only during a woman's period. This approach involves complicated techniques and anxious considerations and removes the joyful spontaneity.
3. *Coitus interruptus.* This tactic can be psychologically difficult and unfulfilling.
4. Use contraceptives. This option is the most unnatural.

All of these put humans in control. Barth cannot recommend any one of them over the others. We must not make our distaste a law for others. Barth follows the convention of his day, thinking that any option motivated by self-seeking, pleasure-seeking, or convenience is evil when it is a "no" to God's "Yes."

The decision must be made in faith, not fear. Both partners must agree in complete freedom. The man must concede the emotional cost for the woman and accept her concerns.

When the two decide to have children, they must recognize that honor comes with obligations. Barth affirms the honor and dignity of an unmarried mother having a special gift from God. The father has honor and responsibility as well.

> Because Jesus is our human brother, every human child is a child of God. God is our true family of origin.

Becoming a father and mother is a significant turning point. They must care for a new person, involving joy and seriousness.

The main task of parents is to care for their children in alignment with God's will. They should live with their children, knowing God sees, knows, loves, maintains, and guides them.

Barth suggests parenting should never be a matter of control, shaping them, or sacrificing for their happiness. They must bring children to know they stand before God, who is their advocate and guardian.

Parental authority must never mean hierarchical control. Authority cannot be reduced to the parent's will or viewpoint. Eventually, children will rebel when they develop their views.

Proper authority is recognized when the children see that their parents also stand under authority—the God who has proper authority.

Parenting can never be wholesome and healthy if only developing the child's individuality. There is a season of growing, beyond which parental guidance fades, and God nurtures their developing self in love.

The law judges and binds. The gospel gives freedom and life; we invite kids into its reality.

Parental responsibility is giving children opportunities to encounter the living God, to know Him, and to love and honor Him.

Childhood is short. Kids are near neighbors for a season and then move on. Parents offer opportunities; they can do little more.

We direct our kids to God, from whom we received them. The Holy Spirit will hold them despite challenging situations.

Jesus stands for our children against the evils of the world. He stands on the border of their lives in a way parents cannot. Their future is rooted in His relationship with them, not our inadequate attempts.

3. Near and Distant Neighbours (pp. 285–323)

Instead of focusing solely on the family, Barth acknowledges a network of relations connects us with humanity, shaping us through our history with them.

Barth describes near neighbors as living close in proximity or sharing a common history, mutually known through sharing everyday life.

Distant neighbors live in different histories, locations, and cultures, only indirectly related. We might call them foreigners; this third sphere exists within wider humanity, the fourth sphere.

Distant neighbors interface at many levels. God's command speaks to them as well as us. He claims all humanity for His service.

Language is one of the challenges with neighbors far and near. Language may unite us when we have a common language and separate us when it is foreign. Communication becomes connection or alienation.

We begin with the language we know. We use our language to build relationships with neighbors. We expand our network by developing language with them.

Near and far are spatial concepts of our geographical locatedness. We live within the boundaries on the map. From home, we see the distance of others from us.

We speak and act as we develop our connection with our place and its inhabitants.

In our home place, we know the history, experiences, and consequences of the path that shaped the community. Foreigners share a different past.

No one has a pure bloodline. We are complex, distinguished by religious, political, cultural, social, and economic factors. Physical differences may be an issue, but histories set us apart.

Our historical outlook informs our attitude about the future. This perspective shapes different assumptions, questions, anxieties, needs, and tasks to consider, and we feel our differences and divisions.

Humanity is one, yet it is made of many groups with different histories. We recognize each other as neighbors, distinguished by language, geography, and stories needing reconciliation.

We leave the past with our neighbors, walking into a new future with Jesus and them. Jesus is the center and meaning of all histories, whether acknowledging or resisting Him.

Staying close to Jesus, we hold near neighbors with one hand and distant neighbors with the other. We belong to humanity. We cannot be rigid in thinking about and responding to others. Our relationships to others are fluid.

We go amiss thinking we can define Americans, Russians, or any group. In every case, God stands with us to break down barriers and build bridges across chasms and confrontations.

Nations are transitory. Past empires have fallen. Who knows the future, except that it will keep changing? The things the world holds as glorious keep passing away.

God is eternal, and His rule over nations is permanent. He is still present as the Lord, Creator, and Sustainer of our sphere.

Our near and distant neighbors are reversible, fluid, and removable. Our current state we must hold lightly and humbly.

God has not commanded the borders, governments, languages, or cultures of people—He commands them to acknowledge His lordship and obey as neighbors.

In this human sphere, the Christian must be bound to Jesus and equally free by the Spirit. One must be conservative in the commitment to love and radical in expressing love.

There is no specific command regarding nationality or the organization of nations. When nations claim they are set up and sustained by God's ordering, they construct a god created to conform to national and cultural values.

Expanding Our Hospitable Embrace toward Others 297

This national god is an idol who demands our sacrifice. It gives humans power in God's name but contrary to His command.

Barth recounts events between the world wars when a people group (the Germans) were set on a level equal to God's arrangement of male-female and parent-child. A nationality was prioritized as part of God's "ordering of creation."

The Holy Spirit breaks national self-centeredness that forgets the neighbors. We must learn the humility of serving the living God.

It is easy for nations to become the primary form of fellowship and its laws the only laws. The state replaces the Church, the government replaces the clergy, and human laws replace the command of God.

The biblical message does not focus on the history of nations; the focus is on God. Nations are secondary characters with which God interacts.

Humans are called to participate in caring for creation and the nations God has given, making space for their histories.

Israel is the exception. It receives its identity from God through His covenant with His people. The same becomes true of the body of Christ in the New Testament.

From this root of belonging, we understand command and obedience as the freedom God has established, embracing and calling us to walk with Him.

The Bible is not concerned with developing a history of nations. We sense their presence and the backdrop of world history. The spotlight shines on the history of God's covenant.

From the story of one family in the opening chapters of Genesis, we move in chapter 12 to the emergence of the world of nations. God's covenant history now stands in distinction from world histories.

After Noah, we see the world of nations reconstituted by his deliverance. God covenants with the nations with a Nevertheless of divine faithfulness for His creatures. The time has come for near and distant neighbors.

We came from one human. The Bible hopes nations will unite again in one human determined by God's revelation.

The problem of the Tower of Babel (Genesis 11) is attempting unity based on human terms and making "a people" equal to God. It is arrogant humans thinking in the form of brick and mortar. This move is a rejection of God.

The nations became distant neighbors with different languages, similar to the first couple leaving the garden.

The result of humanity's pursuit was the loss of one language. They became near and distant neighbors with misunderstandings that come with separation. Their arrogance distanced them from God. All human histories diverge from there.

Humans are called to participate in caring for creation and the nations God has given, making space for their histories.

By God's act, the nations can no longer conspire against God as one people. It is better to be dispersed across the earth than to conspire against God.

God is not against towers, technology, or building civilizations. He is against human arrogance, replacing the providence of God to make ourselves great.

The scattering of humanity is its preservation. Grace prevents the greater evil and creates space for freedom that gives room for many people. The original unity of humankind, lost by arrogance and sin, leaves us homesick for redemption and reunion.

Pentecost is the story of contrast with Babel (Acts 2). The whole Church is brought together and empowered by Jesus. The Holy Spirit brings Jesus' presence to them to extend the kingdom. The Spirit is the gift not owned. With the Spirit comes empowerment for a community united in Christ.

The gift of the Holy Spirit provides a way for people to understand the presence and power of Jesus. He speaks to every nation. Babel is reversed. Many hear the witness to Jesus and experience the works of God.

The words at Pentecost overcame the gulf between near and distant neighbors. The event happens within Israel but is enlarged to a universal Israel with many languages. Israel is not forgotten; it is fulfilled. Israel scattered across all human distinctions as a Spirit-empowered witness.

The new speech of God is given to neighbors near and far by the power of the Holy Spirit. God's goal in human history is fulfilled by His calling and the participation of a people to go with Him.

COMMENTARY:

- Barth includes all human relations within theological ethics.
- Barth avoids focusing on the word *family*. Only God may, in some sense, unveil the meaning of family.
- God creates humanity as male and female, as complementary companions. Only in respect and care for the opposite sex can the image of God be understood.
- Sexual connection is an essential factor in male-female relationships as an act of creating children and serving each other, not to be entered for self-serving.

- Birth control is a complex subject. It is a disruption of God's intent for children. Barth does not discuss abortion here but will in the next paragraph on protecting life.
- Barth affirms parenthood and also singleness. One must follow the vocation God provides.
- Parents do not own children; they are temporary guides and nurturers to direct children to connection with God, their true Father.
- Children are to honor their parents insofar as they represent God's intent.
- Being neighbors is an open category. We are part of the whole of humanity, who are neighbors. We are to love our neighbor, but not each neighbor in the same way.

CONCLUSION FOR THE CHURCH: This section takes on the field of human interactions. The Church still wrestles with relationships between the sexes, the act of sex, the implications for family, parenting, and how we relate to the opposite sex.

The Church often identifies sex with sin. Therefore, gender immediately connects our ethics to relationships. Big topics wrestle with the sexes and sexuality. Pornography, unmarried sex, the breakdown of the family and marriage, abortion, sex trafficking, rape, incest, divorce, domestic abuse, and more reveal a lack of ethical clarity about relating to the opposite sex. Yet sex is a gift of God.

Barth compels the Church to think theologically about God's intentions for men, women, and families. In short, we need to learn from God's love and work within it, articulating what healthy sexuality looks like when lived as the gift of God. The Church has the opportunity not to be an institution of prohibition but to clarify the "Yes" of God when expressing God's love.

I sense that Barth's deepest desire is to let the truth of the gospel be his legacy. He can be nothing more than one who points beyond himself to the living God, whose command we obey sometimes and often fail. Jesus is the gift the Church offers to sinners as sinners.

INSIGHT FOR PASTORS: We have a great challenge before us. We also have a significant opportunity to help men and women see themselves for who they are as God's children. This opening means learning to see through the eyes of grace and not conforming to culture.

Every person wrestles with questions: Am I enough? Will anyone want to be with me, want me, want to love me? Can I accept and give myself to others as a mate, friend, family, or neighbor? These questions begin our wrestling with who we are in the context of other humans, whether intimate or acquaintances. As a pastor, you can reset the field by affirming who we are before Jesus, who establishes our identity as His children.

Healthy sexuality begins by acknowledging we are sexual beings with one another. Fulfillment as a human is not solitary. God creates us to share joy in being who we are with others, who are different from us yet part of our story.

As a pastor, you are the gracious parent to those entrusted to you. You are called to point them to the loving presence of Jesus and not to build fences around them. Learning to live with reverence for Christ in the present moment is the most powerful position one can nurture in this long human journey through the wild.

INSIGHT FOR THEOLOGIANS: This business of human relationships is difficult for theologians trained in principles and arguments. But this is where theology becomes ethics. God made us for Himself and one another, but with some complexity.

Human relationships are a science. We are clarifying the dynamic, personal environment in which we live. Like the weather or the ocean, the object of study—persons—constantly changes. Barth gives us tools for this sphere of study. We must explore the levels of our created orderliness as embodied and relational beings. The best science engages every situation with enough wonder to learn. The theologian must hear from the personal presence of Christ and not merely principles that miss listening to Jesus. Science is always attentive listening.

Relationships are also an art. Artists take time to make something beautiful and meaningful. The Spirit moves us to intuit the moves of love composed into relationships of intimacy, family, or the neighborhood. If we do not see theology with this resonating outworking, we will work in a detached manner that departs from Jesus into theory. This engagement is not textbook theology, like observing a score of music. It is singing from the sheet music with others, creatively improvising as we proceed with others.

CLARIFYING QUESTIONS: Does your theology of human relationships follow a set of rules for marriage, family, parenting, and being neighborly? *Or* do you stand with Jesus, inviting marriages, families, and neighbors to learn a life of serving each other?

CHAPTER 21

A HUMBLY HOSPITABLE LIFE TOGETHER

§ 55. Freedom for Life

FOCUS STATEMENT: The life of God invigorates human life to flourish. In § 55, Barth focuses on making room for others: to live, protect, and serve. We grow together by finding God's freedom through a life that is always hospitable.

Our lives do not belong to us; they are on loan from God. Our contentment requires pursuing life, health, and joy with others. We invest our time and space as we respect ourselves and others, protecting and nurturing all that belongs to God—which is all of us.

We do not merely exist; we are called to love, help, and work actively in the community. This life-in-action participates in God's kingdom, obeying the command to love as we are loved. We have been given life; we pass on what has been offered, pouring into others' lives, and serving beyond our capacities.

INTRODUCTION: We are made as whole beings and now explore living together as embodied beings. Barth switches Jewish philosopher Martin Buber's I-Thou category to Thou-I, signaling that others precede and prepare for our particular existence. The ethical life develops in personal contexts.

Paragraph 55 is the second longest paragraph in *CD* 3 at 241 pages (§ 41 has 288 pages). It contains three sections developing how we live as unique humans. Each person lives actively (section 1) in a life to be protected (section 2) and fully expressed in a life of loving, working, and resting as God accompanies us (section 3).

Barth does not give lists of rules for living. Instead, he explores the dynamics of our particularity lived within our relationships. Freedom comes in answering God's call to live together with love and respect.

CONTEXT: *CD* 3.4
Pages in Paragraph: 241 pages (pp. 324–564)

302   *Church Dogmatics 3.4*

Subsections
1. Respect for Life
2. The Protection of Life
3. The Active Life

📖 **TEXT: § 55. Freedom for Life**

☥ **OPENING SUMMARY: As God the Creator calls man to Himself and turns him to his fellow-man, He orders him to honour his own life and that of every other man as a loan, and to secure it against all caprice, in order that it may be used in this service and in preparation for this service.[1]**

☥ **SUMMARY:**

1. Respect for Life (pp. 324–97)

God the Creator brings us home to Himself and to engage our fellow humanity with welcoming hospitality. Finally, He turns us to respect our particular life through self-caring hospitality.

We exist upwardly, connecting with God. We live horizontally with others to whom our lives are linked. Within these contexts, we are each a specific person.

In theological ethics, we deal with the whole person acting before God. We cannot be distinguished in parts: we are embodied beings who think, feel, intend, act, relate, and respond to God's freeing command to live.

Humans start with intuitions about their lives, thinking each belongs to themselves and exercises some power over themselves, others, plants, and animals. Each person feels as though they live their own life. This perception becomes a false assumption.

All we know through natural observations is the phenomena of being human. Our observations do not help us understand our true humanity as a meaningful life together.

Theological ethics holds that God addresses humans:

1. *Humans exist as independent beings*, given life entrusted to them by God as life on loan for His service. We know ourselves as we are addressed and given meaning by Him.

---

1. *CD* 3.4, § 55, p. 324.

A Humbly Hospitable Life Together

2. We exist with a *distinction of being as a unity of body and soul* as creatures moved by God's Spirit. We perceive, think, desire, choose, and reason as we depend on the life-giving act of God.

3. God acknowledges *each of us as someone, a particular person*, with specific activities that shape us. We are responsible for caring for the life we have on loan. Our lives are not castles to defend ourselves from God; they are His provision for us. God knows our name as the particular person we are.

4. God *made us to live in time, shaped over the journey of one lifetime*. We will be the same person before and after hearing God address us. We live by the free action of the Spirit, accompanied by the Word of God.

5. God *reassures us that we self-determine our lives* as spontaneous authors who accomplish an independent movement. We do not compete with God, nor does He abandon us.

6. God has determined that we *live with Him in freedom, oriented to His life*. Following our nature, we walk toward bondage. But we gather with the Word of God to enjoy His freedom.

7. God has also determined that we *live in freedom in fellowship with others*. We meet with others like ourselves and share the release of our spontaneous interaction. We are made for the interrelatedness of friendship as a loan from God.

8. Barth considers an eighth point regarding *how we stand with plant and animal life*. God does not address our relation to plants and animals. We know He addressed us and gave us responsibility. We are concerned with human life, not all of life. We do not want to diminish our relation to animal life but want to respond to what God has spoken.

> We exist upwardly, connecting with God. We live horizontally with others to whom our lives are linked. Within these contexts, we are each a specific person.

Barth expands on this in six clarifications:

1. When God commands us to live in freedom, we are called to obey *what it means to be human*.

2. We are commanded *to live with human coexistence*. Obedience means to live as ourselves with others.

3. The command *to be human is a divine decree*, accepting God's placement under His care and living by the gift of His life-giving Spirit.

304 Church Dogmatics 3.4

4. We are commanded to *live freely within the benefits of God's grace* that makes us living persons.
5. We live as *a gift that cannot be earned*. God entrusts us with life as a loan to enjoy, use, and be fruitful, to treasure this gift, and freely share it with others.
6. We are commanded to treat the *gift of living as a loan to be renewed daily* with passion. We must take on responsibilities, working to accomplish what is possible within our abilities.

God taking on human form in Jesus reveals His respect through electing and loving human life.

One ought to be shocked that the Christian Church has looked at human sensibilities, religion, and secular humanism to explore ethics. God has given Himself to open our understanding of human behavior in action.

Respect for life means focusing on someone (Jesus), not something (a concept).

We all belong to God as personal beings worthy of the respect He extends. What does it mean to respect others?

1. We live with a *sense of mystery* that allows space for others' uniqueness. While we are similar, we must remain awake to the marvel of each other and not make them an object or take them for granted.
2. We must learn to *appreciate and affirm* the uniqueness of living with others. We cannot focus entirely on ourselves (egoism) or others (altruism). We must affirm the mystery, accepting the gift of sharing life with others.
3. We must become *aware of limitations*. We have time and space as a horizon of constraints within which to live.

God protects life, as is made evident in the command: "Thou shall not kill."

Instincts drive human life, corresponding with the soul of our bodies. Our desires drive choices that form impulses to act, feeding our bodies, sexual urges, and sleepiness. These lower instincts influence the higher spheres of behavior.

Instincts are part of human life in common with animals. But we need not live like animals. By the Holy Spirit, we can make freely loving choices.

For a human to live by instincts does not make them an animal but a sub-animal, who has lost respect in selfish and self-serving behavior that destroys.

A Humbly Hospitable Life Together

When left to instincts, humans do not stop at basic requirements, overcome with an excessive pursuit to fill an insatiable level of satisfaction.

Human impulses and instincts are a gift of God, able to answer the command of God to live. We must respect our instincts created by God. To live is to eat, drink, and connect in love. But these cannot be our guide.

Asceticism, the restriction of meeting specific needs, can help manage one's impulses, not as self-focused suppression, but only when fulfilling the command to love.

We ought not to ask others to do or not do what we will not follow ourselves. This is hypocrisy.

Respect for life accepts the right to our animal instincts until they violate the command to love God or our neighbor. We must protect justice for all human rights within these limitations.

We are all responsible for others when fulfilling the command of God. God is a friend of the poor and hungry and an enemy of those who deprive the needy. God is a radiant humanitarian.

We may abstain from culturally banned practices and still be dictators or narcissists.

We may appear spiritually strict outwardly but be controlling and disordered toward God and others inwardly.

Barth inserts his thoughts on plants and animals. Both have a form of life in a biblical sense. Animals have instincts like humans, but we cannot get inside their life experiences or rationality to discern if they have an animal soul. It is simply unknown.

We can only work from human analogies to describe animal and plant life. We all have physical structures and forms of impulses that allow us to interact with what is other and to survive.

We cannot have a single ethic that embraces humans, animals, and plants as an undifferentiated whole. We may consider the ethics of our relation to plants and animals.

Treating life with respect beyond the human form is a significant issue. We cannot ignore these other spheres. On this matter, we cannot make a doctrine or define what is rightly ethical. We can protest against thoughtlessness and indifference. We do have a responsibility to nonhuman life.

Humans must think and act responsibly in coexistence with nonhuman life. The world of plants and animals occupies the God-given space in which we live and for which we are called to be caring stewards.

The earth and all it contains belongs to God. God has bound us with the rest of creation. He entrusts us to hold a conscious and deliberate recognition of His honor and power, under which we operate as responsible caregivers.

God gives plants to care for as a provision of food. We should not waste or destroy growing plants irreverently.

God also gives animals for human benefit. Domesticated animals support humans in many profitable ways. We are to respect the lives of animals and are not to be cruel.

The big question is whether we can take an animal's life for human purposes. The harvesting of plants participates in the ongoing renewal of plants. To kill an animal is its end. We do not have a right to kill animals, but we have divine permission.

Respect for life includes the will to be healthy. Health incorporates vigor for human life in our soulish bodily existence.

Some may cherish their bodies and minds in self-absorption in pursuit of health and lose what is good in their relations with others. This is unhealthy.

God demands health, giving us the strength to serve with vitality.

Sickness is the negation of health. It is a powerlessness, hindering the functioning of love. One can be sick and still have strength in their impaired condition. As long as we are alive, we should exercise the power in us. Sickness should not define us; we must be oriented to health.

A fundamental demand of ethics is to live with the power to be the person we may be, empowering body and soul to will the operation of love that frees.

Health must be worked out in our physical and mental fields.

Hygiene applies to our physical and mental existence, body and soul. Hygiene guards us against disease or maintains or returns us to health.

Barth affirms a place for doctors. He expresses concern in cases where doctors treat us as an object with general knowledge. He concedes that doctors know more than we do about human health matters.

Within the history of medicine, there have been discoveries and therapies that help. "Medical art and science rest like others on a legitimate use of the possibilities given to man."[2] We should be grateful.

Jesus did not merely dissolve fear from our consciousnesses; He died on the cross to remove sin. Prayer is not just cleansing our thinking; it is an appeal to the living God. Our trust is in the faithfulness of God, not a form of magic that appeals to His provision for our benefit.

---

2. *CD* 3.4, § 55, p. 362.

A Humbly Hospitable Life Together

God has made Himself responsible for humanity. He is the Victor, even where He has allowed space for sin and sickness. We cannot hope to heal ourselves, but we can humbly pray and be consoled by the promises of God.

Health is part of our existence on earth; it is not eternal. It does not belong to us; it is entrusted to us as a gift from God.

Health is the power to exercise our body and soul. Sickness is an impairing of our ability, a deflating weakness. Life, and hence health, begins and ends—thus, it is limited.

God allows sickness and death. He does not will pain, only health and joy; sickness and death are part of life that God has not chosen.

The will for joy, delight, and happiness is the will for life. This call goes beyond just being healthy or satisfying our impulses. It goes beyond working or being virtuous. It even goes beyond loving God and neighbor. The devoted theologian and the sincerest artist both want enjoyment in life.

We must be serious about our willingness to be happy in obedience. This pursuit is as vital as any ethical question.

The Bible is emphatic about pursuing a life of joy. Joy is the summons to arise from the dark places. God has taken the challenging elements of life and intervened. He takes brokenness and revitalizes it to give joy in the morning.

> A fundamental demand of ethics is to live with the power to be the person we may be, empowering body and soul to will the operation of love that frees.

God's gracious action embraces us to joyfully eat, drink, sing, play, dance, and pray.

Joy is a simple form of gratitude. Time stands still as we savor the moments for which we have yearned.

Most joy is anticipatory. We experience some satisfaction and find ourselves wanting more.

1. We should *always be ready* for joy.
   - Joy is like the Sabbath; it interrupts, focuses us, and ignites life for a time. Readiness for joy is renewal in the rhythms of life.
   - Real joy comes when the Holy Spirit comes.
   - Festivals cannot produce joy if they are mere human labor rather than reflections on God's gifts.
2. We will have joy only when we *give it to others*.
   - Joy is a social matter, seldom found in isolation.
   - Joy is created as it is shared.
   - We must ask from the standpoint of others what will give them joy.

3. True joy is *not fixed on one form* but is open to various forms of joy.
   - Freedom in life allows joy to shine through in different ways.
   - We must not measure joy by its quantity but learn to appreciate the smallest joys.
   - We do well to deepen and develop our receptiveness to the artistic side of existence.
4. Joy intensifies and *deepens our whole awareness* of life.
   - We must clarify what gives us authentic joy and what is a pseudo-joy.
   - We cannot pursue joy at the cost of our health, work, or friendships.
   - We cannot have joy contrary to our conscience, meaning our agreement with what God would rejoice in as the giver of life.
5. Our life belongs to God. Only He can reveal to us *what makes for authentic joy* and pleasure.
   - We must find God's glory in the shadowlands stretching from the cross of Jesus.
   - The proof of our joy is included in the acceptance of our suffering with gratitude at the mystery and wonder of the life given to us by God.
   - Life's beauty, blessing, refreshment, comfort, and encouragement can only be a gift of God—even when we do not recognize it.
6. Joy is a *provisional fulfillment* in a life accepted with gratitude.
   - We expect union with God's eternal life yet to come.
   - In the meantime, we endure with gratitude, with the limitation and frailty that require our acceptance.
   - For now, joy is the faith that clings to what has been accomplished as the future is present in our current moment.

Schleiermacher had a sense of the human being fully alive. But he neglected to acknowledge that we are loaned life from God, whose presence penetrates our lives to bring a deep respect for life as belonging to God's realm. What followed developed personality cultures and individualistic humanism.

The attempt to hide oneself from God is a denial of understanding who we are, like Adam and Eve's first disorienting move. This withdrawal is an act of conflict with God from the human side. God patiently asks, "Where are you?" (Genesis 3:9) like one playing hide and seek, who wisely

A Humbly Hospitable Life Together

knows what the one hiding does not know—He knows us right where we are.

To be obedient to God's command is to come to God as one addressed by Him, desiring to be the unique person God frees us to be within His love.

We do not force our "I will be" before God. Instead, we surrender to become thriving souls by the Spirit, blossoming in the connection of a Thou-I relation with God.

To affirm the uniqueness of who we are is an act of obedience, as long as it agrees with God's embrace and does not turn away to find oneself apart from God.

In trying to find oneself, one runs into a dead end, a cul-de-sac. Alternatively, to go with God is to pursue a path of discovery in God's world as a unique gift.

"I" exist only in a Thou-I relation with God. He comes first, and I live in response. My soul exists attached to the Spirit of God.

The power of the Spirit forms our character in the struggle between flesh and soul. We are called to accept who we are and grow into who we are in the life God allows us.

God made us dynamic and always in process toward our particular service.

The will for life is a particular form of the will for power, in this case being capable of fulfilled living with others, not having power over them.

For Nietzsche, the will to power meant overcoming Christian morality and pursuing dominance over others.

Contrary to the power of Goliaths in the world, the appropriate form of power:

1. God provides, allowing humans *to live this life, loaned* with gratitude to God.
2. God entrusts to each person to have the *capacity to live life as an individual.*
3. God gives as *that which is necessary*, not as a luxury. The only necessary power is *for service to others.*
4. Rests in God's hands to *empower humans to fulfill His purposes.* It is the power of the cross as well as the resurrection. It is the true human capacity to be the gift of God.

> The power of the Spirit forms our character in the struggle between flesh and soul.

God makes His strength perfect even in our weakness.

2. The Protection of Life (pp. 397–470)

Protecting life discusses the biblical command not to kill.

Humans are not to murder other humans or extinguish any group of people.

Respect for life is a positive affirmation to pursue. *Protection* of life focuses on what is prohibited.

All human life belongs to God. God has inhabited created life in Jesus. Therefore, respect is due to it.

This subsection focuses on exceptional cases. We cannot willfully disregard the value of human life. But exceptions may arise.

The case of just killing is an exception in both Testaments as the judgment of God, not as open permission for humans.

Murder is at the top of the list of wrongs between humans. Yet Jesus died for the sins of humanity as the exceptional case. We must always argue against taking the life of another and only permit the most justifiable with extreme resistance.

Suicide is a first consideration—the taking of one's own life. Our lives belong to God and are lent to us as an act of divine favor, not to throw away. Jesus did not throw His life away; He sacrificed it for the restoration of the world.

End-of-life questions are challenging. We are not to sustain life at all costs, a rebellious desire to *avoid the end* of earthly existence. This is different from *willfully ending* it.

Sacrificing one's life may be necessary to save others. One may lay down their life for their friends, not choosing death but willing to give life. We cannot make judgments in the case of war other than to recognize the service offered for others.

Suicide from feeling a failure, a burden, or needing release is a tragic act for procuring freedom. Mental or medical breakdowns are heartbreaking causes of suicide.

Barth asks why the last moment of a person's life should be judged in isolation. We cannot see a person's heart and should consider this an exceptional case.

Self-destruction as murder is denied to us, taking what belongs to God. This does not mean it is an unforgivable sin. If there is forgiveness of sins, there is forgiveness for suicide. Suicide is rebellion against God, who forgives sins and is gracious in Jesus Christ.

Barth argues that we believe that we *must* live. This belief leads to a sense of needing to control our lives. This conclusion makes us feel empty and pressured to make something of ourselves. We are lonely and stressed.

In actuality, we *may* live. We are granted freedom from God to will what is permitted as we live with the Lord of life. We are never alone. We live with gratitude for the grace provided. We belong to God.

Homicide, the killing of another, is forbidden in the civil codes and is a common rule across humanity. Yet many humans are ready to kill for compelling reasons in contentious contexts. It is not our nature but the corruption of our nature that enables us to kill. Those who kill try to justify the act, knowing it is wrong.

A killer decides that taking the life of another is justifiable. Private morality takes over and permits depriving another of life, solely based on the killer's opinion.

Abortion interrupts a life developing in pregnancy. The ethics of the situation have considerations for the mother, father, doctor, family, and unborn child. Barth boldly states it is the killing of a human life.

Barth believes abortion takes the life of a human given by and belonging to God. It is not the child's fault that others want to end their life.

The Roman Catholic church stands against abortion. Modern conventions have been estranged from the Church, denying the place of God in the life of the unborn child. We need more insightful engagement than a monolithic "no."

Legal considerations are inadequate to bestow the mystery and awe of human life that comes from God.

Freedom and grace allow life not to be forced; practicing mercy is permitted. We still may say "no" with kindness, hoping to find other ways.

The knowledge that God says "No" also requires that we acknowledge that God can forgive for this act.

We should stand with clarity that we need God's grace and forgiveness that summons us as we are unmasked. God's "No" stands, yet His "Yes" is not to be forgotten as the more profound stand.

Barth allows for considering exceptions. Human life is not absolute. Those involved should desire a healthy life for the child.

In some cases, the termination of the child's life is not murder. It is a life choice to balance the child's survival against the mother's life. It is valid to choose to live with the consequence of the loss of the other. Barth gives four considerations:

1. What is at stake must be a life against a life where one must be sacrificed to save another.

2. One must be bound with a resolute conscience before God to make a free decision.
3. The choice must be responsible to God and not to humans, considering what seems reasonable to them.
4. One must be assured that this is an exception, believing God will forgive what is against His will.

Euthanasia asks whether anyone is permitted to will certain sick, insane, or deformed persons to end their lives. These are the incurable who are often deemed "useless." Barth says, "No."

Euthanasia can become a form of negative eugenics, weeding out those considered undesirable. Who is to say that older people are spent and should be removed? The question is: Who is precious in the eyes of God?

A strong community carries its weak members; rejecting those we feel are unfit is sinning ourselves.

Euthanasia, as a beautiful and painless death, is to unburden the community or release the person. In this case, it is a question of medical ethics. Like abortion, advanced technology opens questions about what is permissible within defined limits.

> All human life belongs to God. God has inhabited created life in Jesus. Therefore, respect is due to it.

Barth honors the intentions of humanitarian impulses but cannot affirm taking the place of God, who protects human life. Dying can be a blessing only when it comes from the hand of God.

For Barth, euthanasia is not an emergency event or a life saved for one lost. It is about suffering, and we must defer to God. Barth concedes that the artificial prolongation of life may be arrogance on the human side that will not let God's action find completion.

Self-defense is an act against someone attacking, with possibility of the aggressor being killed. The danger must be direct and otherwise unstoppable. Self-defense is not encouraged, but it may be justified.

For our purposes, we are only asking what is right before God. It is natural to defend oneself, but does love call us to love even the neighbor attacking by not taking their life?

We are pointed toward peace. When one's life is in danger, one can defend oneself as God has commanded to protect life.

Capital punishment is a drastic means of defense. In this case, a collective body responds to the assailant. The judgment passes to an individual executioner as an act of retribution on behalf of a family or society.

A Humbly Hospitable Life Together

Tragically, capital punishment has intensified as Christianity has spread. The Church's compliance is one reason the gospel has been discredited.

Does the individual, in cooperation with the culture, have the right to avoid the command not to kill? There are three theories put forward to justify this taking of life:

1. To *protect* society, the violator might be made an example for others or prevented from further opportunities.
2. Retribution is a *payment* with one's life to satisfy a debt to society or offended persons. Christians often feel this fulfills God's retributive justice.
3. *Punishment* teaches a lesson to the offender to acknowledge wrongdoing. But with the death penalty, it is hard to make much improvement. Why not rehabilitate if that is the concern?

Barth holds that capital punishment should end if the command to protect life is accepted.

Barth does concede the situation where killing protects the state as a whole. True enemies must be taken seriously. These persons do not merely disrupt the state; they attack with the intent to destroy. Resisting the attack may preserve life.

Conditions for the exceptional use of capital punishment:

1. Recognizing that one person should die rather than the whole nation perish.
2. Recognizing that it is the will of God fulfilled as the reconciling expiation of God.
3. Recognizing that causing the person to die is the only mercy for all humanity.

These criteria are possible with treason in war. The person has acted for war and not for peace. Also, tyrannicide may justify removing a cruel tyrant from leadership, eliminating a dangerous person who threatens the nation. Hitler is a prime example.

War raises a serious issue regarding how we protect life. Illusions about a war that must be addressed:

1. The illusion that we can be *uncommitted spectators* in war. Some may think of the military or soldiers as a class set apart for war;

the rest are not involved. This view is a myth; all are affected by war at some level.

2. The illusion that war is about *the greatness of a nation or its freedom*. War is about economic power. It seeks to acquire and protect land and property. It struggles for influence by employing power to gain more power. It claims to prepare for peace but makes ready for conquest and control.

3. There is an illusion that war aims to *neutralize the enemy with courage and skill*. Instead, it is about killing as many of the enemy as possible. Modern technology has reduced even seeing the enemy, who becomes an impersonal object to be deactivated.

War has become objective, a military science with methods and machines that make killing efficient. We must soberly admit that whole nations are out to destroy one another.

War is about killing, so a just war must have a compelling exception for any justification.

War may save many things, but it does not help people be better. Trauma lives on for a lifetime.

Pacifism will always have a better possibility of bringing life, not death, as a gospel outworking, but it is not the gospel.

Pacifism is not the message of the Church, which should seek to bring light to a dark world, exposing the horror of war.

Christian ethics should emphasize that war is not a normal form of engagement. The Church should plead for the preservation of peace among nations.

Barth thinks that the Church should have a voice against armies that prepare for war (who almost invite it) and only help the voice of pacifism be heard. Pacifism should not be preached in its services, never howling with the wolves with a call that makes it the main focus.

The Church should have learned to keep war at bay by developing strategies to avert war. An emergency may arise that calls for protection with military aid.

Conscientious objection must be a choice to align with God, standing with the proper godly role of the state and contending for peace. This revolutionary act may have a price, but it knows it is to side with God and His future.

Radical pacifism's problem is that it will not stand with God and the oppressed when protection becomes undeniably necessary. When we stand absolutely for or against war, we avoid loyalty to God and follow a principle. There is a time to call out the evil of the enemy and, other times, one's own state.

The Church must stand ready to support or rebuke the state as a necessary frontier, ready to confirm or contend with the actions to express divine order.

> War may save many things, but it does not help people be better. Trauma lives on for a lifetime.

3. The Active Life (pp. 470–564).

We now look at human life as a task, actively corresponding to God's acts, in freedom under the command to love.

We follow God, progressing forward where His love commands. He invites us, and we creatively join, adventuring with God.

Humans desire freedom. Their active nature is the creaturely form of their existence, distinct from plants and animals, experienced through their freedom in sharing God's unique freedom. This freedom is the fruit of responding to the command to love.

Humans live in a sequence of acts that become a history. They never do so alone—always with God, with other humans, and within their environment.

Finding purpose comes through respectful relationships and investing in them to fulfill love's freedom.

An active life is one lived in obedience to God, working in the service of God and others.

The term *work* is easily misunderstood. Work means living here and now in relationships that respond to and participate in the love command of God. It is not human self-effort as a means to acquire by meeting conditions.

Western civilization elevates work to the level of a myth to build great civilizations, even sometimes thinking that is what God wants.

Jesus assumes the value of all kinds of labor, not advocating for any particular form. Jobs cannot become the means to the good life.

Paul was a tentmaker who earned his living. Work was not his focus, but it was meaningful for sustaining life.

Work is not the command of God. Work lies in the background of the Bible; it is not the framework of human life.

The Ten Commandments speak of taking a break on the Sabbath, leaving other days open for human activity.

The Bible does not depreciate work. It has a place of importance in human life.

The Bible calls for relaxation more than modern cultures encourage. The economic drive has made work a master, with pressure for personal and cultural development.

God does permit humans to work as a means of self-focused satisfaction.

God calls humans to go out into the world and share life. This outward orientation allows one to achieve an existence that acts out the gift of God's freedom.

Those who value the contemplative life may see the active life as less spiritual. But each needs to be reaffirmed and reintegrated as life with God.

We must learn the essential nature of the active life from Jesus as the kingdom of God comes down and accompanies us.

We do not merely continue what God has started, as if He passed us a baton. We do not perfect what God began. We participate by responding to what God has done in restoring us to correspondence with Him.

God has come from heaven in Jesus to serve. We place ourselves in His service, choosing God as our priority in love.

To hear, serve, and fear God are all descriptions of obedience.

The first act of serving is to worship God, the central act of our freeing relationship.

In the Old Testament, worship is led by priests. Jesus is our leader in worship in the New Testament.

Ministry is the form of service engaged in the life of Jesus, including men and women to serve with Him as He is with them.

Israel was constantly distracted from serving God. In the New Testament, God acts as the focused servant on behalf of all humanity.

None of God's creatures exists for itself. Each exists for another, and another stands in need of it. Humans are integrated into the order of all creatures and participate in the freedom of every creature.

Freedom for human existence is beyond being a creature. Humans need the neighborliness of the world and its sustaining environment. But all that and the whole universe are not enough. Having fellow humans is not adequate either.

True freedom for human life comes from being summoned by God's command.

The world is bursting with life as we exit the closed circle of our individuality. We embrace loving service as we are loved and served by God. We become other-centered and focused on helping all that God has made.

But mostly, our freedom comes as we burst into the speaking presence

A Humbly Hospitable Life Together

of Him who alone can satisfy His creature as a partner. In relationship with Him, we discover the grandeur of our human existence.

God comes with fatherly accompaniment in the space where we are honored to be His children.

God is not a stranger to us. He comes to us in Jesus, where God meets us as our human companion.

God has a voice and speaks to humans so we can hear. That is to say, the Father addresses us through His Son, and the Spirit gives us ears to respond and become free creatures.

In hearing and accepting God's call, humans are set free by joining God's active life. This ordering is the basis of the ethics of the active life.

God is not so high that He cannot invite us into His service. Humans are not so low as to be disqualified for His service. We are created for correspondence. We receive and give back to God the service offered and shared.

We are drawn into God's activity, radiating the glory of God and bearing His fruit and blessing.

God made His covenant the basis of the world He created; likewise, He created His creature to be His covenant partner as a member of His community.

In the Christian community, no one is excluded, and all are invited.

No one is to be pitied if they do not belong. Neither is anyone to be envied if they must belong.

God genuinely holds and protects humans outside this community, sharing His freedom in other forms than this community. A faithful Christian does not need to judge others but serves instead.

Church history is better understood as what God oversees and accomplishes rather than human self-reflection and congratulations for what humans have done.

Israel and the body of Christ serve as the first expressions of the coming of the kingdom of God. These communities echo God's reconciliation as the Creator breaks into human history.

Jesus is the operation of God in His covenant of grace. He is working out what His Father sent Him to do in service for beloved humanity.

The disciples follow Jesus, preparing for the coming of the kingdom of God, workers in the field of God.

The community meets with Jesus and, therefore, with one another. They abandon the place of isolation and enjoy the hospitality of the host of their gathered life together. The feast that is coming is the feast they now share.

> God calls humans to go out into the world and share life.

Church Dogmatics 3.4

Barth has four *affirmations* of what characterizes a concrete Christian community:

1. The Church is *a particular people* set apart from the rest of humanity, gathered from all nations. Its orientation is to the coming kingdom, not a historical domain. It cannot be the Church *of* the people, only *for* the people, serving with Jesus.
2. The Church is affirmed as *a living people* awakened by Jesus for a specific task, not an institution. It may develop its organization and strategies but only to fulfill its service to the kingdom of God. The institution must be utilized to accomplish its task, not vice versa, where the tasks build the institution.
3. The Church *is a commissioned community* called by Jesus for His coming kingdom. It is not committed to self-improvement or world-improvement. It does not work to make God happy. It follows Jesus where He goes and does what He does.
4. The Church is *a united people* summoned to service. We cannot distinguish between real and false Christians, or as useful and useless. All are useless, but all are used. Also, no distinctions should be made between clergy and ordinary Christians. The whole community is called to service. All may serve; no one is off duty.

In light of these characteristics, how does the Church *actively practice* in cooperation with the living God?

1. The Church becomes a body that *attaches members*. This connection begins with baptism, each becoming part of the community, being invited to die with Jesus to the old life, and become new in Christ's resurrection.

2. As an assembly oriented to Jesus, the Church prepares and adapts its ministry, *building up its members to serve* in love. The internal nurturing of the community is for the external practice of serving. Barth further unpacks the needs of the community:
   i. Pursuing *unity to live for one Lord* by being moved by the Holy Spirit. We are not to diverge into disruptions, divisions, or schisms. The unity of the community is in its head. His Spirit empowers us for service.

A Humbly Hospitable Life Together   319

    ii. Pursuing *practices that bring life to the community* so that it is strong and free, ordered to flourish in the world. The community must embody a visible vitality. By the Spirit, its many gifts will have coherence and attentive guidance.

   iii. Pursuing *a life of knowing the Word*, listening that it may speak. The community is built as it learns to announce its Lord to the world. Theology is a matter for every person, guiding us to go with Jesus.

   iv. Pursuing *a love that binds the community together* as a whole. This love comes from the Lord and His Spirit. The unity of love comes on the horizontal plane only as members share a vocation born from their vertical relation. We grant each other space for creaturely freedom to breathe, move, enjoy, express, and develop. The service of brotherly love is the hardest but most necessary to build community.

3. The Church is commissioned to *reach out to the world*. It cooperates within the world as a witness to those who are not Christians. This attitude is set in motion as follows:

    i. The community *represents God's love for the world*. The Church cannot stand against the world, only with it and for it. Even in its corruption, the world is not an enemy. Loving one another includes non-Christians, who ultimately need the freedom of the Spirit. Our love gives credibility to the love of God we proclaim. Jesus died for every person; we must act consistent with His love.

    ii. The community is *committed to the mission of renewal, calling humans out of the world*. We summon those who are strangers and aliens to know Jesus Christ. There is no promise they will answer. Yet He has acted on their behalf. "The community is as such a missionary community, or it is not the Christian community."[3] Thus, every Christian is a missionary.

   iii. The community is to *preach the gospel to the world*. The God who has loved the world has acted to bring the world out of its confusion and affliction. They must hear the revelation of what God has accomplished to bring them into His life. Jesus has come and will come again. This is the gospel. The gospel is

---

3. *CD* 3.4, § 55, p. 505.

320   *Church Dogmatics* 3.4

the "Yes" of God that says "No" to our brokenness. The human "yes" is an acceptance of His ability to heal and bring us home.

iv. The community has *a prophetic task*: addressing the current events and activities it finds in the world. To speak for God at a particular time is prophetic, declaring what God has done and is doing in His kingdom. The voice of the prophetic community has clarity and power to the degree that each member is a glad child of God.

Humans are not merely the object of His love. We are made to participate in His life.

The work of humans corresponds to and realizes the fatherly rule of God.

God's life is centered in His loving communion as Father, Son, and Spirit. It also has a circumference: His will to be for and with His creation in providential care. Human life is centered on God and echoes a corresponding work. Going out in service is our circumference.

Our work affirms our existence as God's creatures, as the Holy Spirit continually renews us. We did not create ourselves this way—we have life on loan as a gift.

Our work synthesizes our inward and outward elements, body and soul, brought together by the Holy Spirit as a whole human being.

Work can be defined as culture, but culture is not an independent realm with its own laws, dignity, and life. Work lives and acts in the creaturely sphere, produced by human thinking, feeling, and willing. It does not reflect the divine work of God when it works for its own sake.

Human work and culture are a second task; the primary task is service to God. This focus does not devalue human efforts; it reveals their more profound calling. To be fully human is to obey God and be wholeheartedly prepared to work. All human work is done in God's service and under His blessing.

Work is an active affirmation of human existence as an act of self-preservation. Humans want to prolong their lives and develop what is possible. They want to provide a common table of life for those dear to them.

Barth wants humans to be involved in beneficial work and gives five criteria:

1. *The criterion of objectivity.* This aspect means that good work has *goals* and strategies to achieve them. A poorly prepared and presented sermon will not achieve its goal.

A Humbly Hospitable Life Together

2. *The criterion of the worth of human work.* This feature evaluates the *value* of the work one engages in. These will enable cooperation for promoting good in situations that meet real needs—to do honest work. We must not default to serving the individual by doing what is most comfortable or lucrative, thereby missing society's network needing support. We need to discuss how we value each person in our time and place. This approach is living the Christian ethos in the community.

3. *The criterion of the humanity of human work.* This element refers to the *motive* for our work. We may work for our interests, but we also must consider how we benefit each other. There must be mutual assistance. The struggle for control sacrifices the freedom of persons to live and build together. This is when work becomes inhumane. The kingdom of God calls for a redemptive response to the command of God to be for one another.

4. *The criterion of reflectivity.* Work often focuses on the externals of the workplace and associated activities. Undergirding this is an invisible affirmation that brings fulfillment to work. It is the emotional and intentional source from which we set out to work. It is *thoughtful consideration* toward accomplishing one's work. The inward work of reflection belongs to our performance in the world. Thus, reflection plays out as a whole-hearted activity. When unreflective, it becomes meaningless, mechanical work.

5. *The criterion of work's limitation.* The free and loving God claims us for life as whole and free persons. Our obedience must be *meaningful participation* to live a free life. God limits us to protect us and keep us in His freedom. God works and rests; we are called to do the same.

To become enslaved to work is to forget God. One becomes a victim of excessive desires and meaningless goals.

Rest from work is a kind of spiritual hygiene. It is a release from self-preoccupation, freely serving God, and maintaining respectful engagement for self.

Human work would be done much better if we took God seriously and engaged work as children in serious and genuine play. It is the heart-work of the artist and is evident in the scientist as well.

> Humans are not merely the object of His love. We are made to participate in His life.

We must be obedient creatures, including having rest intertwined with our work.

Rest is not inactivity. It is re-creative, refreshing, and beneficial to prepare for the return to one's primary work. One needs one or two hobbies or interests to expand one's refreshment.

Contemplation as rest can become navel-gazing. Self-knowledge becomes a cul-de-sac in the self, circling in self-enclosure.

One may transition from the dead end of self to find the place of hospitality, where one hears the Word of God speaking personally.

Hearing and answering are the intended rest for humans. Departing from our detached selves, we find He has already attached us to Himself.

At rest in the embrace of God, we can see who we are and what we are.

Ultimate rest comes in the act of God speaking, as waking and answering His commanding love.

Our work is always to participate in God's rest, looking toward His final rest for His people (Hebrews 4:9).

COMMENTARY:
- Humans are created for an active life as persons, not separated or self-sufficient.
- Freedom is a way of living with God and others.
- Freedom is characterized by respect for each person's life within the whole matrix of connected relations.
- Protecting life acknowledges that all life belongs to God.
- Barth has not set absolutes; he calls us to protect life and only pursue exceptions when truly protecting what needs greater care.
- Work is not the same as a job. It involves all human activities that serve and reach out to others. It is the kingdom of God in action.

CONCLUSION FOR THE CHURCH: This section addresses our ethics as embodied persons. Barth is concerned that each person's character and the Church's combined body live as a dynamic answer to God's command to live in love.

The Church needs a commitment to health and joy. Beyond loving their jobs, providing for the family, and discovering one's dignity, each person needs to be empowered to serve others at home, in the neighborhood, at church, and in the workplace. Ethics is theology at play.

The Church needs to protect those who are threatened. This gets complicated. Thoughtful persons must wrestle with issues ranging from abortion to suicide to war. We must listen for the call of God's love in each situation.

The Church should have a reputation for nurturing every person within the community to make a difference as a unique expression of the kingdom's coming.

INSIGHT FOR PASTORS: We do not give up our individual lives when giving them to Jesus. Our best self is shaped by living life with Him.

Barth clarifies that each person in a congregation is different and has a gift to give. Pastors are charged to create an empowering environment for active service. Each person must sense the presence of the kingdom of God and their place in it. This develops whole-life ethics.

Church activities are a small part of following Jesus. Each day presents the opportunity to live from joy and find a healthy life within the love of God.

Pastors are not information pushers; they are people empowerers. Jesus did not "go to work." His work was to do the will of His Father all day, every day. It is our work as well.

Pastors are privileged to paint a picture of whole-life obedience as the shape of Christian living. This depiction is not a set of tasks or obligations. It is a clear vision of helping people hear and respond to the voice of God with joy at work from a heart of love.

INSIGHT FOR THEOLOGIANS:

This section resists rational, systematic structures for ethics. It requires that we see humans in a dynamic, systemic response to the call of God. We daily answer the call to live, protect life, and work out our salvation in loving service.

Human systems bring rules and strategies to manage ethical concerns. They work from the logic of taking control. As theologians, we release control to be shown the integrated form of God's kingdom priorities.

Theological ethics requires seeing persons in their systemic relation to God and one another in the field of God's care. Theological ethics must be committed to life in the form of the kingdom of God.

We cannot afford to make theological ethics abstract. As Barth suggests, if we cannot do better than fogging the brains of people, we would be better off joining those who drain sewers or pursue some other service that helps others. A theologian must be dynamic in conversation and adept at listening to what is going on in any situation. Furthermore, we must clarify and create what will bring freedom and joy through awakening to God's presence.

? CLARIFYING QUESTIONS: Does following the Christian way imply an active life of working to serve God by your best efforts? *Or* is every aspect of your life an investment in loving, motivated by God's presence, freeing others to follow Him, and playfully serving in every contribution?

CHAPTER 22

LIFE'S ABUNDANCE WITHIN BOUNDARIES

§ 56. Freedom in Limitation

FOCUS STATEMENT: We finish discussing the hospitality of the creator God, considering our lives as sites for God's gracious encounter. God set a particular time and place for life together.

In § 56, we recognize that life occurs between birth and death. This period becomes the playing field of growth opened for life together. The span of time provides our unique opportunity. We may embrace the journey God makes with us, full of possibilities to flourish as children of God to the end.

INTRODUCTION: This section parallels *CD* 3.2, "Man in His Time." That section explored God's time as eternity and all earthly time as God's creation. This section focuses on time unique to our specific life.

This paragraph ends Barth's discussion of the doctrine of creation as a whole (*CD* 3) as well as this specific volume on the ethics of creation (*CD* 3.4). Barth investigates what fulfills God's intent for the created world—namely, His covenant relationship with each of us.

The three subsections affirm that life is an invitation full of opportunities. God provided freedom. Our vocation is to be fully alive as free persons. We must not try to earn or control life; we may acknowledge what is necessary to be free—the honor of being children of God, our Father who created us.

CONTEXT: *CD* 3.4
Pages in Paragraph: 121 pages (pp. 565–685)

Subsections
1. The Unique Opportunity
2. Vocation
3. Honour

325

📖 **TEXT:** § 56. Freedom in Limitation

✠ **OPENING SUMMARY:** God the Creator wills and claims the man who belongs to Him, is united to his fellow-man and under obligation to affirm his own life and that of others, with the special intention indicated by the limit of time, vocation and honour which He has already set him as his Creator and Lord.[1]

✠ **SUMMARY:**
1. The Unique Opportunity (pp. 565–94)

Barth begins with a review to set the context:

- God calls humans to belong to Him with their whole hearts and lives (§ 53).
- God calls us to connect to our fellow humans in relationships of encounter, affirming, honoring, and enjoying each other (§ 54).
- God calls humans to a commitment to respect their own lives and participate in the lives of others with each serving the other as a gift (§ 55).
- In this paragraph, we see that God has set a time and place for each person—unique boundaries exist, creating opportunities within the space defined by life's limits. He calls us into solidarity with Him.

God has prepared a special place to live within His freedom. Like guardrails on roads or walls in a house, the limits affirm that it is a place for life. In this case, living within God's opportunity gives life and helps us not wander off to get lost. Obedience is to live within the relationship, empowered by His love and freedom.

God is not a stranger. He is the companion who made us and sustains us. We dwell within the hospitable place He has determined as our lifetime and location.

Jesus is the ruler who provides and preserves. He speaks to us, and we hear that we are known. We accept His interruption into our brokenness as we discover we belong to Him.

God does not trample or override our human will or nature. We are not to be pitied for the loss of ourselves, as though God limits our nature. Neither is God limited by our nature. We are not a blank sheet of paper for God to write on.

---

1. *CD* 3.4, § 56, p. 565.

Life's Abundance within Boundaries

Knowing that God knows us, we come to actual knowledge that orients our lives.

When God speaks and commands, we see He knows us and commands us to be what He made us: fully alive and free.

God's limitation is not an affliction on our freedom. It is an affirmation that makes space for God to be God and for us to live responsive to His love.

We are limited to being ourselves as God's partners. When we marry, we limit ourselves to another person. This choice is the gain of a partner determined to live within the limits of shared love.

There is no regret, sense of impoverishment, or deprivation when limitation is understood as the gift of an opportunity for life together.

The *first limitation* recognizes that we are born and someday die. The limits define the boundaries of the life given to each human. We look within the unique opportunity God has given. We are to live it to the full!

> We accept His interruption into our brokenness as we discover we belong to Him.

When our time has passed, we will be with the eternal God. Without the promise of God to be with us eternally, we would pass like a shadow on the wall. The drama of our limited lives exists here and now. Our lives are on loan.

The opportunity available for each person's life is unique to them. It may be used or misused.

God's covenant orients us for our unique opportunity.

Life with Jesus is the purpose of our human existence. In this alignment, we do not lose ourselves; He empowers us for our unique opportunity with Him.

God's covenant implies correspondence: God has established a connection with wayward humanity. We are covenant partners despite our unfaithfulness. We discover we are children and friends of the covenant-making God. We are filled like empty cups.

Jesus Christ is the fellow human of every person, whether or not they know it. He is the center and meaning of human existence.

God has lived in a body like our bodies and found His creation a worthy place to dwell with us. His invisible-transcendence has taken on personal presence-immanence in Jesus in the middle of human history.

He is for us all, but not all are "in Him." That state requires recognition. It means hearing the Word and receiving the Spirit. It means gathering with a community of listeners who become servants. It would mean humans turning to the One who holds them to Himself and accepting His faithfulness on their behalf to share His life. Nevertheless, He chose them all to be in Him.

The divine purpose of a human lifetime is to meet Him who has come to us.

The hospitable God creates a place in time for each of us. We are to recognize and occupy our site gratefully. We are not to scan the horizons for other detached places to indwell. We are set on the stage God provides to accompany us.

Humans attempt to *seize* the day for themselves. But the Christian looks from a different horizon, to be *grasped* by the person of Jesus. We are held by Him each day.

Time belongs to Jesus as He makes room for His showing up for us. Time belongs to Him.

1. He is the One who stands at its beginning and end. He limits Himself, patiently waiting for us from when He knocks until He fulfills His purpose. For us, it is a long time; for Him, it is embraced in His one time as the Alpha and Omega.
2. His time is *short* as He works at the heart of human history. He will be revealed as the Lord. Time is short, not by the calendar, but because He stands at the beginning and the end, held in His one person.
3. We do not know how long time will last. We know where it comes from and where it is going, but not its *duration*. No one knows when it will end. We experience temporal urgency to live the life gifted to us.

The big question is whether we are engaging or neglecting the unique opportunities offered to us each day. Do we act in a "timely" way, responding to the command to love in every act?

We are blind to our missed or resisted opportunities. Only God can judge and redeem our time and actions.

How do we live appropriately within our one life's limitations and hiddenness?

1. We are to *embrace the uniqueness* of our lives as gifts from God and not wish for another life.
2. We must *recognize the urgency* of our one life and not wait for another life. We must embrace all that surrounds us as the stories of our lives unfold.

   It is always a delusion of distraction to think we ought to be doing or considering something else.

Life's Abundance within Boundaries

3. We must seriously *acknowledge that we will die, but not be afraid of death*. We know that we will die but have no idea when. The opportunity to live will have passed. Now is the time to consider what we might have done.

A genuine fear of dying can keep us from living. Without God, this fear is unavoidable.

Accepting that we will die someday is accepting ourselves as we are and getting on with the business of living today.

The living God meets me every step of the way, and nothing is left but to place myself in His hands. This surrender is not a loss; it is urgently living in fullness with One who does not wish to take my freedom for life away.

Death is not the final frontier we face; rather, it is the Lord toward whom we move. He tells us to stop being distracted by death and to take responsibility to live freely, ready for the serious joy that rightly belongs to our passing life.

By dying and rising again, Jesus is our hope. Our limited time may be full of joy because we know we will die and may live now until that day and have no fear even then.

> The divine purpose of a human lifetime is to meet Him who has come to us.

2. Vocation (pp. 595–647)

To understand this section, we must think beyond vocation as a calling to a job or field of work. Our human vocation answers the call to move from *being for oneself* to *being known by God* and knowing God.

Calling may refer to an event, responding to God's election; *vocation* embodies the sum of one's life under God's providential care—living within God's accompaniment.

God calls every person. He provides human vocation as a freeing relation.

Our decisions come from discovering God's choice. He calls, and we respond with our lives. We are reoriented by hearing Him speak to us of His love.

We should not look for another place to find our vocation other than meeting God in our particular life, here and now.

Birth and death are limits; vocation refers to the life in between. He commands that we be the person we are as His child.

Our particular life, oriented to God, is called our *vocation*. It is bigger and more involved than being a Christian.

Your particular life, limited by the specifics of your storied, networked life, is what Barth calls your vocation.

God had you in mind all along and requires you to live freely in response to His choice to be with and for you. Your choice can only be secondary, as a response.

Barth distinguishes between *calling as vocation* and *calling as summons*.

Summons make known God's will, a renewing alteration, summoning humans to freedom as life with God. It is the *call* to a fulfilled lifetime.

Vocation points to what God already has created and preserved. We choose what God has chosen for us. It includes knowing oneself as one known and chosen by the will of God. It is the *whole* of our lifetime.

Persons do not live to work; they work to live. It is good when one's *profession* aligns with one's *vocation*, and one's *job* aligns with God's call on one's *life*.

God calls all humans to answer the Spirit. We show up ready to work with unique gifts, to serve and obey *as ourselves*.

Calling cannot be a high and lofty state for a few. They would become aristocrats, managing the law and the lives of others.

God the Creator makes us *who we are*. God the Holy Spirit makes us *who we will be* as He gifts us for new situations.

The reality of human vocations is characterized by:

1. The calling of a human life is *a unique opportunity* to be engaged through the stages of life. We must each accept our life as it fulfills God's command. From the cradle to the grave, we are both becoming and perishing in a series of chapters or stages.

   We do not have a seat in the balcony to observe our lives. We cannot comprehend the process of our development in its many stages. Only God can see who He has called us to be as a whole person as we move forward together.

   Immaturity is when we think we can live independently of God.

   Maturity recognizes when it is time to harvest. Preparation is complete; it is time to do one's life work in obedience to God.

   One is only "old" when one quits listening to God's command and can only look to the past. One in this state has determined they are at the end. One is not walking into the future. This attitude refuses life and the possibilities of God's openings.

   If we are wise, we will always have more to give as God's command empowers us. Wisdom sees the future as a free gift. God is already in our future and with acts of love calls us to move toward Him.

Life's Abundance within Boundaries 331

Wisdom is not accumulated knowledge. Wisdom embraces God's mercy, as God's light reveals joyful hope.

2. The calling of God works in our *specific situatedness in history*. Wisdom requires attentiveness to God's accompaniment and one's present place in human history.

Human vocation includes the historical world one lives in. We live in each moment as fellow humans sharing a story and as children of God.

We are not passive in our situations; we give them meaning, character, and significance to fit our sense of belonging. God values all situations. Each is equally promising.

In the field of human relations, we must choose how to act, what problems to solve, and what tasks call us to serve. Most significant is to whom we will become personal and whom to resist.

In our situation, we have a home. This locatedness is our vocation, place of work and study, worship and friendship—where God awakens us to our chosen service and teaches gratitude, which makes our place holy.

We stand on the foundation of all the encircling features of family and environment that often open us to surprises.

We are what we are before God, located in the loving freedom of His being.

Historical forces do not shape the final form of a person. We are children of the God who is our Father. He does guide us out of nothingness, but He does not control us. He allows us freedom to obey His calling to live with and for Him.

God does not predetermine what must be but determines to have grace for each one of us.

We are not caged animals; we are given a cradle and learn to walk and grow as we mature into openness with God. We discover life's possibilities by going with God.

Humans are responsible for what they make of the space in which they live. This calling means to conserve what is good and bring obedient change where love calls.

3. God's calling recognizes *our unique abilities and inclinations*. Who we are as created beings will influence our choices as we listen. Our situations are not permanent.

The inner life of a human is relevant to answering our calling. Aptitudes, inclinations, and capabilities all play into the shaping of one's vocation. Our context and capacities are all at play.

We live at the intersection of our inner and outer worlds of experience. We all have strengths and weaknesses that shape our contributions and limits. God requires us to be faithful to who we are.

We are equipped, endowed, and enabled by God Himself. We are not to compare or desire to be someone else.

We must discern whether our gifts are being used in alignment with God's intentions. We are most fully ourselves when loving God and our neighbor with our whole being through our unique abilities.

The command of God is to wake us up to all we can be. Obedience is living true to God's love in our particular manner.

Vocation is not *a part* of our lives; it is the *whole of us*. His calling moves us to answer His already-infused possibilities, unique for each of us—an ongoing discovery throughout our lives by His Spirit.

God integrates our lives. Partitioning our lives is not helpful, with public and private segments. By the Holy Spirit, we are prepared to steward our gifts for service every moment.

As humans learning our vocation, we must be open, eager to learn, capable of modification, not limited by our ideas of our ability and capacity, and ready to be shown who we are in continual disclosure.

4. God's calling affects *our everyday activity within our field of operation*, making our contribution to the tasks shared with humanity.

We intersect with others' fields of activity. This interconnection includes what is commonly called vocation or one's job.

Our job may be only a small part of what makes us persons. We have our sphere of tasks, cares, and accomplishments, as do all others.

Each choice we make is limited within the sphere of God's sovereignty. Within this sphere, we have options.

Humans choose. When done rightly, we obey God's command, leading to freedom. Wrong choices forfeit freedom, as we are enslaved to sin. All choices constitute the vocation of our lives.

Life's Abundance within Boundaries

Human freedom does not limit, challenge, or control the lordship of God.

We reap what we sow. But we are never out of reach of the will of God.

The hand of God faithfully stays the course, whether with our obedience or disobedience. Thus, in our sphere of operation, vocation, and daily activities, we are always within the sphere of God's work.

Even when we sin, we are not outside God's accompaniment. We live not in a strange land but within our Father's house. Indwelling the hospitality of God is our vocation every day.

God's framework of providence has the superior sway, yet human choice is at play and cannot be ignored.

We must ask three questions:

i. What is the correct or obedient choice within the *sphere of God's providence*?
ii. What is the best choice in the *sphere of our choosing*?
iii. How do we make the appropriate choice when moving from *one sphere to the other*?

God's calling is always at work as we make our choices. He will oversee the consequences, but we are responsible for making a decision in the face of the opportunities.

We often contend with what feels desirable, listening to our inward urges. Our choice must resonate with the command of God.

We should interpret the command of God in the external world and the internal world, be open to opportunities and be constrained by obedience to God's call to love.

We are listening for the voice of the Creator. The voice is a creaturely medium for God to speak. We must ensure it is God's voice and not us grasping for self-service.

Vocation requires listening to God's voice and choosing what God wants as our contribution. The way of obedience finds harmony between the voice calling from within and coming to us, leading to one responsible choice.

We come to peace with ourselves as we recognize that God was present in our past and present, and we need not be the judge.

We judge at the moment; He judges with grace from eternity in our present moment.

From a human perspective, not all of life is good and beautiful.

God works all things together for good; that is His justifying work in which we trust.

God's presence daily calls us to hear the Word of God. We humbly follow within our vocation and sphere of operation.

The world is full of problems. We are called to make a difference in the specific sphere in which we operate.

We may develop our gifts in forms addressing our sphere of operation. We must be modest to do great things, content, and resilient within our sphere.

Ministers face a particular danger of expecting too much of themselves and then from others. They may think they know better than anyone else. They become the village oracle and divert from proclaiming the kingdom of God.

Living within God's call leads to renewal and transformation. We must learn to hear with new ears and see with fresh eyes.

We must leave the well-worn tracks of security and familiarity to go on an adventure with God, possibly in the same place but with God's perspective.

> God calls all humans to answer the Spirit. We show up ready to work with unique gifts, to serve and obey *as ourselves*.

We always remain within God's divine calling but may change our sphere of operation.

We are on an adventure and should continue as His servants, ready when an opportunity arises that echoes His voice and calls for obedience.

3. Honour (pp. 647–85)

The end is near! We have seen the limitations of our hospitable space as one lifetime, with a specific vocation, and limited to an adventure of listening to and following Jesus.

There is freedom in our limitation, not as a restriction, but as specific provisions. God fills our lives with meaningful connections. His command is to live with Him in active, loving response.

Now, we turn to the limitations of honor: specific valuing granted by God and developed in life.

With God, honor is a gift; with humans, respect develops in recognition of our service and contribution.

When we hear and respond, we are honored, lifted up, encouraged, and established as His children—God exalts us to live under a new law.

This new, gracious bond is the law of the Spirit of life. Where the Spirit of the Lord is, there is freedom.

Life's Abundance within Boundaries   335

God commands us to be His children, not against our will but in response to an unsurpassable love that holds us to Him, and we discover we are home. "To be with this Father as the child of this Father is freedom."[2]

The release into freedom, acknowledging we are the children of God, comes as we indwell God's imparting of honor.

Looking from outside of God's valuing of us as His children, we are but dust in the wind, a passing flower in the field, a summer breeze. This assessment is valid for all humanity.

We have short expiration dates. But God has given us time to live in freedom with all its limitations.

God could rule far above us without consulting humans. He decided to stand on our level as a partner. Barth calls this God's great condescension, meaning He came down to where we are to be with us.

God wants one supreme thing from us: to recognize His embrace of us and live in communion and agreement with Him in covenant friendship.

He calls us to be disciples, following where He goes, echoing the life of God as beloved children, and working together with Him.

What is demanded of us is to accept God's cherishing. We do not have to obey, but we may.

To obey is to be glad that God has honored us as His children and may serve with Him.

The command of God is not like a falling star coming from heaven, alien to our world. He comes to us in person and leads us to Himself. He calls us by name.

Humans may forget God. Having gone astray, they may not see the humanity of their fellow creatures. We do not stop being humans when we forget God, but we may act inhumanely.

God honors us by remembering who we are as His creatures, even when we forget.

Humans can be godless. However, God cannot be humanless. The idea that we are godless is only in our head; one can only be a theoretical atheist.

One cannot think God away; one can only contend for a void in one's thinking where God is not currently honored.

All honor is God's honor in which humans participate as created and called covenant partners. "God does not will to be God without man."[3]

---

2. *CD* 3.4, § 56, p. 648.
3. *CD* 3.4, § 56, p. 654.

Dignity is granted to even the most despicable of humans because God, as a human, hung on the cross to reveal His glory and remove our shame. Every human has honor as one created and called by God before they can do anything.

The cross removes the shame of what dishonors us so that love alone remains.

Honor is not built into our bones. It is the distinction of being recognized by God's concrete estimation. It comes from God, who knows and preserves us through our ups and downs.

Jesus died to cover our disgrace so His grace would be revealed in the story of salvation.

He speaks to people like those named and unnamed in the Bible, visibly declaring that He loves and acts for each of them in whatever state they may be found.

Many never recognize what they seek is already entirely given. They live under the delusion that we are on our own. However, most people notice something exceptional about their existence but are blind to the source of its distinctive honor.

> We are on an adventure and should continue as His servants, ready when an opportunity arises that echoes His voice and calls for obedience.

Each of us is created uniquely. Each of us counts.

We spend a lot of time convincing ourselves and others of our value. We act to create value in the eyes of others. This honor is humanly sourced, echoing what God has already established for us.

Barth gives criteria as to what makes actions honorable and, therefore, obedient:

1. God honors humans by *calling them to service*. Service in action reflects honor through obedience. The Father calls His child, and the child willingly responds with an expression of honor within the relationship.

    God wills to need us, no matter how small the contribution. Prayer, lending a hand, or other acts of kindness are expressions of honor in the human that honors God.

    It is in service that we come to know and esteem each other.

    We discover who we are when our honorable acts correspond to God's honor. We have an illusory honor when we depend on our acquisitions and accomplishments.

    There is no escape; we are called to serve. We are commanded to live fully, find joy, and engage in rest.

Life's Abundance within Boundaries

2. God honors humans who receive God's honor in an event engaged with modesty.

Honor is the supreme earthly good. It never comes from anywhere but God. It never passes on to others who seek to possess or guard their honor.

Honor comes by the Spirit, the living breath of God; like the soul of a human, both depend on this divine Other. It also depends on Jesus Christ, who has honored us to be made whole in Him. It depends on the Father, who calls us His child.

One can be honorable only with sincere thankfulness, profound humility, and freely open humor.

We stand before our Creator with His giving and gift with *thankfulness*. We are grateful the honor comes from God and not from our efforts.

We have deep *humility* because God is there for us. Honor does not belong to us; it embraces us in the arms of God.

When we are genuinely thankful and humble before God, we become aware of our inadequacy. Humor overflows in us, and we laugh at our urge to self-praise, delighting in God's disarming honor.

3. God honors humans in a manner that *only God can decide*.

Human concepts of honor are full of standards and demands, meeting conditions to earn honor.

Human ideas of honor prove to be inadequate. They can only create false modesty, rejecting the higher dignity given by God.

Whether we become martyrs, heroes, sufferers, or live simple lives like children without problems, we are all needed in the service of God to His honor.

4. God honors humans *as a gift of His grace*. We do not need to earn or defend our honor.

Humans may feel they need to protect their lives, rights, property, and honor. But only God can give honor, and only God can take it away.

We may be comforted that God knows everything and will not abandon us.

Our task is to obey our calling, attempting to be clear, committed, and not misinterpreted.

A legitimate defense of our honor involves self-respect so that we may honestly and appropriately request it from others.

We must be advocates for the honor of our neighbors and thus contend for our honor as well, as we stand for and with them.

Human honor reflects the glory of God. Human honor exists in life with God the Father, who made and granted us dignity and worth. God has honored us by becoming our brother in Jesus.

> One can be honorable only with sincere thankfulness, profound humility, and freely open humor.

Our recognition of the honor of being the children of God is confirmed in the ability to state: I believe in God the Father Almighty, Maker of heaven and earth, and in Jesus Christ, His only Son, our Lord.

 COMMENTARY:
- God limits us only to call us to a life together.
- Limitation means providing boundaries, like the parameters of any lifespan, house, or committed relationship.
- Death is not our end; Jesus is, and we are moving through our lifetime toward Him.
- Vocation is the call to be oneself as God's child.
- Life is a maturing process with God within our sphere of activity.
- Our life is to be one of service, living to the glory of God with joy and honor.

 CONCLUSION FOR THE CHURCH: The Church today invites all humans to live to the full, compelled by the love that sets us free in Jesus. Unfortunately, Jesus and the Church have been misconstrued as institutional attempts to manage humans.

Many today desire the liberation of the individual, free from the limitations of the Church, culture, or whatever threatens self-fulfillment. Barth reveals a more profound freedom found in the gift of God. This is the fullest expression of freedom, connecting with Him and caring for others.

The ethical role of the Church is to awaken humans to our uniqueness, united in being children of God, with the great honor that renews our lives. This ethical imperative calls us to act responsively to God and each other with all our differences and treat each other respectfully.

To say the Church is limited in its power is not to say it is powerless, only that it has one lifetime with each person, a time to discover and empower each person, encouraged to live well as their gift to God.

INSIGHT FOR PASTORS: We must develop a community of unique persons with distinct but integrated lives. Each person becomes a resounding note in the harmony that plays God's melody, each as a unique part of His body. Jesus attends to each life, helping us to develop their gift as His companion.

This section of the *CD* brings home the pastor's work to be constant in exploring opportunities for each person's lifespan in the world. Their "success" will be about service given to fulfill their personhood and the needs of those within their sphere of activity. Pastors may become coaches who discover each person afresh as God's child. They must discern the call of God that activates God-given and human capacities, finding what gives joy in life, not just a job.

Barth wants everyone in our care to feel valued, not for what they do but for who they are as God's children. Honor is given unconditionally by God. Waking up to God's valuing of them instills dignity and value. We persistently need to confirm God's ability to create a community of nurturing and creativity. We must pay attention to God's opening of possibilities for each person in His service.

 INSIGHT FOR THEOLOGIANS: The ethics of creation cannot be generalized or made into principles. Because it is theology, we must start with God's place in the scenario. God has covenanted with each person. Therefore, each person may discover who they are as God's child.

"One life to live" is the unique opportunity a lifespan provides. The truth in this section is that the ethics of God are at work where each person awakens to who they are within the time given, with the abilities provided, and are to be knowingly honored for who they are.

Barth's ethics of creation is a dynamic ethic. The right choices are the loving choices that serve God's honor and reflect the glory of God as lives lived in the freedom to love. This approach is theology in motion, not a notion to think about. It is profoundly integrated into our lives with God and others we interact with.

Barth's God makes the whole world the playground of hospitable grace. The posted rule is to love God and the others you engage, asking, "How can I serve here?" The science of freedom ensures your presence brings joy, awakening gratitude and delight in others. Be fully alive to investigate what it means for others to find they are God's children and act like it.

 CLARIFYING QUESTIONS: Does your theology look for God to be a judge in each life situation and ensure you do the right thing? *Or* is God the ever-present encourager who calls out the best in each opportunity to act in a way that forms and transforms every situation along the journey?

 VOLUME SUMMARY: In *CD* 3.4, we have seen that God is the ultimate event host. God is a participant in the singular event of all human history; He promises to be fully present and in charge, to invite, connect, and be the One whose presence creates a gracious atmosphere. This means to be personally engaged with all persons in a manner that promotes everyone's best behavior with respect and meaningful interactions. The planning for the event, the organization of its details, and the provision and oversight in the history of the event all find their final fulfillment in living out all that was intended in love.

PART 6

VOICES VALUING
CD VOLUME 3

The Doctrine of Creation

THE VALUE OF *CD* 3 FOR BIBLICAL STUDIES

Samuel Adams

Samuel V. Adams is head of school at Seven Peaks School,
Bend, Oregon, and has been director of graduate studies
and assistant professor of theology and social justice at Kilns
College in Bend, Oregon. He was the founding pastor and
still serves as pastor of Bend Mennonite Church. He is
the author of *The Reality of God and Historical Method:
Apocalyptic Theology in Conversation with N. T. Wright.*

Why should the biblical scholar or the pastor who is committed to careful
study and responsible exegesis bother to read the dogmatic work of Karl
Barth? In the present case, why venture into the sprawling pages of his treatment of the doctrine of creation? As a theologian who preaches regularly,
I would like to offer an answer with two mutually supporting claims. First,
Karl Barth's approach to the witness of Scripture is an essential corrective to
a scientific approach that would, in effect, place scholarship prior to God's
revelation. Second, Barth's articulation of the doctrine of creation offers the
proper context for rigorous exegetical work.

Modern biblical scholarship developed into its many forms today for
various reasons and within multiple traditions, so much so that it's hard to
speak of a monolithic "biblical scholarship." Nevertheless, across ideological
divides, those who study the Bible as scholars of the text do so according
to similar methodological commitments, and for whatever purposes people
study the Bible, the work is essentially the same. Do the linguistic work. Do
the historical work. Check your perspective and biases. Present an interpretation that is nuanced, careful, and defensible.

As reasonable as these approaches are, to read Karl Barth in the context of modern biblical scholarship is to be confronted with something that
many of us who have been trained on good exegesis may have been ignoring
for some time: something else is going on with the text, but we don't have
the right method to get after it. Into this methodological quandary, Barth
might drop this bombshell of a question: "*Who* is addressing us when we

read Scripture?" For the biblical scholar, this question can be frightening or, at the least, discomforting. This is so even if the scholar has an acute understanding of the subjectivity inherent in scholarship. But to read Karl Barth is to read an exegete whose engagement with Scripture is grounded in the subjectivity not of the scholar but of the God who comes to us in Scripture.

When we discover that Barth's third volume of *CD*, which is on the doctrine of creation, is structured in such a way that immediately we are confronted with God's self-witness in Jesus Christ and then discover that his exegetical engagements throughout the volume are determined in advance by this "confessional" perspective, it is understandable that our methodological commitments are disrupted.

The biblical scholar, looking into the question of creation, will go to the Bible to carefully understand ancient thought patterns so that the text can be understood as an ancient text to be read now by us, removed from the contexts in which the texts emerged. Yet, to be confronted by Barth's way of reading, we need to see that the Bible is much more than "a repository of all sorts and degrees of pious knowledge."[1] Even scholars for whom a confessional reading is their acknowledged point of departure may hold a methodological commitment to a reading of the text that "thinks it can talk about God the Father and Creator on the basis of scripture, i.e., in the light of this or that passage of scripture, without allowing itself to be taught by Scripture, i.e., the whole of Scripture, to know the Father through the Son, the Creator through the Redeemer."[2] This is the crux of the matter for Barth: the center of Scripture is Jesus Christ.

While this may seem to be a simple hermeneutical choice that merits exegetical scrutiny, for Barth, the reality of Jesus for Scripture's readers goes beyond the hermeneutical, or even confessional, to an actual engagement with the living agency of God. "It is true enough that the statement about God the Creator has its infallible basis in the fact that it is in the Bible. But even on this basis it will be seen by us only if we halt before this centre of the Bible, directing our question of its basis to Jesus Christ *and allowing Him to answer it.*"[3]

To engage the question of creation in the Bible is to engage in the direct questioning of the Creator, which is to encounter the person of Jesus Christ. To not do this is to exclude the very ground of the doctrine of creation. If we bracket out the agency of the Creator in trying to know the creation, we have

---

1. *CD* 3.1. p. 23.
2. Ibid.
3. Ibid., italics added.

The Value of *CD* 3 for Biblical Studies

dramatically limited ourselves before we have even begun. If we engage with the Creator through Jesus Christ, we encounter the creation through the very covenant of the Creator's grace for us.

The question of the value of critical exegetical work still presents itself to us, as it should. Barth is not one to reject critical scholarship. But Barth's contribution to the biblical scholar is to demonstrate what exegesis looks like if we take the active, living agency of the Creator as a determining principle in our scholarship. Perhaps *principle* is the wrong word here. If God has spoken and continues to speak through scripture, our critical engagement with the text will always be subject to the One who is living, active, and present to us in our reading. The agency of God is a *relationship* within which we engage in scholarship.

Within this relationship, the biblical scholar can enter the historical and linguistic work of careful exegesis confident that "the aim of creation is history."[4] The fact of creation validates our study within the limits of creation. If so, let the scholar embark on the important work of linguistic and historical study but never lose sight of the immediacy of history and language to God.[5] This immediacy implies the important insight, found especially in the doctrine of creation but also in the doctrine of the resurrection, that historical study will never be adequate to the task of reading those accounts faithfully since neither are the outcome of historical processes. They may have occurred in history but are not given to history. The act of creation itself, of course, "predates" history, and the resurrection, as another act of God, occurs in many ways like the first, as an act of the one "who gives life to the dead and calls into existence the things that do not exist."[6]

> To read Karl Barth is to be confronted with the priority of the living God in our reading and study of Scripture.

To read Karl Barth is to be confronted with the priority of the living God in our reading and study of Scripture. This may disrupt our commitments to certain methods of study—or not—but at the very least, and in a way that makes all the difference in the world, our study of the Bible is caught up in the freedom and agency of the Creator, who is known first and foremost through the reconciling work of grace in Jesus Christ.

---

4. *CD* 3.1, p. 59.
5. *CD* 3.1, p. 80.
6. Rom. 4:17.

THE VALUE OF *CD* 3 FOR SYSTEMATIC THEOLOGY

Gary Deddo

Gary Deddo is professor of theology, Grace Communion
Seminary, and the author of *Karl Barth's Theology of Relations*.

The answer as to what theologians would gain by reading this four-part
volume of Barth's *Church Dogmatics* is the same as why to read the *CD* at
all. It serves as a powerful witness as to how Christian theology can be done
so that it points beyond itself to the God revealed in Jesus Christ according
to Scripture. It exemplifies theology contributing to doxology. These part-
volumes on the doctrine of creation are a poignant example of living faith
seeking true understanding (*fides quarens intellectum*) of the Object/Subject
of Christian worship.

Of course, these four part-volumes stand on the shoulders of the preceding two volumes of the *CD* ("The Doctrine of the Word of God" and
"The Doctrine of God"). Addressing the particular articles covered in *CD* 3
faces a significant additional headwind. Focusing not on realities that are
God but on those things which God makes—creation, the history of the
God-world relation, human creatures, heavenly creatures—as well as the
question of good and right human action, resist a thoroughly *theological*
treatment.

How does one address subjects that are not God and remain decidedly
theocentric? How does one avoid becoming anthropocentric, even idola-
trous, when bringing into the spotlight that which is not God, other than
God? How do we avoid turning theology into anthropology, becoming
humans speaking in a loud voice about a transcendent being (Feuerbach,
Leibnitz, etc.)? Can the temptation of using theological language as a
supreme means of self-justification be avoided? Can theology save us from
the ultimate antitheological act of turning in on oneself or one's own "tribe"
(*in curvatus en se*, Martin Luther)? Karl Barth took on this task in *CD* 3.

The greatest challenge would be for anyone to remain engaged in

346

The Value of *CD* 3 for Systematic Theology 347

theological science, knowing the God revealed in Jesus Christ while addressing that which is alien to the being and character of God. The force and power of evil are incorrigibly opposed to, in rebellion against, and implacably in denial of the reality of the triune God. That challenge is what Barth attempted to accomplish in *CD* 3.3, § 50, "God and Nothingness," and the last part of 3.3, § 51, "The Kingdom of Heaven, the Ambassadors of God and Their Opponents."

Following Barth through this challenging and often misunderstood material on evil can be rewarding for those seeking, with theological humility, to find a witness to the living God at the extreme edge of human limits. Great patience and biblical knowledge are required, but Barth offers all theologians a content-rich model on such precarious themes.

That's an overview. But each of the four part-volumes of *CD* 3 deserves its own recommendation.

Part 1, "The Work of Creation," being thoroughly theocentric, is about the God who creates and how what this God creates reflects outwardly (*ad extra*) the true nature and character of the Trinity inwardly (*ad intra*). Consequently, Barth brings together how God's relationship to his work of creation established a covenant relationship exhibiting God's goodness, calling for a response of faith in God and his purposes. Identifying all of what exists apart from God as being "creation" is a theological statement of faith/belief/doxology. Of particular interest is Barth's profound and memorable expansion on creation being the theater of God's glory (Calvin). He characterizes creation as the "external basis of covenant" and the covenant as the "internal basis [or meaning] of creation." If you're interested in the meaning of creation as an act of the triune God to establish a real, actual, and beneficial relationship with humanity rather than attempting to ferret out the mechanics or chronology of it, these 415 pages will fit the bill. This section is a masterpiece of theological integration, holding a thoroughly Christian view of the God-world relationship.

Part 2, "The Creature." With this section, Barth makes up for what could be considered a lack in the history of theology, a dedicated Christian anthropology. But more than simply focusing on that topic, Barth has provided a genuinely *theological* treatment, that is, theocentric and christocentric. If you're looking for a foundational model of *theological* anthropology, you should not miss this second part-volume. Barth brings together for our consideration the essential interconnections between our knowledge of the Word of God, Jesus Christ, and our understanding of all human beings—there is no such thing as a godless humanity—and does so with no intention

348 **Voices Valuing *CD* Volume 3**

to make Christology into anthropology, or anthropology into Christology. That is a theological achievement rarely attempted.

Jesus Christ not only reveals God to us but, having assumed our human nature, reveals the truth and nature of humanity. Humans cannot be understood apart from the covenant history of God with his creation—and, more particularly, understood in a way that enables humans to become his covenant partners through Jesus Christ, the "Man for God," the "True Man," and the "Man for Other Men."[1] In this way, Jesus Christ indirectly reveals who, in general, human beings are.

In his discussion of what it means that humans were created "according to the image of God," Barth sets forth his notable argument against an analogy of being (*analogia entis*) between God and human beings and injects his alternative understanding. We can affirm an "analogy of relations" (the *analogia relationis*) as a being in personal "encounter." Thus, Barth affirms a real and actual relationship of God and humans (through Jesus Christ) without hazarding an identity of being. He maintains the fundamental ontic distinction between the Creator/Redeemer and the creature/redeemed. Reading what Barth said offers a distinct alternative to the standard range of understandings regarding humans being "made" or "according to" the *imago Dei*, who is Jesus Christ.

Of particular pertinence today is Barth's prescient discussion of human beings constituted as the asymmetrical relationship of soul and body. "Man as Soul and Body" in "interconnection," "particularity," and "order" is a must-read since it is relevant to so many contemporary controversies. In our modern and postmodern context, the loss of God in our discourse leads predictably (on a theological basis) to the loss of what it means to be human. Barth can be instructive for illuminating our current loss, at least in the West, of the meaning and identity of who and what human beings are and ought to be.

The final section on "Man in His Time" continues to explore the theme, again rarely touched on thematically, of the goodness of the *limits* of the creatures of God. Human beings live not only within the limits of being body and soul but also as creatures of time between birth and death. Are limits a blessing or a curse? The answer, for Barth, is theological—it lies in the person and work of Jesus Christ as the new Adam, working out our salvation from within time and space, within flesh and blood between birth and death. The true humanity of Jesus Christ conducted within our creaturely

---

1. *Man* here translates *der Mensch* and means all human beings, humankind, not the male. The German much more easily avoids the linguistic problem of reference that English has by the use of *der Mensch* (all humanity) and in distinction from *Mann* which refers more directly to the male of the species.

The Value of *CD* 3 for Systematic Theology 349

limits is an absolute counter to human beings who, despising their creatureliness and dependence upon a Creator and Redeemer, aspire to become gods intent on establishing their own universal kingdom.

The third part-volume of *CD* 3, "The Creator and His Creature," addresses an arguably underrepresented and often narrowly addressed topic of providence. His treatment provides exceptional depth and breadth and, as expected, does so in a thoroughly theological and christocentric way. His explorations are integrated with his foundational understanding of the love and freedom of the Trinity, the nature of creation, and humans within it, in light of the divine purposes revealed in Jesus Christ, Lord and Savior. This part-volume calls for reforming the mind regarding the dynamics of the relationship between the Creator and the creature. It calls into question assumptions of that relationship being causal, predictable, or worked out apart from God's mercy and grace. The value here is the thoroughly integrated comprehension of providential oversight with the biblical revelation fulfilled in Jesus Christ. A distinct option for apprehending the Trinity's preserving, accompanying, and ruling arises within that larger sphere of the universal lordship of God the Father. Barth's option overcomes the standard dichotomies that characterize so much thinking about the providential relationship between the Creator and his creatures.

Paragraphs 50 and 51 take on the matter of evil within the context of all that has preceded it to this point in the *CD*. Consideration of who Jesus Christ is and what he accomplished by his saving life, death, resurrection, and ascension are crucial, not secondary, in his theological exposition. Section 50, "God and Nothingness," is perhaps the most challenging in the *CD*. As Barth notes, both too much and too little can be said. How can evil be understood if it makes no sense, cannot be rationalized or justified, and has its own indescribable kind of existence, unlike God's or his creation's? How can one speak theologically, in terms of the God who is good, about what is anti-God and anti-God's creation? The difficulty is intrinsic to the topic but unavoidable. Why bother? Neither to explain evil nor to defend God. The topic is addressed because what Jesus Christ overcame was not nothing but *something*, represented by the abstract suffix *-ness* in *nothingness*. Compared to the goodness of the Trinity, evil is all but nothing. And in the end, it will not be.

Barth states that there appears to be no other way to say it but that evil is the "impossible possibility."[2] Putting it this way is not a sheer contradiction,

---

2. *CD* 3.3, p. 86.

as some have charged. How can one explain, as a matter of biblical Christ-centered faith, that evil is a temporary antihuman, anticreation, and anti-good possibility that God has ensured is all but entirely impossible—and, in the end, will be impossible? Grasping the near impossibility of putting into words the truth of what Barth is bearing witness to is essential to track with him—but apprehending the grandeur and glory of Christ's gracious victory over evil calls for understanding the nature of evil in contrast to the goodness of the triune God. How successful Barth was in this task will be best ascertained by those who exert a thoughtful grappling with it.

Since the creator God's providential oversight includes both the unseen heavenly realm and the earthly, the heavenly creatures of biblical revelation must be given their due attention. Thus, in section § 51 of this part-volume, Barth considers the biblically attested angelic messengers—a subject he takes seriously, intending to avoid speculation. With a dedicated section on the kingdom of heaven, Barth's theological treatment provides insight beyond popular treatments. He brings to the surface what should be obvious yet is rarely touched upon: the relation and ontological distinction between the created earthly and heavenly realms and their respective inhabitants. Finally, Barth is compelled to glance seriously at the demonic, but no more. The biblical record requires some consideration in light of the opposition it represents to God, humans, and even to the angelic creatures and their vanquishing as seen inaugurated in Jesus' earthly ministry. Barth's Christ-centered exploration of evil/nothingness, the heavenly realm, and the demonic will be welcomed by theologians wanting to engage these topics with theological depth and biblical breadth.

The fourth volume of *CD* 3 builds upon what has preceded it, providing a theological foundation for its subject, the "Command of God the Creator." Barth sees "special ethics" (§ 52) as the task of the doctrine of creation and, ultimately, a matter of faith in the creator God. No ethical considerations can be discerned apart from a relationship of freedom and responsibility before this God through Jesus Christ expressed in worship, confession, and prayer—a personal, dynamic, and interactive covenant communion (§ 53). Thus, all obedience to this God is an obedience of trusting faith in the nature and character of the Trinity revealed in Jesus Christ.

On that particular foundation is Barth's exposition of the key and universal relations in which all created humanity exists: (1) as man and woman, (2) as parent and child, and (3) as near and distant neighbors. The biblical revelation gives special attention and concentrated commands regarding these human-to-human relations. They all consist of "Freedom

The Value of *CD* 3 for Systematic Theology   351

in Fellowship" (§ 54). Barth considers these relations based on a theological analogy of the relation of Jesus to the Father and the Holy Spirit. Barth provides ample expositions for ongoing reflection. These essential and unavoidable relations are being questioned today—order, structure, and the shape of proper relations—by being transposed and reduced to modern sociological and psychological terms such as race, class, gender, and family considered apart from any purpose or relationship with the Creator. These are the most fundamental categories by which human beings and their interconnections can be understood. Barth says "no." These inaccurate terms describe only the outward phenomena of human existence and cannot provide meaning and significance. If you have a hunch Barth may be right, this part-volume is for you.

Barth characterized obedience within these relations as "freedom in fellowship." They are to mirror in a limited and creaturely way (*analogia relationis*) the triune relations and character of the creator God. Barth sees that these relations, given by the good triune Creator, have a further purpose, a *telos*, to which they all contribute, namely, "Freedom for Life" (§ 55). The special ethics of Christian obedience cannot be discerned apart from this particular purpose/*telos*.

Freedom for life cannot be construed capriciously but must mirror the Creator and Redeemer's freedom to love in freedom—as we see in Jesus Christ. Such freedom and life are first received from the Creator and are then passed on to others. The coordination between the particular form of being human and the commands that correspond to it calls for obedience by every human individual as soul and body. Barth proposes relations ordered and structured this way will lead to life when pursued with "respect," "protection," and "actively" taking up the task of our Creator and Lord. He establishes in us the uniquely human and personal form of life. Barth's theologically integrative understanding takes us deep into the nature of human life in relationship, understood as a gift our triune God lends us—we are not our own.

> Freedom for life cannot be construed capriciously but must mirror the Creator and Redeemer's freedom to love in freedom—as we see in Jesus Christ.

The final section of this fourth volume, "Freedom in Limitation" (§ 56), gives us much to contemplate. Barth acknowledges human rebelliousness against the limits of our creaturely givenness; we are humans who resist the tasks set before us by God's commands. Barth refocuses by considering the goodness and graciousness of God, who sets limits and calls us to the freedom of obedience found within them. The limits discussed here are not those common to all but those given to each one specifically and individually, although all come under his universal will as Lord and Creator. The categories expounded are not entirely surprising but welcome—since they are viewed within a profoundly theological and not a utilitarian/pragmatic framework. These are (1) seizing a unique opportunity between life and death, (2) choosing the particular vocation to which God calls each individual within and under God's general calling, and (3) living into the honor of being called into fellowship and communion with the triune God himself by this obedience in freedom that corresponds to the willing of God and the limits of his creaturely being. If the notions of limits, obedience, and God's providence over evil seem difficult to reconcile with freedom for loving fellowship with God and/or others, *CD* 3 will undoubtedly contribute to anyone sorting through these issues on a decidedly theological, Christ-centered basis.

The four parts of *CD* 3 provide anyone looking for a complete and coherent theological treatment of the God-creation-humanity relations with a corresponding Trinitarian theological anthropology and ethics, including a profound account of evil. One will not be disappointed but certainly challenged.

THE VALUE OF *CD* 3 FOR EMBODIED THEOLOGY

Cherith Fee Nordling

Cherith Fee Nordling is a sessional lecturer at Regent College, Vancouver. She speaks and writes on Incarnational theology and life in the Spirit. She is the author of *Knowing God by Name: A Conversation between Elizabeth A. Johnson and Karl Barth.*

You may have heard something like this: "As a human sinner, your soul is damned to suffer the eternal torments of hell. But if you accept Jesus as Lord and Savior, your soul will be saved for eternal life in heaven. So become a Christian, and you'll soon be free of your problematic, temporary body." While this may sound familiarly "Christian" to some, it's the antithesis of the gospel of our Lord Jesus Christ and its expression in Karl Barth's *Church Dogmatics*, volume 3. Barth saw the theological dangers and practical effects that lurk in this disembodied, gnostic idea—that we are valuable souls trapped in corrupted, disposable bodies—and the ease with which certain bodies are considered more corrupt, less human, and thus degraded and disposable, by other bodies that hold power. When we attempt to nail down properties that make us human in God's image, like our souls, we end up with a hierarchical dualism that regards the human being as two things, one good (soul) and one bad (body). The peril is that this dualism almost inevitably excludes some human beings from being considered fully human. It scaffolds binaries of gender, race, ethnic or national identity, class, and so on that assign "normativity" or value to one group and "difference" or ignobility to the other and end up underwriting violent embodied assumptions, ethics, and atrocities.

In *CD* 4, however, Barth argues that Jesus' ascension unveils a human-divine love story in brilliant contrast to the gnostic one above: God so loved the world that he gave his only begotten, incarnate Son to become like us unto death so that we become like him unto resurrection. In short, salvation means we finally get to be human. And we discover that humanity is in the hypostatic union of the one human-divine person, Jesus Christ. He is the indissoluble union of Creator and creation, heaven and earth, soul and body. In his own human existence, Jesus' divinity is not his "real self," borrowing an incidental body. Jesus' nonnegotiable oneness is that of divinity and full, psychosomatic humanity. So, says Barth, the body cannot be understood dualistically as a "prison" that keeps our souls from union with God, nor can we divide up the actions of human beings between the body and the soul. He calls this separation of body and soul "an absurd distraction."[1] Instead, we await our resurrection as those who, body and soul, are born of the Spirit in resurrected, cosuffering, self-giving love to enact the will of our Father "on earth as it is in heaven" in distinction and communion.

Hence, Barth exclaims that we're "wondrous beings"—"Bodies of our souls, and souls of our bodies." As humans, we are *one thing*, a union of "the visible world of bodies" and "the invisible cosmos," made for earth and heaven together in material relation to both as "a representation of the whole cosmos."[2] And we're not for earth now and heaven later, but for *both now*, as embodied persons, restored and renewed, transformed and transfigured by the Spirit into Jesus' image.

This is Barth's love language in volume 3 of the *CD*. In Jesus Christ, we discover that human embodiment belongs to the life of God. Barth reminds us that what makes us human is not the body *or* the soul but our psychosomatic relationship to God. Only in Jesus can we know and learn to become who we are as whole human beings made to embody divine love. In *CD* 3.1 and 3.2, specifically, Barth beautifully expounds the creedal affirmations and Chalcedonian implications for human beings as "*covenant partners*" of God.

> The divine and creaturely communion we are uniquely created for is fully embodied in Christ. All that belongs to the body and the soul are united in him.

The divine and creaturely communion we are uniquely created for is fully embodied in Christ. All that belongs to the body and the soul are united in him. "What does soul or body mean for Him to the extent that either implies an importance or function of its own, different from and opposed to the other?" Furthermore, the New Testament holds "not the slightest hint of an emancipation of the bodily life of Jesus from the soul nor of an aesthetic conflict of the soul of Jesus against the body.... [His incarnate exaltation] does not permit his body to become the enemy and conqueror of his soul;

---

1. *CD* 3.2, p. 393.
2. *CD* 3.2, § 46, "Man as Soul and Body."

nor does it consist in the soul masquerading as the enemy or conqueror of his body."[3] In other words, our psychosomatic unity is actual because it's real in Christ.

As Jesus is one subject, body and soul, in what he does for humanity, the human being is one subject, body and soul, in her response to Christ. Moreover, as God holds body and soul together, not in association but in *union*, then what we claim of one we can claim of the other. In somatic and hypostatic unity, this one Lord redeems us indivisibly, body and soul, in relation to God. This leads Beth Felker Jones to reflect: "Just as we cannot divide the works of Christ and ascribe suffering to Jesus' human nature and saving to his divine nature, we cannot divide our live before God by ascribing, for example, our relatedness to God to our souls and our sexuality and love of macaroni and cheese to our bodies."[4] We are eschatologically made for and related to God, one another, mac and cheese, and all creation together as whole beings!

The most profound affirmation of our present and future glory as God's body-souled children is the ascended Word become flesh. Sharing in our suffering and glory and calling us to do the same with him, Jesus has perfected our humanity and restored in us the glory befitting the "sons and daughters" of our heavenly Father. Ascended with the marks of his wounds and ours, he waits to "transform our lowly bodies so that they will be like his glorious body" (Philippians 3:21). This is the hope for which we've been saved, declares St. Paul—"the redemption of our bodies."[5] Until then, as Hebrews 2 aptly notes, our renewed humanity *can only be seen* in the resurrected body of Jesus.

Reflecting on this, Jones reminds us that this means we can only speak about the human body-soul relation in a way that is faithful to our resurrected Lord: "We cannot fully understand our bodies outside of grace: our bodies meet their true nature only as they are taken up into grace, as they are transformed in relationship to the risen Christ whose body still bears the wounds of crucifixion."[6] If we want to know what a body is, we cannot begin with an apparent natural reference from our broken bodies. Our access has to begin from the other direction. As *CD* 3 emphasizes, we must start with the particular body of Jesus, who reveals the holy body not first through creation but through redeemed "new creation."

---

3. *CD* 3.2, 327, 338.

4. Beth Felker Jones, *Marks of His Wounds: Gender Politics and Bodily Resurrection* (Oxford: Oxford University Press, 2007), 81.

5. Romans 8:23.

6. Felker Jones, *Marks of His Wounds*, 88.

As the "true counterpart" of humanity, Jesus reconciles and unites all to himself *and* upholds our particularity in his particular body, connecting us distinctly to God's triune unity-in-distinction. And precisely because there is no hierarchy in the hypostatic union of the Trinity, or Jesus himself, or our human body-soul union, no hierarchical priority can be assigned to any embodied person in relation to another. Ironically, and not without great harm, Barth suddenly forgets this essential reality regarding men and women. Forgetting his warnings against a natural theology and his emphasis on Jesus as "the true counterpart" of every person, he slips into a natural theology of "male-female encounter" and differentiated "fellow-humanity" that prioritizes maleness. This blind spot that reimposes gendered hierarchical ordering occludes Barth's otherwise incarnational clarity. We must not do the same.

CD 3 offers a faithful witness to Scripture (and the Church's earliest interpretations) in proclaiming that Jesus has assumed our full humanity, body and soul, to heal *each of us*, body and soul, and raise us to become like him in glorious, cruciform humility. We're reborn by the Spirit precisely to be conformed to Jesus, individually and communally, to practice our embodied future together in his image of self-giving, cosuffering love. Our embodied life, even now, is a foretaste of our future human glory made possible through Jesus' life, death, and resurrection for and with us, sealed in love by our Father through the empowering presence of the life-giving Spirit.

This is our destiny. This is the Christian life. However, as Christians, we generally are not on speaking terms with our bodies, and we have a disastrous record when it comes to considering the embodied lives of others as more important than our own.[7] Perhaps this is because we don't take Jesus' life seriously for our own. We need help. And in *CD* 3, help can be found.

---

7. Phil. 2.

THE VALUE OF *CD* 3 FOR PASTORS

Will Willimon

Will Willimon has been a pastor, college minister, professor, and United Methodist bishop. He is professor of the practice of Christian ministry at Duke Divinity School in Durham, North Carolina, and director of the doctor of ministry program. Will is the author of dozens of books on ministry, including *Conversations with Barth on Preaching* and *The Early Sermons of Karl Barth*. His 2021 Beecher Lectures on Preaching at Yale, *Preachers Dare*, arose from Will's longtime interest in Barth's *Göttingen Dogmatics* and its relevance for contemporary homiletics.

Karl Barth's *CD* 3 has been a sustaining partner, critic, and sometimes an uncomfortable prod in five decades of ministry. When I found myself lying in the ditch of despondency in reading "Jesus, Lord of Time," *CD* 3.2 threw me a lifeline and hoisted me back into the fray.[1] In the middle of a church fight with my detractors, who were unhappy about my protest against the draconian Alabama Immigration laws, *CD* 3.3, "The Divine Accompanying," gave me strength to go on, though I'm not sure why.[2] Only a week later, *CD* 3's brilliant exposition on "nothingness" rendered suspect some of my self-righteous prophetic posturing, forcing me to look at the shadow side of my ministry, even when I didn't want to.[3] (Don't seek help from Barth if you're risk-averse to the possibility of being smacked by him.)

Where Are We?

One of the major challenges of pastoral work is the mundane, quotidian, humdrum quality of parish life and its incessant *thereness*. I'm called to preach God's word, but I'm now stuck in the church fellowship hall setting up chairs and tables for tonight's sure-to-be-boring board meeting. Ordained to equip the saints, I have just blown an eternal hour, refereeing a squabble

---

1. *CD* 3.2, § 47.
2. *CD* 3.3, § 49.2.
3. *CD* 3.3, § 50.1–4.

over the proper color to paint the church parlor. How did a person of my gifts get stuck out here in the boondocks with losers like them?

How? Barth answers, *Jesus Christ!*

Pastors are located as part of the Creator's determination to incarnate, to be present and situated as God with us. Pastoral ministry participates in the dynamic of God's tendency to go local. Therefore, all pastoral work is parochial, tied to a specific place and people, whereby God takes up room in God's world. Context heavily determines our preaching, pastoral care, and congregational leadership.

Where are we? is, therefore, a crucial question for those who lead congregations. The answer to that question determines the answer to another: *Who are we?* Both of these questions are Karl Barth's major concern in *CD* 3. Neither question can be answered without first asking and answering, *Who is God?*[4]

CD 3 celebrates the wonder that we are located as God's creatures and given time to do God's work in God's creation.[5] God has benevolently created a wonderful space for us to be in covenant with God. We and our world are products of God's overflowing love.

Calvin began his *Institutes* by reasoning from what he thought he knew of the world to what he hoped could be known about God.[6] For Barth, there's no way to know where we are and what we are here for without knowing the truth about God, otherwise known as Jesus Christ. This is how Barth explains why the most important questions in church life or pastoral work are all theological. And, by the way, the only good reasons for persevering as a pastor are theological.

Many educators urge pastors to exegete our congregations, to study the demographics, economics, and ideology of our congregational context. My reading of *CD* 3 says that while such anthropological data can't hurt, they contribute little to pastors' answering, *Where are we?* (Much less do they answer the pastor's *Why am I here?*) Barth has convinced me (in *CD* 1) that we know more about who God is (Jesus Christ, in the power of the Holy Spirit, is relentlessly revealing) than we'll ever know about our cagey, arcane, self-deceptive, and secretive people, God bless 'em.

We know for sure that God is whoever made a unilateral covenant to have humanity as God's partner. And what we know about God through the gift of God's self-revelation in Christ makes a world of difference.

---

4. *CD* 3.2, § 44.
5. *CD* 3.2, § 45.
6. *Institutes*, 1.1.

What Are Pastors For?

Pastors are significant as those who are called by God and the church to care for and to keep talking to God's people about the God who, in Jesus Christ, is determined to be in conversation with them. Pastors talk to, about, and for the God who is, rather than waste time prattling about the assorted gods we wish might have been.

Barth's "Doctrine of Creation" affirms the service to which we pastors give our lives. Sometimes, you feel discouraged and think your work is in vain, tempted to throw in the towel and take up a less dangerous occupation. *CD* 3's sweeping reassertion and reiteration of God as continuing Creator could revive your soul again.

From eternity, God has self-determined not to be confined to heaven. Everything begins with Genesis 1, "And God said...." The Creator locates among us and insists on telling us all about it. A new nation is promised into being, unilaterally made covenant partners with God so that God can have a people who have the guts to listen to God and the chutzpa to speak up, in word and deed, for God. That's where we pastors come in.[7]

Pastors have no greater purpose and are engaged in no more significant work than all the ways that we insist on asking and answering the theological.

In response to my smug episcopal jeremiad against a hapless rural congregation, an Alabama pig farmer replied, "So you're saying that when Jesus Christ called people like us to follow him, he didn't know what he was doing? We may not be the greatest church there ever was, but we're all he's got out in this part of the county. Bishop, it's a shame you don't see us like Jesus does."

Daddy Barth shouted, "*Richtig*!"[8]

CD 3 critiques some contemporary performances of pastoral work. Preaching need not labor to create the emotional conditions whereby people might feel spiritually roused, nor must a sermon offer a strategic stairway from us lowly, wayward creatures up to the omnipotent God. Preaching must simply announce the facts of life: we are located in God's world, the theater of God's redemption, and have been chosen by God to play our part in God's glorious pageant by letting everyone know the truth about where they are, who they are, and what God's up to where they are.

Two affirmations of *CD* 3 keep rescuing my ministry from irrelevance:

---

7. I work these Barthian themes in William H. Willimon, *How Odd of God: Chosen for the Curious Vocation of Preaching* (Louisville: Westminster John Knox, 2015).

8. "Correct!"

1. Partners

The first thing the Creator did after creating a world and calling it good was to call humanity creatively to partner with God in caring for and cultivating the world. This sharing is our vocation. For all our many faults, pastors have been made God's partners. We are accountable to and under the authorization of God: Father, Son, and Holy Spirit. Our vocation is to help God call and equip all the baptized to engage God's gracious invitation to God-human partnership.

In creation, God did not just give us life; God gave us a task—actively called to partner in playing our bit parts in God's reconciling retake of God's creation. Over the years, some of Barth's critics accused him of having little room in his theology for human agency. Don't believe it.

To be human is to have been summoned and assigned. The purpose of the God-pastor partnership is to serve a human community. It has been created and called for no greater purpose than creaturely partnership with the Creator. Pastors equip the saints for the work of ministry.[9] Whether or not our people know it, they are created to work with God to accomplish God's creative purposes in God's world.

The test of my vocation as a pastor is the quality of discipleship of the saints committed to my care. Forgive me for peppering my sermons with examples and illustrations of ordinary Christians in my congregation who, in word and deed, extraordinarily get discipleship right. If God doesn't deign to produce at least a couple of credible Christians each decade of my ministry, you're justified in asking, "What, in God's name, are you doing?"

Pastors help those under their care realize their humanity by discovering their God-given purpose and vocation, whereby God continues to carry on with creation through their baptism into Christ. Pastoral care bandages the wounded to be sent back to the front lines rather than soothing the anxieties of the upwardly mobile, relatively affluent. Preaching gives disciples the words they need when they must say something before the powers that be, not evoking pious, poetic feelings among spiritual eager beavers. Congregational leadership prepares the faithful for service where the battle rages in the world, not soothing the hurt feelings of the self-consumed within a religious club for older adults.

Somebody in the congregation whispered to me that, after a youthful screw-up, Fred had once done six months in jail. I asked Fred to tell me the story. He described the horrors and enlightenment he had been given while

---

9. Ephesians 4:12–16.

incarcerated. I told Fred that he and our Lord had something in common; much of the New Testament was written in jail.

"I bet the Lord had something in mind when he busted you out of jail," I said, posing the partnership question. "I wonder what?" Long story short, Fred founded, equipped, and led our church's first foray into prison ministry at the Youth Incarceration Center: Bible study, literacy training, and a miraculous mission.

Pastors work with their people under the assumption that everyone has been created and called to partner with God—if we can help them figure out how. A tired or overstressed and anxious pastor is inevitably a cleric with an inadequate theology of baptism, vocation, and partnership. Running errands to soothe the aches and pains of taciturn, disengaged, narcissistic consumers who think they're a church isn't worth your life. (Am I cutting too close to the bone?)

In Jesus Christ, God has chosen to save us together. There is no such thing as a solitary disciple of Christ. Therefore, pastors are community persons called by God and the church to keep talking to the church about corporate communal concerns, to worry about what makes for a community, and what keeps us in relationship with one another and God.

As a rule of thumb, if a layperson spends more than fifteen hours a week hanging out at the church, running errands for the pastor, that person wastes time. The baptized have their ministry in the world, not the church, joining an active, present Christ in his work.

> Pastors work with their people under the assumption that everyone has been created and called to partner with God—if we can help them figure out how.

By implication, if a pastor spends more than fifteen hours a week running about the world, campaigning for a seat on the school board, managing the shelter for the homeless, and harassing City Hall, the pastor wastes time. Pastors are called to teach, preach, counsel, convene, organize, and pray, equipping the saints, not relieving them of their baptismally bestowed responsibilities to be in the world in mission with Christ.

2. God in Action

Barth thinks that God matters. God is an active agent, a living, present person, not a passive principle. From the first, God likes to start things (see Genesis 1–2 and 17). God's love is love in action. God's "Yes" to God's creation is an active, resourceful "Yes" to which the congregation modestly but determinedly replies "yes." Whatever Jesus Christ wants to do in the world, he has chosen to do it, not without the likes of us.

God is completing the work that God began in Genesis 1. God in action is called *providence*. We do not belong to ourselves, nor are we abandoned to our own devices. Therein is our hope. It's not all left up to us. "My Father is still working, and I am working too."[10] I don't have to preach the best sermon ever; I need to preach well enough for Christ to condescend to have his say to his people through my sermon. I don't have to bring in the kingdom of God before I'm done at this church; God already has and is.

With it, we acknowledge that we don't preach solo, that it's up to Christ, in the power of the Holy Spirit, to make our words into God's word addressed to them. I preach under the assurance that Barth was right in his portrayal of a relentlessly revealing God. I can confidently speak about God because the God who covenanted with Israel is a big talker.

God is even busy beyond the bounds of my church. God didn't give his Son only to the church; Jesus is God in action on behalf of the whole world.[11] Therefore, my congregation is not free to be introverted. Every congregation must be helped to ask, "What is God already up to in this neighborhood? How can we hitch on to what God's already doing?" The congregation's mission is determined not by what a community thinks is realistically possible or fits the congregation's assessment of itself. God assigned our mission as our part in the cosmic *missio Dei*.[12]

God has created us to participate in God's goodness. God has said "Yes" to God's creation. Pastors do many things to help Christ's Body be in motion. In a congregation's witness, it's as if God told us, "I've enjoyed creating something out of nothing, letting light shine in the darkness, speaking into the silences; now you try it."

"This is the most loving and caring congregation in town," she said to me as a visiting preacher that Sunday. "We're like family here."

"That's not good enough," Barth made me reply, in love.

---

10. John 5:17 CEB.

11. John 3:16.

12. Barth is generally credited with revolutionizing missiology with his stirring speech at a 1932 world mission conference in which he asserted the *missio Dei*—mission is the activity of God himself. See David J. Bosch, *Transforming Mission: Paradigm Shifts in Theology of Mission* (Maryknoll, NY: Orbis, 2012), 398–403.

THE VALUE OF *CD* 3 FOR ORDINARY PEOPLE

Jeff McSwain

Jeff McSwain founded Reality Ministries, Durham, North Carolina: "Creating opportunities for adults with and without disabilities to experience belonging, kinship, and the life-changing reality of Christ's love." He is the author of several books, including *Movements of Grace: The Dynamic Christo-Realism of Barth, Bonhoeffer and the Torrances*; *"Simul" Sanctification: Barth's Hidden Vision for Human Transformation*; and *Hidden in Contradiction: Humanity in Christ before, during, and after the Fall.*

I came to Barth through J. B. and T. F. Torrance, who introduced me to North African church father Athanasius, "The Father of Orthodoxy" (born in 296). Having come from a tradition that pronounced that we must believe in order to belong to God, it was a transformative joy to find a long stream of church teaching that reversed the familiar order, instead proclaiming, "You belong, therefore believe" and "You are forgiven, therefore repent." Instead of asking Christ into my life, I began seeing my life in his. I no longer needed to rely on a decision-based appeal whereby people effectively adopt themselves into God's family. I belong to God not because of what I have done or not done but because of what Christ has done. The reality of this belonging and its claim upon every person propelled me into a new approach to ministry. From this new starting point of belonging, I increasingly began to appreciate varied expressions of human believing, verbal and nonverbal.

Barth's "Doctrine of Creation," part-volume 3.1, is like the unappreciated, overlooked mustard seed of the whole of *CD*. This smallest part-volume anticipates the full reach of all Barth's biblical-theological branches and all that I need to make my points below.

In 3.1, we catch Barth's vision for creation and its goal in the closest possible connection; we discover that the end is like the beginning (and the middle is too!). That is why we arguably learn more in 3.1 about what Barth intended for his proposed volume 5 than in any other part-volume. On page 13, he provides a harbinger of redemption: "The statement that God has created heaven and earth speaks of an incomparable perfect, and tells us that this perfect is the beginning of heaven and earth. It is also true that this beginning does not cease."[1] Did you catch our Swiss friend's drift? He insists that in one sense—one dimension, you might say—as bad as sin and evil are, they can never change the truth of God's "perfectly good" (not just "good") creation.[2]

Barth's approach saves us from a low view of creation, completely trashed by the fall. It is not as if God chalks Genesis 1 up to a false start and says, "Let there be a do-over" because Plan A didn't work very well. Before engaging reconciliation in volume 4, Barth wants to ensure that what is done in the atonement is unrelated to a second creation. Reconciliation is not a second creation. Re-creation is not like creation, which was from scratch. "The creation of man . . . , in the image and likeness of God, is not overthrown by the episode of the fall, but remains even in face of the total contradiction between it [the fall] and the being of man."[3]

Humanity's indelible, irrevocable honor is that every human *person* is created in Christ,[4] the *person* who has always shared life with the *persons* of the Holy Trinity. When the fall inexplicably occurs, God doesn't let go. Nothing can separate us from his love, for we, warts and all, belong to the Great Physician. The gospel of our belonging declares that the doctor became the patient to heal us. Christ's cross demonstrates how the wrath of God serves his love, making all of the separations in the right places, delivering his beloved children from the things that are not part of his creative purpose and are out to destroy them. The redemptive goodness of judgment separates not Christ from God, nor humanity from God, but sin and brokenness from humanity. Good news indeed!

> I belong to God not because of what I have done or not done but because of what Christ has done.

Ultimately, we will have eyes to see what has been perfect. "In Him," notes Barth, "the created world is already perfect in spite of its imperfections, for the Creator is Himself a creature, both sharing its creaturely peril, and guaranteeing and already actualising its hope." On that Day, he continues, "its justification and perfection will infallibly be perceived and it will be seen to be the best of all possible worlds."[5]

---

1. *CD* 3.1, 13.
2. *CD* 3.1, 364.
3. *CD* 3.1, 190.
4. Ephesians 2:10.
5. *CD* 3.1, 385. See 366–88 for one of the richest sections in *Church Dogmatics*, "The Justification of Creation."

The Value of *CD* 3 for Ordinary People

It's no wonder that Barth's ethics are concentrated in the last part-volume on the doctrine of creation. Barth's ethics are based on a perspective directly connected to how persons are created, as revealed by how they are reconciled and redeemed.

This is what Barth calls a "seeing through" since we always look through a glass dimly in this world.[6] The gospel receiver "sees through the imperfections of being to its perfection. That this is not a direct vision, but a seeing through, makes it a struggle," notes Barth, but even if through a mirror dimly, "it can be and may be a true seeing."[7] With resurrection retrospection, the Spirit gives us a cruciform filter to envision the pure creaturely goodness of Genesis 1, "to see in the sign of that end the sign of the beginning."[8]

It is an elementary principle, even if it's not easy. But by the revelation of Jesus Christ and Him crucified, we are better equipped for each specific situation than if we focus first on the situation itself. The latter can only be a train wreck of self-projection. With this emphasis on "general ethics" (as guiding principle), Barth leaves room for adjustments in the realm of "special ethics."

Using his revelation-based principle, Barth tackles myriad ethical dilemmas in 3.4. For instance, even if the other person is my brother, is there ever a time when killing him is more congruent to the overriding principle than not? Was Bonhoeffer right, Barth asks, to risk his own life for the chance to take Hitler's? Considering that we are all Genesis 1 creatures, is there ever such a thing as a just war? What about abortion? Euthanasia? Capital punishment? Marriage?[9] Barth weighs in all of these areas, using his guiding principle that we are all created in Christ as Genesis 1 creatures, purposed for Revelation 22.

Then there are issues we might consider more current. What about our beloved family member with Alzheimer's who acts like a completely different person? Is the person we knew "gone," or are they still there? Can we say that the person is fully present in their wholeness despite their brokenness?

Regarding gender identity, can we avoid making the simple projection from biology (our mortal material bodies) to ontology (our spiritual material

---

6. 1 Cor. 13:12.

7. *CD* 3.1, 380. As will be true throughout, I have maintained the British spelling from the T&T Clark translation.

8. *CD* 3.1, 281.

9. Regarding Barth's own marriage, his over forty-year relationship with scholar and co-worker Charlotte von Kirschbaum will always be controversial. For the best treatment of the complex web of relationships that included von Kirschbaum and Barth's wife and children in one household, see Christiane Tietz, *Karl Barth: A Life in Conflict* (Oxford: Oxford University Press, 2021).

bodies, which are always dimensionally present)?[10] Can we think of gender as deeper than sex? Can we refuse to define ourselves simply by what we see in the mirror or simply by what we feel about ourselves? Flesh and blood will not enter the kingdom of heaven. We will all be changed.[11]

When it comes to intellectual disabilities, is a distinction between how we are created and how we are born helpful even if we can't "see through" to our Genesis 1 body? With Barth's principle, can we hold on to the baseline that we are fearfully and wonderfully made,[12] even while acknowledging that we are sinful from the moment we are conceived?[13] Based on our present perspective being indirect at best, can we avoid conflating Genesis 1 with a conviction about what *we think* is normal?

If my child was diagnosed with carrying a cancer gene in the womb, should I pursue genetic engineering to remove that gene if I could? Would I be messing with creation (which I wouldn't want to do) or the fall (which seems appropriate)? If I decide that there is no difference between creation and procreation, what do I do with the haunting notion that God created my child with cancer?

There are no easy answers because even with our christologically informed guiding principle, "seeing through" the cross to Genesis 1 (or retrospectively from redemption to creation) is not easy, even if it provides a preferable starting point.

How do you see others around you as you implement Barth's general principle?

Are they whole or broken? Yes.

Are they God's friends or God's enemies? Yes.

Are they created perfect just the way they are, or are they a fallen sinner? Yes.

Are they lost or found? Yes.

Are they a prefall or postfall human? Yes.

Are they living or dying? Yes.

Are they innocent or guilty? Yes.

---

10. Ephesians 2:6, Colossians 3:1–3.

11. 1 Corinthians 15:50–51. See *CD* 3.1, 321–22. For Barth, "male and female" refers to gender or sexuality only in the third sense, after Christ and his body (Ephesians 5:22ff.), and second, Yahweh and Israel. Such an interpretation obviously gives a different emphasis to "be fruitful and increase in number" (Genesis 1:28), biological procreation now bearing only relative witness to the deeper spiritual call to fruitfulness (cf. John 15:16). Conversely, if procreation is the primary point of gender differentiation and fruitfulness in Genesis 1:28, single and celibate people are immediately marginalized as humans, not to mention others.

12. Psalm 139:14.

13. Psalm 51:5.

The Value of *CD* 3 for Ordinary People

Are they righteous or wicked? Yes.

Are they sheep or goats? Yes.

Are they a child of light or a child of darkness? Yes.

Yes, but in all these things, never the second without the first.

Past the polarizing projections that plague us, we find refreshment in the reality of Jesus Christ, where there is no "us versus them."

On judgment day, the wheat and tares of our lives will be plain to see. In the meantime, we do our best, and we have compassion on ourselves and others around us as we make judgment calls in the name of the one judge who is compassion incarnate. We don't know why God would set it up this way, giving such a berth for human evil and suffering. But we can return to the consoling fact that the compassionate one would have never subjected us to these things without first submitting to them himself.[14] God is not a stranger to our situation. As Barth says, "The Creator Himself willed to endure, and has endured, and still endures, the contradiction in creaturely life. . . . He does not stand aloof from the contradiction of our being."[15] "For the love of us, God has made the problem of existence His own."[16] We will never feel more understood than on that day of redemption.[17] On that day, in the light and embrace of the One who knows us the best and loves us the most, we may discover the joy set before us in Christ as a Genesis 1 community, a Trinitarian community "that does not cease."[18]

---

14. In Barth's words, "He first placed Himself under the stern law of the twofold aspect of being. What are all the severity and relentlessness of its contradiction as known and experienced by us in comparison with the relentlessness and severity which He caused to be visited on Himself, on His own heart, even before He acted as Creator?" *CD* 3.1, 381.

15. *CD* 3.1, 380–381.

16. *CD* 3.1, 382. These references hail from one of the richest sections in *Church Dogmatics*. See 3.1, 366–88.

17. Ephesians 4:30.

18. *CD* 3.1, 13, quoted in note 1.

THE VALUE OF *CD* 3 FOR MENTAL HEALTH

Daniel J. Price

Daniel J. Price pastored churches in California, Scotland, and Switzerland until his retirement in 2018. He is the author of *Karl Barth's Anthropology in Light of Modern Thought* and other essays in theology and ethics. He has taught church history, psychology, and introduction to Christianity courses at Cal Poly Humboldt University and North Coast Bible Institute. He has been married to Dr. Karen McCarthy Price, a practicing clinical psychologist (recently retired), for forty-seven years.

I am inviting the reader to discuss Karl Barth's doctrine of creation and its implications for mental health in part three of the *Church Dogmatics*. This discussion is especially relevant over fifty years after Barth's passing for several reasons.

First, there is less animosity between the mental health disciplines and religion today than during Barth's lifetime. Perhaps the reader has heard of the pinched philosophical school of logical positivism. Until the mid-twentieth century, positivism cast a long shadow over many disciplines, including psychology. In sum, positivism doubted the validity of any statements that were not either empirically verifiable or logically necessary. Freud's work in the developing field of psychology assumed that proof for his theories must be filtered through the Enlightenment findings of empirical science—especially Newtonian physics. This reductionist approach explains why the early twentieth-century psychological theories of Freud and others were highly skeptical of any dialogue with religion or theology. Today, things are beginning to change. Even with the recent decline in religious practice, many therapists are prone to see religious faith as an aid to mental health rather than a hindrance.

Second, from the theological side, Barth's massive *CD* has altered the form and content of Christian theology to such a degree that his ideas are still being developed and considered in many fields. This dialogue might surprise those with a cursory understanding of Barth and the controversies in which he was engaged. Barth was sometimes accused of invoking a *theological* positivism, grounded not so much in logic or empirical truth as *revealed* truth.[1] When we couple this with Barth's ongoing controversies with Emil Brunner over the place of natural theology and our capacity, or incapacity, to establish a "point of contact" with God apart from divine revelation,[2] the prospects for finding mental-health insights in *CD* 3 might seem dim. Despair not. Barth's volumes in *CD* 3 contain countless references to God, self, and others. These discussions prove fascinating when understood and therapeutic when taken to heart. This essay will counter the assertion that revealed truth necessarily divides nature from grace or mental health from theological anthropology.

Third, the human condition in the twenty-first century has significant similarities to the early twentieth century. Barth's battle cry of crisis theology, first shouted out in his *Epistle to the Romans* and later resolved in his *Church Dogmatics*, has renewed relevance for probing deeper into human sin and goodness. What follows are a few examples to whet the appetite of those unfamiliar with the *CD* and encourage deeper probing for those already familiar with Barth.

Barth begins his four-volume doctrine of creation in *CD* 3.1, reminding us that this doctrine, no less than any other, is a doctrine of faith. It must be believed to be understood. By faith, we understand that while the Creator could be self-existent, the creation cannot; creation exists because God creates. It follows that creation is the external basis of the covenant. In other words, without the created order, there would be no covenant with Israel or the church since neither would exist.

Conversely, Barth asserts that the covenant is also the internal basis of creation. This insight clarifies that the covenant provides meaning and purpose to the creation, especially to the apex of creation: humans created as male and female in the image of God. The connection between creation and covenant also means that humankind is put here for a purpose; our lives are not random because we are creatures beloved by our Creator. Barth puts it this way: "The creature does not exist casually. It does not merely exist but exists meaningfully. In its existence, it realizes a purpose and plan and order."[3]

---

1. Dietrich Bonhoeffer first ascribed this term to Barth (*Offenbarungspositivismus*), *Letters and Papers from Prison*, trans. Eberhard Bethge (New York: Macmillan, 1973) 280–81, 286, 328–29. But later critics were a bit less irenic. Cf. Simon Fisher, *Revelatory Positivism? Barth's Earliest Theology and the Marburg School* (Oxford: Oxford University Press, 1988); and Wolfhart Pannenberg, *Theology and the Philosophy of Science*, trans. Francis McDonagh (Philadelphia: Westminster, 1976) 32ff.

2. *Natural Theology: Comprising 'Nature and Grace' by Professor Dr. Emil Brunner and the Reply 'No!' by Dr. Karl Barth*, trans. P. Fraenkel (London: Bles, Centenary, 1946).

3. *CD* 3.1, 229.

This purposeful assertion is where theology can assist mental health and its many disciplines.

Most importantly, Barth affirms that as God's creatures, humans are the object of divine love.[4] Creation is the framework for the covenant of divine love and, therefore, an expression of divine love. For those who insist that mental health paradigms must be reduced to empirical observation alone, I would add that every discipline contains elements of faith in its method and within the community that sustains the research in its respective field. Further, the context of faith and community provides a greater likelihood for the therapeutic practitioner to achieve their goal than the reductionist models of early Freud or behavioral psychologies.

In *CD* 3.2, Barth deals with familiar themes of Christian anthropology. In broad strokes, Christian theology had long held in balance the opposites of the two Creation stories found in Genesis, differently affirming the Creator's immanence and transcendence. Barth engages this, establishing that humans are creatures, not the Creator. Barth upheld God's transcendence as "Wholly Other" early in his theological career.[5] On the other hand, we *are* creatures created uniquely in the image and likeness of God. For centuries, theologians have debated what Genesis means when it affirms our image and likeness to God. These discussions center around the theological topic called *imago Dei*.[6]

Barth interprets the *imago Dei* in terms of Christology and incarnation, thus introducing a relational component to our essential humanity that was both dynamic and novel. In Barth's incarnational theology, we are encouraged to see the common humanity in all people: those within and without the church. Barth urges us not to disparage or insult those outside the covenant. In contrast to some of the Reformed theologians of the Calvinistic tradition, Barth insists, "Human nature is not isolated but dual. It does not consist in the freedom of a heart closed to the fellow-man, but in that of a heart open to the fellow-man."[7]

Barth develops his christological interpretation of humankind in *CD* 3.2, in the section he calls the "Basic Form of Humanity."[8] He repeatedly

---

4. The "goodness of the Creator toward his creatures" is a theme that runs throughout this entire doctrine of Creation. But see especially *CD* 3.1, 3.

5. Cf. *The Epistle to the Romans*.

6. Latin for 'image of God.'

7. *CD* 3.2, 278. It is unfortunate the Barth's translators used the term *dual* in this context because he is anything but a dualist. Here Barth is using the term *dual* as a contrast to solitary or autonomous.

8. *CD* 3.2, § 45, 2.

The Value of *CD* 3 for Mental Health   371

reminds us that to be human is to be *with* and *for* others. Barth posits this in stark contrast to Nietzsche's *Ubermann*, who dwells in "azure isolation, six thousand feet above time and man."[9] He continues to say that Nietzsche "encounters [Christianity] as an enemy because it opposes to Zarathustra or Dionysius, the lonely, noble, strong, proud, natural, healthy, wise, outstanding, splendid man, the superman." This isolated Superman stands in stark contrast to the Christian message, which makes the "claim that the only true man is the man who is little, poor and sick, the man who is weak and not strong, who does not evoke admiration but sympathy, who is not solitary but gregarious—the mass-man. It goes so far as to speak of a crucified God, and therefore to identify God Himself with this human type."[10]

Based upon Christology, Barth concludes that to be fully human is to encounter (*Begegnung*) others. And what does that encounter look like—especially since many human encounters end in either isolation or subjugation? It means, Barth says, "I am as Thou art." He then defines the basic form of our humanity by describing four important aspects of being-in-encounter.[11]

First, it means seeing eye to eye. When we look *at* a person, we may see them as objects. When we look into someone's eyes, we see them as a living subject—an equal who is not "I" but who encounters us on a personal level. Barth says, "The human significance of the eye is that we see one another eye to eye."[12] There is a reciprocity of seeing and being seen at a deeply personal level. Seeing eye to eye implies we see each other as equals: if not equals regarding station—equals in Christ—then equals as creatures made in the image of God. We don't look down on others with contempt; neither do we look up with reverence. But in the person-to-person encounter, we are equal. However, seeing and being seen, while a necessary first step, is open to misinterpretation. Therefore, words are essential in moving on to the next level of encounter. Barth puts it this way, "What is needed at this point is speech—the human use of mouth and ears. Humanity as encounter must become the event of speech."[13]

The second aspect of being in encounter is mutual speaking and hearing. We must not only see others—we also listen. After listening, we speak. After speaking, we listen. Again, Barth clarifies that we do not talk down to

---

9. *CD* 3.2, 240.

10. *CD* 3.2, 239.

11. Barth would not have known that he was talking about what later psychologists and therapists would call "attunement." More on that below. The fuller ethical implications of relationally defined personhood become clearer where Barth develops his explicit ethics in *CD* 3.4.

12. *CD* 3.2, 250.

13. *CD* 3.2, 253.

others as if we are superior. Though Barth doesn't put it this way, I'd say we listen from the heart for things coming from the heart of the other.

The third aspect of interacting with others is rendering assistance. We render assistance when asked. However, if someone has been injured, we may pull them out of harm's way, much like the Good Samaritan. But we usually wait for the person we encounter to ask for help so that we do not rush in where we should allow them space to keep their dignity. We are not called to patronize, much less act as a savior. In this sense, Barth is characteristic of theologians influenced by existential thought (especially Kierkegaard). To speak is cordial; freely acting on another creature's behalf is essential.

Fourth and finally, we do it all joyfully. When we see, listen, and render assistance, we do it with joy. When we mutually speak and listen, we do it joyfully, not assuming we do the other a favor. We do it joyfully even when the conversation goes longer than we expect. We do it with joy even when we see the pain in the eyes of others who cannot or will not see our pain. We do it with joy whether or not the person we encounter is pleasant or able to give us something in return. We do it joyfully because the person we see is made in the image and likeness of God. Whoever they are and whatever their condition, we know they are, like me, one for whom Christ died.

Barth's view of our basic humanity can provide a therapist with a strong resource for empathy and warmth toward others—especially patients. This insight has led some psychologists to propose that the Rogerian method of psychotherapy, characterized by accurate empathy, congruence, and warmth, is partly a result of Barth's theology. This association likely developed as people read the *CD* and realized that Barth's Christology and doctrine of reconciliation lead us to a different conclusion than double predestination. This correction arises because while the Calvinist doctrines tended to espouse the great divide of humanity between elect and nonelect, Barth's theology reminds us of our common election in Jesus Christ. Christ, says Barth in *CD* 2.2, is electing God and elected man rather than accuser of the reprobate and mediator for the elect. The overwhelming influence of Barth's christocentric view of election urges us to engage with other fallen humans. We help even when we are not sure we have the right insights or techniques to help them, even when we are not confident that their past behavior warrants our help. With Barth's guidance, there can be little doubt that each client, patient, hurting neighbor, relative, or friend is a person created in the image and likeness of God and redeemed in Christ. Barth's God scans the prodigal on the horizon and rushes to welcome him home. While our

The Value of *CD* 3 for Mental Health

dysfunctional relationships tend to be the source of our deepest wounds, Barth clarifies that our restored relationship with God in Christ draws us back to the Father and, necessarily, to one another.

In *CD* 3.3, Barth deals with the doctrine of divine providence. This topic follows logically from the previous two volumes, where he dealt first with creation in general and then the creation of humankind in particular. In this volume, Barth compares and contrasts the Creator and the creature. Barth traces the seminal intersection between God and humanity back to Genesis 22 and the story of Abraham and Isaac.

The term *providence* is preferred by Barth over *predestination*. Why? Most likely because Barth wishes to sustain the sovereignty of God without derailing God's freedom. Similarly, the term providence keeps humanity anchored to the creation as God's creature without necessarily surrendering to the double predestination of Calvinism. Barth again anchors providence in God's grace of election revealed in Jesus Christ.[14] While this is a particular act in history, it does not single out elect from nonelect. Instead, it holds out hope for every human being. Barth prefers to keep the universal scope of Creation in play with this vital term: *providence*.

I offer a few concluding words from a surprising source: modern studies of brain physiology. Contemporary studies of the human brain have yielded striking correlations between interpersonal bonding (I-Thou) and brain function. Perhaps the primer of twenty-first-century neuropsychology can be found in *A General Theory of Love*.[15] The authors argue, "The brain's ancient emotional architecture is not a bothersome animal encumbrance. Instead, it is nothing less than the key to our lives. . . . As individuals and as a culture, our chance for happiness depends on our ability to decipher a hidden world that revolves—invisibly, improbably, inexorably—around love."[16] The part of the brain that the authors credit with forging emotional, interpersonal connections is found primarily in the limbic region; therefore, "limbic resonance" is the way neuropsychology often describes our powerful mutual attraction. It can be summarized in these words: "In a relationship, one mind revises another; one heart changes its partner. This astounding legacy of our combined status as mammals and neural beings is *limbic revision*: the power to remodel the emotional parts of the people we love, as our

---

14. *CD*, 3.3, 7.

15. Thomas Lewis, Fari Amini, Richard Lannon, *A General Theory of Love* (New York: Vintage, 2001).

16. Lewis, Amini, and Lannon, *A General Theory of Love*, viii.

Attractors activate certain limbic pathways, and the brain's inexorable memory mechanism reinforces them."[17]

While finding the bridge between theology and mental health may seem awkward, I think Barth would be amused and pleased to hear that recent studies of brain physiology reinforce the efficacy of interpersonal encounters. It's no stretch to suppose the brain is the organ of limbic resonance, an organ hardwired for I-Thou. This is precisely what Barth said we should expect to see in creatures fashioned after the image and likeness of their Creator. Therefore, any genuine seeing and listening has the potential to heal the human heart. The primal resonance between humans, which Barth calls "being in encounter," is remarkably similar to limbic resonance—but without reducing all human interactions to a deterministic sequence of brain synapses.

In *CD* 3.4, Barth defines humanity's moral condition and purpose as he develops his Christian ethics theologically. Barth's doctrine of creation beckons further conversation with all disciplines seeking to understand our moral obligations. Barth is Reformed but not a theologian who impugns human dignity using terms such as total depravity to describe the human condition. Neither is Barth naive about human sin. He balances a stark realism about human behavior with an undaunted hope for humankind's future.

Regarding the sixth commandment, "Thou shall not kill," Barth admits that we humans sometimes treat one another with unspeakable cruelty:

> *Homo homini lupus.* There exists in man a very deep-seated and almost original evil readiness and lust to kill. The common murderer or homicide is simply the one in whom the wolf slips the chain. This is no excuse. It must not obstruct his lawful punishment. But it means that his action is a question addressed to all others and an accusation against them, not merely in the sense that this social environment is partly responsible for the loosing of the wolf in him, but in the sense that this wolf is only too well known to all those who belong to the same society.[18]

Nevertheless, Barth's insight about our wolflike proclivity is countered by this immediate qualification:

---

17. Lewis, Amini, and Lannon, *A General Theory of Love*, 144. Limbic revision is the way the therapist employs limbic resonance in therapy, or healthy deep relationships can bring about the same.
18. *CD*, 3.4, 413.

Moreover, the point has also to be considered that no single man and therefore no criminal is identical with the indwelling wolf. It is not his nature. It belongs to the corruption of his nature. All men know, either in an obscure and feeble or perhaps a clear and forceful way, that they are ordained and disposed to respect human life, and this in a far more original form than can be said of the evil readiness to kill. In this respect, too, man has been created good and not bad.[19]

The science of mental health can thus continue to explore, expecting to uncover not only human pathology but also a human essence that is *originally good*. The latter is our destiny more than the former, according to Barth. Therefore, any therapy that provides genuine help can be viewed joyfully by the Church and its people, for it brings out the temporal goodness of the creature, reflecting the eternal goodness of our Creator.

---

19. *CD*, 3.4, 414.

THE VALUE OF *CD* 3 FOR SPIRITUAL FORMATION

Geordie Ziegler

Geordie Ziegler serves global Christian leaders through *Imago Christ*, the spiritual formation team of *Novo mission*. He is author of *Trinitarian Grace and Participation: An Entry into the Theology of T. F. Torrance* and numerous published articles on the intersection of trinitarian theology and spiritual formation, including "Is it Time for a Reformation of Spiritual Formation," in the *Journal of Spiritual Formation and Soul Care*.

At over six million words, Barth's *Church Dogmatics* occupies twenty inches of prime shelf space in my study, dominating an otherwise multicolored, irregular cacophony of books with a slate of drab grey reminiscent of cold-war communist architecture. Yet inside this monolithic mountain of ink lies one of the twentieth century's greatest gifts, replete with treasures to be received and explored.

A week from this writing, I will be on another mountain as I trek the ninety-three-mile Wonderland Trail with my son around Mount Rainier. The mountain, ascending 14,410 feet, is the largest thing I've ever seen, and the prospect of walking all the way around it sounds a bit crazy (25,000 feet of elevation gain). Taking on a mountain, be it a paper mountain penned by a theological giant or a physical mountain created by God Almighty, is no small feat. One might get lost on a mountain.

Yet to the mountains we go, seeking treasures we have yet to imagine. We venture out because courageous others have gone this way before and lived to tell—like John Muir, who, during a ferocious wind storm in December 1874, chose to rush out to experience it fully:

> Instead of camping out, as I usually do, I then chanced to be stopping at the house of a friend. But when the storm began to sound, I lost no time in pushing out into the woods to enjoy it. For on such occasions,

The Value of *CD* 3 for Spiritual Formation

Nature has always something rare to show us, and the danger to life and limb is hardly greater than one would experience crouching deprecatingly beneath a roof.[1]

Muir didn't just saunter outside for a peek before rushing back into the "protection" of a roof against the elements. No, he hiked the highest ridge and then climbed the tallest tree so he could *know* the weather in every pore of his being, body, mind, and soul, feel it, and take it in: "I kept my lofty perch for hours, frequently closing my eyes to enjoy the music by itself, or to feast quietly on the delicious fragrance that was streaming past."[2]

To those willing to settle for a simple bed under a solid roof, Barth comes rushing in from the weather to coax us out of ourselves. We protest, complaining that there is nothing more to see. We already "know" what weather is like. We've seen it through our windows and on our screens. But Barth keeps ringing the summons for over 2,000 pages in *CD* 3 alone. He has immersed himself in the truth of the weather and lived (and died and lived again) to tell.

What's the big deal, we wonder? And more specifically, what's the value of *CD* 3 for spiritual formation? It had better be worthy because my life is already full of church business and the business of the church . . . and besides, my bed is pretty comfortable.

With Barth as our experienced mountaineer tour guide, he summons us to venture outside and into God's world. We have much to learn if we humble ourselves and listen.

SPIRITUAL FORMATION'S CONTEXT: We Are Already in God's World

Barth knows us (ordinary people and theologians alike) too well. He knows how apt we are to start with ourselves and what we know before we hear the word of Jesus Christ. He warns, "Hold on there. Talk about creation and human beings is theological talk."

Barth considered one of his primary tasks to be "the re-Christianizing of these doctrines,"[3] so he roots and grounds his doctrine of creation in his doctrine of Jesus Christ. "I believe in Jesus Christ, God's Son our Lord, in order to perceive and to understand that God the Almighty, the Father,

---

1. John Muir, *The Mountains of California* (New York: Century, 1894), 249.
2. Muir, *The Mountains of California*, 254.
3. John Webster, *Karl Barth*, 2nd ed. (New York: Bloomsbury Academic, 2004), 94.

is the Creator of heaven and earth. If I did not believe the former, I could not perceive and understand the latter."[4]

God's relation to creation is christological from the start, and as such, no general (i.e., nonchristological) relation exists between God and his creation. This simple move changes everything. We do not begin with creation and then figure out how God fits into it. We do not start with our projects and plans and then petition God to bless them. We begin with Jesus Christ revealed, and by doing so, creation and creatures are immediately and intrinsically gifted with purpose. "Creation sets the stage for the story of the covenant of grace."[5] The "internal basis of creation" is the covenant.[6] This is the reason there is something rather than nothing. Creation is "equipment for grace."[7]

I love Marty Folsom's hospitality metaphor for *CD* 3. The story we find ourselves in is one in which we exist in God's house, like it or not, with Jesus Christ as our eternal brother and the Spirit, the breath that fills our lungs. The triune God is our gracious host, and this world (creation) exists purposefully as the space and time for meaningful relationship (covenant) with this God. We do not need to get in to God's house or story; we are already caught up in it. We breathe christological air. This being the case, our attention should be awakened. God is in all things, and all things are in God. Spiritual formation begins with this announcement: "Wake up, sleeper, rise from the dead, and Christ will shine on you."[8]

SPIRITUAL FORMATION'S END: to Become Human as Jesus Is Human

When we follow Barth outside of ourselves to experience the Weather, we discover Jesus Christ is much more than the Weather, he is the Mountain itself. We considered religion a slim slice of life labeled "spiritual" but with Barth as our guide we discover the human God is the ground of our innermost being.

We were like the deep-sea fisherman fishing for minnows while standing on a whale. Like Augustine we confess, "You were within me and I was outside myself."[9]

---

4. *CD* 3.1, p. 29.
5. *CD* 3.1, p. 44.
6. *CD* 3.1, p. 94.
7. *CD* 3.1, p. 231.
8. Ephesians 5:14.
9. Augustine, *Confessions* 10.27.38.

The Value of *CD* 3 for Spiritual Formation

To be human and live a human life in the theatre of God's creation is to be drawn into a covenant relation with God. At the center of this relation stands Jesus Christ and his human response of faith and obedience. His being human is ontologically determinative for all human beings.[10] In him, human nature itself is established and revealed. His is the only human nature that exists. Every human being, whether she knows it or not, is "the fellow-man of Jesus."[11]

> A decision has been made concerning the being and nature of every man by the mere fact that with him and among all other men He too has been a man. No matter who or what, or where he may be, he cannot alter the fact that this One is also man. And because this One is also man, every man in his place and time is changed.[12]

"Spiritual" formation refers to the activity of the Holy Spirit in the life of the Christian, not with some abstract part of ourselves we call *spiritual*. Our lives are lives of utter and complete dependence; the self we are is a self-in-relation with the Father, through the Son, by the Spirit. At no point along the way do we have life in ourselves independent from the triune God. Even our very soul "owes its being and existence to the Spirit."[13] It is a "spiritual soul and entirely from the Spirit. . . . The breath of the creature is never more than the answer to the breathing of the Creator."[14]

If this is the case, that the Spirit of Jesus is at work in and among us, and we didn't put him there, then once again, we are not in charge. We find ourselves immersed in the weather of a world that is Jesus' from first to last. Our part is to repentantly reorient ourselves to think and act from a center in God rather than self. This is the heart of Christian discipleship and spiritual formation: to habitually think and act in Christ, with Christ as our center, until we become human as God is human in Jesus. From this christological center, the primary work of the Holy Spirit in formation (i.e., spiritual formation) is training us to listen, trust, obey, participate, and bear witness to the triune God who is with us.

---

10. *CD* 3.2, p. 132. Whether one believes or not, the being of every human being is "grounded in Christ and ontologically bound to his humanity." T. F. Torrance, "Karl Barth and the Latin Heresy," *Scottish Journal of Theology* 39, no. 4 (1986): 481.

11. *CD* 3.2, p. 134.

12. *CD* 3.2, p. 133.

13. *CD* 3.2, p. 372.

14. *CD* 3.2, p. 373.

SPIRITUAL FORMATION'S METHODS: Participation in and with Christ—So Let Us Receive Our Yoke alongside Him

All that sounds well and good we say, but in the end, isn't spiritual formation just churchy language for the practices, disciplines, and activities we do to respond to all that God has done for us?

Barth just stands there and shakes his head, "Nein!"

A bit baffled, we push back at him. We even toss in a mic-drop Dallas Willard quote for emphasis, "Grace is not opposed to effort; it is opposed to earning. Effort is action. Earning is attitude. You have never seen people more active than those who have been set on fire by the grace of God."[15] While Dallas may be right, he does not say all that needs to be said about human effort and action. Barth steps in to posthumously correct: Grace is not a thing; Grace is Jesus Christ. And Jesus Christ is opposed to all action that does not obey himself. Sheer action is neither here nor there and most often somewhere over there. What the Christian is called to is participation in Christ. God wants willing covenant partners. Yoked in with the truly human one, we learn to become ourselves in him.

This is good news. It is good news because how many of us have found ourselves weary and heavy-laden with an overwhelming variety of programs, systems, strategies, books, podcasts, and blogs—you get the idea—telling us how to "do" spiritual formation? How many of us have tried hard, *so, so hard*, to work the program, and at the end of the day, looking back, see that nothing has really changed and we were mostly just killing time? Barth has good news for weary and frustrated travelers: *it is not about you.*

> This is the heart of Christian discipleship and spiritual formation: to habitually think and act in Christ, with Christ as our center, until we become human as God is human in Jesus.

Jesus, who defines and determines human nature, does not step back when it is our turn to step up. Instead, he welcomes us to his side. Human action takes place within the economy of grace. In Christ, human action is real, yet our freedom and responsibility to act are not in competition with divine sovereignty. When we go outside to play in the spacious country of salvation, the weather does not stop. We do not recite incantations to conjure up weather. Weather is present whether we recognize its presence or not. Spiritual formation does not bring one closer to God. That is an impossibility. Spiritual formation is waking up to the living and active presence of the triune God.

---

15. Dallas Willard, "Live Life to the Full," *Christian Herald* (UK), 14 April 2001, https://dwillard.org/articles/live-life-to-the-full. See also Willard, *The Great Omission: Reclaiming Jesus's Essential Teachings on Discipleship* (San Francisco: HarperSanFrancisco, 2006), 61.

To read Barth's *Church Dogmatics* is to be battered (in love) by the summons to begin again at the beginning with God revealed in Jesus and then to proceed to understand all things in the light of Jesus Christ. Ultimately, the mountain of words he has amassed could wrongly be construed as one man's vain attempt to define or "figure out" God. His mountain expresses his love for the weather and his desire to be immersed in it. Six million words can be summarized in one finger of John the Baptist pointing to the crucified One, the true Mountain. Barth was reminded every day when he fixed his eyes upward above his desk to Matthias Grunewald's depiction of Christ crucified on the cross watching him from above, the true Mountain.

THE VALUE OF *CD* 3 FOR MISSIONS

Ross Lockhart

Ross Lockhart is dean of St. Andrew's Hall and professor
of mission studies at Vancouver School of Theology. He is
the author of *Lessons from Laodicea: Missional Leadership
in a Culture of Affluence*; *Beyond Snakes and Shamrocks:
St. Patrick's Missional Leadership Lessons for Today*; coauthor
of *Better Than Brunch: Missional Churches in Cascadia*; as
well as *Christianity: An Asian Religion in Vancouver*; and
editor of *Christian Witness in Cascadian Soil*. Ross is an
ordained minister in the Presbyterian Church in Canada.

Whether at work on the University of British Columbia campus, with its
breathtaking views of the Pacific Ocean, or at home in North Vancouver
nestled into the side of Grouse Mountain, I encounter God's creation daily
as a place of profound revelation. I am aware, however, as a missiologist and
a disciple of Jesus, that what I see so clearly as God's creation, my affable
agnostic neighbours view as nature. Kindhearted secular friends look at
the natural world with awe, wonder, and respect but devoid of any revealed
presence of the triune God: Father, Son, and Holy Spirit. A long-standing
tagline from the local tourist board where I live is "Super, Natural British
Columbia," dissecting the divine with a comma to emphasize the natural
beauty of my West Coast province. Surrounded by such stunning environmental beauty, many Vancouverites enjoy nature blissfully unaware of John
Calvin's urging that humans should take a "pious delight in the clear and
manifest works of God" in the "beautiful theatre of creation."[1]

Karl Barth was right to be more than a little suspicious of natural theology. And yet, when it comes to a missional reading of our North American
context, finding overlapping consensus with our non-Christian neighbours,
relatives, coworkers, and friends may be rich soil for the gospel to take root.
Karl Barth's theology of creation in volume 3 of the *Church Dogmatics* is a

---

1. John Calvin, *Institutes of the Christian Religion*, trans. Henry Beveridge (Grand Rapids:
Eerdmans, 1998), 1.14.20, p. 210.

gift to those thinking through a missional engagement of the world and alert to God's divine action in our midst. From David Fitch's missional call for us to attend to God's "faithful presence" to Alan Roxburgh's invitation for Christians to be "detectives of divinity," Barth's teaching in *CD* 3 offers the human creature an expectation of revelation, of the triune God made known in the covenant and creation.

Karl Barth remains a key interlocuter for the missional-theology conversation in church and academy, as the Swiss Reformed theologian was influential in laying the theological groundwork for the missional turn over the last several decades in the post-Christendom West. As early as 1932, Barth argued for a greater emphasis upon the missionary vocation of the church and the missionary nature of the triune God that David Bosch later described as changing from a "church-centered mission . . . to a mission-centered church."[2] Darrell Guder argues that by the Willingen Mission Conference in 1952, the Protestant churches achieved a "strong, global consensus" that the church was missionary by its nature, and that was echoed a decade later by the Roman Catholic Church at Vatican II in the formulation of a missiological ecclesiology.[3] According to Craig Van Gelder, this significant shift meant that the church could no longer serve as the starting point for thinking about mission. Instead, a theology of mission required Christians to understand mission in relation to the Trinity.[4] After Willingen, the term *missio Dei* was used more widely to describe the church's understanding of the triune God's activity in the world and the church's participation in that mission.[5] This evolution of Christian understanding of both church and mission in the world shifted the language from "theology and mission" to "theology of mission" to "mission theology" or "missionary theology," as David Bosch described it.[6] Darrell Guder, editor of *Missional Church: A Vision of the Sending of the Church in North America*, has been

---

2. Darrell Guder, "From Mission and Theology to Missional Theology," *The Princeton Seminary Bulletin* 24, no. 1 (2003): 43.

3. Guder, "From Mission and Theology to Missional Theology," 43. Guder notes that while Willingen International Missionary Council marked the public event in which *missio Dei* began to form the integrating consensus for mission theology, debate continued for decades later regarding the meaning and impact this understanding had on ecclesiology and missiology.

4. Craig Van Gelder and Dwight J. Zscheile, *The Missional Church in Perspective: Mapping Trends and Shaping the Conversation* (Grand Rapids: Baker Academic, 2011), 27.

5. As Jeppe Nikolajsen notes, however, there was disagreement on the nature of the church's participation with the Triune God in that mission. Those who interpreted God's activity to be independent of the church in the world adopted the language of *mission Dei generalis*, while those who understood God to be participating with the church in a redemptive mission expressed their missional ecclesiology with the language of *missio Dei specilais*.

6. Guder, "From Mission and Theology to Missional Theology," 45.

deeply influenced by Barth's writing and notes, "Missional leadership, centred upon the Word and practiced with evangelical collegiality, must serve the gathered church by preparing each member for his or her apostolate. How do we equip each other to walk worthy of our calling in the personal apostolates into which God sends us every time we make the transition from gathered to scattered community?"[7]

What kind of world does God gather people from, equip through the Word of God, and ultimately send us out into? It is a world facing environmental crisis, a world where the doctrine of creation and questions of human stewardship are pressing, and a world that Barth makes clear is the theatre of God's covenantal dealings with humanity, grounded in the person and work of Jesus. According to Barth, this is a world in which God gives a "Yes" to humanity. We discover more of who God is through the revelation of covenant, creation, and community. As Barth writes, "Creation is blessing because it has unchangeably the character of an action in which the divine joy, honour and affirmation are turned towards another."[8]

From a gospel perspective, articulating how "This Is My Father's World" (to borrow from an old hymn) is a key act of missional witness today in a cultural context where public theology often finds itself on the margins. Vancouver theologian Jonathan Wilson laments the "far-reaching and damaging effects of the loss of teleology" in what he describes as "the transformation of creation into nature."[9] Wilson argues that this turn to nature is the conviction that the world is all that there ever has been and will be. Echoing Canadian philosopher Charles Taylor in *A Secular Age*, Wilson notes that even Christians in this "imminent frame" are conditioned to see the world around them within the self-governing norms of nature. What I have identified elsewhere as "Christian Functional Atheism,"[10] Wilson describes in this way, "people are most often 'practical naturalists,' confessing belief in God and creation and afterlife while living as if this world were all there ever has been and ever will be."[11]

Paul Bramadat at the University of Victoria suggests that in the Pacific Northwest region of North America, known as "Cascadia," this widespread care for the planet unites people of different values and understandings in

---

7. Darrell Guder, *Called to Witness: Doing Missional Theology* (Grand Rapids: Eerdmans, 2015), 159.

8. *CD* 3.1, 331.

9. Jonathan Wilson, *God's Good World* (Grand Rapids: Baker Academic, 2013), 37.

10. Ross Lockhart, *Lessons from Laodicea: Missional Leadership in a Culture of Affluence* (Eugene, OR: Cascade, 2016), 49.

11. Wilson, *God's Good World*, 38.

what he calls "reverential naturalism." He defines reverential naturalism as "a broad and naturalized schema that helps to explain the ways Cascadians think and talk about religion, spirituality, and nature" that "favours an orientation that is both accepting of scientific approaches to nature and inclined to perceive and imagine the natural world in ways that are redolent of mysticism, panentheism, animism, pantheism, and inclusive forms of theism."[12]

With a broad consensus in society that care for the planet is good and urgent, the need for a clear and compelling doctrine of creation is evident, as Christians make claims that "This is my Father's world: He shines in all that's fair,"[13] amongst a cacophony of secular, new age, and other belief traditions. For Christians, however, leveraging the overlapping consensus of environmental concern shared by their affable agnostic neighbour through a missional approach offers the ability to articulate the gospel through the lens of creation care. This missional turn enables Christian communities to espouse "a theology with a robust doctrine of creation" that "would help us see that our environmental crisis is not rooted in our struggle to manage scarcity or to allocate resources properly in a zero-sum game; it would help us to see rather that our environmental crisis is rooted in our misuse and abuse of the superabundance provided by God."[14] Missional theology's emphasis on the *missio Dei* is vital here as Christian witness is conditioned by a deep trust in divine agency at work.

> Barth's doctrine of creation continues to stoke the imagination of missional thinkers who seek to join God's redeeming and reconciling work in the world, trusting that creation is indeed our "Father's world."

Furthermore, Christian articulation (and lived practice) regarding the doctrine of creation that Barth addresses in *CD* 3 provides other conversation partners in the missional discussion, including Indigenous peoples. As my faculty colleague and leading Indigenous scholar Ray Aldred notes, "A people closely connected with the earth help define a spiritual way of living that is

---

12. Paul Bramadat, "Reverential Naturalism in Cascadia," in *Religion at the Edge: Nature, Spirituality and Secularity in the Pacific Northwest*, ed. Paul Bramadat, Patricia O'Connell Killen, and Sarah Wilkins-LaFlamme (Vancouver: UBC Press, 2022), 24.

13. Maltbie D. Babcock, "This Is My Father's World," hymn, 1901.

14. Wilson, *God's Good World*, 23. Even the language of Creation Care is problematic, as Leah Kostamo reminded my students recently while discussing her book *Planted: A Story of Creation, Calling, and Community*. Kostamo is a founder and Spiritual Care Coordinator of A Rocha Canada, an environmental ministry on a farm in Surrey, BC. She noted while in conversation with my students her own movement away from the language of "Creation Care" given the power and patriarchal tones that risk leaning into an unhealthy understanding of language that leaves everything up to us as human beings to control.

thoroughly grounded within the here and now. This moves spirituality and perhaps 'religion' out of the category of the private inner world and into the public real world. Indigenous peoples have this 'earthly' spirituality that is situated in the land and is living in a good way in all my relationships."[15] As Christians, we are ambassadors of reconciliation (when we are at our best by God's grace), having been entrusted to proclaim Jesus Christ to the world through our witness of words and works. As Barth notes, "(God) has reconciled the world to Himself in Jesus Christ, i.e., as the One who in His death reveals the end of all creatures, and at the same time their new beginning in His resurrection."[16] Barth's doctrine of creation continues to stoke the imagination of missional thinkers who seek to join God's redeeming and reconciling work in the world, trusting that creation is indeed our "Father's world." We witness and proclaim, "The Lord is King: let the heavens ring! God reigns; let the earth be glad!"

---

15. Ray Aldred, "The Land, Treaty, and Spirituality: Communal Identity Inclusive of Land," *Journal of NAIITS: An Indigenous Learning Community* 17, no. 1 (2019): 3. Aldred gives an example of the specificity of the land in Indigenous culture when he translates John 3:16 in his own Cree language to read, "God so loved the land that he gave his son." Aldred notes, "The land takes in land, oceans, rivers and lakes, plants and all creatures. Not a generic land, but a specific place, *a Cree world, Askiwina*."

16. *CD* 3.1, p. 28.

THE VALUE OF *CD* 3 FOR THE ARTS

David W. McNutt

David W. McNutt is senior acquisitions editor at Zondervan
Academic, associate lecturer of core studies at Wheaton
College, and an ordained Presbyterian minister. He is
the coauthor of *Know the Theologians*, and he is writing
a book for IVP Academic's Studies in Theology and the
Arts series on Barth's doctrine of creation in relation
to the arts. He is also the cofounder of McNuttshell
Ministries, a teaching, preaching, and writing ministry
that serves both the church and the academy.

If you were looking for a passionate theological advocate for the significance
of the arts in the Christian faith and life, you could do better than turning
to Karl Barth. That, at least, appears to be the case on the surface. Since
the days of Zwingli and Calvin, the Reformed tradition has often expressed
reservations about the arts, and Barth stood squarely and unapologetically
within that tradition. He once quipped, concerning the incarnation, "A well-
intentioned business, this entire 'spectacle' of Christian art, well-intentioned
but impotent, since God Himself has made His own image."[1] Yet Barth's
work, especially the oft-overlooked third volume of his *Church Dogmatics*,
has deep theological significance for the arts.

Readers of *CD* will find it helpful to remember that Barth was a pastor
before he was a professional theologian, and he preached throughout his
life. The preacher's task to relate the good news of Jesus Christ to today—
symbolized by the pastor holding the Bible in one hand and the newspaper
in the other—was never far from his mind. Barth's commentary on and personal involvement in pressing social and political matters of his day (e.g., his
early affiliation with the Social Democratic Party, his role in the Confessing
Church movement, and his later critique of atomic weapons) all suggest
that he would have developed a keen eye and ear for the arts as well. It is not
surprising, then, that throughout *CD*, one finds references to visual artists

---

1. Karl Barth, *Dogmatics in Outline* (New York: Harper & Row, 1959), 41.

(Grünewald, Michelangelo, and Rembrandt), musicians (Bach, Mozart, and Beethoven), and authors (Shakespeare, Goethe, and Dostoevsky), among others. This is not the work of some culturally isolated hermit.

At the same time, Barth admitted that he was not an expert in the arts. More importantly, he was unwavering in his commitment to the absolute priority of the triune God's self-revelation through the person and work of Jesus Christ. This belief rings throughout the entire *CD*, and it is evident in *CD* 3, his doctrine of creation, which raises several questions pertinent to the arts and artists: What does it mean to create? Does the creativity of artists define what it means to be human? How can we make art in the midst of a broken and fallen world? What does it mean to fulfill an artistic vocation?

In the first case, Barth's discussion of God's work of creation in *CD* 3.1 emphasizes that the triune God's act of creation is intimately related to Christ's fulfillment of the covenant. Creation and redemption are not isolated events; they are understood as belonging to God's one work of grace. What it means to create, then, is not defined by humanity's artistic activity. As impressive as composing music, painting, filmmaking, and other artistic activities might be, creation as an act is determined by the unique work of the triune God. Similarly, Barth's theological anthropology in *CD* 3.2 answers what it means to be human by looking to Christ. While some (e.g., Dorothy Sayers) argue that humanity's creative capacities reveal what it means to be made in the image of God, Barth argues that the answer to the puzzle of the *imago Dei* is found in Christ, who alone is the image of God (2 Corinthians 4:4, Colossians 1:15, Hebrews 1:3). Once again, Barth's christological commitment determines how he responds to fundamental questions. Understandably, such a focus might seem to threaten any genuine agency on the part of humans, including artists. Helpfully, within his doctrine of providence (*CD* 3.3) and his theological ethics (*CD* 3.4), Barth affirms the role of human agents by placing our activity in its proper context. And there is perhaps no better example of this in *CD*—and no better example of Barth's engagement with the arts—than in his reflections on the music of Mozart.

Barth's passion for Mozart finds expression in a heavenly desire, stated elsewhere: "I even have to confess that if I ever get to heaven, I would first of all seek out Mozart and only then inquire after Augustine, St. Thomas, Luther, Calvin, and Schleiermacher."[2] Too much? Perhaps. But Barth's

---

2. Karl Barth, *Wolfgang Amadeus Mozart* (Grand Rapids, MI: William B. Eerdmans Publishing Company, 1986), 16.

extended excursus about Mozart in *CD* 3.3 demonstrates that his comments cannot be dismissed as mere sentimentality. Somehow, in Mozart, Barth found "music which for the true Christian is not mere entertainment, enjoyment or edification but food and drink; music full of comfort and counsel for his needs."[3] One might ask what led a Reformed theologian like Barth to such a conclusion, especially since, he confesses, Mozart "was not a father of the Church, does not seem to have been a particularly active Christian, and was a Roman Catholic, apparently leading what might appear to us a rather frivolous existence when not occupied in his work."[4]

Within his doctrine of providence in *CD* 3.3, Barth tackles a topic that has vexed theologians throughout the church's history: the reality of evil and suffering in God's good world. For his part, Barth distinguishes nothingness, *das Nichtige*, from the negative or "shadowside" of creation, *die Schattenseite*. Whereas the former, Barth states in Augustinian fashion, is a privation of the good and an evil that opposes God's providence, the latter points to the reality of creaturely limitations and the finitude found within creation. And this is where Mozart comes in.

Barth reminds his readers that Mozart was born shortly after the infamous Lisbon earthquake of 1755, which raised difficult (though not entirely new) questions for theologians and philosophers: How do we account for the reality of evil? What does this mean about belief in a good God? To Barth's ears, Mozart's music was the artistic equivalent of (and superior to) the various philosophical and theological responses that followed. While he acknowledged both the positive and negative sides of creation, both its "Yes" and "No," Mozart affirmed the goodness of creation, even in its limitations, and demonstrated that "in its totality, creation praises its Master and is therefore perfect."[5] Mozart "heard, and causes those who have ears to hear, even today, what we shall not see until the end of time—the whole context of providence."[6] This music, composed in the shadow of Lisbon, resonated with Barth as he sought to affirm God's goodness and providential care while writing *CD* 3 after the horrors of World War II. As gifted as he was, then, Mozart was not some superhuman artist. Rather, he "simply offered himself as the agent by which little bits of

> Barth's lasting significance for the arts is his thoroughgoing attention to what God has done in the person and work of Jesus Christ, who illumines all aspects of human existence.

---

3. *CD* 3.3, 297–8.
4. *CD* 3.3, 298.
5. *CD* 3.3, p. 299.
6. *CD* 3.3, p. 298.

horn, metal and catgut could serve as the voices of creation."[7] He praised God within his creaturely limitations and thus fulfilled the vocational task that each of us bears, whatever our specific calling may be.

Barth's devotion to Mozart is undoubtedly his best-known interaction with the arts in *CD*. Yet his greatest contribution to the arts is not his reflections on any one work of art or any one artist, even Mozart. Instead, Barth's lasting significance for the arts is his thoroughgoing attention to what God has done in the person and work of Jesus Christ, who illumines all aspects of human existence. Christ reveals what it means to create, what it means to be human, and what it means to offer oneself in praise of God.

Carry on, then, artists! Bring all your God-given gifts and Spirit-led creativity to bear upon your craft. But know that you do so not to define creation or human nature but rather to glorify the triune God, who called light out of darkness and gave life to things that were not.

---

7. *CD* 3.3, p. 298.

THE VALUE OF *CD* 3 FOR SCIENCE

Jonathan Lett

Jonathan Lett is associate professor of theology at Letourneau University. He is the director of the Faith, Science, and Technology Initiative. He wrote the essay "Barth on the Ethics of Creation" in *The Wiley-Blackwell Companion to Karl Barth*. His doctoral dissertation explored *The Challenge of "Nature": Rethinking the Created Order with Karl Barth*.

It is no surprise that many do not consider Karl Barth to be a friend of the sciences. His relentless emphasis on the particularity of God's self-revelation in Jesus Christ appears to foreclose the possibility of knowledge obtained by reason rather than faith. To claim that the "doctrine of Creation is a doctrine of faith and its content a secret" and thus "belongs to the creed and to Church dogmatics" sounds like the end of constructive dialogue, not its beginning.[1] Barth was aware that his first volume on creation might give such an impression. In the preface, he anticipates the criticism that he has not addressed the "obvious scientific questions" posed in the opening chapters of Genesis. Although he had expected to tackle challenges related to the doctrine of creation—presumably from the fields of evolutionary biology, geology, and physics—he discovered that the sciences have no bearing on what "Holy Scripture and the Christian Church understand by the divine work of creation."[2]

The reason for this is simple. The doctrine of creation articulates the world in relation to the triune God. The Creator-creature relationship is defined by God's eternal decision to become incarnate in Jesus Christ to share nothing less than his very self with humanity. Although creation took place before the incarnation temporally, election in Christ was logically and eternally before the act of creation. God creates to share his triune life with human creatures by becoming incarnate in Jesus Christ. This pretemporal

---

1. *CD* 3.1, p. 4.
2. *CD* 3.1, p. xi.

decision determines the being and nature of all things. Therefore, creation's nature and order are designed to facilitate eternal covenant fellowship with God in Christ. The fundamental structure of reality is thus "covenantal."[3] The secret of creation can only be accessed in Christ by faith.

In this essay, I will sketch how Barth's doctrine of creation implies that the sciences offer genuine but incomplete accounts of creaturely phenomena. According to Barth, this view of the limited nature of science allows it to be truly scientific in its study of the world.

The covenantal nature of creaturely being distinguishes the doctrine of creation from all scientific accounts of the world because the subject matter is materially different. Creation is a metaphysical and ontological category. By *metaphysical*, Barth means that Jesus Christ is the grounding structure that orders and unites all creation.[4] Barth follows New Testament passages like John 1:1–18; Hebrews 1:3; and Colossians 1:15–20 that link Christ and creation, describing reality as determined by the Word made flesh, in whom all things were created and are now held together.[5] By *ontological*, Barth means that the very structure of human nature is equipped for human beings to have fellowship with God through Jesus Christ. Since the sciences do not seek to describe creation in relation to Christ, they can describe the world as nature but not as creation.[6]

Despite these material differences, Barth believes that the doctrine of creation and the sciences share important methodological commitments.[7] First, neither begins with a prior worldview or pre-metaphysical picture of the world. Second, both attempt to describe the nonhuman world in relation to the human observer. Third, both recognize the "distinct spheres" occupied by what can be observed by human methods and what lies beyond the reach of those methods. According to Barth, if the doctrine of creation and the sciences maintain their boundaries *and* overlapping methodological commitments, each will remain true to itself as a scientific approach to its subject matter.[8]

> Barth's doctrine of creation implies that the sciences offer genuine but incomplete accounts of creaturely phenomena. According to Barth, this view of the limited nature of science allows it to be truly scientific in its study of the world.

For Barth, the boundary between theology and the sciences does not stem from

---

3. See Barth's exposition of the relationship between creation and covenant, *CD* 3.1, § 41.
4. *CD* 3.1, p. 341.
5. *CD* 3.1, pp. 51–56.
6. *CD* 3.2, p. 19.
7. *CD* 3.2, pp. 14–15.
8. *CD* 3.2, p. 19.

The Value of *CD* 3 for Science 393

different sources of truth, such as God's Word and the world. It is not that the Bible teaches us about faith and nature teaches us about science, but that these two domains cannot contradict one another since God's Word and the world cannot conflict. Instead, Barth sees only one source of truth: God's self-revelation in Jesus Christ. And this revelation includes the knowledge of the world disclosed in the "secret of creation." As Barth writes, "The whole cosmos exists in no other way than by the Word of God, which is already the secret of its creation, existence and nature. Human beings may deny this Word, but by no denial can they remove or abrogate it."[9] Jesus Christ, the secret of creation, is the unified metaphysical and ontological framework enabling us to know and understand nature as it truly is.

This view of creation gives a distinct coordination of theology and the sciences. Instead of separate spheres, Barth would have us think about creation's "inner" and "outer" dimensions.[10] Science deals with the latter, not the former. The sciences give an account of the phenomena of the world, the observable and empirical. Scientific accounts of the world speak accurately insofar as they remain simple descriptions of outer phenomena of the world. But suppose science extends its analysis from the outer phenomena to the inner metaphysical and ontological reality of creation. In that case, that science has ceased to be scientific and is now doing theology—and from a source that is not revelation. This is not only untheological theology but also unscientific science.

How does Barth understand the positive relationship between the doctrine of creation and the sciences? If creation's covenantal ontology is real, then nontheological disciplines will bump up against the reality of creation. Barth states that we should not be surprised to discover that "non-Christian wisdom" has produced "approximations and similarities" to theological claims.[11] The sciences will describe aspects of reality, such as a recurring pattern in the world or a human capacity. But they will be unable to appreciate the phenomena in its full import and meaning in connection to God's purposed order for fellowship. Science describes natural phenomena that have their basis in the reality of the human. Still, it cannot articulate the actual human as those created and called to covenantal fellowship with God in Christ. On the one hand, various scientific descriptions of humans could fit with the view of humans as creatures and covenant partners. On the other hand, some scientific descriptions will be rejected, altered, or reframed

---

9. *CD* 3.1, p. 111.
10. *CD* 3.2, pp. 25–28.
11. *CD* 3.2, p. 78.

because they contradict the inner reality of the human that lies beyond the reach of scientific description and explanation.

Two brief examples will help illustrate the relationship between theological descriptions of the inner secret of creation and its outer phenomena. First, theological claims about the inner reality of creation lie beyond what science can access. For example, scientific theories about the beginning of the universe—whether it's the Big Bang or the eternality of the universe—do not describe God's "incomparable act" of creation.[12] The act of creation lies "behind" and "beyond" scientific investigation, which cannot extend to the act of creation itself. God's act of creation is not the first cause among others in the universe's great chain of causation. Since God is categorically different from God's creation, divine action cannot be studied as a species of causality as conceived in modern science.[13]

Second, conceptions of the inner nature of creation frame our interpretations of outer phenomena. Scientific accounts of creaturely phenomena depend on some prior, inescapably metaphysical conception of nature because they presuppose an unobservable conception of the human.[14] The world does not interpret itself. Scientific knowledge cannot be read off the surface of the physical world, like words on a page there for the taking. Instead, a hermeneutical lens must be supplied for the scientific process to begin. And the scientific process could be marshaled to support several competing interpretations of phenomena. For example, Barth argues that evolutionary biology will never be able to definitively say what makes humanity unique (or not) regarding nonhuman creatures. Only a theological claim about the inner reality of creation can identify what distinguishes humanity from other creatures. When this presupposition is established, it can help us correctly interpret the differences and similarities to nonhuman creatures that the sciences genuinely articulate.[15]

Barth draws a hard line between the doctrine of creation and the sciences, not to separate but to unite them. He offers a comprehensive metaphysical account of the world in which genuine but not ultimate knowledge of the world *as creation* can be obtained through sciences. Created reality exerts itself so that scientific disciplines can investigate and conceptualize the world in ways that produce knowledge of the world. Theological claims about creation are primarily metaphysical and ontological, but they also

---

12. *CD* 3.1, pp. 14–15.
13. *CD* 3.3, pp. 103–104.
14. *CD* 3.2, pp. 79–89.
15. *CD* 3.2, pp. 89–90.

imply a particular empirical picture of the world's nature, purpose, and order. So long as the sciences recognize that their depictions of the world depend on certain metaphysical and ontological commitments about the inner reality, they will be "genuine" because they will be true to their discipline's provisional and incomplete nature.[16] To return once more to Barth's preface to the doctrine of creation: "There is free scope for natural science beyond what theology describes as the work of the Creator. And theology can and must move freely where science which really is science, and not secretly a pagan *Gnosis* or religion, has its appointed limit."[17]

---

16. *CD* 3.2, p. 200–202.
17. *CD* 3.1, p. x.

AFTERWORD

This book was a monumental journey, distilling four substantial volumes of *CD* into one pleasant and enriching drink of God's goodness in creation and hospitality toward us. So much more could be said, but this helpful guide will get you to the table of meeting with the Creator.

I have loved comments that reflect on these volumes as life-giving and speaking to the heart. Barth listened to the music of heaven and wrote for the harmonizing of earth with heaven and God's kingdom coming. I am delighted that these volumes are not just books about a set of books—they are an adventure into knowing God, who has come to host us within His triune life.

I again thank the team at Zondervan for their enthusiasm and teamwork in creating these books that take years to sculpt into the work of art in your hands. Abigail, my daughter, continues to thrill with her creative work to accompany the journey of discovery at the entryway to each chapter. Anna Lyn Horky is a servant of extreme value in fine-tuning words to make them flow with clarity.

Cindy and I have moved to Camano Island, Washington. She is my patron saint who makes this work possible; she is a gift whose support is grace in the deepest sense. It has been a moving season in every sense of the word.

The chorus of essayists for this volume are stellar beacons of light for their various disciplines. I added two disciplines, one on embodied theology (Cherith Nordling) and one on missions (Ross Lockhart) beyond the previous eight. These essays help fill out the "for everyone" vision.

Summarizing is an improvisational task that has expanded my horizon and charted new trails in the expansive wilderness of God's grace and goodness. May this book take you to sit with the Great Host. God's hospitality created and provided all that is necessary and beyond for the shared life of love. He is waiting patiently and persistently yearns to wake you to His presence.

Marty Folsom
All Saints' Day, 2023

FURTHER READING

SPECIFIC SECTIONS IN *CD* 3
Creation (*CD* 3.1)
Gabriel, Andrew. *Barth's Doctrine of Creation: Creation, Nature, Jesus and the Trinity.* Eugene, OR: Cascade, 2014.
Sherman, Robert. *The Shift to Modernity: Christ and the Doctrine of Creation in the Theologies of Schleiermacher and Barth.* Edinburgh: T&T Clark, 2005.
Watson, Gordon. *The Trinity and Creation in Karl Barth.* Adelaide: AFT, 2008.
Whitehouse, W. A. *Creation, Science & Theology: Essays in Response to Karl Barth.* Grand Rapids: Eerdmans, 1981.

Humanity (*CD* 3.2)
Deddo, Gary. *Karl Barth's Theology of Relations: Trinitarian, Christological, and Human: Towards an Ethic of the Family.* New York: Lang, 1999.
Hunsinger, Deborah van Deusen. *Theology and Pastoral Counseling: A New Interdisciplinary Approach.* Grand Rapids: Eerdmans, 1995.
McLean, Stuart. *Humanity in the Thought of Karl Barth.* Edinburgh: T&T Clark, 1981.
Miell, David. "Barth on Persons in Relationship: A Case for Further Reflection?" *SJT* 42 (1989): 541–55.
Price, Daniel. *Karl Barth's Anthropology in Light of Modern Thought.* Grand Rapids: Eerdmans, 2002.
Torrance, Alan. *Persons in Communion: Trinitarian Description and Human Participation.* Edinburgh: T&T Clark, 1996.

Providence (*CD* 3.3)
Gorringe, Timothy. *God's Theatre: A Theology of Providence.* London: SCM, 1991.
Green, Christopher. *Doxological Theology: Karl Barth on Divine Providence, Evil, and the Angels.* Edinburgh: T&T Clark, 2011.

Kennedy, Darren. *Providence and Personalism: Karl Barth in Conversation with Austin Farrer, John Macmurray, and Vincent Brümmer*. New York: Lang, 2011.

Wallace, Layne. *Karl Barth's Concept of Nothingness: A Critical Evaluation*. New York: Lang, 2020.

Ethics (*CD* 3.4)

Biggar, Nigel, *The Hastening that Waits: Karl Barth's Ethics*. Clarendon: Oxford, 1993.

Gorringe, Timothy. *Karl Barth: Against Hegemony*. Oxford: Oxford, 1999.

Haddorff, David. *Christian Ethics as Witness: Barth's Ethics for a World at Risk*. Eugene, OR: Cascade, 2010.

Mangina, Joeseph. *Karl Barth on the Christian Life: The Practical Knowledge of God*. New York: Lang, 2001.

McKenny, Gerald. *The Analogy of Grace: Karl Barth's Moral Theology*. Oxford: Oxford, 2010.

Migliore, Daniel, ed. *Commanding Grace: Studies in Karl Barth's Ethics*. Grand Rapids: Eerdmans, 2010.

Nimmo, Paul. *Being in Action: The Theological Shape of Barth's Ethical Vision*. Edinburgh: T&T Clark, 2007.

Webster, John. *Barth's Moral Theology: Human Action in Barth's Thought*. Grand Rapids: Eerdmans, 1998.

Werpehowski, William. *Karl Barth and Christian Ethics: Living in Truth*. New York: Routledge, 2014.

Willis, Robert. *The Ethics of Karl Barth*. Leiden: Brill, 1971.

ONLINE RESOURCE

Karl Barth Resource Guide, https://issuu.com/ptsem/docs/barth_resource _guide